W9-CEU-392

Qualitative Research in Psychology

BF
76.5
.Q34

Qualitative Research
in
Psychology

PROCEEDINGS OF THE INTERNATIONAL
ASSOCIATION FOR QUALITATIVE RESEARCH
IN SOCIAL SCIENCE

Edited by

Peter D. Ashworth
Amedeo Giorgi
André J.J. de Koning

DUQUESNE UNIVERSITY PRESS
PITTSBURGH, PA

472967

Copyright © 1986 by Duquesne University Press
All Rights Reserved
Manufactured in the United States of America

No part of this book may be used or
reproduced, in any manner whatsoever, without
written permission except in the case of
short quotations for use in critical
articles and reviews.

Published in the United States of America
by Duquesne University Press
600 Forbes Avenue, Pittsburgh, PA 15282

Distributed by
Humanities Press International, Inc.
Atlantic Highlands, NJ 07716

First Edition

Library of Congress Cataloging-in-Publication Data

Main entry under title:

Qualitative research in psychology.   /

   Proceedings of the first symposium on qualitative
research of the International Association for Qualitative
Research in Social Science, held at the Casa del Sacro
Cuore in Perugia, Italy in the Summer of 1983.
   Includes bibliographies.
   1. Psychology—Research—Congresses. I. Ashworth,
Peter D. II. Giorgi, Amedeo, 1931–   . III. Koning,
A. J. J. de (André J. J. de) IV. International
Association for Qualitative Research in Social Science.
[DNLM: 1. Psychology—congresses. 2. Research—
congresses. BF 76.5 Q15 1983]
BF76.5.Q34 1986   150'.72   85–27415
ISBN 0–8207–0187–4
ISBN 0–8207–0189–0 (pbk.)

Contents

Introduction

André J. J. de Koning

Scientific research and discoveries always presuppose a certain stance in the world which makes it possible to investigate phenomena from a perspective which enables the researcher to answer his question. The perspective might shift so radically that a new way of looking at phenomena brings to light certain findings which were previously invisible and unheard of. To study light in the way Newton did, presupposes an attitude and a perspective quite different from the usual way of seeing sunlight. Romanyshyn (1982), for instance, showed how Newton, in order to study light, had both to stand with his back to sunlight and use shutters to exclude almost all of it before he could study the small portion that penetrated the gap and passed through his prisms. This stance, this perspective, enabled him to analyze the sunlight, which was useful since the results can be applied and can answer questions coherent with the nature of the research. It becomes another matter if we "forget" that a number of metaphors have been used and that the results are taken to be the whole of "reality."

J. H. van den Berg (1959), the author of quite a number of books on the historically changing nature of phenomena, indicated that, prior to the "discovery" or "invention" of the nature of the circulation of the blood by Harvey, people believed in Galen's theory of the movement of blood as flowing back and forth like the tide. Simple calculations would have shown that the old theory could not possibly make sense, considering the enormous amount of blood the heart would have to deal with if there were no circulation. Yet nobody looked upon the body from this objectifying perspective, just as no one considered space from an outside perspective before lived, heterogenous space was transformed by science into an abstract, homogenous space. In natural science such shifts in perspective, which lead to new paradigms in, for example, the increasingly more complex fields of physics, have led to ways of looking at phenomena which could only be possible because of a new qualitative perspective and the inclusion of the researcher in the research. Whilst in physics research of a qualitative nature goes on, most of the research in social science does not seem to get beyond a Newtonian phase, in which the method more or less determines the questions asked and the themes of investigation are limited to phenomena which lend themselves to a quantitative method of research.

Brentano expressed his concern about an overemphasis upon method in the field of psychology as early as 1874, in his "Psychology from an Empirical Standpoint." He was interested in investigating the presuppositions underlying empirical psychology, as well as investigating by means of experimental, qualitative procedures. Psychological research, like any scientific investigation, includes the formulation of questions as well as approach and method, and should not limit itself to questions which can only be dealt with through statistical procedures. Giorgi has stressed this point in many of his writings (e.g. 1970, 1975) and has argued that psychology has not found its paradigm yet.

Psychology, though it often deals with human beings as its subject of science, has often imitated natural science by using quantitative methods without being critical of its own presuppositions and assumptions. What, for instance, can we learn about "experience" from psychology? Certainly, we read in psychology textbooks that experience plays a part in learning. Learning, a theme much studied in psychology, is a change in behaviour through experience. Quite a few textbooks come up with such a broad, fairly meaningless, definition of learning. One can read about the change of behaviour but little about the experience. First of all, learning has been studied so extensively, because other human phenomena are more difficult to quantify, but then there is a consequent overemphasis on the change of behaviour, leaving out experience. The experience of the subject under investigation is often regarded as irrelevant or even a disturbing factor in the "scientifically" controlled experimental situation. In other words, it is as if the subject is being studied without the researcher taking advantage of a consideration of the variation in experience and meaning which both researcher and subject go through during the experiment.

Such "subjective" factors only interfere, it is thought, with the "real" findings, but quantitative procedures are only fruitful if the research question demands such an approach and such a method, but lead to trivialities if the focus of the research and the question asked require research of a qualitative kind. Human psychological phenomena such as anguish, fear, joy, grief, anger, love, sadness, etc. all have experiential aspects with their qualities which are left out of textbooks because there is no qualitative research which is generally accepted as scientific. One does see, however, that after the research has been done, that scientists make qualitative statements and are all of a sudden competent in fields which they have dismissed as unscientific from the start. This is also typical of natural scientists, when they mix their research findings with arguments which demand another approach. For instance, a discussion about accounts of people's experience of being clinically dead can lead to an argument in which medical scientists declare that the visions experienced by such people do not mean much, since it might be merely that the occipital lobe has been stimulated in one way or another. This is like saying that experiences do not mean anything, since there are such things as physiological reactions. The observation that nor-adrenaline starts to flow when someone is angry should not therefore imply that there is no meaningful experience.

This confusion of quantitative findings with qualitative arguments is something that happens more frequently than one would suspect when listening to scholars. Dealing with experience and their meanings cannot be done by methods which are not suitable and certainly should not lead to the dismissal of research which attempts to come to grips with meanings in order to increase knowledge of human phenomena. In order to do justice to the phenomena as they are experienced by human beings, one has to approach the matter in a certain way and apply methods consistent with the approach as well as the content.

The reaction against the violence of science to human existence and experience, has taken shape in movements within the field of psychology which have done away with research altogether, sometimes ending up in cults pretending to have gained knowledge through stereotyped rituals. Just as scientists can appear to be qualified in hermeneutics without ever having studied the matter seriously, there are also plenty of people trying to overcome, or rather deny, problems in research by abolition or negation.

Luckily enough, there is also a movement within the fields of social science which tries to do justice to the phenomena as they are experienced, while at the same time to maintain a critical dialogue with their own assumptions and presuppositions. In many countries in the West there are signs of a development in psychology in which the qualitative aspects of research are brought into focus. This book contains the proceedings of our first symposium on qualitative research in psychology of the International Association for Qualitative Research in Social Science, initiated by Amedeo Giorgi some years ago. The symposium was held at the Casa del Sacro Cuore in Perugia, Italy, in the Summer of 1983. Here, in Perugia, the Collegium Phaenomenologicum has held conferences where phenomenology has been discussed and studied by philosophers and social scientists for quite some years. Though our symposium was quite distinct from the Collegium, the reader will find that phenomenology has had a major influence on quite a few contributors to this work. The approach itself does not restrict the method or style, but rather makes it possible for research to be conducted in such a way that a dialogue between approach, method and content is consistent and therefore maintains its rigor. The fact that there is no single style or method, does not imply that there is no rigor. On the contrary, a question which leads to research of a qualitative nature takes into account the context in which the research takes place. This also implies the social context and culture of the researcher, who has to carry out his dialogue with fellow-researchers. So, different questions concerning different aspects of psychological research within different contexts should also lead to various methods and styles if the research is to be coherent. This is one of the reasons why there is such a variety in style and method to be found in this text. Research should not be independent from time, place and people; just as truth does not appear in a sterile fashion deprived of dynamics. It is often the attempt of traditional research in Western psychology to destroy these variations which ultimately leads one away from enrichment of knowledge.

In the opening chapter, Giorgi points out more specifically what the background of the problems are concerning the issue of descriptions in qualitative research. The bias of positive empiricism has led to an over-emphasis on sensory-perceptual 'givens', but on a theoretically scientific level arguments can be given for a phenomenological approach. Giorgi says: "a phenomenologically grounded science uses a descriptive approach in order to obtain the facts of a given experience in order to clarify their meaning" (p. 7). He furthermore argues that the implications of the phenomenology of meaning with respect to intentionality and reflections lead to consequences for the problem of perceptual presences and their descriptions. In this philosophical, Husserlian analysis of the problem of meaning, he furthermore clarifies why *meanings*, as opposed to *facts*, are central when trying to understand behavioral acts. The appearance of meanings to reflective consciousness enables one to be directly present to meanings, just "as directly as pointer-readings can reveal numbers" (p. 18). His analysis warns one against judging descriptive research by the wrong standards; that is, another system's presuppositions about psychological reality cannot be applied here. The implications of these reflections for research, especially within the field of psychology, are discussed and detailed examples and elaborations can be found in the research of Aanstoos and Wertz. Aanstoos has investigated the pattern of thinking in chess-players and drawing from a whole range of descriptive protocols in the field, he has enriched both the theory and research in the psychology of thinking by allowing the subjects to express their very own thoughts while playing chess.

Wertz conducted an original research project by taking a taboo–situation (people looking at porn —magazines in a bookshop) in order to study perception in the life-world. Both these researchers take a phenomenological approach and give clear examples of the actual practice of qualitative research using descriptions of people's experiences. Justice is done to these experiences as lived by the subjects and there is a clear dialogue between the method and content, leading to knowledge of a psychological, scientific kind about such phenomena as thinking and perception.

Apart from the phenomenological approach, we also find qualitative research with a different approach. There is, for instance, the approach to which Hakkarainen and Hedegaard refer to in their chapter when they compare the phenomenological approach with the theoretical emphases which the researcher Ference Marton gives. Psychologists who are familiar with the qualitative approach in education might be familiar with Marton's distinction of first and second order perspective, in which the latter is a perspective of the world as perceived and the former

the factual perspective, where these perspectives apply to categories of conceptions of subjects. According to him the goal and the
content of psychological research is to construct a map of different conceptions of phenomena and Marton therefore speaks of
"phenomenography." Hakkarainen and Hedegaard furthermore
elaborate on the research project on "evaluating teaching-
material to pre-school children from the children's play with the
material" and the use of the instructional method in this project
which enabled children to understand new conceptions.

Discussions of these two trends in qualitative research are to be
found in the chapters by Engeström and Svensson. Engeström
has made a critical analysis of phenomenography and points out
some of the antinomies inherent in this approach. He defends
"dialectics" as an alternative. The paper is highly reflective and
will clarify a host of issues involved when practicing research of a
qualitative kind.

Svensson deals with the difference between approaches and its
relation to the fact that there have been "turns" in the search for
appropriate methods. He does not only describe the phenomenological approach as an aspect of the "philosophical turn" but
also "the scientific turn" which proceeded it and "the linguistic
turn" or the turning to language as a guide for the development of
methods. The reader will find detailed descriptions of the practise
of qualitative research as well as treatment of the different kinds
of description involved in the different approaches.

Säljö has introduced a discussion in the field of educational
research, by treating the different issues at stake in research in the
pedagogic phenomena. The difficulty of developing a language in
terms of which pedagogic issues can be articulated is the central
theme and the object of inquiry would be the communication
developing between teachers and learners and teaching and learn-
ing-situations.

Apart from these issues, the reader will also find an excellent
paper by Steinar Kvale on the psychoanalytic enterprise as a
process of ongoing qualitative research. He gives seven characteristics of psychoanalysis as a research method, which makes it
possible for the reader to get an insight into the nature of
psychoanalysis as a way of obtaining knowledge and its relation to
treatment.

Kruger has presented us with a well-written paper on the
phenomenological approach to psychotherapy and research is

psychology and in this paper an outline is given of the major themes dealt with in the clinical field.

At the symposium there was, in the clinical field, also a presentation and discussion on the research into the phenomenon of dreams, of which a summary of Meijer's presentation has been included in this clinical section.

Van Zuuren's original investigation into rule-breaking behavior must be most stimulating for the social and clinical psychologist, but also for anyone interested in the development of alternative strategies to cope with a situation in which a person is deviating from normative or rule-abiding behavior.

I shall not go into further detail here, but the reader will notice that some themes, already discussed and elaborated on by different authors, also return in the two chapters by Ashworth and Hagan. Hagan's chapter on the problem of interviewing will make clear what the arguments of a qualitative kind of research are, when confronted with practical situations in the field when interviewing the downtrodden. Once more the reader will notice how complicated the field of research can be when one is not just following a set of rules derived from a theory about interviewing. Practice and theory are in constant dialogue with each other in order to deepen the research. This issue, strongly relates to the problem of methodology which Ashworth has made a theme in his study on "Approaching Social Attitudes." He points out the many presuppositions found in the formation of theory and method, especially with regard to the tendency of equating method with technique. His thoughts on hermeneutic fore-understanding are themselves hermeneutical and therefore lead to a deepened understanding of what methodology actually is and what the implications are when studying social attitudes.

Here then, the proceedings of the first symposium of scientists from different cultures and different fields within psychology, challenging the need to apply quantitative methods and reflecting on research as a much more comprehensive enterprise of science than is usually considered to be the case. It is, of course, up to the reader to what extent and in which way she or he wishes to become involved with alternative kinds of research. Whether it will lead to fruitful results and a continuing process in which knowledge will be attained, depends for a good part on our own understanding of truth. There is a nice story about this with which I like to complete this introduction.

AJMAL HUSSEIN AND THE SCHOLARS*

Sufi Ajmal Hussein was constantly being criticised by scholars, who feared that his repute might outshine their own. They spared no efforts to cast doubts upon his knowledge, to accuse him of taking refuge from their criticisms in mysticism, and even to imply that he had been guilty of discreditable practises.

At length he said:

"If I answer my critics, they make it the opportunity to bring fresh accusation against me, which people believe because it amuses them to believe such things. If I do not answer them they crow and preen themselves, and people believe that they are real scholars. They imagine that we Sufis oppose scholarship. We do not. But our very existence is a threat to the pretended scholarship of tiny noisy ones. Scholarship long since disappeared. What we have to face now is sham scholarship.

The scholars shrilled more loudly than ever. At last Ajmal said:

"Argument is not as effective as demonstration. I shall give you an insight into what these people are like."

He invited "question papers" from the scholars, to allow them to test his knowledge and ideas. Fifty different professors and academicians sent questionnaires to him. Ajmal answered them all differently. When the scholars met to discuss these papers, at a conference, there were so many versions of what he believed, that each one thought that he had exposed Ajmal, and refused to give up his thesis in favour of any other. The result was the celebrated "brawling of the scholars." For five days they attacked each other bitterly.

"This," said Ajmal, "is a demonstration. What matters to each one most is his own opinion and his own interpretation. They care nothing for truth. This is what they do with everyone's teachings. When he is alive, they torment him. When he dies they become experts on his works. The real motive of the activity, however, is to vie with one another and to oppose anyone outside their own ranks. Do you want to become one of them? Make a choice soon."

*In "Wisdom of the Idiots," I. Shah, quoted in full with permission of Octagon Press, P. O. Box 227: London (1979).

References

Berg, J. H. van den. *Het menselijk lichaam*. Nijkerk: Callenbach, 1959.

Giorgi, A. P. *Psychology as a human science, a phenomenologically based approach*. New York: Harper & Row, 1970.

_____. Phenomenology and the foundations of psychology. In J. K. Cole and W. J. Arnold (Eds.), *Nebraska symposium on motivation 1975*. Lincoln: Nebraska University Press, 1975.

Romanyshyn, R. *Psychology as metaphor: From science to metaphor*. Austin: University of Texas Press, 1982.

PART I

Discussions of General Methodological Issues

Theoretical Justification for the Use of Descriptions in Psychological Research

1

Amedeo Giorgi

I. Introduction

The use of language in science is like the air we breathe: it is omnipresent, taken-for-granted and its necessity is appreciated only in its absence. Imagine for a moment going to a psychological convention and not hearing a word spoken! What you would see instead would be only experiments or demonstrations of experiments or the actual performance of therapy. In such a case, how could we know that we would be observing what the researcher would want us to observe? How could we discriminate a particular therapist's special technique from the rest of the therapeutic process? Or imagine if professional journals simply consisted of the publication of raw data without any statistical treatment. How could we make any sense of such data, especially if categories and labels were missing? At least in the examples given so far, there was something to present or demonstrate, but if there were no language, how could theories ever be developed, let alone communicated? No, it is clear that language is as essential to science as it is to human life in general.

The above exercise in imaginative variation helps us to see the paradoxical role that language plays in scientific affairs. On one hand, the imagined lack of language enables us to see the critical role that language plays in the very organization of science. For example, an analysis of variance design does not treat numbers that were obtained haphazardly, but it specifies which kind of number can appear; it helps organize the meaning of treatment

*A modified, shortened version of this paper was presented at a symposium entitled "The Value of a Descriptive Method for Psychology" held at 90th Annual meetings of the American Psychological Association, Washington, D.C., August 24, 1982.

and non-treatment groups; it helps to establish what is permissible and what is not, etc. A good psychophysical design will define a stimulus so precisely that only a narrow range of energy can count as a stimulus. This is the truth of the Whorfian thesis: language influences how reality is perceived. On the other hand, if language did not in some way express the non-linguistic, it would have fallen into disuse long ago. Think, for example, of the millions of words that are used at a convention to communicate to audiences things and events that are not perceptually present. It is obvious that all of these presenters believe that somehow essential aspects of their theories or research are getting across to listeners despite the lack of perceptual presence of the matters about which they are speaking. The very possibility of science depends upon this power of language to communicate the non-linguistic and therein lies the paradox: science both needs and is limited by language. Husserl (1960, pp. 13–14) captured both aspects when he wrote: ". . . the sciences aim at predications that express completely and with evident fitness what is beheld prepredicatively . . . Owing to the instability and ambiguity of common language and its much too great complacency about completeness of expression, a new legitimation of significations . . . and fixing of words are expressing significations thus legitimized (will be necessary)."

This paradox undoubtedly accounts for the mixed attitudes that psychologists hold with respect to language or descriptions (A description is the use of language to articulate the objects of experience). On one hand, it is implicitly trusted so that even the most hardnosed scientist describes his apparatus and procedure in words with the clear implication that anyone who wanted to replicate his study could read his descriptions and do so. The assumption is that descriptions can be precise enough for the important scientific step of replication to be carried out. This same scientist also assumes that the descriptions of his results and interpretations in his scientific reports are precise enough so that they will be understood as he intends them to be. Yet, on the other hand, if the same hardnosed scientist would obtain reports of experiences from subjects, he would consider such reports to be untrustworthy data. At best, these descriptions could serve as pilot data, but only performance data would count as scientifically valid. The arbitrariness of this attitude can also be seen by the fact that at least half of our profession, the therapists and clinicians, make extensive use of language and find it to be effective.

Clearly, the issues surrounding language are too complex to sort out in a single stroke. The purpose of this paper has the more modest if difficult aim of merely trying to justify theoretically why descriptions can be a legitimate source of data in psychological research. The inspiration for such a justification is the already noted fact that if humans, as scientists, can, under proper conditions, use descriptive reports with precision, then it seems to me that humans, as subjects, should also, under the proper conditions, be able to generate valid descriptive reports. This paper will try to explore why.

II. Background of Problem

One cannot raise the question of the legitimate use of descriptions without raising thorny philosophical issues as well, but unfortunately, the philosophy of description is itself still unsettled (Mohanty, 1983). While in this paper I ultimately want to argue at a theoretically scientific level, it is impossible not to begin without a preliminary statement of certain philosophical positions.

In my view, the reason for the difficulties surrounding the use of description as data lies with the positivistic and empirical philosophical views that were dominant when psychology became independent and which psychology adopted in its haste to be scientific. I would say that the heart of the matter seems to be the absolute privilege granted to the sensory-perceptual givenness of a physical thing and the way in which it is interpreted by positivistic empiricism. It is assumed in this view that a discrete material reality that is publicly verifiable and that can somehow silently impress itself on a perceiver is the ultimate criterion. It is further assumed that once we begin to speak about our impressions distortions enter. If such be the criterion, then descriptions seem vulnerable because they are reports about things and events rather than direct perceptual presence to them. Being "once-removed" they seem to be vulnerable to distortion and/or deliberate violation. The ultimate guarantee, therefore, is direct perceptual presence to some physical thing or material event that can in principle be given to many.

This formulation raises two questions: 1) whether this criterion is formulated as precisely as it can be and 2) whether or not it was developed specifically for psychological reality. Concretely, it is a known fact that a fully adequate empirical theory of perception does not yet exist and empiricism is especially vulnerable with respect to just how material objects impress themselves on perceptual consciousness without involving consciousness. If consciousness is active, then of course, pure empiricism is surpassed. In addition, an implicit assumption is that the material thing is first and foremost a discrete, independent reality that only subsequently comes into relation with consciousness. Our view will challenge that assumption. Lastly, empiricism uses a material object as a test case and it is dubious at best whether criteria derived from a material object *as such* are best suited for the perception of psychological reality. For scientific psychology, criteria should be derived from how psychological objects present themselves to consciousness. Ultimately, it is positivistic empiricism that has to be surpassed and so I adopt a phenomenological approach because it is my conviction that this philosophy can do more justice to the difficult double demands of scientific rigor and psychological reality, and I shall, within the space allotted, try to indicate why.

III. Phenomenology

Phenomenology is the discipline that devotes itself to the study of how things appear to consciousness or are given in experience. Thus it is concerned with phenomena in the strict sense: that is, how things and events are for the consciousness that beholds them and not how they are in themselves. Whatever presents itself in experience is to be understood precisely as it presents itself even though one may know that the given contains more than appears or may be different from how it presents itself. Illusions provide a perfect example of the point we are making. One may know that the lines of the Muller-Lyer illusion are equal, but one can still experience the illusion. It is to this presolidified realm of consciousness or experience that phenomenology directs us and this example shows that it is not equivalent to knowledge. The phenomenal realm would be better characterized as a living presence than knowledge. That is why the phenomenological approach includes the procedure known as bracketing—the putting out of play of what we know about things in order to experience them freshly.

It should also be mentioned that in the phenomenal realm one is talking about appearances or presences and not existences. This is a consequence of the adoption of the phenomenological attitude as opposed to remaining in the natural attitude where things are presumed to be as they appear. In the phenomenological attitude, whatever is given is taken only as a presence and existential claims are withheld. In the phenomenological attitude we will speak of presences and in the natural attitude of existences.

Now, precisely because a phenomenological approach does not assume that we already understand psychological reality, it was able to tease out an essential feature of consciousness, viz. intentionality, that differentiates consciousness or experience from things. To say that experience is intentional is to say that it is essentially directed toward the givens of experience. These givens may be internal or external to consciousness but they always transcend the acts in which they appear. In other words, creatures possessing this characteristic enjoy a direct openness to things or events that transcend them and consequently they themselves cannot be sheer material things in the same sense that the objects of physics and chemistry are material. We may note in passing therefore that to use the sensory-perceptual givenness of a material object as a criterion for psychological reality is to falsify the latter. It does not mean that the object of psychology is not given perceptually, it simply means that the object of perception is not necessarily exhausted by its material aspects.

Because experience is essentially directed to things or events that transcend it, the object of psychological analysis becomes inherently relational. It is not consciousness understood as a separate entity, on one side, and then an existential material object that first exists independently, on the other, that are the units of analysis, but rather the structure: act of consciousness directed toward a transcendent object that is directly but partially grasped through an aspect. Phenomenology, of course, understands behavior as being on the side of consciousness, so if one were to speak specifically about behavior, the structure of the object of psychology would be: a behavioral act directed towards a transcendent situation that is directly but perspectively modified. In other words, the object of psychology is a complex whole consisting of discernible but inseparable parts. This is what phenomenologists call a categorial object because it includes material aspects that could be given simply but in ordinary experience most frequently are not, and the claim I am making is that the genuine object of psychology has to presuppose something like a categorial object because it can never be reduced to simple materiality because it is always relational, and as relational, requires non-sensory aspects as well as sensuous givens to make up a whole. The point is that the unified object that is the perceptual object presents itself as a synthesis of existential presences and absences, but within phenomenology this always means some sort of phenomenal presence.

Thus, the phenomenological reduction is an important procedure for being able to depict precisely how perceptual objects are given to experience since it helps us to delineate how things present themselves regardless of their ultimate "reality status." Vague and ephemeral aspects should be included along with physical and non-physical attributes of the perceptual object. Indeed, even "absences" present themselves as certain present gaps, tensions or anticipations. In effect, it is precisely description that the reduction invites us to perform so that an adequate ground can be obtained in order to ascertain the fullness of perceptual objects in the world.

Phenomenology is also the discipline that seeks the meaning of experience rather than its sheer facts. Facts are obtained, of course, and indeed they are necessary, because they are the points of departure for the discovery of meanings. Reference to a subject is intrinsic to the understanding of a meaning, but facts can be known without such references. If a phenomenologically grounded science is different from other sciences, it is because of its rigorous pursuit of the clarification of meaning (including an awareness of its limits). Thus, a phenomenologically grounded science uses a descriptive approach in order to obtain the facts of a given experience in order to clarify their meaning. Let's try to thematize some of the problems surrounding the two activities, description and meaning, that are the heart of phenomenological analysis.

IV. Phenomenological Philosophy of Description

While in my view positivistic empirical philosophical assumptions have created problems for a descriptive approach to research in psychology, there is no ready alternative to which to turn. I find the assumptions of phenomenological philosophy, however, more sympathetic to the aims of descriptive psychology because it, too, proceeds descriptively and it, too, seeks meanings. The justification for the use of description in phenomenological philosophy is also incomplete but some of the arguments and themes that such a justification would take have been provided in a recent paper by Mohanty (1983). While the points raised by Mohanty help to provide a context within which our scientific theorizing can take place, it will be seen that the major contribution of Mohanty in the paper referred to, while extremely important at this stage of development, is still basically propaedeutic in the sense that it merely clears the way for a specific theory of scientific descriptive psychology.

The major implication of Mohanty's article for me is that descriptive philosophy and descriptive science must be judged by their own internal criteria and not by the criteria of other philosophical systems. This point will become obvious as I elaborate the contributions of Mohanty to this task. The chief implication for descriptive psychologists, or descriptive scientists in general, is that we have our work cut out for us in these early years. Specifically, it means that until the criteria for descriptive work get specified, we must present our criteria with our research. This is a double burden, but it is inevitable in the early years of the development of a science.

Let us now turn to some of Mohanty's (1983) contributions. Mohanty begins by saying that what is meant by description in philosophy is still not completely certain. Different interpretations of the term currently exist. However, phenomenologically speaking, Mohanty mentions two points: a description must stay "close to the given" and all descriptions must be based upon intuitive experience. Or to say the whole thing most succinctly, a descriptive method is one in which one "restricts oneself to making assertions which are supported by appropriate intuitive validations" (Mohanty, 1983, p. 24). Thus a description is meant to relate how a given presents itself to conscious experience.

Now, of course, the very idea of the given is itself problematic. We cannot go into all of the philosophical issues here, but Mohanty (1983, pp. 6–8) discriminates the sense of the given he would want to maintain from several historical philosophical interpretations. For example, he says that the given need not be simple or not further analyzable; it need not be what is given in immediate experience only; it need not be defined as what is passively given; it need not be indubitable; it need not be what is only determinate and self-complete; it need not be obvious or what is merely on the surface; and finally, in order to have access to the given, reflection, analysis and thought may be required. By detaching the given from being essentially related to all of the above characteristics, Mohanty has provided a real service because we are now free to turn to the given with a renewed freedom to see how it is constituted.

Mohanty (1983, pp. 8–9) provides another great service to phenomenological scientists when he differentiates the frame of reference within which a phenomenologist interprets descriptions from other philosophical systems. Thus, Mohanty distinguishes a phenomenological, descriptive approach from: a deductive philosophical system; a hypothetical-confirmatory-disconfirmatory system; an approach that constructs interpretive frameworks or theoretical models; a rational reconstruction of experience; an analytical reflection that seeks the conditions of the possibility of the given; and lastly, from explanatory systems, i.e., those that develop theories to account for underlying processes behind manifest appearances. He also mentions in passing that the ability to predict is not the measure of a description.

Now, the above listing makes abundantly clear, I think, that part of the difficulty in doing descriptive scientific work in psychology is that criteria drawn in a helter skelter way from the above systems are used to judge the value of descriptive research. But since it is now clear that descriptive work is not motivated by the same criteria that such systems use, it will have to be judged differently.

Like all other human activities, descriptive work takes many forms. Mohanty (1983, pp. 24–27) lists some of the types of philosophical description actually in use: descriptions can be direct, they can be by negation, they can proceed in such a fashion that better acquainted phenomena are arranged in a series which points towards the thing to be described as its limit, they can proceed by classifying and Mohanty even finds in hermeneutics nothing but description. This list is obviously not exhaustive. In this paper, we will be primarily concerned with the first type: direct description.

However, before turning to our own analysis of direct description, two other issues that Mohanty raises with respect to description should be mentioned. The first is a suggestion for a test for a good description. Mohanty says that a good criterion would be to make sure that there are no preconceptions vitiating the description. The aim of philosophical description is to make explicit the intelligibility that resides in experience from within experience. Other criteria may also be necessary, but at least the one Mohanty mentions is a good point of departure.

The other sticky issue Mohanty synopsizes is the number of objections that have been made to descriptions and he provides, briefly, the direction for answers. The two basic types of objections that Mohanty reports are: (1) the "given" cannot be described because nothing is given or else it is "unknowable" and (2) "pure description" is impossible because various factors enter in to contaminate it such as language, conceptualizations, the perspectival nature of experience and the existence of subjective meanings all of which require interpretation. Mohanty indicates how each objection is a genuine problem but that plausible solutions to the problems also exist. However, here we cannot enter into these discussions because they would take us too far afield. We merely want to state that all of Mohanty's points listed above would constitute the assumptive framework of a descriptive science.

V. The Phenomenology of Meaning

The philosophy of meaning is another area in which much has been written but little consensus achieved. Ogden and Richards (1952/1923), for example, distinguish sixteen different senses of meaning grouped into three categories. Debates about whether meanings are objects, ideas, mental images, linguistic characteristics or mere fictions are still going on in philosophical circles (Christensen, 1961). What everyone does agree upon is that the problem of meaning is a complex one and one that can only be analyzed with great difficulty.

Since we are limiting ourselves to a phenomenological perspective here we will only mention some of the key features of a phenomenological understanding of meaning. This sketch will help provide an interpretive framework for the psychological analysis to follow. Drawing from Mohanty (1976) we may state that the following points are critical for phenomenological philosophy of meaning: (1) The idea of expressive act as intentional,

(2) The distinction between meaning-intending acts and meaning-fulfilling acts, (3) The distinction between sense and reference, and (4) The idea that meanings are discovered in a reflective act of consciousness.

In order to be clear of the charge of psychologism, Husserl wanted to affirm the objectivity of meanings, which meant that they could not be real parts of mental states in the way that images are. Because of the general intentionality thesis of consciousness, Husserl could affirm that there were special acts, called expressive acts or speech acts that bestow meanings (Mohanty, 1976, pp. XVI–XVII). Meanings are the "'intentional correlates' of acts" or "'ideal contents'" of these conscious acts (Mohanty, 1976, p. XVII). Meanings are to be understood as "ideal unities" rather than entities. Husserl (1970/1900, I, p. 322) writes: "Pure logic . . . is exclusively concerned with the *ideal* unities that we here call 'meanings'" (Italics in original). To say that meanings are not self-subsistent entities is also to say that Husserl's theory of meaning is not ontological (Mohanty, 1976, p. XVII).

The core meaning of intentionality is that consciousness is always directed to something that is beyond the act of consciousness in which that something appears. The second point above refers to the fact that Husserl has delineated two poles of his relationship, the act side or noetic sphere and the object side or noematic sphere. In addition, he has distinguished meaning-intending acts, which in the narrow sense are defined by the possibility of intuitive fulfillment from meaning fulfilling acts in which the intuitive fulfillment of the meaning-intending acts actually takes place. For Husserl, meaning, properly speaking, is independent of the intuitive or fulfillment side and wholly based upon the meaning-intending acts.

Thirdly, Husserl goes along with the more or less traditional distinction between the sense of an object and the reference to an object. The reference is that about which an expression says something, the sense is what it says about it. The two never coincide perfectly. But that they are different can be shown by the fact that the same expression can refer to different objects (e.g. "dog" may refer to a stray dog near the garbage pail or my pet Digby) and different meanings can refer to the same object (e.g. the victor at Jena and the vanquished at Waterloo both refer to Napoleon). As stated above, in Husserl's theory, as opposed to more scientific theories of meaning or to certain analytic theories, the object referred to does not have to exist in order for there to be meaning (Mohanty, 1976, p. 45).

Lastly, meanings are discovered only reflectively, not straightforwardly. Experiences are spontaneously directed toward the objects or states of affairs in the world and not directly to the meanings. In order to grasp or clarify the meaning of an experience, one has to reflect upon it. This would mean that one would capture the sense of the experience rather than the reference.

With these brief background expositions on the phenomenological approach to description and meaning, we shall now move on to the main point of the article, viz., the justification of descriptions for psychological research. We shall return to the problem of perceptual presence again.

VI. Consequences of Phenomenological Approach For Problem of Perceptual Presence

We said earlier that we questioned whether the issue of perceptual presence was formulated precisely enough by the positivist-empirical approach. Let's see what the phenomenological approach will enable us to achieve. First of all, we've seen that the intentionality thesis describes consciousness in terms of a series of upsurging acts directed to objects that transcend the acts. This means that consciousness is both active and relational in the sense that it is spontaneous as well as contributory with respect to the objects of conscious acts. Secondly, to say that consciousness is relational and active in the above senses also means that an independently existing material object cannot be the model from which criteria for the nature of consciousness should be drawn. Rather, phenomena such as believing, wishing, perceiving, etc., and their objects should be used as exemplars. Thirdly, the intentional relation also means that even when a material object is used as an intentional object, it should be taken as a presence (related to consciousness), and thus cannot be understood as a discrete event with only external relations with other events. If this last point can be grasped the reason why analyses of descriptions are workable can also be appreciated because the solution to the problem of description rests upon showing that the material aspects of perceptual experience are but moments of a complex structure.

From a phenomenological viewpoint descriptions can serve as legitimate data because the focus of the positivist-empiricist approach, the sensory-perceptual given, is but a moment in a system that already includes the labor of consciousness and language. In fact, the clarification of the system itself is but a prolongation of the labor begun by consciousness and language and further clarification actually enhances the perceptual moment. To understand the actual sensory-perceptual given as but a moment of a system of profiles that constitute the whole perceptual object also means that at any given instant only one profile enjoys actual sensory givenness while all of the other profiles are cointended as possible profiles. In other words, each moment requires a complex set of supplements to be able to exist as such a sensory moment for consciousness. From the viewpoint of consciousness, the supplements are seen as copresent if not coexistential. If the supplements change, the sensory given also changes; and if the supplements can be articulated more adequately, then the sensory moments, in turn, will also appear to be more articulate. Thus the articulation of the perceptual system by means of language is not just a copy of what the perceptual given is, but an actual articulation of the perceptual system.

Let's explore this a bit further. We know that empiricism has been stressing perceptual presence for validity, and we know that science is concerned with facts. Now the curious thing is that even facts are not simple perceptions, but highly elaborated cultural perceptions created by humans. Facts are in the world in a way different from the way that perceptual objects are because facts arise when we want to make statements about things. Facts are things in their articulated intelligibility. Or for phenomenologists a fact is a categorial arrangement articulated in objects (Sokolowski, 1974). A fact is a categorial object. For example, if one could merely stand before a tree for the first time and merely absorb it, it would be the closest one could come to sheer perceptual presence, but as soon as one murmurs "tree" or says "the tree is tall" or "the tree has many leaves" one has gone beyond sheer perceptual presence and established a fact, which is an articulated arrangement of aspects of the object which includes language and other references. While science likes to get its answers in terms of "meter readings," think of the complicated machinery used today in order to get such meter readings. An intelligent comprehension of such a reading goes way beyond mere perceptual presence.

Let's look at an example from everyday life. Suppose you observe the following incident. Someone is sitting and working at his desk and you both hear a voice say "The door is locked." Then you observe the person get up from his desk, open the door and let the visitor in. Now the fact that the person who was working at the desk let the visitor in is observationally simple but analytically very complicated. We do such things all the time in everyday life. But the object of the perception was the whole unified act and not just a momentary slice such as a photograph would give. When we behave the total behavioral act has to be understood as a unity in which what is actualized at a given time is but a moment against a series of possible actualizations that are yet to come or have just passed. And it is the unified totality with its momentary actuality and its horizon of possibilities that is the object of perception. Thus we see that it is complex, articulate and ordered and that is why we can call it a categorial object.

Now the reason that language can express the non-linguistic is because consciousness, which is the root of language, is already at work in the articulation of the world. So, again, one does not have to go from one system to another, but because of consciousness, one is unfolding two aspects of a single system. The very givenness of an articulated presence contains a non-sensorial ground from which the sensory can stand out. Thus, to differentiate the man from the desk and the desk from the floor and the floor from the door shows consciousness at work in discriminating, and in relating the man and the door, it shows consciousness in the act of relating, and when I say "the man is going towards the door," the use of "is" shows consciousness in the act of predicating, etc. The use of "not," or "and" or "is" is what philosophers call syncategorematic aspects of categorical objects and they are non-sensorial, but necessary functions required by categorial objects. "Syncategorematic" means incomplete aspects of a meaningful expression. In brief, the very "standing out" of the man from the desk, etc. is not a passively received imprint but the result of labor of perceptual consciousness and thus a languaging of this "standing out" extends the work of perceptual consciousness.

Thus facts as categorial objects already express a subject–world relationship and that makes description in terms of linguistic specification possible. But here again, a system is at work. Following Sokolowski (1974, 1978) let's say that registration means making statements about objects that are present and reporting means making statements about objects that are physically absent. Once a fact has been discerned, the linguistic activity involved between registering and reporting is not so different. The difference between the two is due to the lack of possible intuitive richness in the case of reporting. Indeed, the identical fact is the core of numerous intellectual processes such as registering, reporting, judging, doubting, etc. and if it were not, discourse would make no sense. The fact can remain identical in part because the syncategorematic moments of the categorial object provide a bridge for the different forms of expression.

All of the above comments refer to facts, but there is even a stronger reason that descriptions can serve as a ground for psychological research from a phenomenological perspective and that is because phenomenological psychology concentrates on meanings rather than facts and the way in which language expresses meanings is no different in registration or reporting. Let's recall that in the phenomenological reduction we deal with presences and not existences. So we're not so much concerned with the way things actually are or were as the way in which they appear to the subjects. Psychology very much depends upon such presences, i.e., the *way things are experienced* by subjects. Pathologies, for example, are based upon such subject references as are emotional experiences, illusions, etc. Now, while it may be theoretically possible to observe subjects over the long haul and makes inferences about their worlds, a psychology based exclusively upon such an external procedure would still fall far short of what would be necessary to have a complete science. Memories and expectations, to mention but two phenomena of intrinsic interest, could never be known in this way. Thus, the only way to know presences for sure is to have subjects express them but whether these expressions are based on registrations or reports is indifferent to their validity because it is the meaning-intending acts that count. We might say that reporting is to registration what the reflective is to the prereflective. Just as prereflectively lived meanings are available for a reflective act that will deepen or elaborate them, so too are the prereflectively registered events available to acts of reporting that can enrich or elaborate them.

The alleged problem of distortion here is only a problem for those concerned with facts from within a "copy theory" of experience which is not a phenomenological presupposition.

To make this point in a technical phenomenological way we would say it as follows. Phenomenologists distinguish among signitive acts, intuitive acts and fulfilled acts. The correlate of the signitive act is an empty intention or meaning (I'm looking for my glasses). The correlate of an intuitive act is presence to an object (Here are a pair of glasses). The correlate of a fulfilled act is the identity between empty meaning and intuition (*These* are *my* glasses). Now, when we express meanings, the meaning expressed is dependent upon the signitive act and not upon the intuitive or fulfilled acts. The latter two serve a function, of course, but they are not the acts that are critical for an analysis of meaning. Even when intuition or fulfillment are present, they are valuable only insofar as they are implicitly revelatory of the signitive acts. Consequently, the expressions of signitive acts are directly visible in descriptive accounts as long as one is looking for meanings rather than facts. The researcher analyzing descriptions in a phenomenological way is actually registering meanings as they appear to a reflective mode of consciousness and they should be present to other researchers just as directly if the procedures are sufficiently specified. In other words, descriptions by subjects can reveal meanings just as directly as pointer readings can reveal numbers.

VI. Phenomenological Psychological Meaning and the Implications For Research

The above was an essentially philosophical and Husserlian analysis of the problem of meaning. We would now like to move to a level where the analysis is more sensitive to psychological concerns. It is important to stress, however, that we are still short of a final solution to this problem because it presupposes a correct grasp of the essense of meaning as well as the essence of the psychological and both, in my view, are not as yet historical achievements. Nevertheless, they won't become achievements until solutions are attempted and the flaws in the attempts are corrected.

As a point of departure, however, we shall try to circumscribe, but not define, the region of the psychological and of meaning.

The psychological is for us the realm of subjectively-coherent pararational or paraobjective patterns of conduct. By the term conduct we imply both the experiential and behavioral aspects of situated human subjects. Psychological reality is the situation understood precisely in terms of its subjective constitution or in other words, in the terms of a subject's dependencies.

The best way to grasp a situation as subjectively constituted is to try to ascertain the lived meaning of the situation for the subject. Such meanings already presuppose intentional relations. Only because of the gaps, lacks or "tensions" created by intentionality can meanings be present. They are synthetic ideal moments embedded within the totality of subject-world, subject-subject and intra-subject relations. With situated behavior, meanings can be directly ascertained. With respect to meanings embedded in persons' experience or presences, language, gesture or other modes of expression are necessary to grasp the lived meanings.

The next important task is to differentiate psychological meaning from philosophical meaning. We mentioned above the four factors necessary for a phenomenological philosophical approach to meaning, and of the four, the second factor, the distinction between meaning intending acts and meaning-fulfilling acts, is the most crucial for distinguishing philosophical meaning from psychological meaning. For one thing, as opposed to philosophical meaning, psychological meaning is much more dependent upon *personal* subjectivity. While it is part of the essence of meaning to transcend subjectivity, the nature of the subjectivity constituting the meaning differs in the two cases. In the constitution of philosophical meaning a level of consciousness that is more suprapersonal or impersonal, than personal, is operating to constitute the meaning. The personal more or less gives itself over to the impersonal and thus meanings that transcend personal subjectivity can be created. On the other hand, psychological meanings are dependent upon a level of subjectivity that is personal. The idea of a suprapersonal consciousness is not a mysterious phenomenon since everyday life already gives much evidence of the derealization of the personal as when, for example, one assumes the attitude of another, or a consciously unprejudiced attitude, or a distant attitude, etc.

A second difference is that the objects of fulfilled acts become equally important for the psychological analysis of meaning.

Since we are dealing with a personal subjectivity rather than an impersonal one, and since the psychological is understood as pararational or paraobjective it becomes important to analyze the noematic achievement as a clue for the noetic analysis of the meaning constituting activity. In other words, at the level of the psychological, the noematic object is much more the result of personal consciousness than of the object as it would be "in itself." Thus a person in a fearful mood sees "frightening dark woods" whereas one in a more objective frame of mind is capable of seeing them merely as a dark woods. In such a case one would want to understand the world or the past history of the personal subject to know why fearfulness is haunting him just now. The "frightening" aspect of the woods is totally dependent upon the acts of that particular subject as a person and that is what a phenomenological psychologist would want to understand. Note, we are dealing with noemata and not facts here, so once again this information is directly available to the reader of a description.

Given, then, the phenomenological theory of psychological meaning just sketched, how can one, in principle, detect such meanings in a description? Descriptions contain words and sentences that are capable of depicting a situation as it exists for the experiencer. Words, or more accurately, sentences, are conveyers of meaning. Linguistic meaning, a mode of conscious expression, presupposes and extends the labor of consciousness begun by prelinguistic presences. Thus descriptions have to be understood as relating levels of consciousness, not two entities such as consciousness and non-conscious matter. But meanings are like bridges and they reveal as much about the consciousness that produces them as they do about the non-conscious affairs toward which they are directed. And since it is analysis of conscious beings in which psychology is interested, an analysis of meaning can lead to psychological discoveries.

Generally speaking, it is the act of speech (writing) that expresses meaning and the act of hearing (reading) that detects it. However, in reading a sentence we do not initially experience a jostling of the meaning of each word and then a delayed welding of them into the unified sense of the sentence. Rather, the meaning of the sentence itself, in a unified but articulated way, is what is directly grasped. It should be noted that for phenomenologists, meanings do not have to be unified, but are directly grasped (Sartre, 1956/1943). For psychological meaning, however, a special attitude (the psychological attitude) is necessary in order to detect the psychological meaning of a text as opposed to its everyday meaning or its philosophical meaning.

Let me try to exemplify these differences in a brief way. In doing some research on learning, subjects were asked to describe situations in which they learned. One subject, an ardent chess player, described a situation in which he gave to his son one of his cherished chess sets in what was for him a solemn manner. The subject then described how the situation evolved into a learning one for him because his son did not want the chess set for chess purposes but because the chess pieces contained leaded weights that he wanted to use for his own ends. The subject described how he learned that the same situation can be seen from different perspectives and how, within limits, each person had a right to his or her own perspective. He realized later that his son was simply never present to the solemn ritual with which he transferred the chess set to him.

Now, in this situation, the objective meaning is that the chess set is a chess set, that is, implements with which a certain game within a certain culture can be played according to certain rules. Without this most universal meaning, the rest of the analysis could not proceed. It is the most invariant base against which more relative meanings can emerge. The everyday meaning of the above situation is that a father gave his son a cherished chess set that he expected the son to receive in the same manner. The psychological meaning of the same situation, which could only emerge after some probing, was that the father simply assumed the priority of his perspective on the situation without allowing for the fact that other perspectives were possible. Note, other perspectives were logically always there, but they were not ex-perienced as possible by the subject. He learned later, however, not only that they were possible, but even dominant. He had to cope with this actuality and a consequence of this coping was that he learned not to assume the priority of his perspective all the time. But this discovery was possible because the chess set and its transferral were seen, not in their objective or everyday sense, but primarily in terms of the personal projects of the two princi-pals. For the father, chess was a significant value in his life and in giving the son his treasured chess set he thought he was doing about as much as a father could do for a son and he expected the son to react appropriately. The son, on the other hand, saw the chess set as a gift out of the blue and appropriated its value in terms of his own projects, and that was to take this pieces apart so that he could use the lead weights for another project. These are acts of "personal subjectivity" embedded in "personal projects." The psychological meanings have to do with the acts of "giving," "expecting," "receiving," "using," and how these acts are lived out in a personal way. Descriptions can reveal such psychological acts adequately because the type of description that reveals the situation for the experiencer also reveals how the experiencer is in the world and the acts of reading and understanding grasp these meanings. Of course the above analysis does not explain *how* meanings can be directly grasped. But the feasibility of descriptions and their analyses is one thing; their explanation is another.

Overall, then, descriptions of situations by subjects can form the base of a research program when the psychological meanings of such descriptions are being sought rather than the objective facts. Indeed, as most therapists know, it's precisely when the expressed facts deviate from objective facts that psychological interest is aroused the most. That is because that is when the lived meanings are most significant in revealing the subjects' personal projects.

As a reminder, it should be noted that the descriptions of situations by the subject and the description of the meaning of the situation for the subject as grasped by the researcher are not reducible to each other. The two, in principle, do not have to be identical because the experience of the situation as described belongs to the subject, but the meaning transcends the subject and is available to others once it has been expressed. The experience takes place prereflectively, but the discovering of the meaning requires reflection. It would be necessary to ask the subject to reflect on his or her experience in order for any chance for identity to be possible but even then it would assume that the subject could assume a psychological perspective as well. For research purposes, it would seem to be better not to ask the subject to play the role of psychologist.

We can see that nothing elaborated in this section is inconsistent with what we said about the phenomenological philosophical approach to description. The issues revolve around description and meaning, only it is psychological description and psychological meaning rather than philosophical description and meaning that is being sought. The difference is simply that psychological meaning adheres more to the concrete and is more delimited than philosophical meaning, but some sense of the Husserlian theory of meaning and description is presupposed.

References

Christensen, N. E. *On the nature of meanings*. Copenhagen: Munks-gaard, 1961.

Findlay, J. N. Translator's introduction, In E. Husserl, *Logical investigations*, Vol. I. N. Y.: Humanities Press, 1970.

Husserl, E. *Cartesian meditations* (Trans. by D. Cairus). The Hague: M. Nijhoff, 1960, (German original, 1950).

_____. *Logical investigations* (Trans. by J. N. Findlay). N. Y.: Humanities Press, 1970 (German original, 1900).

Mohanty , J. N. *Philosophical description and descriptive philosophy*. Paper presented at First Annual Simon Silverman Center Conference on Phenomenological Thought entitled: Phenomenology: Descriptive or Hermeneutic in April, 1983.

_____. *Edmund Husserl's Theory of meaning*, Third ed. The Hague: Nijhoff, 1976.

Ogden, C. K. and Richards, J. A. *The meaning of meaning*. N. Y. : Harcourt, Brace and Co., (1952/1923).

Sartre, J. P. *Being and nothingness*. (Trans. H. Barnes). N. F. Philosophical Library, 1956 (French original, 1943).

Sokolowski, R. *Husserlian meditations*. Evanston: Northwestern University Press, 1974.

_____. *Presence and absence*. Bloomington: Indiana University Press, 1978.

Three Approaches to Descriptive Research

2

Lennart Svensson

Introduction

Within the social and human sciences, communication with people participating in investigations is very often the form for collecting data. The treatment of such data involves interpretation. When meaning is not defined in advance but considered to have to be justified on an empirical basis, the research is descriptive in a fundamental sense. The aim of the research, then, is description of meaning. The descriptions are arrived at by interpretation and qualitative analysis. In relation to this research, some methodological questions may be raised. These concern how to collect the data, how to analyse the data and how to represent the data and the results at different stages of development of the descriptions. A meta-question concerns how to argue for the methods used. In this paper, three different approaches giving somewhat different answers to these questions will be compared.

The three approaches compared have some important characteristics in common, which narrows or concentrates the discussion to a certain variation of methods within descriptive research. In all three approaches, the importance of interpretation and its intuitive nature is emphasized. An algorithmic treatment of data is not accepted as a possible way to arrive at the kind of descriptions aimed at. The three approaches are compared because they represent some differences against the background of the similarity mentioned. The differences in methods reflect general differences in the ways of delimiting the field of research and the phenomena studied. An important factor is also the conception of

*This study was financially supported by the Swedish Council for Research in the Humanities and Social Sciences.

the kind of knowledge aimed at. The field of research delimited and the conception of the results aimed at are manifested in the methodological approach. The specific differences in methods have to be understood in relation to the differences in the general methodologies. The general differences between the approaches are related to the fact that they represent different "turns" in the search for a basis for and for support in answering questions about methods. The three "turns" will be labeled "the scientific turn" (S), "the philosophical turn" (P) and "the linguistic turn"(L).

S means a "turn" to the conceptions of the specific phenomena studied and the field of inquiry as the basis for the development and justification of methods. In this turn, answers to questions about methods are given relative to the phenomena studied. There is an emphasis on the specifics of the methods in relation to the specifics of the phenomena. General ontological and epistemological assumptions are considered as they are represented in the conceptions of the phenomena dealt with and the methodology concerns the implications for the treatment of data about the phenomena. The approach of the present author and his colleagues at the Department of Education, University of Góteborg will represent this "turn". Because it represents the author's position, it will also in a sense represent the framework for the comparison.

P means a "turn" to philosophy to get the answers to the methodological questions. A philosophical position includes positions on ontological, epistemological and methodological issues. The "turn" means that these general positions are considered as assumptions in the empirical work. The assumptions give the frame for answering questions about methods. The development of methods means an exploration of the philosophical framework in relation to the field of inquiry. The phenomenological approach at the Department of Psychology, Duquesne University, Pittsburgh will represent this "turn". Especially, the work of Amedeo Giorgi will be referred to.

L means a "turn" to language, i.e., to forms of representation, as a guide for the development of methods. This means an emphasis on the results and the formal characteristics of the descriptions aimed at and developed. However, the concern is usually not restricted to the end result of research but represents a general concern for representation also as a part of the analyses. L is well represented within the philosophy of science. In the present case, it also represents a turn to the field of linguistics to obtain a framework or a starting point for developing methods. Work carried out by Joan Bliss and Jon Ogborn at the Center for Science Education, Chelsea College, University of London will represent this "turn".

It is not the aim of the present report to give an extensive account of the three different approaches or the work of the researchers referred to. The aim is the more restricted one of illuminating some aspects of the treatment of verbal data by comparing the approaches in some main respects. The aim is to present the different models for dealing with descriptive research. The comparisons will be developed successively starting from some general aspects of the "turns" and going to more specific characteristics of the analyses of data.

The Commitments of the "Turns"

The three "turns" represent somewhat different overall commitments, although the commitments said to characterise the "turns" are not exclusive. In S, the commitment is to the conception of the phenomena studied, based on earlier research (and common sense). Methods are selected, adjusted and developed on the basis of their compatibility with the conceived possible nature of the phenomena. The general assumptions about the phenomena are not taken for granted but temporarily accepted as a basis for judging the consistency between these assumptions and the methods used. The immediate aim is to transcend present knowledge about the specific character of the phenomena studied. Thus S emphasises descriptions of phenomena in terms of their specific nature.

In P, the commitment is to explore the philosophical frame in relation to a general field of inquiry under the assumption that this frame is fruitful. The field is that of psychological phenomena in general. The exploration is also dependent upon knowledge of the field. The research is seen as a development of the implications and possibilities of the philosophy within the field. It is not a question of straightforward derivations but of creating correspondence between the philosophy and the empirical work on main points. The commitment is to integrate the philosophy and the empirical work on the basis of the philosophy. This also includes a development of the philosophy on the basis of the empirical work. The justification of the methods is that of having specified the general assumptions of the philosophy in the most appropriate and fruitful way.

In L, the commitment is to provide forms of representation of data. The aim is to systematise the descriptions of verbal data and to make the descriptions comparable. To fulfill this aim, general forms of representation are suggested. The "turn" as discussed here is not an absolute commitment to certain forms but a commitment to a general system of representation and to the task of finding general categories and combinations of categories that may, within the system, represent the results of exploring interpretative analyses of items of verbal data. The general system is seen as capable of representing within it a great variation as to the specific content of the categories developed. Thus, it is only the general forms of the categories and their relations that are thought to be general while the content of the categories is expected to be based on the analyses of the empirical data.

The three "turns" emphasise the conceptions of the phenomena studied (S), the philosophical assumptions behind the studies (P), and the forms of representing the research data and the results (L). What is emphasized is different aspects of the research and, on a general level, these are complementary. The three approaches to descriptive research, of course, each include all three aspects. The difference in emphasis on one or the other of the aspects is, however, related to differences in ways of dealing with all of them. These differences are not only dependent upon the general nature of the "turn" but also depend on the more specific meaning of the "turn" in the three specific approaches compared.

Fields of Research

The "turns" are important in the search for a basis for finding the specific methods to be used. This basis is a methodology in the broadest sense. The delimitation of the field of research and the phenomena to be investigated is apparently the first step in any empirical investigation and it is crucial for the whole design of an investigation. Phenomena always exist in a context and they may be delimited in different ways in relation to this context. The phenomena are constituted through the intentionality of the researcher in relation to the world. The three "turns" represent some differences in this respect.

In S phenomena similar in content are grouped together and investigated. The investigations are motivated on the basis of earlier research and practical interests. Thus the investigations concern phenomena similar in a rather specific sense or closely related in their existence in the world. In the present case, our own research, the phenomena concern peoples' conceptions or understanding of phenomena and messages; peoples' thinking and learning about different phenomena and themes, and students' study activities and study results. In these investigations, the specific content conceptualized, thought about and/or learned is the basis for delimiting and grouping the cases. Thus, in S, the focus of the delimitation and grouping of phenomena is on the specific content and/or situation. The progressive delimitation, grouping and description of the specific phenomena is the aim of the research and it is carried out by the researcher on the basis of the data provided by the participants. The phenomena described are units of activity, of thinking and doing, carried out by the participants.

In P, the delimitation of phenomena is based on the general philosophical-methodological approach. In the present case, the philosophy of phenomenology is "applied" to the field of psychology. The delimitation of phenomena is a part of developing a phenomenological psychology. The starting point is then taken in some main fields and kinds of phenomena in psychology, for instance perception and learning. It follows from the philosophy that these phenomena should be studied as experiences. Through the phenomenological approach, the true fundamental meaning of the experience, the essence, will be revealed. This essence is expected to be of a general kind and common to many specifically different phenomena.

In P, the starting point in the empirical work is taken in a wide range of phenomena such as very different experiences of learning. The concern is with what the participants have experienced as a real case of the kind of phenomena investigated. Descriptions and groupings of phenomena are based directly on the participants' descriptions, i.e., the data have the character of and are treated as reports on the phenomena studied. The aim of the research is to collect such reports and to find the essence of the individual phenomenon through these reports. Phenomena may then be grouped into fundamentally similar and different phenomena according to their described essences.

In L, the focus is not on individual phenomena per se, but on many phenomena together and extensive materials of verbal data. The concern is with forms of representing the data. In our present case, the forms of representation are modelled after descriptions developed within linguistics. What is modelled is a system of forms representing a hierarchical structure and a network that might be illustrated by a tree diagram with nodes representing options. Superordinate categories or nodes are qualified as to their meaning by subordinated nodes, options or categories. Categories on the same level in the system may be combined to represent a larger part of the data. Such combinations are considered to represent the phenomena and phenomena will finally be described and grouped according to these combinations. The concern thus is with the description and combination of specific verbal data within different fields of research.

Design and Collection of Data

The general commitments and delimitations of fields of research are manifested in the design of the investigations and the collection of data. Within the "turns" the methods of analysis have been developed in relation to restricted sets and kinds of investigation. In S, the design is usually based on a certain group of persons and their relation to a situation, a message, a phenomenon and/or problem. The investigation varies as to number of participants, occasions of data collection and kinds of data collected. Interviewing has been the dominant method of data collection. The interviews are rather unstructured but focussed on one or more themes. They are based on the introduction of the theme by the interviewer and the asking of a very open or general question in relation to the theme, followed by follow-up questions in relation to the participant's answers. How many themes and opening questions that are given in advance and how extensive the follow-up is on each theme varies considerably between investigations.

The interviews contain two kinds of verbal data. One is the participants' explication of their thinking about the content of the themes. This kind of data constitutes the basic data in the investigations. The other kind of data is complementary to the first kind and consists of the participants' reports on their own activity (thinking, reading, studying). In some investigations, only the first kind of data is collected. In other investigations, the two different kinds of data are collected and related for the same occasion and participant to give descriptions of understanding, studying and learning. The analysis and relating of data in the individual case is also based on comparisons within the group participating in the investigation. Thus, the investigations include comparisons between individuals and between groups. The forming of the groups is a part of the analysis and a main result.

In line with the philosophical basis for P and the commitment to develop a phenomenological psychology, the concern is with the common nature of large groups of phenomena rather than with the specific content of some individual phenomena. The interest is in the foundations of psychology and the starting point is taken in some general concepts or groups of phenomena rather than in the specific instances. Particular interest has been devoted to learning because this concept has been seen as especially problematic. The concern then is for the general nature of learning. Fundamental to the design of the investigations is the aim to reveal the nature of learning by describing experiences of learning. Two quite different designs have been used in this case. One is represented by a study by Collaizzi (1973) and builds on an arrangement of a number of learning occasions. The emphasis is on covering different kinds of learning. The participants carry out the arranged tasks and the data collection concerns reports from the participants on different aspects of change that might have been experienced while carrying out the tasks. In this case, the data collection was carried out by the use of a questionnaire.

A quite different design was used by Giorgi (1978). He does not start from any arranged tasks or situations but asks the participants to select examples of learning from their past experience. This design involves more reliance on and use of the participants' experience and less concern for the covering of a general variation. What is common to the two kinds of design is that the concern is with learning in general. The second common characteristic is that the concern is with the participants' reports on their experience of learning as a change. Giorgi (1978) collects these reports in the form of interviews which have the form of the participant telling the story about once when he/she really experienced that he/she learned something.

The forms of representation focussed on in L are not meant to be bound to any specific designs or methods of data collection. However, they seem to have more to offer to investigations characterised by many participants and many different pieces of data. The need to deal with this kind of extensive data has been the background for developing the forms of representation. Several applications of L have been made (Bliss and Ogborn, 1977; Ogborn, 1977; Bliss, Monk and Ogborn, 1983). What makes the system of representation especially relevant is a fairly extensive data material in combination with a concern for description of specific parts of the material and combinations of such specific parts. The characteristic of extensiveness does not necessarily have to apply to each particular investigation. The investigation may be seen as a part in building up a more general system of representations together with other investigations.

Kinds of Descriptions Developed

In the preceeding sections, we have briefly described some general characteristics of the three approaches to descriptive research. In this and the following section, we will focus on the two aspects of the approaches that are our main concern in this article. The first aspect is the kind of description developed and the second is the kind of analysis through which the description is developed. The kinds of descriptions aimed at are seen as the most immediate basis for how the analyses of data are carried out. By giving an example for each approach in this and the next section we hope to be able to clarify some main characteristics of the approaches and some main differences between them.

Categories of description

In all three approaches, the aim is to describe the phenomena studied, but in somewhat different senses. In S, the aim is to both preserve the specific content of the phenomena in the description and to focus on some more fundamental characteristics. The characteristics searched for are those representing whole-characteristics of the phenomena. The aim is to describe the phenomena in terms of their essential meaning. The aim is not to describe the organization or structure of the phenomena per se but to describe the organized content. Still, the descriptions are given in a rather brief and general form, in the form of categories. These categories are considered to represent the content and form of the phenomena together and to summarise a more extensive specific content.

The kind of description aimed at and developed may be exemplified by the following categories. They represent a description of the main similarities and differences among a group of university students in their conception of the main point made in an article about the examination pass rates at the Swedish universities.

Selective measures. Measures are to be taken for some students but not for others (only for those groups of students that do not fulfill the necessary requirements).

Differential measures. One has to consider differences between students in 1) taking measures in university education and 2) making investigations, about university education.

Measures. Something is wrong with university education and/or something must be done about it.

Differences. There are differences between groups of students in examination pass rates and there are differences in the study conditions related to the differences in pass rates.

Greater precision and specificity in the meaning of the categories has to be given in relation to the variation in the answers grouped in the categories. The categories express what is found to be common to the answers in each category, and this also has to be understood against the background of the differences within each category. The categorisation is also based on what is found to be the main differences in conception of the main point of the message. This gives a relation between the categories which is empirically based. When describing conceptions, the focus is on a unit of content. By emphasizing the content per se the description becomes static and represents the result rather than the process of thinking. In other cases, the descriptions concern the activity of thinking, reading, analysing or describing as a whole and the content as a part of the activity. Also, as has been said earlier, there is a great variation in the kinds and extensiveness of the activities researched.

A part of the scientific turn and the concern for the specific characteristics of the conceptions and the thinking is that the analyses and descriptions are also based on comparisons between instances to reveal significant similarities and differences. The categories developed may be said to each stand for themselves by accurately describing each case in the category. However, the significance of the descriptions is revealed through the similarities and differences described by the whole categorization. Thus, the problem of significance is already dealt with in the development of the categories.

Description of essence or structure

In P, there is a strong emphasis on the descriptive nature of the knowledge aimed at in the sense that what are to be attained are descriptions of the essence of experienced phenomena and this delimits the field of research as described above. It is seen as important to avoid premature analytic or explanatory constructs in the descriptions of phenomena, i.e., phenomena are described as they present themselves as meanings for us without taking the further step of stating that they really are what they mean to us. (This is the meaning of the phenomenological reduction.) The knowledge aimed at are the essences of the phenomena and the uncovering of the intentionality of experience. The reduced naive descriptions are the necessary conditions for achieving this aim.

In P, the descriptions concern other peoples' experiences (in contrast to what is the case in philosophy). Thus the naive descriptions of others represent the researcher's data. These are reflected upon by the researcher in order to attain descriptions of essences and intentionality. The essences or structures are not the end of the analyses but are seen as means of bringing to light all of the actual living relationships of experience. The aim is thus to describe the nature of experience and the description of essence is a means to this end. The meaning of essence is not one but several. In philosophy, the main emphasis has been on essences as representing a universal level of analysis. In P, the interest is more in essences or structures that are context-dependent and relevant for typical situations rather than universal. The aim is thus to describe a typical essence which means that the reflection is stopped (or at least halted) short of complete universality. What is aimed at is a level of description that is neither universal nor particular but general.

We shall now give an example from Giorgi (1978) of the kind of descriptions aimed at and developed. The example concerns a report on an actual case of learning. The report was an answer to the following request: "Describe for me a situation in which you learned something". The subject described how she learned to make yogurt. Her "naive description" was transformed to the following description, headed 'General Description of Situated Structure of Learning'

> Learning is the acquisition of knowledge concerning, and the actual execution of, as well as the belief in one's ability to execute on one's own, on demand, a progressive step-like procedure which initially involved the clarification through the mediation of others, of ambiguously lived through moments on account of lack of knowledge or wrongly posited assumptions (p. 46).

As can be seen from the example, the general descriptions aimed at are general in that they do not contain any of the specifics of the naive description. The description is given in general psychological terms which are intended to reveal the essence or structure of the experience described in the naive description. The aim is to leave out the specific content. Still, the approach focusses, in a sense, on the content. The aim is to describe all of the content in an exhaustive way, but in general terms. This means that although the general description is based on the whole of the specific content it does not contain any specific content. This makes the relation between the naive description and the general description one that has to be ascertained through the way of doing the analysis, a general method, which will be described below.

A second example of a naive description reflected upon is given in the same presentation (Giorgi, 1978). It concerns a restaurant owner's learning about the relation between him and the waitresses who are working for him (that they are cheating him and why). The difference between the examples is due to the way of collecting data. It also illustrates that the comparison between cases is not part of developing the general descriptions, but that the general descriptions are based on the individual naive descriptions. Comparisons and groupings of the descriptions of structure may be done as a later systematization of research results. This could include a further analysis and revealing of more general essences common to the experiences grouped together.

Network and artificial coding languages

In L, there is less concern for the delimitation of the phenomena and the field of research as mentioned above. The aim is to develop forms of representation that will be applicable to a great variation in the kind of phenomena described. The aim is to describe the data and the results as combinations of general categories within a system of general forms of representation. L means a turn to linguistics for this general system of forms of representation. The aim is to use these forms to represent the results of intuitive analyses of data. The turn is not for formal linguistic analyses to constitute the relation between data and the descriptions developed. The meaning of the categories is developed on an empirical basis. The crucial question then concerns whether the forms of representation developed are in correspondence with the empirical content to be represented.

The kind of description aimed at is a network that represents the essential meaning of many different statements and at the same time the significant differences between the statements and cases within the perspective of the investigation. Each case is represented by a combination of options within the network. The focus is not on the individual cases but on the network. The following network was developed to represent a set of data consisting of students' stories about experiences in their studies (from Bliss, Ogborn and Grize, 1979, p. 433).

The network is supplemented with a description of the cases in an artificial coding language in which each term not only has its normal range of meaning, but also a fixed and definite meaning assigned by the network. The idea is to invent rules for relating the network to the data by means of a code which reads like a direct analysis of each item of data. By means of this code, a summary description of each case is given. The code has a dual function. It is both a language which is close to the data and at the same time a formal language with fixed meanings assigned by the network.

The concern for representation is a rather specific one aiming at representing specific items of data from a certain perspective and interpretation. Categories referring to items of data and with meanings general across different cases are developed. The individual cases are described as the combination of such categories with generalised meanings. Thus generality is developed for

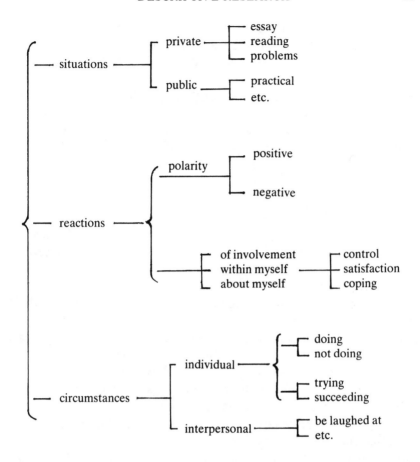

descriptions of rather specific parts of the data. This makes different cases comparable on this specific level, but the assumed correspondence in meaning between cases at the same time presents a problem of justification. The categories provide a basis for comparing and aggregating specific similarities and differences between cases, and also for comparing combinations representing more extensive data about each case.

The Analyses

In the preceeding section we have described what kind of descriptions that are developed within the three approaches. In this section, we shall comment further on the treatment of data using the same examples as above. Within the three approaches, the methods are given somewhat different roles. In S, the methodology concerns the kind of treatment of data and not the procedure. The more specific methods and techniques are not prescribed, but are expected to vary and to be evaluated on the basis of the specific results attained. In P, the procedure is more specified and the methods are seen as a guarantee of the proper results. In L, the main restriction on the methods is that they shall produce the kind of representation of the data intended. In all three approaches the analysis starts with the data being read. However, there are differences in the way of reading the data and in the further treatment of the data.

Contextual analysis

In S, the data material is first read for a whole group of cases in order to obtain a general overview of the material. The material is also read to find out what seem to be significant parts of the data and what seem to be the main aspects in which there are differences between cases. Significant parts and aspects are delimited on the basis of the theme or perspective of the investigation. In the earlier example used, the theme is given through the question referring to the text as a whole. The perspective adopted in the analysis is that of discovering how the students have understood the phenomenon or the author's message as a whole.

In the case of the example given above, what is common to the parts, which are delimited as significant, is that they all refer to the situation at the univerities and what to do about it. It can be further specified that the basis for the categorization is the statements about the differences in pass rates and the statements about measures and their interrelation. For instance, statements about the conditions for, the causes of, or reasons for, the differences are not central for the categorization. Thus, the significant parts are not those referring to the situation at the universities generally but those referring to differences in pass rates and ideas about measures. These parts in many cases represent less than half of the student's retelling of the message of the article.

The significant parts of the retellings, delimited in the way described, clearly form a part of the wider context of the whole retelling and the interview situation. This should be considered when using the descriptions developed. Also, other delimitations of significant parts could, of course, be made for other purposes. What has been illustrated here is that in this approach significant parts of the data are delimited and that this is done on the basis of the referential meaning of the data. Also the descriptions are based on and refer to these significant parts of the data, leaving other parts as background or context.

In the example it is with respect to the ideas about measures that we find the most clear qualitative differences between the students and it is this that is the reason for these statements becoming the focussed ones. When it comes to the arguments for the measures, then other differences are mentioned or left out by individual students. Furthermore, it does not matter which specific differences in pass rates are refered to when it comes to the meaning of the general relation between the differences in pass rates and the ideas about measures — only that the pass rates were high (and satisfactory) for some groups and low (and unsatisfactory) for others. Thus, the categorization describes the most important qualitative differences in the conceptions of the message of the article.

Reduction through transformation

In P, there are four or five distinct steps in the analysis. The first step is an exploration of the whole naive description by reading it enough times to develop a sense of the whole statement. The second step is to read through the text with the specific aim of distinguishing "meaning units". This distinction is made from a psychological perspective and in our present case within the set that the text gives an example of learning. The perspective and set are general and the essence or structure of learning has to be discovered within this general perspective and set. The third step is a transformation of each "meaning unit" from a description close to the subject's language to a description using general psychological categories. We shall now give a brief example of the second and third steps of the analysis of the naive description of the case concerning learning to make yogurt. We just present the first two meaning units delimited and their transformation according to Giorgi (1978).

| Descriminated meaning units expressed as much as possible in S's language based upon perspective that description was an example of learning. | Descriminated meaning units expressed more directly in psychological language and with respect to relevancy for the phenomenon of learning. |

1. In health food store, S and friend get recipe for yogurt.	1. S gets instructions (she desires) from "expert other."
2. S remembers recipe as 1/2 gallon milk and 1/4 cup yogurt — keep mixture at 90°–110° for 5 hours — chill to make firmer.	2. Instructions consist of step-procedures wherein subsequent phases presuppose correctness of earlier phases. Three essential steps are given.

The biggest change made within the first three steps of the analysis in relation to the preceeding steps and the reading of the naive description is made through the transformation in step three. Every unit here is described in a more general way, substituting more general concepts for more specific ones. To get a recipe for yogurt is described as a matter of getting instructions, the prescribed mixture of given quantities of milk and yogurt and the heating and chilling of the mixture become step-procedures wherein subsequent phases presuppose the correctness of earlier phases, and so on. On the basis of this unit for unit transformation done within the set of giving a general description of a case of learning, one or two summary descriptions of structure are developed. The most general of these two kinds of descriptions was presented above.

The second kind of description is called "Specific description of situated structure of learning" and it is somewhat more extensive compared to the general description of structure. It follows the sequence of the "meaning units" and the actual experience. The specific description may be seen as a step in between the transformation of "meaning units" and the general description and/or as a means to clarify the relation. Both descriptions are given in the same kind of general psychological language. The specific description of structure describes the experience of learning as a progressing event while the general description of structure describes the structural characteristics of this event rather than the event per se.

Construction of networks

In L, the analysis starts with a question concerning the relation between students' reactions and the circumstances in which the reactions arise. In relation to the research question, it is assumed that the empirical data can be accounted for by using three general categories: situations, reactions and circumstances. These categories present a starting-point for the analysis of the empirical data, which have to be described as combinations of more specific categories within the three main categories. For this reason, the network presented above begins on the left with the three main categories. The rest of the network is constructed in the form of guesses or hypotheses concerning what will be options within these categories specific enough to account for individual items of data and general enough to apply to many items of data. Decisions have to be made concerning how delicately to distinguish between different items of data by further splitting the options. These decisions depend on the variety represented by the data and the importance assigned to the distinctions that could be made.

Hypotheses or guesses in the form of sketches of a network are checked against the data. Each item of data should correspond well enough with one network combination or pattern (paradigm). This also implies that the whole data material could be divided into items corresponding to network combinations. Questions about whether the items of data represented by the same options are really to be considered the same or not, have to be answered as well as questions about whether the different options really describe the differences between the items of data.

This problem can be illustrated in relation to the network presented earlier. The aim of the analysis was to describe students' reactions to study situations. Two of the reactions described were given the following fixed meanings in the network within the main category of reactions.

A: Positive satisfaction and positive involvement.
B: Positive satisfaction and positive coping.

These combinations of options in the network corresponded to the following descriptions in the artificial coding language.

A: I felt elated and beauty-of-ideas.
B: I felt pleased and able-to-cope.

Questions then to be asked are if it is satisfactory to give "elated" and "pleased" the same meaning of "positive satisfaction" and if the difference between "involvement" and "coping" in the network is enough to distinguish between "beauty of ideas" and "able to cope". These questions have to be answered in relation to the meaning of the corresponding data in the two cases.

The codings in the network and in the artificial coding language are codings of the following parts of the descriptions given by the students.

> A: -and things came out so well I felt like kissing the book . . .
> B. . . .that made me feel very good . . . for the rest of the term I felt so good I could have tackled anything . . .

The code "positive satisfaction" seems to refer to very different experiences in the two cases, the experiences of feeling like kissing a book and feeling like one could have tackled anything. This difference in meaning also illustrates the difficulty of separating the meaning of the reaction from the situation and the circumstances. In the second case, the situation is that of having written a very good essay. It is a general problem in developing the network to delimit the options in a way that as far as possible does justice to the meaning of different items of data as they exist in contexts of larger units of data. As the analysis proceeds, these questions are given their specific answers. It is the dual property of being at once a descriptive language which is rather close to the data and a formal language with fixed and definite terms and meanings, which is seen as making the artificial language code and the associated network useful in handling large bodies of qualitative data.

Main Differences Between the Three Approaches

In this article, some general characteristics of three approaches to descriptive research within the human sciences have been described. They have been described as representing three different "turns" in finding a basis for answering methodological questions. The "turns" also mean some differences in the commitments of the research. The specific cases of research represent associated differences in the delimitation of fields of research and phenomena to be investigated, which are also reflected in the designs and the ways of collecting data. These different aspects of the research were described as a background to comparing the kinds of descriptions developed and the kinds of analysis used to develop the descriptions as the two main concerns of the article.

The differences concerning kind of description are clearly related to the different "turns" and commitments and also to the differences in delimitation of phenomena and data collection. There are two main interrelated differences between the categories of description in S and the descriptions of structure in P. The first concerns the content of the descriptions and the second the assumed or expected generality of the descriptions. In S, the descriptions concern the content of the whole-characteristics of the phenomena (conceptions). In P, the descriptions concern the structure of the phenomena (experiences) with no specific content.

The difference in the content of the descriptions is related to a difference in the treatment of the problem of generalization. In S, there is an emphasis on the general (and the structural) as it appears in the specific cases. There is a concern for differences in the meaning of general structures depending on differences in the contents of which they form parts. In P, there is an emphasis on the general structure as general and on finding the truly general structure. Thus, the most fundamental difference behind the different descriptions seems to concern the belief in the significance of general structural characteristics or the conception of what is the more crucial problem: to find general structural characteristics (P) or to find the characteristics of structure and content together (S).

In both S and P, the descriptions concern whole-characteristics of a delimited phenomenon. The main difference in the nature of the descriptions compared to L concerns this focus on the whole of the individual case. In L, the concern is for a more general system of representation, a network, which is general across all cases studied. This network is made possible through a representation of specific parts of the data and the phenomena in the form of categories given a fixed general meaning. The emphasis is on generalization in the form of generalized descriptions of specific items of data and combinations of such descriptions.

Thus, the three approaches represent three different ways of dealing with content; S describes the content of whole-characteristics, P describes the structure of the whole content and L describes the general meaning of specific contents and constructs a general system of combinations of such general meanings. These kinds of descriptions imply three different kinds of generalization. In S, the generalizations concern the relation between the form (structure) and content of whole phenomena; in P, the generalizations concern the structure of whole phenomena and in L, the generalizations concern the similarity in the meaning of specific parts of phenomena.

There are also some main differences in the ways of carrying out the analyses which are related to the differences between the descriptions. The contextual analysis in S is analytic in the sense that the main focus is on differentiating parts of the data. One differentiation concerns the delimitation of the phenomena to be described. Another differentiation concerns significant parts of the data representing fundamental whole-characteristics of the phenomena. In differentiating significant parts of the data, comparisons between cases are important. The significant parts make up a whole and this is summarized in a description in the form of a category.

The differentiation and selection of parts of data is based on the referential meaning of the data and the justification for the reduction of data is that the fundamental or important characteristics of the referential meaning are focussed on and described against the background of the total set of data. The categories of description give the content of the significant referential meaning of data. The content is given in a summarized form. The categories of description both summarize the result of the analysis on the level of data and give this summary in a general form which is a means for generalization, for developing and testing theoretical hypotheses.

In P, there is also a reduction of the data, but the principle for this is different and it is not analytic as in S. The reduction is achieved through transformation and summary descriptions of transformed data. The transformations are based on the identification of "meaning units". The meaning units are transformed intuitively from having a specific every-day language content to having a general psychological content which corresponds to the every-day language content. The justification for this transformation lies in the relevance of the psychological perspective, the intuitive method and the psychological language used. The transformation gives the basis for a reduction of the extensiveness of the description by giving a description of the structure revealed through the general meaning of the transformed meaning units. Thus, there are two kinds of reductions of the data involved: first, a reduction of the specific every-day language content to its corresponding general psychological meaning and then a reduction of the extensiveness of the description by means of a description of the whole of the transformed meaning units.

In L, the reduction of data is in the form of a code representing specific items of data. This is also a reduction through transformation. The basis for the transformation is an understanding of the specific data (or meaning units) and their general characteristics. The justification is found in the general applicability of the code to à larger material of data. The description of individual phenomena is reduced through the use of a reducing code and it is made a whole through the combination of terms in the code. Both the relevance of and the level of generality-specificity of the terms/categories are tested against the experienced richness of the data and the intended use of the code.

The possibly most apparent differences concern the procedural aspects of the analyses. In S, there is no clear general procedure. What is general is that the starting-point is taken in the data and that the treatment of data involves differentiation and organization of parts and selection of significant parts. In P, on the other hand, there is an emphasis on the procedure. In L, there is also an emphasis on procedure but not as strong as in P. In contrast to S and P, the procedure is clearly deductive. However, the procedure, although it may be the most visible characteristic of the analyses, is not all there is or what is most important. There is another sense in which the analyses represent important differences. It concerns the relation created between the data and the descriptions developed.

In all three approaches, there is a delimitation of the data collected which implies assumptions about the phenomena studied. In S, the further basis for the analysis is that different parts of data may refer to different phenomena or aspects of a phenomenon and that a differentiation of parts may be made on the basis of an interpretation of data concerning their referential meaning. It is further assumed that certain such differentiated units may be focussed on and further analysed and described as to their whole-characteristics. It is considered fundamental to base the delimitation of these parts not on the sequence of the data but on the content of their referential meaning. The content and form of the units/wholes are considered together, which makes the organization of content central in the description.

The descriptions of organized content are developed by means of a discovery based on comparisons between cases and general knowledge about the content and principles of organization. In the example mentioned above, the knowledge concerns universities, groups of students, examination pass rates and so on. The second kind of knowledge concerns forms, structures or principles of organization, like for instance the structure of selective measures and the organizing principle of arguments — conclusion.

This knowledge does not constitute any special theoretical knowledge used as a starting point in the analysis but general knowledge drawn upon when it is discovered to be relevant on the basis of the interpretation of the data and as a part of the data. Thus, in S there is very little specific dependence on theory in the analysis and much dependence on the data and common sense knowledge on the level of the data.

In P, the procedure is prescribed and stepwise which also means that the steps in the analysis are made explicit. The nature of the procedure is intended to guarantee a total account of the data. This is accomplished by differentiating meaning units and transforming all the units into a general description. The descriptions of structure are then based on all the transformed units. The transformation presupposes the existence or creation of a psychological language, into which the intuitively experienced meanings of the "meaning units" are transformed. The intention is to give a description of the whole of the experience to be described, but in a reduced form representing the essence or structure of the experience.

The reduction has the form of a transition from everyday language to psychological language. However, the delimitation of the psychological language used is not clear at the outset but is a part of the transformation. Thus, the reduction represents a step-wise procedure through which the data are transformed into a psychological language. The generalization achieved through this transformation and through the creation of the psychological language is seen as based on eidetic intuition. The essences arrived at are seen as theoretically neutral, i.e., not dependent on any specific theory about the phenomena described.

In L, the hypothetical-deductive procedure would be expected to mean an extensive dependence on theory or on general assumptions. This also seems to be the case. The broad categories started from in the analysis are assumed to be relevant on the basis of the conception of the research question and not on the basis of any analysis of the research data. The following testing of the correspondence of the description to the data is restricted to the variation within these categories already assumed. The development of options within the three main categories are made dependent upon the variation in a rather extensive empirical material. This dependence has the form of comparisons and analyses of similarities and differences between specific items of data. However, also this part of the analysis includes a dependence on general assumptions concerning the significance of different possible options or terms that might be used in the code.

The use of a coding system to represent data means a transformation of data. In L, the transformation concerns individual items of data. This transformation presupposes the existence or development of a code which is different to the ordinary language in which data are given. This relation between the two languages implies that the assumptions built into the construction of the code will influence the interpretation of the data and this is also the reason for developing such a language. Thus, the use of a code always means a theory dependence in the sense of a dependence on the assumptions built into the code. In the present case, the dependence on general assumptions is strengthened by the deductive way of developing the network. The most fundamental need for general assumptions in the analysis concerns the encoding of individual items of data and the basis for separating the data and transforming them into general categories.

Thus, the three approaches include different principles of analysis in line with the differences in the descriptions aimed at and developed. The S-analysis is analytic although in an interpretative sense. It differentiates, organizes and selects data on the basis of their referential meaning and then it describes the meaning of the differentiated, organized and selected data as representing the essential nature of the phenomena, of the conceptions. The P-analysis transforms the whole of the data material into a theoretical psychological language. The nature of the transformed data provides the basis for describing the structure of the whole phenomenon, of the experience referred to by the original specific data. The L-analysis transforms the specific data into terms in a code which is expected to be generally applicable to a set of cases. The original specific data are described in terms of combinations of such terms where the meaning of the different terms combined, are shared with all other cases. Thus, the three approaches may be labelled interpretative-analytic (S), interpretative-transformational (P) and interpretative-aggregative (L).

References

Bliss, J. and Ogborn, J. *Students' reactions to undergraduate science*. London: Heinemann Educational Books, 1977.

Bliss, J., Mark, M. and Ogborn, J. *Qualitative data analysis for educational research*. London: Croom Helm, 1983.

Bliss, J., Ogborn, J. and Grize, F. The analysis of qualitative data. *Eur. J. Sci. Educ.*, 1979, *1*, 427–440.

Collaizzi, P. F. *Reflection and research in psychology: A phenomenological study of learning*. Dubuque: Kendall/Hunt Publ. Co., 1973.

Giorgi, A. *Phenomenology and psychological research*. Paper presented at Duquesne University's Centennial Symposium on Phenomenology and Psychology, Pittsburgh, 1978.

Marton, F. On non-verbatim learning. I. Level of processing and level of outcome. *Scand. J. Psychol.*, 1975, *16*, 273–279.

Ogborn, J. *Small group teaching in undergraduate science*. London: Heinemann Educational Books, 1977.

Svensson, L. *Study skill and learning*. Göteborg: Acta Universitatis Gothoburgensis, 1976.

The Concept of Content in Phenomenography and Dialectics[1]

3

Yrjö Engeström

1. Introduction: The Problematic Intentions of Qualitative Research

Most characteristically, qualitative psychological and educational research questions the value of generalizations reached through traditional quantitative research.

> Starting with a number of cases and identifying and quantifying a limited number of factors, a typical study might ordinarily derive statistical correlations between factors and statistical probabilities that such correlations occur or do not occur by chance. . . . These generalizations may or may not hold for any of the individual cases that went into formulating the collective quantification of each factor (Willis 1978, p. 7).

This is actually criticism against *formal empirical generalizations* as the ultimate outcome and objective of research. However, most proponents of the qualitative approach indentify formal empirical generalizations with generalizations in general. The conclusion is:

> In contrast, qualitative evaluation aims at *particular* understanding (Willis 1978, p. 8).
>
> . . . the most general message is that we should not remain with generalities (Marton 1981b, p. 168).

Thus, generalizations are given up and the focus is switched to the specific, the unique and the individual. This switch is entailed in the development and use of a number of qualitative research techniques and skills. At the same time, fundamental epistemo-

1. The study reported in this paper is a part of a research project concerning the teaching and learning of theoretical concepts, financed by the Academy of Finland.

logical and methodological questions are often tacitly set aside. For example: How does the researcher find the essential qualities in the first place?

> Depending on the insightfulness and skill of the evaluator, qualitative techniques may or may not focus on the most significant characteristics and qualities of an unfolding situation and may or may not generate perceptive or even adequate meanings and explanations. . . . (Willis 1978, p. 8).

The outcome of this endeavour is often the replacement of statistical correlations with singular descriptions, of 'objective' causal connections with subjective experiential interpretations. It is not unusual to see qualitative methods used simply for the purpose of confirming, enriching and illustrating the more or less finished and conscious theoretical framework of the author. As in the case of mainstream quantitative research, one is left with the feeling: 'no surprises, we already knew this.'

Methodologically conscious proponents of qualitative research are no doubt aware of these pitfalls. Thus some philosophically more ambitious attempts have emerged within the qualitative movement during the last few years. These attempts are aimed at overcoming the typical methodological subjectivism and arbitrariness characterized above. The recent work of Ference Marton and his colleagues, associated with the heading *phenomenography*, may be regarded as one such attempt in the area of human thinking and learning.

In the following, I take a critical look at the tenets of phenomenography. This critical assessment leads me to a discussion of the general qualities required of a viable qualitative methodology. Finally, I shall consider dialectics as a possible basis for a qualitative research methodology. The concept of *content* shall be analyzed as a point where certain essential differences between phenomenography and dialectics are condensed.

2. Phenomenography as a Scientific Endeavour[2]

Marton distinguishes between asking questions about the world around us *and* asking questions about people's ideas about the

2. After finishing this paper, I have become acquainted with Marton's new theoretical contribution 'Toward a Psychology beyond the Individual' (Marton 1984). The new article represents a major development in Marton's approach but it cannot be assessed here in detail.

world around us. The former is called the first-order and the latter the second-order perspective in research. Marton advocates the second-order perspective (Marton 1981a).

Marton uses another dichotomy, too, namely that between a *relational or contextual* approach and the standpoint of *naive realism*.

> The experience of a certain aspect of reality is a relation between that which is experienced and the one who is experiencing and, to the extent we can discern a number of qualitatively different ways of experiencing a certain aspect of reality, our reality is socially constructed. . . . Fundamental 'givens' of our existence are man-made. We have simply learnt to experience reality in one way instead of any of a number of other possible ways.

> The alternative to thinking in terms of possible multiple realities is the philosophical standpoint of *naive realism*. According to this view we more or less have a direct access to reality. Reality is what we experience through our senses (Marton 1981b, p. 160).

Needless to say, Marton defends the first position.

These dichotomies, however, do not distinguish Marton from many other qualitative researchers. To the contrary, research directed toward experiential description of people's conceptions, feelings and intentions is quite typical of the phenomenologically oriented qualitative research. Marton's phenomenography goes one step further. Its aim is to:

> find and systematize forms of thought in terms of which people interpret aspects of reality — aspects which are socially significant and which are at least supposed to be shared by the members of a particular kind of society; namely, our own industrialized Western society (Marton 1981a, p. 180).

> We should put all the findings together which concern the experi-ence (conception) of, for instance, time (or power or learning or justice) irrespective of whether the studies from which they origi-nate stem from pre-school children in Massachussets, Samoan aborigines, medieval writings or the daily life in a London suburb.

> This would of course bring the content of thinking into focus. The relational, experiential and content-oriented points of view of human thinking very obviously go together (Marton 1981b, p. 168).

In other words, Marton wants to relate individual conceptions to the 'collective mind' of a society. Instead of the sources of variation in people's conceptions, Marton wants to focus on the contents of that variation. The outcomes of this kind of research are *categories of description*.

> . . . the uncovering of the distinctly different ways in which a certain aspect of reality can be experienced is a *result* in itself and . . . such results should be compiled . . . (Marton 1981b, p. 167).

For Marton, the concept of content is rather unproblematic. Content, or rather *perceived content* (Marton 1981b, p. 168), is manifested and embodied in people's *conceptions*. Conceptions are studied by asking people about their views and by letting them produce answers or solutions to different problems.

In pedagogical terms, this implies the study of learning and teaching in the *learner's* perspective. This can be expressed as the demand to *make the pupils' conceptions the content of instruction*.

3. The Antinomies of Phenomenography

Marton's approach contains fundamental problems which can be formulated as antinomies. Four such antinomies may be identified.

1) Marton advocates the *relational* view according to which the experience of a certain aspect of reality is a relation between that which is experienced and the one who is experiencing. All concepts and conceptions are dependent on the context, they are social constructions. In other words, we are dealing with *relations* between reality and conceptions, between the first order and the second order. This is an exciting and promising idea. But it turns out that Marton denies this very idea as soon as he has put it forth. He concentrates exclusively on the conceptions as such, cut off from their 'first order' basis. This means among other things that Marton is not interested in the 'truthfulness' or substantial validity of the conceptions.

> What we want to thematize . . . is the complex of possible ways of viewing various aspects of the world, the aggregate of basic conceptions underlying not only different, but even alternative and contradictory forms of propositional knowledge, irrespective of whether these forms are deemed right or wrong (Marton 1981a, p. 197).

Thus, the relational intention vanishes and we are left with a very un-relational and static approach. Clearly people get their conceptions — though mediated in manifold ways — through their sense organs from the surrounding reality. If the tension-laden relations and interactions between conceptions and reality are eliminated, it is impossible to study the change, the dynamic development of the conceptions.

The mediating link between reality and conception is human object-oriented activity. In the phenomenographic analysis, the researcher looks at the statements and conceptions as such, not as expressions and reflections of the subjects' life activities. Marton himself notes this fundamental problem:

> A conception exists in the real world only in terms of a mental act and it is exhibited by someone who does something in a certain setting. In talking about categories of description, then, we 'bracket' the dynamic-activity perspective and we consider the categories almost as if they were 'frozen' forms of thought, (Marton 1981a, p. 196).

This important and potentially self-critical statement is, however, left hanging in the air. In his programmatic writings, Marton cannot avoid incorporating actions into conceptions; he asks us to study how persons 'perceive the situation', how they think and how they experience (Marton 1981b, p. 162).[3] But when he gets closer to the practical research, the focus is narrowed down to the collection, description and classification of statements representing different conceptions.

The problem of ignoring activities in the study of conceptions leads to serious questions concerning the validity of the empirical results obtained. Knowledge becomes easily identified with an imaginary static structure — the 'conception.' Yet knowledge exists only in the form of material and mental actions. If these actions and their wider contexts — activities — are not studied, it remains unclear and unknown, just what actions constitute the 'conceptions' obtained from the subjects in different situations and what is the overall importance of the given 'conception' in the

---

3. Marton (1981b, p. 165) even cites Smedslund's (1977) contention that we should consider " . . . only children's concrete activities in concrete situations as real". The concept of activity, however, receives no further theoretical attention from Marton. It does not fit into his conception of phenomenography, but at the same time it is difficult if not impossible to eliminate.

subject's activity. In her study of students' perceptions of evolution, Margaret Brumby provides an example of this problem.

> These students had studied Darwinian evolution . . . and therefore 'knew' that Darwin's theory is based on the selection or survival in the nature of 'the fittest'. Their difficulty was not in having the knowledge, but in being able to *use* their knowledge in unfamiliar problems (Brumby 1979, p. 224).

Even Brumby shares the misconception of knowledge as something that can be 'had', i.e., the separation of knowledge and activity. There is no knowledge 'as such' in the subject, existing outside actions as if stored in a container. But Brumby's example shows how hopeless it is to study human thinking, learning and understanding without a truly relational and processual theory of these activities, understood as forms of societal practice.[4]

The first antinomy of phenomenography may now be defined as that between *the professed relational approach and the actually realized un-relational, static study of conceptions*, or between *activity and conception*.

2) According to Marton, there are two distinctly different ways of dealing with human thinking. The first one takes the subjects' logic for granted and studies the different ways of understanding some particular aspect of reality among the subjects. The second one takes the subjects' understanding for granted and seeks to explain the different solutions provided by the subjects on the basis of different developmental levels in their logic (Marton 1981b). This dichotomy understanding/logic is borrowed from

---

4. Thus Brumby's conclusion must be completed with the remark that the contexts and activities of the usage and generation of knowledge are societal and not merely technical 'problem situations.' Knowledge about evolution, for example, is used in different ways and with different contents in classes of natural sciences and in classes of religion (see Engeström, 1981). It is noteworthy that certain approaches within or close to cognitive psychology have realized the action-character of individual knowledge (though not its socio-historical character). Thus, proponents of 'ecological pscyhology' "prefer to talk about knowing as something that the organism does rather than knowledge as something the organism has" (Michaels & Carello, 1981, p. 62). And the prominent student of problem solving, James Greeno (1980, p. 20), points out that "the concepts to be acquired are components of a decision process, rather than simple labels."

It is symptomatic that Marton writes programmatically about the social construction of conceptions of reality. Yet the processess and dynamic mechanisms of this very construction are left outside of his practical research interest.

Smedslund (1970). Marton strongly opposes the second alternative, i.e., the use of some general logic as the basis of assessing individual variations in thought.

In Marton's opinion:

> To the extent that we move to a more abstract and general level on which thinking is characterized, *what* is thought about is left behind (Marton 1981b, p. 165).

In other words, there is an inverse relation between the level of logical generality and the richness of content in our study of thinking. This idea implies a strict divorce between logic and content. Logic is a set of formal rules of correct thinking, content is something upon which these rules are applied.

In effect, Marton is criticizing *formal logic* as the criterion of the level of thinking. Formal logic is indeed indifferent to specific contents upon which it operates. This is most clearly expressed in Piaget's work where the level of formal operations is supposed to be independent of contents. But Marton identifies formal logic with all logic, with *logic in general*. This leads him to a peculiar antinomial position. On the one hand, he totally denies logic as the criterion of thinking, demanding it to be taken for granted, as something self-evident in every individual. On the other hand, as he sees no logical alternative to formal logic, he is forced to recognize and partially accept the formal-logical apparatus of Piaget.

> Even if our philosophical standpoint and an overwhelming amount of empirical evidence force us not to speak of concrete-operational or formal-operational *children*, we may still find it most revealing to speak of concrete-operational or formal-operational *ways of thinking* . . . (Marton 1981b, p. 166).

In other words, logical categories are after all necessary for the adequate description and analysis of human thinking. The only kind of logical categories known to Marton are formal-logical categories. Thus, he ends up willy-nilly using the very same logical apparatus that originally has caused his distress with logic, namely the apparatus that is totally divorced from the substantial contents and only interested in formal relations.

The second antinomy of phenomenography may now be defined as that between *the professed logic-independent approach toward thinking and the actual use of formal-logical categories in the description of thinking*, or between *logic and content*.

3) Marton attacks the standpoint of naive realism. According to that view, we have more or less *direct access* to reality. Reality is what we experience through our senses (Marton 1981b, p. 160). Marton wants to replace this approach with a relational approach which recognizes that our reality is socially constructed.

To be consistent with his own tenets, Marton should apply this principle to his own way of treating research data. For Marton, the essential data are statements representing the 'second-order reality,' i.e., the conceptions. How is this data treated?

For Marton, this seems surprisingly unproblematic. The conceptions are to be compiled, described, interpreted and classified. We are supposed to "discern *fundamental differences* in the way individuals approach a certain kind of task or think about a certain aspect of their world" (Marton 1981b, p. 166, italics mine). But what are fundamental differences and how do we find them? Shouldn't we have some kind of substantial theory of the aspect of reality (including the formation of the 'second order' conceptions about it) under investigation? — These questions are left unanswered.

In fact, it seems that Marton is treating his data, the 'second order reality,' in much the same manner he is criticizing in the tradition of naive realism. He seems to suppose that we have, indeed, *direct access* or at least intuitive access to phenomena of the 'second order.' Conceptions (= the second order) are what we experience through our senses. Instead of naive realism, we might here speak of 'naive phenomenologism.'

Marton's approach implies that the researcher looks at his or her data with no bias, putting his or her previous theories and concepts temporarily aside into 'brackets'. This is essentially the same idea the traditional positivist research formulated as the demand "*all theorists accept all the facts*" (Hilgard & Bower 1966, p. 9). In other words, first we have a certain amount of neutral sensory data or facts (be they of the 'first or second order' makes little difference here). After this, we start describing, classifying, generalizing — and eventually formulating explanations and theories.

It is well known that our perceptions and experiences are always 'theory-laden.' This is accepted as one of the points of departure in Marton's programmatic presentations. But the closer we come to the recommendations concerning practical research procedures, the more obvious it becomes that the role of theory in the initial apprehension of empirical, sensory data is neglected or, at best, explained only in terms of the *subjective, individual* bias or involvement of the researcher.

That reality is *objectively, not only subjectively socially constructed,* is not pointed out. The objects of our perception (including statements) are themselves socio-historically formed and produced. The practice under our eyes is already theoretical and cannot 'speak for itself.' It cannot be directly or spontaneously grasped. It has to be *reconstructed theoretically,* using consciously conceptual *instruments* that correspond to the nature of the means and methods with which the objects of reality were originally produced.

> The world confronts the individual as the thought of preceding generations realised ('reified,' 'objectified,' 'alienated') in sensuously perceptible 'matter' — in language and visually perceptible images, in books and statues, in wood and bronze, in the form of places of worship and instruments of labour, in the designs of machines and state buildings, in the patterns of scientific and moral systems, and so on. All these objects are in their existence, in their 'present being' substantial, 'material,' but in their essence, in their origin they are 'ideal', because they 'embody' the collective thinking of people, the 'universal spirit' of mankind (Ilyenkov 1977, p. 81).

It is symptomatic that Marton does not stress the researcher's knowledge about the particular aspect of reality reflected in the conceptions under scrutiny. Somehow the researcher is supposed to be able to classify conceptions concerning any arbitrary aspect of reality, simply on the basis of the subjects' statements. That these statements are adequately understood only as mediated manifestations of historical processes of societal practice, of the thought of preceding generations, of the 'universal spirit' of mankind, seems to be an alien idea to phenomenography. The researcher casually obtains a flavor of omnipotence without any deeper substantial and historical insight in the contents he or she is classifying.

The third antinomy of phenomenography may now be defined as that between *the professed denial of 'direct access to reality' and the actual empiristic treatment of research data as something to be directly described, interpreted and classified,* or between *theory and data.*

4) Every scientific concept contains a certain method. Modern scientific knowledge is essentially methodological. It contains not only the cognition of an object of study but also consideration of itself, of the method of its own generation: "its typical feature is the direct inclusion of methodological techniques into the content of knowledge" (Ovchinnikov 1979, 105).

The central concept of phenomenography is *conception*. Its operative counterpart is *category of description*. According to Marton

> . . . we regard categories of description simply as tools used to characterize ways of functioning . . . (Marton 1981b, p. 167).

The central concepts of phenomenography are thus essentially of descriptive nature. This is in line with the programmatic tenets of the approach. But another tenet is *content*-orientation. What is the content of the concept of conception? In other words, what essential *inner relations* of the phenomena called human thinking does the concept conception contain?

We find that the concept of conception is essentially empty, to be filled with arbitrary contents. Conception as such is a formal vessel with no apparent inner relations of its own. Such a formal concept is essentially a product and an instrument of *formal, empirical generalization*. It is obviously generated by recognizing that people have all kinds of different subjective experiences, images, conceptualizations, opinions, solution patterns etc. The common denominator is that all these are subjective reflections of some aspects of reality — so let's call them conceptions (the term could be any other as well). And let's use this term as a formal instrument of classifying different subjective reflections.

A concept (better: a term) of this type is an example of *separating content and method, theory and methodology*. Since it contains no visible inner relations, it is void of the *historical self-movement* characteristic to genuine theoretical concepts. Paradoxically, Marton (1981a) stresses the evolutionary, continuously developing character of conceptions. But his very concept of conception is generated and applied in such a manner that it cannot reveal that movement. In other words, to be a truly theoretical concept, it should reveal the inner relations that constitute the 'mechanism' of the birth and continuous change of conceptions. Now it is only a formal label, an empirical term. As such, this term explains nothing and cannot function as the wellspring of new theoretical knowledge.

The fourth antinomy of phenomenography may now be defined as that between *the professed content-orientation and the actual formality of the central concepts*, or between *theory and methodology, content and method.*

4. Necessary Qualities of a Qualitative Methodology

The four antinomies characterized above may be divided into two subgroups. The first two antinomies are specific in the sense that they concern one defined research area, namely the study of human thinking and learning. These two first antinomies deal with concepts like *activity, conception, logic of thinking* and *content of thinking.*

The latter two antinomies are of a general nature. They are not restricted to any specific field of study. We may safely say that these two latter antinomies must be consciously elaborated and overcome if we are to develop a qualitative methodology in general. In other words, the relations between *theory and data* on the one hand and between *theory and method (methodology)* have to clarified in a viable qualitative methodology of human sciences.

At this stage of our discussion, we may attempt a preliminary formulation of the necessary qualities of a qualitative methodology of research in human sciences.

Firstly, the new methodology must take the theoretical nature of practice, the theory-laden character of empirical observations and experiences as its point of departure. It must give us tools to observe and analyze reality theoretically from the beginning, i.e., give us a method of seeing the 'facts' or objects of perception in their social and historical origination and functioning, in their interdependence and developmental determination. In other words, the new methodology must lay out the *general principles of theory formation* which enable us to overcome *both* the hypothetico-deductive/experimental-inductive *and* descriptive-experiential empiricism, characteristic of the 'normal science' and much of the 'qualitative research', respectively.

Secondly, the new methodology must give us a method of deriving systematically the central explanatory concepts of our research and a method to use them to create new theoretical knowledge. In other words, the central concepts must be *substantial*, they must reveal the essence of the phenomena studied, i.e., their *inner relations*. At the same time, the central concepts must be *functional* as *procedural tools*, they must contain the method of their own creation and development. Thus, the new methodology must be a methodology of *concept formation through concepts*; it must unify the theory and the method of inquiry.

The prime candidate claiming to answer these demands is *dialectics* as a general theory and method of cognition.

5. Dialectics as a Theory and Method

During recent years, we have witnessed an increasing interest in dialectics within the behavioral and social sciences of the west. The 'dialectical psychology' of Klaus Riegel and his followers is but one example of this trend (see Riegel, 1979).

Much of this new interest is, however, plagued by what may be called *pseudo-dialectical formalism* (or formal pseudo-dialectics). Central categories of this formal brand of dialectics are *interaction* and *dialogue*.

In this mode of reasoning, interactions are analyzed as such, as pure forms. The object contents of interaction play a minimal role. The historically formed substance of interaction, i.e. the substantial character and quality of both the objects and subjects of interaction, is neglected. Charles Tolman (1981) has aptly called this approach 'the metaphysic of relations'.

> In short, from a dialectical point of view, the dialogue or any other interaction cannot explain anything; it remains itself to be explained — by metaphysics or mechanism in terms of outside forces, by dialectics in terms of the internal contradictions of the entities or persons interacting (Tolman 1981, p. 46).

This criticism applies well to the version of formal dialectics which reduces dialectical logic to a method of tracing and analyzing contradictions *between interpretations* of an object or event. Dialectics becomes here a mode of debate. Attention is thus diverted from the substance and inner contradictions of objects themselves. Dialectics becomes a 'pure method' void of any statements concerning the content of the world around us (e.g., Mitroff & Kilmann, 1978; Mitroff & Mason, 1981).

Modern proponents of formal dialectics justly refer to Hegel as the founding father of scientific dialectics (e.g., Riegel 1979, pp. 35–55). Their interpretations, however, do not do justice to the quality of Hegel's thinking. Grasping the essence of the real Hegel is a necessary prerequisite of materialist, that is, *substantial, content-bound* dialectics.

It is well known that *reason, thought* was for Hegel the prime mover and infinite power through which and in which all reality finds its being. But reason or thought was *not* something purely mental, taking place within the individual's head and manifesting itself in words only. Hegel demanded that thought should be investigated in all the forms in which it was realised, above all in human actions and activities, in the creation of things and events outside the head of the individual.

> Thought revealed its force and real power not solely in talking but also in the whole grandiose process of creating culture and the whole objective body of civilisation, the whole 'inorganic body of man' (Marx), including in that tools and statues, workshops and temples, factories and chancelleries, political organisations and systems of legislation (Ilyenkov 1977, pp. 175–176).

On this basis, Hegel correctly saw the logical forms of the individual consciousness as being objectively determined by things outside the individual psyche, by the *entire spiritual and material culture*, collectively created and transformed by people, surrounding the individual and interacting with him from the cradle. This collective process, the intellectual development of humanity, could be objectively traced in the history of science and technique. According to Hegel, this process also included, as a phase, the act of realising thought in object activity, and through activity in the forms of things and events outside consciousness. Here Hegel "came *very close* to materialism," as Lenin (1963, p. 278) noted.

Thought had to be investigated as collective, co-operative activity where the individual performed only partial functions. In really taking part in common work, the individual was subordinating himself to the laws and forms of universal thought, though not conscious of them as such.

For Hegel, dialectics was the form and method of thought that included the process both of elucidating contradictions and of concretely resolving them on a more profound level of understanding the essence of the same object. In other words, the contradictions could be resolved only "in the course of developing science, engineering, and 'morality', and all the spheres he (Hegel) called the 'objective spirit'" (Ilyenkov 1977, p. 190). The practical outcome of dialectical thought was not individual adjustment but collective societal development and qualitative change of human culture.

Hegel's essential superiority to the modern proponents of formal dialectics lies in two facts: (1) Hegel pointed out and defended the *objectivity* of logical forms of thought, their origination in the universal forms and laws of development of human culture — science, technique, and morality; (2) Hegel introduced *practice*, the process of activity on sense objects that altered things in accordance with a concept, into our conception of thought and logic.

> The subject matter of logic then proved to be those really *universal* forms and patterns within which the collective consciousness of humanity was realised. The course of its development, empirically realised as the history of science and technique, was also seen as that 'whole' to the interests of which all the individual's separate logical acts were subordinated (Ilyenkov 1977, p. 197).

But where did these universal forms and patterns of logic come from? How did universal spirit originate?

In order to understand Hegel's view, we have to realise that he did not take any easy answers from religion. His conception was an accurate reflection of the real conditions under the spontaneously developing division of social labor, the separation of mental work from physical labor in particular. Under these conditions,

> the separate human individual did not prove to be the bearer, i.e., to be the subject, of this or that universal faculty (active power), but, on the contrary, this active power, which was becoming more and more estranged from him, appeared as the subject, dictating the means and forms of his occupation to each individual from outside. The individual as such was thus transformed into a kind of slave, into a 'speaking tool' of alienated universally human forces and faculties, means of activity personified as money and capital, and further as the state, law, religion, and so on. (Ilyenkov 1977, p. 230).

Science also was transformed into a special profession, above of and opposed to the majority of human beings, to practical physical labor.

Registering and reproducing this condition, Hegel actually counterposed man and his real thought to impersonal 'absolute' thought as an eternal force which had actually created man and the world of man. Logic became an absolute form, in relation to which the material world and real human activity were something derivative, secondary and created. The scientist, the mental worker, appeared as the representative of the universal thought, approaching and formulating its categories. The sensuously objective activity of physical labor, creating the material body of culture, remained outside Hegel's view. It appeared to him only as the 'prehistory' or 'application' of thought.

> Thought was thus transformed into the only active and creative force, and the external world into its field of application. Naturally, if the sensuously objective activity (practice) of social man was represented *as the consequence*, as the *external objectification of ideas*, plans, and concepts created by thought (i.e. by persons occupied in mental work), it became in principle impossible to say either what was the source of thought in the head of theoreticians or how it arose (Ilyenkov 1977, p. 237).

It follows quite logically that the *word* (speech) appeared as the primary tool of the externalization and objectification of thought. "The real tool — the stone axe or cutting tool, scraper or wooden plough — began to appear as the second and secondary, derived tool of the same process of objectification . . ." (Ilyenkov 1977, pp. 239–240). Labour only realised what the thinking spirit had found in itself in the course of its dialogue with itself.

According to Hegel, man thought initially and then acted accordingly. The initial form of existence of thought was the word. Thus, Hegel's schema can be expressed as follows:

WORD — ACT — THING MADE BY THE ACT — WORD.

Ilyenkov sums up the essence of Hegel's position:

> The Hegelian logic described the system of objective forms of thought within the limits of which revolved the process of *extended reproduction of the concept*, which never began, in its developed

forms, 'from the very beginning', but took place as the *perfecting of already existing* concepts, as the transformation of *already accumulated* theoretical knowledge, as its 'increment' (Ilyenkov 1977, pp. 247–248).

According to Engels, dialectics is "nothing more than the science of the general laws of the motion and development of nature, human society, and thought" (Engels 1975, pp. 168–169). In other words, dialectical logic is not only the science of the laws and patterns of thought, but also, and above all, the science of the development of all things, both material and 'spiritual'. It is the science of "the reflection of the movement of the world in the movement of concepts" (Ilyenkov 1977, p. 9).

Hegel was also interested in the world around us, in the human culture and labor. But he considered them as derivatives of the universal thought. This rendered him unable to study the different forms of nature and culture *in their own right*, independently of the eternal universal spirit. Even so, Hegel never reduced dialectics to pure 'dialogic interactions' or 'procedures of debate', void of objective contents. Hegel may have seen the relation between thought and external material world upside down, but he certainly didn't exclude the world from his eyesight: ". . . thinking is not an activity which treats the content as something alien and external; it is not reflection into self away from the content" (Hegel, 1966, p. 113).

Hegel directed devastating criticism against abstract formalism.

> If the knowing subject carries round everywhere the one inert abstract form, taking up in external fashion whatever material comes his way, and dipping it into this element, then this comes about as near to fulfilling what is wanted — viz. a self-origination of the wealth of detail, and a self-determining distinction of shapes and forms — as any chance fantasies about the content in question. It is rather a monochrome formalism, which only arrives at distinction in the matter it has to deal with, because this is already prepared and well known (Hegel, 1966, p. 78).

In contradistinction to formalism, Hegel defined the proper nature of dialectics:

> The abstract or unreal is not its element and content, but the real, what is self-establishing, has life within itself, existence in its very notion. It is the process that creates its own moments in its course,

and goes through them all; and the whole of this movement constitutes its positive content and its truth. This movement includes, therefore, within it the negative factor as well, the element which would be named falsity if it could be considered one from which we had to abstract. The element that disappears has rather to be looked at as itself essential, not in the sense of being itself fixed, that has to be cut off from truth and allowed to lie outside it, heaven knows where; just as similarity the truth is not to be held to stand on the other side as an immovable lifeless positive element (Hegel, 1966, p. 105).

In other words, dialectics deals with real *substantial contents*, both material and spiritual. Moreover, dialectics deals with the *movement* of objects. This movement is characterized by two essential features: it is *self-movement*, not externally caused but internally generated (*causa sui*), and it is movement in the form of *inner contradictions*. Dialectical thinking "should sink into and pervade the content, should let it be directed and controlled by its own proper nature, i.e. by the self as its own self, and should observe this process taking place" (Hegel, 1966, p. 117).

The process of dialectical thought is compared with the process of formal understanding.

> Instead of making its way into the inherent content of the matter in hand, (formal) understanding always takes a survey of the whole, assumes a position above the particular existence about which it is speaking, i.e. it does not see it at all. True scientific knowledge, on the contrary, demands abandonment to the very life of the object, or, which means the same thing, claims to have before it the inner necessity controlling the object, and to express this only. Steeping itself in its object, it forgets to take that general survey, which is merely a turning of knowledge away from the content back into itself. But being sunk into the material in hand, and following the course that such material takes, true knowledge returns back into itself, yet not before the content in its fullness is taken into itself, is reduced to the simplicity of being a determinate characteristic, drops to the level of being one aspect of an existing entity, and passes over into its higher truth. By this process the whole as such, surveying its entire content, itself emerges out of the wealth wherein its process of reflection seemed to be lost (Hegel, 1966, pp. 112–113).

This process unifies the content and the form, the theory and the method.

> The concrete shape of the content is resolved by its own inherent process into a simple determinate quality. Thereby it is raised to logical form, and its being and essence coincide; its concrete existence is merely this process that takes place, and is *eo ipso* logical existence. It is therefore needless to apply a formal scheme to the concrete content in an external fashion; the content is in its very nature a transition into a formal shape, which, however, ceases to be formalism of an external kind, because the form is the indwelling process of the concrete content itself (Hegel, 1966, p. 115).

According to Hegel, the truth is the whole. "The whole, however, is merely the essential nature reaching its completeness through the process of its own development" (Hegel 1966, 81). The whole "comes to the stage to begin with in its immediacy, in its bare generality. A building is not finished when its foundation is laid; and just as little is the attainment of a general notion of a whole the whole itself" (Hegel, 1966, p. 75). Theoretical thought has to find the initial and truly general essence of the complex whole, it has to reduce the whole to its abstract foundation.

> But the actual realization of this abstract whole is only found when those previous shapes and forms, which are now reduced to ideal moments of the whole, are developed anew again, but developed and shaped with this new medium, and with the meaning they have thereby acquired (Hegel, 1966, p. 76).

The dialectical method is a method of grasping the essence of the object by reproducing theoretically the logic of its development, of its historical 'becoming.' The dialectical method is thus a unity of the historical and the logical. The history of the object is purified of its arbitrary details and secondary features, it is elevated to the level of logical succession.

The bare, abstract generality is the point of departure in the theoretical reproduction of the development of the object — of 'the whole,' in Hegel's terms. The bare generality, the initial *'germ cell,'* is the original contradiction that has given birth to the concrete system under investigation. It is the fundamental inner relationship of the system. The mental reproduction of this germ cell through substantial abstraction is the first step in the procedure of *ascending from the abstract to the concrete*, i.e., of understanding the rich forms of the totality, of the 'unity of the manifold,' in their lawful inner determination and movement.

But what is the quality of the 'general'? How is the germ cell found and how does it function?

For formal logic, 'general' means an attribute common to a number of 'examples' of that common attribute.

> In other words, 'a scientific consideration of the world' consists in a purely formal, verbal uniting of a handful of odd facts by subsuming them under one and the same term, under one and the same 'general.' The 'general,' interpreted only as the 'meaning of the term or sign,' always turns out to be something quite arbitrary or 'previously agreed upon,' i.e., 'conventional' (Ilyenkov, 1977, p. 64).

The most famous example of the application of the dialectical method is Karl Marx' *Capital*. In the analysis of the economic system of capitalism, Marx begins with *the commodity*, or the 'commodity form of the labour product,' or the 'value form of the commodity.' This is his germ cell, the bare generality. Marx points out certain requirements that have to be fulfilled by the germ cell. Wolf Fritz Haug summarizes them in the following four: (1) the initial germ cell has to be something commonplace, known to everybody, (2) it has to imply a definite, strictly determined continuation and development, (3) it has to be logically elementary for the system under investigation, (4) it has to be historically the earliest, genetically the initial and undeveloped within the system under investigation (Haug, 1976, p. 35–45).

The nature of the general, of the germ cell, has been most thoroughly analyzed by Ilyenkov (1977, 1979). In his analysis, the fourth of Haug's requirements obtains a decisive role. The general, the germ cell, is above all something genetically initial, literally giving birth to its various subsequent manifestations. To clarify this, Ilyenkov uses the image of a common ancestor, of a father, as an example.

> The image of a common ancestor, . . . of a progenitor, cannot be reconstructed by abstracting those attributes, and only those, that are genetically preserved by all his (or her) descendants. There simply are no such attributes. . . . Among the attributes of a common ancestor who continues to live among his descendants, one has to presuppose a capacity to give birth to something which is opposite to itself. . . (Ilyenkov, 1977, p. 347).

The general or universal is something quite real and material. It is not just an abstraction, based on the observation of external similarities. Furthermore, the general is not only the beginning of the system — it also continues to live as a part of the complex whole to which it has given birth.

> The ancestor, as a rule, does not die but continues to live alongside all its offspring as an individuum among other individua, and the problem consists in discovering among the *existing separate individuals* the one that was born before the others and therefore could have given birth to all the rest (Ilyenkov, 1977, p. 347).

The general is above all the regular *connection* of two or more individuals, a connection that converts them into moments of one and the same real unity, into a concrete system. " . . . the general functions as the law or principle of the connection of these details in the make-up of some whole, or totality, as Marx preferred to call it . . ." (Ilyenkov, 1977, p. 350). The outward expressions of the universal within the system may be and often are seemingly separate and even opposite to one another.

The general or the universal in nature is a law. But a law of nature is not realised as an abstract, mechanically functioning rule or algorithm. It is realised in the form of a *tendency*, manifesting itself in the behaviour of a complex ensemble of individual phenomena, through the negation and breach of the universal in each of its separate manifestations.

> The general includes and embodies in itself the whole wealth of details, not as the 'idea' but as a quite real, particular phenomenon with a tendency to become general, and developing 'from itself' (by virtue of its inner contradictions) other just as real phenomena, other particular forms of actual movement (Ilyenkov, 1977, p. 369).

The general is not eternal. Historically it may have previously existed as an individual exception, as something particular and anomalous. "Only capitalism made value (the commodity form of the product) the general form of the interrelations of the components of production" (Ilyenkov, 1977, p. 368). Before that, this form appeared as a particular relation taking place from time to time between people and things in production.

Genuine scientific breakthroughs have always proceeded from a more or less conscious and consistent conception of the universal or general within the system under investigation. It may be claimed that every researcher is in fact guided by some such conceptions, however vague and erroneous they may be and however fanatically the researcher may believe he or she is working with 'pure facts.'

6. The Concept of Content in a Dialectical Approach to Thinking and Learning

In their seminal work on the meaning of meaning, Ogden and Richards (1936) present a convenient diagram depicting the inner relations of 'meaning' (figure 1).

THOUGHT OR REFERENCE

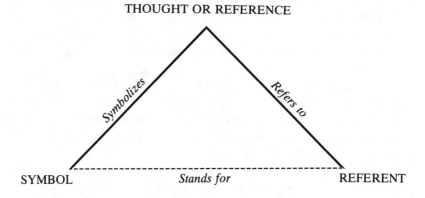

SYMBOL   *Stands for*   REFERENT

Figure 1: Meaning as relations between thoughts thoughts, words and things (Ogden & Richards, 1936, p. 11).

The authors point out the specific nature of the bottom line of the triangle, i.e., the relation between symbol (word) and referent (thing).

> Between the symbol and the referent there is no relevant relation other than the indirect one, which consists in its being used by someone to stand for a referent. Symbol and Referent, that is to say, are not connected directly . . . but only indirectly round the two sides of the triangle (Ogden & Richards, 1936, pp. 11–12).

This is indeed an important realization. It means that there is no direct correspondence between a symbol and a thing it symbolizes, between words and things. This relation is always *constructed* by man and thus historically changing.

> We shall find, however, that the kind of simplification typified by this once universal theory of direct meaning relations between

words and things is the source of almost all the difficulties which thought encounters (Ogden & Richards, 1936, p. 12).

So far, the basic idea of Ogden and Richards seems to be a fruitful point of departure in our inquiry concerning the problem of content. It presents content (= meaning) in a *relational* manner which enables us to study its inner dynamics, movement and contradictions.

But this conception contains certain serious weaknesses. Ogden and Richards conceive of the construction of the relation between symbol and referent purely and exclusively as a *thought process*, as a mental act *of the individual*. Furthermore, they see meaning embedded exclusively in *symbols and language*, not in material things and artifacts. This renders them rather helpless at the face of the problem of the *origination of thought, symbols and language*.

It is also symptomatic that Ogden and Richards restrict the *indirect, mediated nature* to the bottom line of the triangle. The other two relations, that between thought and symbol and that between thought and thing, are seen as "more or less direct" (Ogden & Richards 1936, p. 11)[5].

But can these two relations really be direct? Let's consider first the relation between thought and symbol. Symbols are sociohistorically produced and transmitted artifacts. They are abstracted and generalized from the production and use of material objects. The relation of an *individual* to a symbol *appears* direct. But the *cultural development* of symbols can never be understood in direct individual terms. It is an *over-individual, collective* process, based on the *mediated, indirect interaction of subjects with symbols via objects (referents)*. Furthermore, even an individual can really grasp and creatively use symbols only as he or she relates them with the world of objects which they represent and stem from.

This origination of words and symbols from practical material actions is pointed out by Malinowski:

> Thus, when a savage learns to understand the meaning of a word, this process is not accomplished by explanations, by a series of acts of apperception, but by learning to handle it. A word *means* to a

5. The triangle of Ogden and Richards has been discussed, criticized and further eleborated by numerous authors, among the them Bunn (1981), Eco (1979) and Meredith (1972).

native the proper use of the thing for which it stands . . . . (Malinowski, 1936, p. 321).

The relation between thought and thing may be analyzed in a similar vein. Things are not just simply there, to be thought about and referred to. They are produced and used by human beings in their collective life activities, in their practice. This production and use of things does not take place directly but *always with the (visible or invisible) help of symbols, i.e. tools and knowledge, concerning the qualities and behavior of these things*. Thus, as we look at an individual referring to a material object, it appears that he or she has a direct relation to that object. But beneath the surface of this seemingly simple act, internalized symbols, products of collective cultural-historical development are working. The act is not direct, not even when it proceeds automatically; the mediating symbol is there and becomes visible whenever the individual confronts more demanding tasks.

We may now return to the triangle of Ogden and Richards. The prime mover in that triangle is the uppermost corner, the *thought*. Everything begins with the thinking individual. But there is no thought without a material carrier, without a subject. The subject not only (and not even primarily) thinks but, above all, acts practically, molds the material environment. Furthermore, the subject does this co-operatively, not individually. Thus, we may change the title of the uppermost corner and name it *subject*.

But this means that we have to reconsider the other corners, too. The corner *referent* has to be redefined as *object* of activity. In its original form, the object of human activity is some natural entity not created by man (plants, animals, rocks etc.). But the very origination of *human* activity implies the production and use of *generalized tools as mediating links beween the subject and the object of activity*. These generalized tools are the primary form of symbols. For the sake of clarity, let us name the third corner *tools* (= *objectified knowledge*). We now obtain the following new triangle (figure 2).

This triangle means that the meaning, the real *content* or essence of any phenomena can only be approached and understood concretely when the phenomena are studied as *systemic formations, as relations and continuous transformations between subject, object and tools*. The meaning of a cup of coffee can be grasped only when the object cup is studied as something

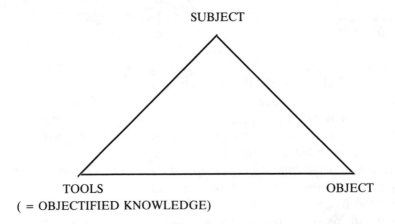

SUBJECT

TOOLS   OBJECT
(= OBJECTIFIED KNOWLEDGE)

Figure 2:   Meaning as relations between subject, object and tools.

produced and used in certain ways by certain concrete historical
subjects with the help of certain tools (knowledge, words, sym-
bols). As the cup is cut off from these systemic relations, it ceases
to be a meaningful object and becomes just a piece of certain
material having certain form and color.

The transformations between the corners are essential.

> In activity there does take place a transfer of an object into its
> subjective form, into an image; also in activity a transfer of activity
> into its objective results, into its products, is brought about. Taken
> from this point of view, activity appears as a process in which
> mutual transfers between the poles 'subject-object' are accom-
> plished (Leont'ev 1978, 50).

Consider the reciprocal movement between object and tools.
What originally was a generalized tool, an artifact created for the
purpose of molding natural objects, becomes itself an object to
be handled and molded by more advanced tools, e.g., theoretical formulae or computer programs. A tool becomes an object
and an object may become a tool as it is used for a general
purpose. A cup of coffee is both an object and a tool.

The transformations signify the *unity of activity and meaning.*
Meaning can be understood only as a socio-historically formed
system of activity. In its original, primitive form this unity can be
found among children and primitive tribes.

> Words are to a child active forces, they give an essential hold on
> reality, they provide him with the only effective means of moving,

attracting and repulsing outer things and of producing changes in all that is relevant (Malinowski 1936, p. 321).

Meaning . . . does not come to Primitive Man from contemplation of things, or analysis of occurences, but in practical and active aquintance with relevant situations. The real knowledge of a word comes through the practice of appropriately using it within a certain situation. The word, like any man-made implement, becomes significant only after it has been used and properly used under all sorts of conditions (Malinowski 1936, p. 325).

This unity of activity and meaning found its early psychological formulation in Vygotski's work 'Tool and Symbol in Children's Development' in 1930.

Every elementary form of behavior presupposes a *direct* reaction to the task set before the organism (which can be expressed with the simple S → R formula). But the structure of sign operations requires an intermediate link between the stimulus and the response. This interemediate link is a second order stimulus (sign) that is drawn into the operation where it fulfills a special function; it creates a new relation between S and R. The term 'drawn into' indicates that an individual must be activity engaged in establishing such a link. The sign also possesses the important characteristic of reverse action (that is, it operates on the individual, not the environment).

Consequently, the simple stimulus-response process is replaced by a complex, mediated act, which we picture as:

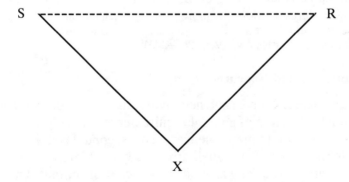

. . . Careful studies demonstrate that this type of organization is basic to all higher psychological processes, although in much more sophisticated forms than that shown above. The intermediate link in this formula is not simply a method of improving the previously existing operation, nor is it a mere additional link in an S-R chain. Because this auxiliary stimulus possesses the specific function of reverse action, it transfers the psychological operation to higher and qualitatively new forms and permits humans, by the aid of extrinsic stimuli, *to control their behavior from the outside*. The use of signs leads humans to a specific structure of behavior that breaks away from biological development and creates new forms of a culturally-based psychological process (Vygotsky 1978, 39–40).

Recently Marx Wartofsky has summarized essential parts of this line of argumentation:

> In summary, then, what constitutes a distinctively human form of action is the creation and use of artifacts, as tools, in the production of the means of existence and in the reproduction of the species. *Primary* artifacts are those directly used in this production; *secondary* artifacts are those used in the preservation and transmission of the acquired skills or modes of action or praxis by which this production is carried out. Secondary artifacts are therefore *representations* of such modes of action, and in this sense are *mimetic*, not simply of the *objects* of an environment which are of interest or use in this production, but of these objects as they are acted upon, or the mode of operation or action involving such objects. Canons of representation, therefore, have a large element of convention, corresponding to the change or evolution of different forms of actions or *praxis*, and thus cannot be reduced to some simple notion of 'natural' semblance or resemblance. Nature, or the world becomes a world-for-us, in this process, by the mediation of such representations (or more broadly, such canons of representation), and thereby, in accordance with our varying modes of practice (Wartofsky, 1979, 202–203)[6].

7. Summary and Conclusions

In this paper, I have sketched an argumentation on two levels. The first level is that of general requirements of a truly qualitative methodology in human sciences. The second level is that of specific problems of the qualitative study of thinking and learning, centering especially around the concept of content. On both levels, I have criticized Marton's phenomenography by identifying certain antinomies within its own line of argumentation. I

---

6. Wartofsky's approach accounts also for imaginative constructions, dreams, fantasies etc. as 'tertiary' artifacts (see Wartofsky, 1979, p. 209).

have contrasted phenomenography with certain aspects of materialist, content-oriented dialectics.

The concept of content appears as something self-evident and unproblematic within phenomenography. It is actually identified with people's conceptions, which in turn are dealt with as relatively discrete and static pieces of data, cut off from the life activities they reflect.

The dialectical concept of content must be relational and possess self-movement through inner contradictions and transformations. It must be at the same time both an object of research and a tool (a means, a method) of research. In other words, it must say something essential and substantial about the quality of content and simultaneously function as an instrument of analyzing and constructing contents. Furthermore, the dialectical concept of content must unify *and mediate* the subjective and objective, personal and cultural-historical aspects of content. This corresponds to what Michael Otte (1984) calls the principle of complementarity of scientific concepts. The mediation is accomplished through the unification of the concept of activity with the concept of meaning.

References

Brumby, M. *Students' perceptions and learning styles associated with the concept of evolution by natural selection.* Unpublished dissertation. University of Surrey, 1979.

Bunn, J. H. *The dimensionality of signs, tools, and models.* Bloomington: Indiana University Press, 1981.

Eco, U. *A theory of semiotics.* Bloomington: Indiana University Press, 1979.

Engels, F. *Anti-Dühring.* Moscow: Progress Publishers, 1975.

Engeström, Y. The laws of nature and the origin of life in pupils' consciousness: A study of contradictory modes of thought. *Scandinavian Journal of Educational, Research* 1981, *25*, 39–61.

Greeno, J. G. Some examples of cognitive task analysis with instructional implications. In R. E. Snow, P-A Federico, & W. E. Montague (Eds.), *Aptitude, learning and instruction, Vol. 2.* Hillsdale, N. J.: Lawrence Erlbaum, 1980.

Haug, W. F. *Vorlesungen zur Einführung ins 'Kapital'. 2. Aufl.* Köln: Pahl-Rugenstein, 1976.

Hegel, G. W. F. *The phenomenology of mind.* Transl. by J. B. Baillie.

London — New York: George Allen & Unwin — Humanities Press, 1966.

Hilgard, E. R. & Bower, G. H. *Theories of learning.* 3d ed. New York: Appleton-Century-Crofts, 1966.

Ilyenkov, E. V. *Dialectical logic: Essays on its history and theory.* Moscow: Progress Publishers, 1977.

Lenin, V. I. Philosophical notebooks. In: *Collected Works, Vol. 38.* Moscow: Progress Publishers, 1963.

Leont'ev, A. N. *Activity, consciousness, and personality.* Englewood Cliffs, N. J.: Prentice Hall, 1978.

Malinowski, B. The problem of meaning in primitive languages. Supplement I in Ogden & Richards, *The meaning of meaning.* 4th ed. London: Kegan Paul, Trench, Trubner & Co., 1936.

Marton, F. Phenomenography — describing conceptions of the world around us. *Instructional Science 1981, 10,* 177–200. (a)

Marton, F. Studying conceptions of reality — a meta-theoretical note. *Scandinavian Journal of Educational Research,* 1981, *25,* 159–169. (b)

Marton, F. Toward a psychology beyond the individual. In K. Lagerspetz & P. Niemi (Eds.), *Psychology in the 1990's.* Amsterdam: North Holland, 1984.

Marx, K. *Grundrisse.* London: Penguin Books, 1973.

Meredith, G. P. The origins and aims of epistemics. *Instructional Science* 1972, *1,* 9–30.

Michaels, C. F. & Carello, C. *Direct perception.* Englewood Cliffs, N. J.: Prentice-Hall, 1981.

Mitroff, I. I. & Kilmann, R. H. *Methodological approaches to social science.* San Francisco: Jossey-Bass, 1978.

Mitroff, I. I. & Mason, R. O. *Creating a dialectical social science.* Dordrecht: Reidel, 1981.

Ogden, C. K. & Richards, I. A. 1936. *The meaning of meaning.* 4th ed. London: Kegan Paul, Trench, Trubner & Co, 1936.

Otte, M. The work of E. G. Judin (1930–1976) on activity theory in the light of recent tendencies in epistemological thinking. In P. Hakkarainen, M. Hedegaard & Y. Engeström (Eds.) Learning and teaching on a scientific basis. Aarhus: Aarhus Universitet, Psykologisk Institut; 1984.

Ovchinnikov, N. Problems of theoretisation of knowledge. *Social Sciences,* 1979 *10*:2, 104–118.

Riegel, K. *Foundations of dialectical psychology.* New York: Academic Press, 1979.

Smedslund, J. Circular relation between understanding and logic. *Scandinavian Journal of Pscyhology 1970, 11,* 217–219.

Smedslund, J. Piaget's psychology in practice. *British Journal of Educational Psychology 1977, 47,* 1-6.

Tolman, C. The metaphysic of relations in Klaus Riegel's 'dialectics' of human development. *Human Development 1981, 24,* 33-51.

Vygotsky, L. S. *Mind in society.* Cambridge, Mass.: Harvard University Press, 1978.

Wartofsky, M. W. *Models: Representation and the scientific understanding.* Dordrecht: Reidel, 1979.

Willis, G. Qualitative evaluation as the aesthetic, personal, and political dimensions of curriculum criticism. In G. Willis (ed.), *Qualitative evaluation.* Berkeley, Calif.: McCutchan, 1978.

PART II

Thinking and Learning

Phenomenology and the Psychology of Thinking

4

Christopher M. Aanstoos

Introduction

There is an old folk saying in the United States that goes something like this: the proof of the pudding is in the eating. Undoubtedly a reflection of American pragmatist philosophy, it nevertheless seems relevant to our discussion here as well. Research methods, after all, are only as good as the results they can produce. While it is still premature to expect qualitative methodology to have generated a complete corpus of findings, it is not too early to begin applying it to significant, or paradigmatic, problems in psychology. Only then can our disputes with more traditional approaches merit the attention of the wider academic community. For that reason, I'd like to use this forum to share with you a phenomenological study I conducted on the psychology of thinking. Let me begin my presentation with a brief overview of contemporary developments in that field, in order to situate the importance of phenomenological work in this area.

Review of the Literature

Thinking is almost universally acknowledged to be a crucially important topic for psychology. A quick survey of psychology's introductory textbooks, for example, reveals that thinking is identified as "the most significant activity that humans engage in" (Haber & Runyon, 1978, p. 135), "the most uniquely psychological subject" (Marx, 1976, p. 179), "absolutely central to our notions of who we are . . . one of the principal hallmarks of being human" (Lefrancois, 1980, p. 234). Texts on the psychology of thinking in particular, which may be expected to take a more partisan interest, have also long affirmed the key role of the topic of thinking. For example, Humphrey (1948, pp. 1–3) asserted

79

that "thinking is incomparably the most important thing in the world . . . thinking is vital . . . we must learn to understand thinking." And Guilford (1960, p. 6) has stated that no psychological problem is more important than that of thinking, and that "it is imperative that we understand more about the processes of human thinking."

Despite its recognized importance, psychology has consistently failed to explicate the phenomenon of thinking. By 1949 this failure was decried as the "essential weakness of modern psychological theory" (Hebb, 1949, p. xvi). By 1959 a text on the psychology of thinking was forced to conclude that "we still have a long road to travel before our knowledge is anything better than speculative" (Thomson, 1959, p. 209). By 1969, a conference on thinking whose stated goal was "to reach agreement on the general nature of thought" still could not even do that (Voss, 1969, p. vi). This lack of foundational clarity continues to be widely noted (Bourne, Ekstrand & Dominowski, 1971, p. 8; Bruner, 1978, p. vii; Hunt & Poltrock, 1974, p. 277), and has led to the conclusion that thinking is the most "difficult" (Haber & Runyon, 1978, p. 135), "frustrating" (Guilford, 1960, p. 6), or "intractable" (Weimer, 1974, p. 6) of all psychological phenomena.

It was on the ground of this continuing disillusionment with its ability to understand thinking that psychology recently embraced the now dominant information processing approach with its alluring promise of a method suited to the complexities of the subject matter. The pioneering efforts of Allen Newell and Herbert Simon have deservedly earned for them the recognition as the founders of the information processing approach to psychology. Their basic premise is that the person, like the computer, is an information processing system, whose thinking can therefore be demonstrated with computer simulation models (Newell, Shaw & Simon, 1958b; Newell & Simon, 1961, 1972; Simon, 1978, 1979; Simon & Newell, 1964, 1971). According to their view, the computer simulation program is taken as a precise model of how thinking proceeds (Newell & Simon, 1972, p. 5). Hence their fundamental methodology has been to design computer programs capable of simulating human performances in order to demonstrate what it requires. Their model yields the conclusion that thinking is essentially symbol manipulation in the same sense that computer processing is. In other words, thinking is viewed as a series of elementary or primitive processes, combined serially according to explicit, pre-determined rules, each process of which is a formally definite operation for the manipulation of information in the form of elemental and discrete symbols.

How can the validity of such a model be determined? Newell and Simon first sought to validate it by recourse to the argument of sufficiency: that is, if a program contained all of the statements required for the computer to perform a task that requires a person to think, the program can be taken as a simulation of thinking (Newell, Shaw & Simon, 1958b, pp. 151–153; Newell & Simon, 1961, pp. 2012–2013; Simon & Newell, 1964, p. 282). And, from the beginning, chess playing was chosen as the "type case" (Newell, 1955) or "natural arena" (Newell, Shaw & Simon, 1958a) of such a task. Indeed, chess playing has become so important a task for computer simulation efforts that it is now referred to as the "fruit fly" of that field (Hearst, 1978, p. 197). Although chess programs have never attained the playing strength that overly optimistic early estimates claimed they would (Simon & Newell, 1958), the best recent ones have exhibited considerably improved capabilities. However, the criterion that similarity of results alone could establish the validity of the computer model was eventually acknowledged to be inadequate, after it was pointed out that similar results were no guarantee that they had been attained in a similar manner (de Groot, 1978, pp. 387–388; Gunderson, 1964; Hearst, 1967, p. 32). For example, airplanes can fly, but that result is not a simulation of birds flying because they do not fly in the same way (Simon, 1980, p. 76–77). Most information processing theorists now admit that it is the processes themselves that must be simulated, and not merely the results (Simon & Newell, 1971, p. 147; Simon, 1980, pp. 76–77). But this requirement led to an additional problem: the lack of data on how human thinking actually proceeds. This question is so problematic because the information processing approach sought to simulate thinking before it understood thinking, presuming to know the very phenomenon that nedeed to be disclosed.

Some information processing researchers have attempted to fill this gap by searching for similarities between the steps taken by computer simulation programs and protocols spoken by human subjects engaged in solving the same problem (Newell 1977; Newell & Simon, 1961, 1972). Such comparisons can be quite ambiguous because of the differences between the computer language of the simulation program and ordinary language used by the human subject (Boden, 1972, p. 111; Simon & Newell, 1971, p. 148; Kendler, 1981, pp. 362–363). To insure fidelity under these circumstances, a rigorous analysis of the human protocols in their own right should be the necessary pre-requisite. But this has not been done. Instead information processing preconceptions have biased these comparisons in ways that can be severely criticized (Frijda, 1967; Wilding, 1978, p. 171). Even Newell's (1977) more thoughtful effort to specify a means of protocol analysis that would be helpful "for developing theory rather than for validating theory" remains faithful to inferred information processing preconceptions, as its aim is to identify the presumed elemental "operators" applied to a "problem space" to incrementally change a "state of knowledge."

Advocates as well as critics are increasingly recognizing that efforts to improve simulation programs are reaching an impasse, limited by a lack of understanding of how people actually think, and that this impasse can be remedied only by a direct investigation of human thinking (Charness, 1978, p. 35; Hearst, 1978, p. 200; Neisser, 1976, pp. 7–8; Newell, 1973, pp. 303–304; Raphael, 1976, pp. 284–285; Wilding, 1978, p. 176). This gap is precisely the sort of deficiency in traditional methodology that can best be remedied by phenomenologically based research. For that reason, I conducted an empirical phenomenological study of thinking exemplified during chess playing (Aanstoos, 1983b). The method used in that research will be outlined in the next section, after which the results will be summarized.

Method

Subjects

Five highly skilled chess players were used as subjects in this study. It was decided to obtain subjects across the range of competitive ability claimed by today's best computer chess programs, so as to facilitate a more clearcut comparison of results. Fortunately, a standard evaluation of chess playing ability was available: the rating system devised and used by the U.S. Chess Federation to rate its members on the basis of their tournament results. These ratings are strictly performance based, and are stratified into levels, each of which is identified by a particular term. Those relevant for this study included: Master, Candidate Master, Category I, Category II, and Category III (in the remainder of this article, these subjects are identified as S.1, S.2, S.3, S.4, and S.5, respectively). Subjects were recruited to fill these positions by means of an advertisement placed in the Pittsburgh Chess Club's newsletter, and by posters displayed at two U.S. Chess Federation tournaments. None of the subjects knew the researcher, and none were involved in psychology, either as students or as professionals. All subjects were male, and they ranged in age from late teens to mid-thirties. Subjects were paid for their participation in this study. The amount of money, specified and agreed upon in advance, was $20.00 each for the Master and Candidate Master, and $15.00 each for the others.

Procedure

Each subject played one game of chess, having the white pieces (and so making the first move), against an assistant of the researcher. Each subject played against a different assistant, matched as closely as possible with the subject's own level of skill. Each game was played on a separate occasion, always at the same location, a quiet room in the researcher's house. The researcher did not remain in the room while the game was in progress.

Before the game began, the subject was given a page of written instructions to read and an Informed Consent form to read and sign. These specified that the subject was to "think out loud as completely as possible all of the thoughts you are having throughout the game . . . exactly as they occur to you." This basic instruction was repeated redundantly in the various ways that pilot studies had demonstrated to be most clearly understandable.

The subject then played a game of chess against the researcher's assistant, and thought aloud throughout the game. The subject's entire thinking aloud was tape recorded. The opponent was prevented from hearing the subject by wearing headphones through which music was continuously played. The researcher's assistant (the subject's opponent) wrote down the moves of the game for the researcher.

After each game, the subject was interviewed by the researcher. In addition to noting whatever commentary the subjects had to give about the game itself, three specific questions were asked of every subject. The first question was: "do you feel that you were able to say your thoughts aloud without any problem?" All subjects said they had been able to do so. The second question was: "do you feel that having to think aloud interfered with your game in any significant way?" All subjects answered that it had not. One subject (S.4) noted that it helped him to see that he didn't usually use his opponent's time to think very effectively. The third question was: "do you feel that the ability you showed in this game was fairly representative of the games you've played ·recently?" All subjects responded affirmatively. Indeed, one who lost (S.2) even said that he had been making just those same sorts of costly blunders in his recent tournament games.

Next, the tape recorded protocols were transcribed by the researcher. These transcriptions were then compared to the tape recordings by another assistant of the researcher, to ensure that any discrepancies would be discovered. Then a portion of each protocol was set aside for in-depth analysis. The portions to be analyzed in-depth were selected from points at which the games were still relatively evenly balanced, and leading toward an important turning point. For S.'s 1, 2, and 3 this segment went from the beginning of the game to the early middle game. For S.'s 4 and 5 this segment was taken from the late middle game. The remainder of the transcripts served as background for the researcher's understanding of the segments. (The interested reader may find these transcripts in their entirety in Aanstoos, 1983b).

Data Analysis

Unlike information processing analyses of protocol data, phenomenological methods recognize the intrinsic relation of the person to some subject matter. Indeed, that is the meaning of its most important discovery: intentionality — that consciousness is consciousness of something. Hence, fidelity to the data demands that the protocols not be preconceived as 'bits of behavioral responses' for the sake of methodological orthodoxy. Rather, they must be taken as a description of the relation of the subject to the intentional world (see Aanstoos, 1983c, for a more extended discussion of this use of think aloud protocols). This recognition is the starting point for a phenomenological analysis of the data. In such an analysis "the task of the researchers is to let the world of the describer . . . reveal itself through the description" (Giorgi, 1975b, p. 74), in order to remain faithful to the phenomenon as it was lived. This aim is fulfilled in a phenomenological method by rigorously specified means of engaging the naive descriptions and discerning their psychological sense. This method was first formulated by phenomenological philosophers and has since been adapted to psychological research by Giorgi. It consists of the following steps: bracketing, intuiting, describing.

Bracketing. In order to attend to thinking, or any phenomenon, as it is lived, it is necessary to "take what is experienced just as it gives itself in any instance, and thus begin where we must begin" (Husserl, 1925/1977, p. 42). In other words, in order to understand the subject's intentional world of lived experience, one must first arrive at it by a suspension, or bracketing, of all presumptive constructs about it. Such bracketing "slackens the intentional threads which attach us to the world and thus brings them to our notice" (Merleau-Ponty, 1945/1962, p. xiii). In that way, the naturalistic bias which conceives the world as extrinsic and simply there as a thing in itself it overcome, and the world as intended, or meant, is allowed to come into view.

By this bracketing operation, a phenomenological method aims to achieve a direct contact with the world (Merleau-Ponty, 1945/1962, p. vii). Thus, this reduction does not result in the disinterest of the researcher but rather in the suspension of all narrowly confining interests preceding attention to the phenomenon, in order to become fully interested in the phenomenon itself. By so deliberately avoiding concentrating attention on any particular pre-determined aspect, the researcher is able to escape the danger of finding only what one expects to see. Instead, one adopts an attitude of "open-ended presence to the phenomenon that is unfolding" (Giorgi, 1976, p. 313). Giorgi (1975b) identified this first step as an "initial familiarizing" and demonstrates concretely how its achievement is brought about by reading the transcript several times to get a sense of it as a whole, attuned not merely to the linguistic content, but to the intentional, or lived, experience of the subject as intentional, lived experience. For example, in this case, the conception of thinking as simply manipulation of discrete symbols that happen to be passing through short term memory is set aside, in order to inquire about the intentional meaning of that experience. Allowing the subject's thinking to come into view meant that the researcher had to give it priority over questions regarding the objective accuracy of the subject's judgment, for thinking was not to be prejudged by the standards of logic. For example, when a subject thought that a particular move was "forced," then it is as a forced move that it is an object of thought for him, regardless of whether or not another analysis of it could demonstrate otherwise.

Intuiting. The next step was to grasp the essential psychological meanings through a direct, eidetic intuiting. In this way, the phenomenological method aims to bring the phenomenon itself to a self-showing, to "return to the things themselves" in order to bring their very sense to self-evidence (Husserl, 1913/1962, pp. 48–50). In contrast to all probabalistic methods, such essential seeing relies on the standard of self-evidence as its criterion of evidence (thereby attaining an iconoclastic power in relation to all merely inferential frameworks). Phenomenological methods are non-inferential in the sense that there are no hypotheses to be tested. Evidence resides not in the probalistic proving of a hypothesis, but in the description of the essential significance of the phenomenon. That is what van den Berg (1972, p. 124) meant when he wrote that "the phenomenologist never needs hypotheses. Hypotheses emerge where the description of reality has been discontinued too soon."

Since an eidetic intuition is one that reveals itself as a coherence and so resists arbitrary change or variation, it is self-verifying to the extent that it coheres. Merleau-Ponty (1942/1963, p. 130) identified this primordial coalescence of any phenomenon as its "structure," which he elucidated by showing that "situation and reaction are linked by their common participation in a structure in which the mode of activity proper to the organism is expressed." He added that this notion of structure does not imply that the organism knows the structure and attempts to realize it. Rather, it is significant as a structure for the one who grasps it as such (1942/1963, p. 159). Hence, it may be said that structure is the explicit thematization of the implicit dialectic of "situation and reaction," of world and person. The comprehension of this "immanent meaning" (Merleau-Ponty, 1942/1963, p. 184) or "immanent significance" (Merleau-Ponty, 1945/1962), p. 258) is the aim of this step of the phenomenological method.

These essential meanings are not at all self-evident in advance however. They must be brought to a self-showing, and can only be made self-evident through rigorous effort. It is this work that the eidetic intuiting strives to accomplish. A concrete exemplification of the manner in which such essential meanings are brought to a self-showing has been provided by Giorgi (1975a, 1975b), who proceeds by way of identifying meaning units, specifying their central themes, and then articulating their psychological sense or meaning. For the present study, these procedures, were carried out as follows:

1. The researcher read the protocol, attuned to the question of the meaning of thinking. Each time a transition in meaning was perceived (always in regards to the sense of the whole within which it participates) it was delineated. The result was that each protocol was delineated into their constituent meaning units.

2. Next, the phenomenal themes of each meaning unit that had allowed it to emerge as a constituent in the first place were clarified and made explicit. This description of the lived experience of the subject retained its embeddedness in the naive perspective of the subject. The aim of this step was simply to provide a phenomenal description of the meaningful themes of each constituent. Such a phenomenal description is not yet a structural understanding, rather it is that which has to be comprehended structurally.

3. Next, each of these phenomenal descriptions of the meaning units was reflected upon in order to discover what it revealed about the structural psychological significance of thinking, in that situation for that subject. It is at this step that the researcher aims to transform the phenomenal description into a properly phenomenological understanding by laying bare the immanent structural significance therein.

Describing. At this step, the structural meanings achieved were organized into a systematic structural description in order to grasp the relation of the essential meanings through their coherence. Following the guidelines of Giorgi (1975a, 1975b) and Wertz (1983), this procedure consisted of two phases. The first task was to describe the situated or individual structure for each of the empirical cases. These ideographic descriptions remained anchored in the concrete experience of the particular subject, and thus were the systematic structural statements of the essential psychological significances that were grasped in the preceding step.

Then, the second task of this operation was to interrogate those individual structures in order to proceed from them to a description of the structural significance of thinking in chess in general, by retaining those features that were essentially invariant across the particular cases. In other words, the analysis proceeded from the individual to the general by means of its articulation of the "essential generality" of each particular instance examined. Another way of expressing this movement is that it is a disclosure of the essence of the phenomenon, or the essential theme of all its variations. It must be clear that the theme is expressed in its concrete variations, and only in its concrete variations. It is "not a thing which rests in itself" (Merleau-Ponty, 1942/1963, p. 159). The way to the invariant theme of the variations was by "cross checking" the essence of each variation (Merleau-Ponty, 1964/1975, p. 26). In this step, not only were the empirical variations checked against each other, but against other possible variations imagined by the researcher as well. Empirically obtained variations can never exhaust the realm of all possible variations. Instead, they provided the starting point, a set of exemplar cases, which had to be completed through the use of imagined variations (a procedure first employed by Husserl, e.g., 1925/1977, p. 53). Each constituent of the individual structure was varied, and the question asked 'if this were changed, would this phenomenon still be this phenomenon?' In that way, the researcher was able to proceed to the essential generality that was then described as the general structure of thinking as it is exemplified during chess playing.

Results

Levels of Specification

This presentation will provide the final result of the analysis: the general structural description of thinking, as it is manifested in chess playing. The high level of essential generality of this structure will then next be elaborated concretely, especially with regard to the specific points about thinking raised in the preceding critical analysis as needing clarification.

A structural description may be developed with varying degrees of specificity or completeness, depending on the audience for whom it is to be presented. These results, for example, have been presented in brief formats (e.g., Aanstoos, 1983a). The most concise description of the general structure of thinking that was formulated as a result of this research is the following:

Thinking as it is exemplified during chess playing is a telic and pragmatic explicitation of symbolically expressed transformative possibilities through interrogating, characterizing, and fulfilling modes. Thinking apprehends such possibilities by thematizing their implicatory embeddedness within the relational unity of the position, which is grasped perspectivally as a referential network of spatial and temporal implications. Thinking explicitates these implicit references to possibility by means of an 'if — then' structure.

The language in such a statement is necessarily precise, in order to condense so much material so concisely. But after a certain point, such condensation begins to exact a price in comprehension among those readers who are not familiar with the complete individual analyses from which it was derived. The precise statement may be elaborated with a little more detail for such an audience. The following is an example of such an elaboration:

Thinking as it is exemplified during chess playing is a process of discovering and making explicit certain implicit possibilities that are taken to be present in the position. These possibilities are experienced as dynamic currents of force, avenues of virtual action that hold the ambiguous promise of transforming the position. This effort of making such possible transformations explicit is therefore essentially telic in the sense that the aim is to achieve a favorable transformation of the position within the overall aim of winning the game. Thinking concerns itself with these possibilities in three ways: by taking them as a question, by characterizing them as possibilities in their own specificity, and by determining their pragmatic appropriateness to the context of the game. In doing so, thinking thematizes the relation of these possibilities to the position as a whole. In other words, thinking grasps this relational unity by the way that it is implied by the possibilities. This relational unity is itself a network of implications, with both temporal and spatial references to further possibilities. Temporally, it implies relations between past, present and future moves. Spatially, it implies relations between pieces on the board. Thinking grasps this relational unity from the particular perspective of the player, illuminating only those aspects of it that appear as relevant from that point of view. The specific means by which thinking determines the implicatory significance of its possibles is by grasping their 'if — then' relations within the larger referential unity of the position.

Unfortunately, neither of the above statements can adequately disclose the rich and varied texture of thinking provided by the descriptive data. The phenomenon of thinking defies cursory explication. That is precisely the reason for the repeated failure of the psychology of thinking. To do justice to such a complex phenomenon, the complete and detailed structural description that was developed as the culmination of the data analysis must be presented. That description is the following.

The General Structural Description

Thinking is necessarily thinking about something. Hence, its structure includes two constituents: a specific (noetic) act by which it intends an object of thought, and the (noematic) object of thought itself. These two constituents are strictly correlated as a bipolar structure, in that there could be no object of thought without an act of thinking, nor could there be an act of thinking without an object of thought. Though writing, by its sequential nature, requires that they be described alternately, it is important to realize their essential correlation. In this general structural description, first the noetic pole, the act of thinking, will be described, and then the noematic pole, the objects of thought. In each case, however, sufficient mention of the other will be made so that their correlative status will be clear. After that, thinking's structural involvement with other moments of psychological life in chess playing will be described.

The noetic structure of thinking. In chess playing, thinking's own proper intending of its objects is the explicitation of the possible. In other words, thinking is the act of making explicit the implicit possibilities which are the symbolic objects of thought. Thinking explicitates previously prethematic possibilities by thematizing how they are implied, or symbolized, by the configuration of the position in the chess game. Through this thematization of possibility, thinking predelineates a possible future. That is, it discloses the future implications of the present position. In that sense, thinking is essentially future directed, or telic. The apprehension of this telic dimension is itself founded on thinking's aim, which is to determine the most efficacious possible transformation of the present position in order to facilitate the thinker's effort to win the game. Thus thinking is pragmatic. To summarize: thinking is pragmatically and telically explicitative of a symbolic dimension.

Thinking explicitates its objects through three different modes of apprehension: interrogation, characterization, and fulfillment. Though typically unfolded within a phasic temporality, these various modalities cannot be said to comprise a strictly sequential linearity. Their relation differs in two fundamental ways from such linearity. First, any mode may elicit either of the other two. For example, it is often the case after the opponent has just made his move that thinking begins by characterizing a particular theme of that move and then shifting to interrogating it more deeply. S.3 for instance first characterized his opponent's third move as "threatening my king pawn," but then interrogates the significance of that threat. Another example of the differing temporal relations of thinking's modalities is revealed by those occasions when thinking shifts from interrogating to fulfilling. For instance, as soon as S.5 questions the possibility of a particular rook sacrifice, he immediately shifts to a fulfilling mode, simply noting that "I need those rooks," without any intervening characterizing of that need. A second way that the relation of these modes differs from strict linearity is that not every specific instance of thinking involves all three modes prior to its transformation to some other psychological act. For example, thinking can shift to memory following its interrogatory mode. Such a shift is especially typical during the opening moves. At the beginning of S.2's game, for instance, his implicit questioning of what opening to play evoked a memorial attunement to a previous game. Another variation of this point is thinking's shift to another psychological act directly from its characterizing mode. S.3's shift directly to a decision of what move to make after having characterized the dynamics of his opponent's previous move provides an example of that variation.

Thus, one point that must be grasped is that thinking's different modes of intending objects of thought are structurally rather than linearly related. Specifically the structure of their relation is that each may evoke or be evoked by each of the others. And the second point is that not every act of thinking includes all three modes. Rather, thinking can and does occur in more fragmented ways as well. Such instances are not inherently less efficacious. Their utility is preserved by the demand character of the game, which at points renders unnecessary thinking's bringing to bear all three modes of explicitation. Each of these three modes must next be described in some more detail.

As *interrogation*, thinking thematizes a questionableness about the position. Concrete ways by which interrogation raises this questionableness include: possibilizing, projecting, and seeking justification. That questionableness irrupts within previously taken-for-granted facticities, and reveals a gap as that which is to be completed. Subject S.1 provides an apt illustration when, after noting several possible moves his opponent could make, says "I'm not sure how this opening works, if he, if he can develop his king bishop."

Thus, in the mode of interrogation, thinking addresses itself to and thematizes a prethematic questionableness as an indeterminant significance horizonally present within a more complacent certainty. This horizonal questionableness is itself evoked by more implicit moments of interrogation. Thus, interrogation unfolds as an ensemble of questioning, pulsating between the horizontal and the thematic. The next several meaning units following the one quoted above provide ample exemplification of this unfolding ensemble of implicit questioning, culminating with: "um. I'm not sure where all my pieces ought to be going. Maybe I play bishop to rook three. I've got to think about that. Maybe I should just play, ah, maybe if bishop to knight five I should play bishop to rook three right away, to trade, to keep him from castling. That's an interesting idea."

Such questionableness is never devoid of contextual inherence. Rather, it is evoked by the referential network characterized by thinking (see below), toward whose possibilities for transformation it is directed. Specifically, interrogation takes up the beginnings, or sub-beginnings, or new beginnings, for transformative possibilities. The example just cited illustrates this point well. Another is S.2's: "wonder what he'll play against me." Of course it must be kept in mind that the use of the term "beginning" here refers to its meaning as such for the subject, not to any objective or logical standard. Two different kinds of questions are raised by interrogation: those which seek a single answer that is taken to be determinable and definite, and those for which such answers are not sought (although these are still assumed to be answerable). This distinction is related to that between forcing and virtual types of possibilities (see below). It is revealed especially by whether the subject questions some move he thinks he should make versus some move he merely considers wanting to make. An example of the former type of question is S.1's "maybe I should play pawn takes pawn right away." An example of the latter type of question is S.2's: "where do I want my queen bishop developed. Knight two maybe? King three? Knight five?"

As *characterization*, thinking thematizes possibilities by apprehending how they are implied by both general principles and especially by the position as a network of spatial-temporal references (see below). Thinking does not attend to the entire network of referential relations, but precisely only to those that appear to offer relevant transformative possibilities. These are predelineated by thinking's characterizing an 'if — then' structure, in which thinking thematizes what is implied by explicitating the relatedness between two features or possible moves (see below). In this mode, thinking is concerned with the answerability of thematized possibilities which may be either specific move continuations or more general positional characteristics. In either case the possibilities (as gaps within the facticities) have the character of being fill-able, completable, determinable. To fill in the gap, thinking as characterization strives to discover a necessary positional advantage or a forcing continuation by which the particular transformation may be achieved. The compelling quality of such characteristics, however, are highly relative (see below, under objects of thought).

Some examples of both combinational and positional characterizations are in order. An example of the former type is S.4's characterization of the continuation: "knight takes pawn, pawn takes pawn, queen takes pawn, I don't get anything back. Ffh." This instance is particularly exemplary of a number of aspects of such characterizing. It demonstrates thinking's grasping of the relatedness of the moves and thinking's sense of the determinability of what is being characterized, but it also demonstrates something more. It shows thinking's characterizing being guided by, and elucidating, an implicit contact with a balance of a dynamic tension of force. That concern will be described more fully below, as an object of thought.

Besides combinational characterizing, thinking also characterizes positional features as such. Some examples of such moments include thinking's characterizing: balanced development; a lack of attacking possibilities; a troublesome knight; control of the center. Two important aspects of such characterizing stand out: positional characterizing is typically the result of a prior questioning; and it is through such characterizing that thinking contacts the medium and long range future of the game. The sense in which the game's future is an object of thought will be described more fully in the section on the noematic structure of thinking (see below).

As *fulfillment*, thinking establishes the embeddedness of the possibility within the referential network. That enables thinking to bring a sense of closure to its explicitation of the role of that possibility in the transformation of the position. It distinguishes those possibilities that affect the dynamics in a fundamental way from those that do not. For example, S.1 noted that "knight to rook seven is, is flashy but, but bogus." That move was grasped as not able to fundamentally affect the transformation of the equilibrium because S. grasped that the opponent could still maintain it by making a particular move. Thus, its apparent capacity to affect the equilibrium depended on the opponent not making his own best move. In this mode, thinking thematizes such criteria. In other words, as fulfillment, thinking involves demonstrations of the applicability and the necessity of the thematized possibility. It does so by means of 'if — then' structures (see following section on objects of thought). In this mode, thinking seeks to achieve a reorganization of the field of possibles such that the ambiguity about the future is dissolved. Such a thorough-going clarification is sometimes achieved, but most typically it is not. Rather, the transformative capacity of the possibilities remains beyond the circle of necessity, retaining a peripheral instability, which then evokes subsequent interrogation.

The noematic structure of thinking. The objects of thought are intentional objects, and as such must be distinguished from the transcendent objects which are thought about (e.g., the chess pieces on the board). However, part of the essential meaning of the object of thought is its relation to that which is thought about, and this relation will be articulated as part of the noematic structure.

The object of thought presents itself as a possibility capable of factical completion. Its manifestation as a possibility is through that which "could," "might," or "may" be. It has four essential attributes: it is symbolic, pragmatic, telic, and ambiguous. Regarding the first, the object of thought is essentially *symbolic* in that it has no existence apart from its participation in a referential totality of meanings to which it refers and through which it is expressed (see below for a more complete specification of this referential totality). Regarding the second, the object of thought is *pragmatic* in that it has the character of an action possibility: the possibility of effecting a transformation in the dynamic relations in the position. An example is S.3's: "bishop to knight five, which can go from there to rook four to knight three, attacking his king pawn." Regarding the third attribute, the object of thought is *telic* in the sense that it refers to the future. Usually, this attribute is obvious, but it is even descriptive of thinking's thematizing a past possibility, that is, something that was previously possible but now no longer is. Even then it illuminates the ongoing relations among the pieces. An example is: "bishop takes knight didn't work because of queen takes, knight takes pawn, and ah, knight takes pawn himself. Or he could even just play knight takes pawn." The telic dimension of such an object delineates what the future does and does not now portend. Regarding the fourth attribute, the object of thought essentially presents itself as an *uncertainty*. But uncertainty here must be seen as a quality of the intentional object (i.e., as lived), not a mathematical array of objectively determinable alternatives, for it is the lack of foreclosure rather than the availability of legal moves that founds uncertainty. That was especially exemplified by the subjects' manner of playing opening moves by rote.

In the course of a chess game, thinking intends many different objects of thought. These include: a move, the initiative, a positional feature, the opponent, and the network of referential relations in the position. While a possible move, and particularly the next move, is the most thematically central object of thought, all these objects are structurally related to the network of spatial-temporal relations, whose implicatory or referential character provides the basis for thinking's determination of the sense or meaning of these other objects. This network of spatial and temporal relations is repeatedly delineated, revised, and maintained by thinking.

Thinking's thematization of spatial relations in the position includes both global spatial-dynamic tensions as well as specific spatial relations. An example of the former is S.2's sense that there is "a lot of space advantage" to be won on the queenside. Another, even more general spatial determination is S.4's sense that a particular move will leave his opponent "cramped." An example of a specific spatial relation is S.2's sense that his opponent's knight, if moved to its typical place, "blocks in his queen bishop."

The position is also grasped as being temporally related to past and future possibilities. S.3 notes that it is a "crucial time" in the game. S.1 wonders if it might be "too late" to play a previously thematized move. S.4 consider that his opponent might want to play a "waiting move" to change the temporal flow of the game.

Both the spatial and temporal relations mutually imply each other, and so form a *spatio-temporal network* of relations. These relations, however, are not closed in upon themselves, but imply, or refer to, the possibility of transformation. Their relational structure is an implicatory, or referential, one, such that the meaning of each constituent is not that of an isolated unit, but rather that of a participant in a totality, referring to other possibilities. For example, after a possible move, the spatiality may be so rearranged that a well posted knight now becomes easily dislodged. The transformation of the spatial relations can even refer to the emergence of new possibilities that are not yet thematic. For example, S.4 noted "maybe this brings on some new possibilities with my bishop to there." Hence, this referential network is not a collection of elemental pieces on a geometrically uniform board, but a field of differential forces and tensions carved out by and defined according to their dynamic-actional relations.

Thinking does not thematize this referential network in its totality, but neither are its relations grasped randomly. Rather, it is precisely those whose pragmatic character is most evident (see above). These are grasped by means of an '*if — then*' *structure*, in which thinking delineates what is implied by explicitating their referential significance. This 'if — then' structure takes a variety of forms, their essential structural commonality being an effort to penetrate the opacity of the future possible unfolding of the implications of the present position by extending its referential arcs in order to explicitate what they imply. Actual types of this 'if — then' structure include: 1) a specific move in both the 'if' and the 'then' clauses; 2) no move in the 'if' clause and a specific move in the 'then' clause; 3) a specific move in the 'if' clause and a specific or global evaluation of the position in the 'then' clause; 4) a goal in the 'if' clause and a goal in the 'then' clause.

The *first* type is the most common, and in fact may form compound 'if — then' structures by taking its 'then' clause as an 'if' clause for a new 'if — then' structure, or by combining with the second type. Even in its pure form, there are many varieties of this type of 'if — then' structure. The three most important will be presented here. The first is: 'if move X is made by one player, then the other can make move Y.' Two examples are: "if I go there he can move his queen back"; "if he does play knight' to king bishop three right — knight to knight five — right now, I'll play pawn to king rook three." The second variation of this type if: 'if move X is made by one player, then the other must make move Y.' Examples include: "he can play bishop to king two and I have to retire to king four in frustration"; "if he'd play knight to the king bishop three, I'd have to kick it out with my king rook pawn." The third variation of this type is: 'if move X is made by one player, then he can no longer make move Y.' For example, S.2 noted that if his opponent moved his knight, it would prevent him from then moving his bishop.

In the *second* type of an 'if — then' structure, a move by one player is deliberately omitted. That serves to make explicit what possibilities would be implied if they are not blocked by the player whose move is omitted. Thus, the structure is: 'if no move is made by one player, then the other can make move Y.' For example, S.3 noted during his own turn a particular move his opponent could make were it his turn instead ("if it was his move bishop takes queen would win"). This type may be compounded with the first one and so make explicit the implications of a series of moves by one player. In this case the structure is: 'if one player makes move X, and the other makes no move, then the first player can next make move Z.' Examples include: S.1's considering what his opponent will do the turn after making his next move, without interposing S.'s own intervening move; S.3's noting 'I can play pawn to queen three here, and then queen knight to queen two.'

With regard to the *third* type, a specific move may imply a global significance rather than another specific move. In that case, the structure is: 'if one player makes move X, then positional consequence A will follow.' An example is S.3's noting that his kingside would be weaker after a particular move. Sometimes the resulting global significance remains prethematic. For example, S.2's sense that a "great game" would follow a particular center pawn advance after castling.

In the *fourth* type, a particular goal is grasped as implying the possibility of the achievement of another subsequent goal. In this case, the structure is: 'if goal 1 is achieved, then goal 2 can be.'

For example, S.2 determines that if he can "control" a particular square, he can subsequently occupy it with his own piece. Another example is S.5's sense that if he can gain control of the seventh rank, he will then have checkmating possibilities.

One final point about this 'if — then' structure is that there is a variant of it that is also a thematic object of thought. This variant may be identified as the *'since — then' structure*, as it is a preceding move (rather than a future one) that is taken as referring to the possibility or necessity or foreclosure of a subsequent move by the same or the other player. For example, S.3 determined that since his opponent's last move resulted in an attack on his bishop, he must now back it up on his next move. While such 'since — then' structures occur quite frequently after the opponent's moves, they are typically anticipated prior to that move as an 'if — then' structure. Hence, their referential significance has already been largely delineated by the subject. When that significance has not been so delineated, the move presents itself to thinking as "a very strange looking move" precisely because it lacks referential relatedness. At those times, it is up to the 'since — then' structuring to weave it into the referential network.

A summary of the referential network as an object of thought is in order at this point. Thinking grasps the position not as a collection of isolated units, but as a symbolic network of spatial and temporal references, of implicatory referential arcs. These referential arcs are contacted as being there in the position, but they must be uncovered. Thinking grasps them by making thematic, by making a theme of that which is implicit. That is, thinking is an explicitation of the implications. But how does thinking contact the implications to be explicitated? Implicitly — that is the tacit dimension of thinking. In that way, possibilities that seem to come to mind capriciously or 'out of the blue' — those referred to as 'intuition' — are precisely the implications that were implicitly referred to by these referential arcs. An example is a point is S.1's game when thinking thematizes, seemingly 'out of the blue,' a move the opponent could make next. Even the subject is unclear about the basis for the move, suggesting that the opponent might want to play it "out of curiosity" to "see what happens." Evidently, the subject's curiosity has also been piqued by the move. It becomes clear through the rest of the meaning unit that the move carries with it a set of referential implications. Thematizing that move called thinking to make these implications explicit, which it promptly begins to do: "I suppose if he plays bishop to knight five I play bishop to king two and then follow up with knight to knight five later or something." Thus, the referential arcs disclose the meaning of the spatial-temporal matrix. Indeed, that disclosure is their essential role for thinking, and is taken as such by thinking. For example, after following out such a referential arc, S.5 explicitly noted "which means I have to move the queen." While the spatial-temporal matrix may be focal, its referential implication or meaning may be horizontal. Furthermore, these referential arcs are transformed with every move. Thus, thinking takes as its task the explicitation of the consequences of these transformations. And, lastly, in doing so, thinking distinguishes between necessary (or forced) and contingent (or virtual) possibilities, necessary ones being those that are directly and immediately implied, whereas contingent ones are those that are only potentially implied by the referential network.

These referential arcs imply possibilities which themselves can effect the transformation of that referential totality; hence there is a dialectical relationship between the referential network and the possibilities implied. Most thematically central is the next move or continuation of moves that can be made. It is here that the intentional object of thought participates in the transcendence that is thought about: the chess game itself. As an intersubjective reality which thinking contacts only perspectivally, the chess game provides the foundation for the answerability which is a profile of the objects of thought. That is, it is by virtue of their relation to this transcendent reality that the objects of thought possess their character of possibility-that-is-to-be-filled-in. This completability eludes final realization in thinking, yet exerts a demand on thinking. That is, answerability includes a normative significance: each possibility presents the meaning that 'maybe this is what should be done' (in the sense that it may be the most efficacious way to effect a change in the game in favor of the thinker). This 'should' dimension is particularly evident when the object of thought is what move to make next, as that is precisely when the transcendent object must be effected. It is through its proximal relatedness with the game itself that the next move in particular acquires its demand, or telic, character. An apt example is S.1's wrestling with the idea of making a particular pawn trade. He sees it as something he had "better" do, even though it is something he "hates" to do, and feels it is a "pity" to have to do.

The next move as an object of thought, however, is itself subservient to another object of thought wherein its own telic character is ultimately found. This other object of thought, which remains highly implicit itself, is the final result of the game as a future possibility. As objects of thought, the next move is related to the final result by another object of thought, which is sometimes implicit and sometimes explicit: the initiative, or capacity to force the action to a certain extent by the use of offensive threats that force the other player to parry them in limited, defensive ways. This sense of dynamic force or momentum unites the next move (as an explicit and primarily spatial object of thought) with the final result (as an implicit and primarily temporal object of thought). This unity is possible because both have spatial and temporal characteristics (for instance, the next move is never thought about in isolation from the temporal flow, but always as embedded within a plan or combination), and because 'initiative' is structurally essential to both.

As an object of thought, *initiative* or momentum is a profile of the game as a whole. For example S.2's sense that his position was such that "I got to have a great game." It is specifically revealed through the dynamic balance of offensive opportunities or threats and defensive necessities. This balance is not summatively determined, however, but on the basis of the thinker's capacity to control the transformative flow of the next few moves by being able to force the other player to make defensive moves. When a certain move has the character that it 'has to' or must be made as a consequence of the forcing nature of the other player's initiative, that character differs from the 'should' character that other moves have at other times. S.1 provides an example of his distinction. He thinks that "pawn takes pawn" is a move he "should" have made, but now thinks "I have to retire to king four." In the former case, it was a move he should have made in order to keep the momentum, whereas the latter move is one that he must make for having lost the momentum. Generally, this balance of opportunities is grasped only implicitly until there is a change or impending change in the balance, in favor of either player. At that point it becomes an explicit object of thought. For example, as S.1's own attacking possibilities are blocked, he became aware of the need to keep his queen defensively posted, sensing that his opponent "may be counterattacking there pretty soon." This change may be an increase or a decrease in the offensive capacity of the player who is already considered to have the momentum, or a disturbance of, or re-establishment of, a state of relative equilibrium. The exact shift in the equilibrium may not be clear, only that it needs to be re-evaluated. For example, S.3 finds his hoped for breakthrough of his opponent's defenses stalled, and re-examines the momentum: "uup, this isn't too bad a game now. Thought for a while I was smashing him. Nah, he's not smashing me, I still have all the trumps but, he's not doing too bad."

Another category of objects of thought has to do with the *opponent's intentions*. While the opponent himself remains a highly implicit object of thought, what the opponent may be thinking about is repeatedly thematized as an object of thought. As an object of thought, the opponent's intentions emerge through an imaginal shift of perspective, based on the implicit presumption that the opponent's thinking is no different than the subject's own. For example, S.1 "doubts" that his opponent will fail to block a possibility that he would block. This implied identity is most clear in those cases where a subject thinks a particular move fulfills a particular question. An example is S.4: "I think he wants to move his rook back there." However, it also extends to those instances wherein the subject, still uncertain about the implications of a particular move that the opponent could make, thinks that the opponent is also interested in, but uncertain about, that move as well. A previously cited meaning unit of S.1 also applies well here: he was curious about a move, and so he assumed his opponent was too. But the opponent's thinking, as an object of thought for the subject, is not simply projection, for it always retains a certain impenetrability about it. Indeed, sometimes it is the very opacity of the opponent's intentions that is the object of thought. S.2, for example, wonders what opening his opponent will play, then later wonders what he is thinking, and then where he will move a particular piece. More frequently, it is grasped as ambiguously likely, partially illuminated by some specific characteristics of the position. An example is S.1: "he just plays, probably just plays bishop to ah, bishop takes knight." Sometimes the opponent's intention is not illuminated by the position but by his bodily comportment. For example, at one point, S.4 thinks that his opponent has given up hoping to be able to retain a piece by how hard he depressed the bell after his move: "he punched that clock, punched that bell pretty hard, that means he must have dropped it." The implicit basis for thinking's concern with the opponent's intentions is the pattern of rythmic alternation whereby each player takes a turn at transforming the referential network. While this dialectic remains highly implicit, it provides the structural coherence for thinking's taking the opponent's intentions as an object of thought.

Thinking's involvement with other modes of psychological life manifested in chess playing. Thinking is not the only psychological modality brought to bear in playing chess. Playing chess is properly an action of the whole person, in which many psychological modes are elicited as a unity. Indeed, while thinking 'casts about' in a sea of possibility, it is flanked by shores of facticities given by other psychological modes. Thinking initially relates to these facticities by taking them as a springboard, from which thinking itself emerges. That is, thinking emerges within the gaps in these factically givens. It de-structures them by relating them to the possibilities which are the proper objects of thought, in the service of returning psychological life to the field of the factical, but now a facticity transformed by its possibilization. Thus, thinking, whose intentional objects have the character of possibility, occupies an intermediate position, linking modalities whose intentional objects have the character of facticity. Often it bridges two moments of the same mode, for in the actual flux of a chess game, thinking is both evoked by and also evokes the emergence of these other modes. In that sense, thinking is involved with these other modes as a two-sided dependency. The relations of thinking with these other psychological modes must be addressed next, each in turn. While this description will detail these other modes only in terms of their relation with thinking, it should be recognized that each of them could also be made the focus of an analysis of how each is exemplified during chess playing. But that would be another investigation, and is beyond the scope of this one.

Thinking's relation to *memory* is one of the most pervasive and crucial in chess playing. Memory of the rules of chess (how the pieces are moved, etc.) is of course essential for being able to play chess at all. But that memorial infrastructure does not become an object of thought. Rather, in those instances in which thinking relates to memorial objects, those with which it is involved are memories of one's general stock of chess expertise and memories of previous games. These memorially givens are evoked on the basis of their relevance or similarity to the present game. Yet similarity is not an exact duplication. That is because the memorial object is ultimately not a particular configuration of pieces, but a theme, or idea. In thematizing it, either its essential similarity may be focal or its essential difference may be focal, depending on how the memorial object is related to the present position. An example of the former case is S.1's determination that the position reached so far in the game is essentially similar to that of a previous game: "as in the Bisguier game." The relation with that game also provides an example of the latter case, when later the present game diverges essentially from the previous one. S.1 now memorially thematizes how it differs: "it would be like the game with Bisguier except I'd be a, tempo down." This example reveals the distinction between essential versus inessential similarity. The configuration of the pieces is still basically like that in the previous game, but the tempo is different (whose side has the next move). And the subject recognizes that that essential difference means that the similar features no longer indicate an essential similarity.

Thinking's relation to *perception* is also crucial. Perception of course is involved in chess playing especially visually as the player looks at the pieces on the board for virtually the entire game. Indeed, subjects often used visually based terms: a position "looked" good for example, or "let's see" about a particular move possibility. The sole occasion when another sense modality was used was by S.2. While considering his 22nd move, he said "that sounds pretty good." That followed a quick, superficial synthesis of a possible combination. Perhaps he couldn't yet "see" it, but it sounded right to him (at that same time he was also not "seeing" the material balance accurately, which is quite a blunder for a player of his caliber). But what is thinking's relation to perception such that at some point it almost merges into it, or fails to? Perception thematizes the immediate physiognomies of the position, especially right after it has been transformed by the opponent's making a move. For example S.4 notes: "ah he plays rook to D eight." In that sense, perception provides a starting point for thinking. But the relationship is more complex than that, for thinking also evokes perceptual reorganizations. These are achieved by thinking's clarification of the referential arcs of the spatial-temporal network. For example, thinking founded a perceptual reorganization upon taking up the opponent's perspective for subject S.1. It was specifically when thinking thematized the position as if it were the opponent's turn that the perceptual field is reorganized such that he now sees the relation between the opponent's bishop and his own queen. A second example of thinking's capacity to evoke perceptual reorganizations is provided by subject S.4. Only after thinking has thematized a possible future move that S. could make does S. perceive a particular dynamic relation that his opponent's knight has with his own pieces. He now grasps perceptually a certain configuration of these pieces ("the knight hook") that he had not previously perceived as a configuration. Thus, even though the pieces were not moved at that point, the perceptual field itself is re-gestalted or reorganized as a consequence of thinking's thematization. While such a reorganization comes as a surprise, it would be inaccurate to understand it as a merely fortuitous coincidence. Indeed, thinking does not simply evoke them, it provokes them, so frequent and important are such perceptual reorganizations to the course of the game.

Thinking's relation to *affect* also provides an example of a two sided dependency, in that each can evoke the other. A player's first reaction upon seeing his opponent's move (already within its implied significance) may be an affective one; he may be shocked, surprised, even frightened. Such reactions then evoke thinking to thematize the implicit significance. On the other hand, thinking may in its turn evoke affect, such as relief or frustration. An example is S.1. His frustration at being unable to achieve the aim of his speculative opening gambit mounts and mounts, until it nears the point of "hair tearing frustration." Perhaps the notion of a two-sided dependency here is not even sufficient to grasp the intertwining of affect and thought in chess, for it is an intensely emotional experience for the serious player. S.1 "curses" himself for having "missed a shot here." S.2 becomes quite depressed over his blunder late in the game. S.4 castigates himself as a "dummy" for thinking he had a possible combination when he didn't, and writhes in agony when he feels his opponent's capacity to defeat a particular possible continuation: "ooh, he's got me crunched now." Even when not verbalized, the affective experience of the chess game is expressed bodily, through gestures and comportment. Thought and affect are brought to bear as a unity during chess playing, a relation well grasped by chess masters themselves. Vitale Sevastianov, president of the Soviet Chess Federation, summed this relation concisely by noting that "through chess a human being is able to unite his mind and feelings" (Quoted by Bert, 1981, p. 30).

Thinking's relation to *imagination* is a complicated variant of a two-sided dependency. Certainly it is the case that either can evoke the other. Just as imagination as the evocation of the possible founds thinking's "if–then" structuring, so too does thinking's questioning call forth imagining. But in imagination, the mode of givenness is changed; specifically, they are not posited as questions, as uncertainty. Rather, the imagination serves thinking by projecting its object, such as a move, into a future, but then it is thinking which takes up that future possibility as a question. For example, S.4 considers the imagined possibility of a bishop sacrifice. The imagination simply presents that possibility as a possibility. It then becomes an object for thinking's questioning.

Thinking's relation to *empathy* is also important. One of the ways that the subject intends his opponent's possibilities and intentions is by empathically taking up the opponent's perspective. For example, S.4 feels that his move has surprised his opponent. And S.3 empathically feels at one point that his opponent "is really thinking hard now." Often this empathic sense occurs by virtue of the subject's having been in that position in previous games himself. S.1, for example, thematizes such a time. Thus, empathy provides facticities for thinking to take up.

Thinking's relation to *anticipation* and *judgment* is also important. These are listed together here as they are both typically founded on thinking as its outcomes, or its means of returning to facticity. But there is an essential difference between them. When thinking passes into judgment, the subject remains mindful of the uncertainty character of the intentional objects. For example S.3's judgment that his next move "should protect everything" reveals this mindfulness. In anticipation however, there is a falling toward the future within a forgetfulness of uncertainty, in which possibility is foreclosed and questionableness submerged. For example, S.2's anticipation that "I got to have a great game" just before making a particular move reveals this blinding enthusiasm – he lost that game.

Finally, a word should be added about thinking's relation to *motivation*. There seems to be an intrinsic motivation which founds thinking without being evoked by it, thus in the manner of a one-sided dependency. Specifically, thinking in chess as pragmatic is founded upon the motivation of wanting to win the game. While the motive of wanting to win the game is the way by which motivation interfaces with thinking, it is possible to analyze more deeply concerning the motivational significance of chess playing. While that analysis is largely beyond the scope of this research, some interesting leads did emerge from the data. For example, all of the subjects spoke not merely of attempting to defeat their opponents, but of wanting to thrash them in some more primordial way: to "tear him apart" (S.1), or to "smash him" (S.4), for example. And often, in their distracted moments, subjects' thoughts drifted onto physical sports competitions, for example, S.2 onto baseball, S.3 onto hockey. Lastly, there was also an obscure sexual connection. After thinking of taking control of "the long diagonal" (the diagonal formed by the squares extending from one corner of the board to the opposite corner), S.2 then became distracted by thoughts of his girlfriend. Fine (1967) has conjectured a latent sexual significance to chess playing, which he considered Oedipal in nature.

Discussion

The results of this research bear critically on the view of thinking promulgated by the information processing approach. This critical significance will be discussed in terms of both quantitative and qualitative issues. First, the quantitative differences will be described. Then, ten specific qualitative differences will each be elaborated in turn.

Quantitative differences. Subjects searched far less than information processing models proposed by Newell and Simon. In fact, the continuations they thematized in the time between making one move and the next (thereby including the time during which the opponent made his intervening move) never involved more than sixty-two positions. This maximum is lower than de Groot's (1978, p. 319) finding of a maximum of seventy-six for his experimentally provided position, but within the range he found of twenty to seventy-six. Also, the average number of positions included was far lower than de Groot's. Partly that difference can be accounted for by de Groot's having preselected difficult positions, whereas in an actual game some positions are much less complicated. Also, however, the subject's embeddedness in the game contributes to his being able to focus more narrowly than could de Groot's subjects, who were presented with a position in the middle of a game they had not even seen develop. This difference re-confirms the structural description already presented concerning the role of the previously constituted horizons in the thematization of future possibilities, and is also compatible with Luchins (1960) finding that creative thinking is facilitated to the extent that the subject participates in the formulation or creation of the problem on which he subsequently works. The significance of this embeddedness was not only missed by de Groot (see Aanstoos, 1981), but is essentially overlooked by information processing models.

Another quantitative difference was in the number of beginning moves thematized. Clarke (1971, p. 190) had suggested that one reason that chess programs search many more variations than people was because programs include two or three times the average number of possible first moves in their search as people do (four to seven as opposed to two). That difference is also confirmed and accounted for by these findings. And the anomaly of the information processing model's much larger searching must be seen to be inherent precisely because its search method is structurally different from human thinking. The only exception to such exhaustive searching by a computer program is that proposed by Atkin (1972; Atkin & Witten, 1973). His program analyzes positions in terms of maximizing the values of a position according to a grid of fifty-three dimensions. However, that program cannot play chess, and its sterile description of a position so neglects taking dynamic and tactical possibilities into account (such as imminent piece captures or checks) that its method has been judged to have "quite obviously no relationship with human chess thinking" (Bell, 1978, p. 92).

Uncertainty. Many theorists have tended to describe thinking as a process whereby one choice is selected from among various alternatives. Obviously, such a 'decision making' or 'problem solving' view of thinking is the one employed by information processing, as well as by those they take as precursors (especially de Groot and Selz). Such a perspective is wider than that, however. Writers as far removed from the information processing model as Dewey (1910) and Bolton (1972) have also characterized thinking as beginning with a 'forked road situation' in which an obstacle blocks the way of goal directed activity. Bolton (1972, p. 9) adds that the chosen alternative is selected by applying a set of rules and that "thinking is therefore essentially a matter of judging and evaluating objects and events." Berlyne (1965, p. 276) also argues that "conflict is a major influence in the initiation of directed thinking." He then links this notion of conflict with that of the formal, mathematical concept of "uncertainty" provided by information theory:

> The mathematical truth that information implies prior uncertainty corresponds to the biological and psychological truth that the role of information in animal life is contingent on conflict, the behavioral equivalent of uncertainty. Information will be valuable to an animal only when it prevents or relieves conflict. (Berlyne, 1965, pp. 278–279)

It is partly the wide acceptance of this linkage of uncertainty, as the presence of alternatives, with information, in its formal sense, that is responsible for the current high status enjoyed by the information processing approach. It mathematized and mechanized the taken for granted view of thinking as decision making. But such a view is incomplete, for it considers thinking only within an already explicit field of choices. The results of this study showed that thinking also involves the delineation of that field of possibles, through an interrogatory or questioning, mode. Furthermore, these findings show that this thematization of the possibles is not merely propaedeutic to thinking, but is an essential constituent throughout the thinking process. In that sense, these findings are closer to Green's (1966, pp. 11–12) position. He asserted that the "sterile stages model . . . has led nowhere" and proposed simultaneous rather than serial activities, specifically including an "assimilating" activity. Berlyne himself had noted that the term "question" seemed relevant to the thinking process. However, he prejudged its role on the basis of information theory, and took it in the following sense: "the questioner will be faced with a set of alternative events to which an uncertainty value can be assigned" (Berlyne, 1965, p. 285). As already noted, the results of this study do not support such a mathematical conception of uncertainty. Instead, the research showed that uncertainty is more accurately described by the Gestalt psychologists (especially Wertheimer, 1945) as a stress, strain, or tension. In other words, while uncertainty is an essential constituent, it is best understood as a lived experience rather than as a mathematical array. The subjects experienced uncertainty not necessarily when there was a large number of objectively available moves, but precisely when there was no prior foreclosure of them, as there typically was when a combination was being followed through. Indeed, that is the meaning of a combination.

Look ahead. The information processing model had posited a look ahead function that proceeded in a linear, move by move counting out fashion, to a predetermined depth. The results of this study also include data in which such move by move sequences are taken as objects of thought. However, in contradiction to the information processing model, such move by move sequences were always embedded within thinking's overarching contact with an implicit sense of the flow of the game as a whole. This relation of the particular move to the flow of the game was achieved by thinking as a unity through a sense of 'initiative' as a telic characteristic. And it was that unity that guided thinking's looking ahead, even in the absence of any counting out sequence. For example, S.1 refrained from moving his queen at one point based on thinking that he would need it where it was to counteract his opponent's future attack on that side of the board. That looking ahead involved no specific sequence of counting out at all, but was based on the sense that the initiative was changing toward his opponent. As another example, thinking about the consequences that a move in the middle game had for the endgame was typical for the subjects, yet that is something no model based on a sequential look ahead can simulate. In other words, the results show that the information processing model's problem cannot be resolved simply by lengthening its look ahead to a farther depth. Rather, they indicate that thinking looks ahead in an essentially different way.

Purposiveness The information processing model had posited predetermined heuristic rules as guiding thinking to certain moves and not others. The results of this study do show that general principles are involved in thinking in chess. However, rather than simply adhering to predetermined guidelines as sheer facticities, thinking took them up as guidelines, as objects of thought. As such they were questioned, as possibilities. For example, S.4 followed the principle of posting a knight on the sixth rank when he had the opportunity to do so, as an explicit following of a maxim that it is advantageous to do so. But the maxim itself was thematic as a question, and following it meant extending that questioning to the position on the board. In other words, the maxim did not serve to conclude thinking, but to evoke it. So, even when followed, maxims serve as signifiers rather than as rigid rules. Perhaps an even more clear example of this difference between thinking's flexibility and the model's rigidity occurred in those instances when thinking took up again as questionable the very possible moves it had already rejected. For example, S.1 repeatedly reconsidered playing "pawn takes pawn" after having decided against it "on general principles." Such data provides ample support for the distinction that thinking determines the applicability of guidelines within the context of the game or situation, in contrast to the predetermination that is made for the program's heuristics.

Goal seeking. The information processing model asserts that thinking is essentially serial processing, able to pursue only one goal at a time. The descriptive results are also revelatory on this point, for they show thinking pursuing a multiplicity of goals simultaneously. More specifically, they show this simultaneity is possible because the goals are related to each other as theme and horizon. For example, S.2's pursuit of the goal of controlling the center was thematic and his goal of maintaining the initiative was horizonal. Both could be pursued simultaneously because of their intrinsic relatedness at a structural level. This finding undercuts Newell and Simon's (1972, pp. 796–797; Simon & Newell, 1971, p. 149) argument against such multiplicity, for they had based their argument on the demonstration that a person cannot do two unrelated tasks simultaneously. This understanding of the structural relatedness of thinking's goals needs also to be distinguished from the information processing model's use of goals and subgoals (Newell & Simon, 1972, for example). Such a model achieves a goal by breaking it down into steps, called subgoals, and then establishes subroutines to solve these subgoals one at a time in order to narrow the difference between the present state and the goal state. It would appear that thinking also includes this use of goals and subgoals. For example, S.1 wondered whether to open the long diagonal in order to attain greater offensive threats. To read that as compatible with the information processing model, however, is to miss a crucial distinction made evident in the structural analysis. The difference is that, for thinking, the former (in this case, the open diagonal) is not one small step on the way to the latter (in this case, greater offensive threats). Rather, the latter, as initiative, is the horizonal meaning of the former. The open diagonal, as theme, is not isolated from its horizon as if it were one step on the way toward something other than itself. Rather it is embedded in that horizon specifically by means of a referential unity of implications.

Memory. In information processing models, memory serves thinking by storing an enormous amount of information in the form of isolated bits. This research showed that objects do indeed serve thinking, but in a much more concise and organized form. It is concise because memorial objects are taken up as objects of thought only as they are appropriate to the present game. Thinking's capacity to grasp this essential similarity is what enables it to make more limited yet more effective use of memory. The effectiveness of thinking's use of memorial objects is also dependent on another structural difference with the computer model: the memorial objects are recalled as dynamic wholes — for example, S.1's remembering of his previous game against Bisguier. Indeed, it is only because it is recalled as a whole that he can discriminate its essential similarity.

Overall sense of the task. Two important differences may be noted here between the results of the descriptive study and the information processing model. For the model, the game is incrementally put together, since a game that is constructed incrementally can only be evaluated statically. In contrast, thinking is guided by an overall sense of the game which it evaluates dynamically. One obvious way by which that is repeatedly manifested is through thinking's tendency to provoke reorganizations in the subject's perceptual grasp of the position. Chase and Simon's (1973a, 1973b) PERCEIVER program had no such capacity. This overall sense that unites any individual move within the flow of the game is possible because each move refers to a larger whole (the referential unity) and because the shifting balance of offensive opportunities and defensive necessities is itself an object of thought (as 'initiative'). This overall sense is not an artefact of incremental objects but is itself their telic structure. Similarly, it is 'the initiative' as an object of thought that founds the dynamic evaluations typical for the subjects. S.1 and S.4, for example, continued to regard their position as superior to their opponents' even while they were down a pawn in material.

Level of knowing. Information processing models function

completely on the basis of formal and explicit criteria. The descriptive data, however, reveals that thinking is guided by a tacit awareness of objects of thought that remain implicit. For example, all of the subjects recognized certain moves as significant even without being able to specify wherein their significance lay. This difference may be most crucial to the information processing model, for its whole approach is based on the belief that thinking can be represented as a formal, explicit system. In contrast, the subjects' thinking was guided by the implicit referential significances of the position. An example from the descriptive results is the role that a sense of closure, as an implicit and nonformal characteristic, had for thinking. The importance of closure to the directedness of thinking was in fact suggested by Harrower (1932) as possibly playing a similar role in thinking as it does in perception.

Role of experience. Information processing models seek to explain intuition on the basis of stored patterns from previous experience. But, as in the use of memorial objects in general (see above section on memory), the elemental and predetermined nature of the program's stored patterns differ from the wholistic and contextually relevant patterns the subjects used from their previous experience. And, with regard to the issue of intuition in particular, analysis of those instances wherein a subject thematized a particular move 'out of the blue' as it were, reveals that it is the explicit thematization of a possibility that had already been referred to implicitly before that. This explicitation of a previously implicit object of thought therefore does depend on previous experience in that the object of thought had been previously experienced implicitly. However, it does not require, not arise from, an array of thousands of elemental and predetermined patterns.

Expectations. Though absent from information processing models, expectations were frequent objects of thought for all subjects. They concerned not only the position (for example: "there's got to be something here though. I just know there's got to be something here" by S.4), but also the opponent's intentions (for example: "after pawn to queen three as I expect him to play" by S.3). These expectations are not inferences or calculations, but the temporal adumbrations (given through the referential arcs) of 'initiative' as an object of thought.

Opponent's style. A sense of the opponent's "chess personality" likewise absent from computer processing models, was a common object of thought for the subjects. Wiener, a pioneer in cybernetics, had anticipated the importance of this aspect, when he criticized von Neumann and Morgenstern's (1947) theory of game playing for omitting it. He noted that "naturally, as always is the case with chess, you will come to a judgment of your opponent's chess personality" (Wiener, 1948/1961, pp. 171–172). The descriptive results reveal that this sense of the opponent emerges in the course of the game. At first, the opponent is grasped almost anonymously, simply as "the opponent." Early thematizations of the opponent are based on the subjects' empathically putting themselves in their opponents' perspective. There is a phase of questioning the opponent's ability by some subjects (notably S.4). Then eventually, the opponent's style coalesces as a specific object of thought. For example, S.1 concluded "now I have some kind of idea of what kind of player I'm dealing with . . . take everything in sight, especially when you're down in material."

Conclusion. Taken in their totality, these differences constitute a significant critique of the information processing model of thinking. The basic conclusion supported by this critique is that it is time psychology set aside its presuppositions about thinking. Rather than rely on a computational model of thinking in which discrete elements are processed according to predetermined rules, the psychology of thinking needs to begin with the recognition of thinking as a genuinely explicitative process of bringing to clarity an ambiguous, referential network of possibilities.

References

Aanstoos, C. M. (review of de Groot's *Thought and choice in chess*). *Journal of Phenomenological Psychology*, 1981, *12*, 131–139.

———. A phenomenological study of thinking. In A. Giorgi, A. Barton & C. Maes (Eds.), *Duquesne studies in phenomenological psychology* (Vol. 4), Pittsburgh: Duquesne University Press, 1983. (a)

———. *A phenomenological study of thinking as it is exemplified during chess playing.* Ann Arbor: University Microfilms, 1983. (abstracted in: *Dissertation Abstracts International*, 1983, *43*, 2726-B.) (b)

———. The think-aloud method in descriptive research. *Journal of Phenomenological Psychology*, 1983, *14*, 243–266. (c)

Atkin, R. H. Multidimensional structure in the game of chess. *International Journal of Man-Machine Studies*, 1972, *4*, 341–362.

114   *QUALITATIVE RESEARCH IN PSYCHOLOGY*

Atkin, R. H. & Witten, I. H. Mathematical relations in chess. In A. G. Bell (Ed.), *Computer chess: Proceedings of a one day meeting on chess playing by computer*. Chilton, England: Atlas Computer Laboratory, 1973.

Bell, A. G. *The machine plays chess?* Oxford: Pergamon, 1978.

Berlyne, D. *Structure and direction in thinking*. New York: Wiley, 1965.

————. Behaviorism? Cognitive theory? Humanistic psychology? To Hull with them all! *Canadian Psychological Review*, 1975, *16*, 69–80.

Bert, A. The FIDE reports. *Chess Life*, Nov. 1981, pp. 29–32.

Boden, M. A. *Purposive explanation in psychology*. Cambridge, Mass.: Harvard University Press, 1972.

————. *Artificial intelligence and natural man*. Hassocks, Eng.: Harvester, 1977.

Bolton, N. *The psychology of thinking*. London: Methuen, 1972.

Bourne, L., Ekstrand, B. & Dominowski, R. *The psychology of thinking*. Englewood Cliffs, N.J.: Prentice-Hall, 1971.

Bruner, J. S. Foreword. In A. Burton & J. Radford (Eds.), *Thinking in perspective*. London: Methuen, 1978.

Charness, N. Human chess skill. In P. Frey (Ed.), *Chess skill in man and machine*. New York: Springer-Verlag, 1978.

Chase, W. G. & Simon, H. A. The mind's eye in chess. In W. G. Chase (Ed.), *Visual information processing*. New York: Academic Press, 1973. (a)

————. Perception in chess. *Cognitive Psychology*, 1973, *4*, 55–81. (b)

Clarke, M. R. Some ideas for a chess compiler. In Elithorn & Jones (Eds.), *Artificial and human thinking: Report of the NATO symposium on human thinking*, 1971 (San Francisco: Jossey-Bass, 1973).

de Groot, A. D. *Thought and choice in chess*. (2nd ed.). The Hague: Mouton, 1978. (Originally published, 1946).

Dewey, J. *How we think*. Boston: Heath, 1910.

Fine, R. *The psychology of the chess player*. New York: Dover, 1967.

Frijda, N. H. Problems of computer simulation. *Behavioral Science*, 1967, *12*, 59–67.

Giorgi, A. An application of phenomenological method in psychology. In A. Giorgi, C. Fischer & E. Murray (Eds.), *Duquesne studies in phenomenological psychology* (Vol. 2). Pittsburgh: Duquesne University Press, 1975.(a)

————. Convergence and divergence of qualitative and quantitative methods in psychology. In A. Giorgi, C. Fischer & E. Murray (Eds.), *Duquesne studies in phenomenological psychology* (Vol. 2). Pittsburgh: Duquesne University Press, 1975. (b)

————. Phenomenology and the foundations of psychology. In W. Arnold (Ed.), *Nebraska symposium on motivation* (Vol. 23). Lincoln: University of Nebraska Press, 1976.

Green, B. F. Current trends in problem solving. In B. Kleinmuntz (Ed.), *Problem solving*. New York: Wiley, 1966.

Guilford, J. P. Basic conceptual problems in the psychology of thinking. *Annals of the New York Academy of Sciences*, 1960, *91*, 6–21.

Gunderson, K. The imitation game. In A. R. Anderson (Ed.), *Minds and machines*. Englewood Cliffs, N.J.: Prentice-Hall, 1964.

Haber, A. & Runyon, R. P. *Fundamentals of psychology* (2nd ed.). Reading, Mass.: Addison-Wesley, 1978.

Harrower, M. R. Organization in higher mental processes. *Psychologische Forschung*, 1932, *17*, 56–120.

Hearst, E. Psychology across the chessboard. *Psychology Today*, 1967 (June), 28–37.

————. Man and machine: Chess achievements and chess thinking. In P. Frey (Ed.), *Chess skill in man and machine*. New York: Springer-Verlag, 1978.

Hebb, D. O. *The organization of behavior*. New York: Wiley, 1949.

Humphrey, G. *Directed thinking*. New York: Dodd, Mead, 1948.

Hunt, E. & Poltrock, S. The mechanics of thought. In B. Kantowitz (Ed.), *Human information processing*: tutorials in performance and cognition. Hillsdale, N.J.: Erlbaum, 1974.

Husserl, E. *Ideas* (W. Gibson, trans.). London: Collier, 1962. (Originally published, 1913).

————. *Phenomenological psychology* (J. Scanlon, trans.). The Hague: Nijhoff, 1977. (Originally published, 1925)

Kendler, H. H. *Psychology: A science in conflict*. New York: Oxford University Press, 1981.

Le Francois, G. R. *Psychology*. Belmont, Calif.: Wadsworth, 1980.

Luchins, A. S. On some aspects of the creativity problem in thinking. *Annals of the New York Academy of Sciences*, 1960, *91*, 128-140.

Marx, M. *Introduction to psychology*. New York: MacMillan, 1976.

Merleau-Ponty, M. *The phenomenology of perception* (C. Smith, trans.). London: Routledge & Kegan Paul, 1962. (Originally published, 1945)

————. *The structure of behavior* (A. Fischer, trans.). Boston: Beacon Press, 1963. (Originally published, 1942)

————. Maurice Merleau-Ponty at the Sorbonne. *Bulletin de psychologie*, *236*, 18, 1964. (trans. under A. Giorgi by the Duquesne University Psychology Department, 1975, unpublished manuscript).

Neisser, U. *Cognition and reality*. San Francisco: Freeman, 1976.

Newell, A. The chess machine. *Proceedings of the 1955 Western Joint Computer Conference*, 1955, 101–108.

————. You can't play twenty questions with nature and win. In W. G. Chase (Ed.), *Visual information processing*. New York: Academic Press, 1973.

————. On the analysis of human problem solving protocols. In P. N. Johnson-Laird & P. C. Wason (Eds.), *Thinking: Readings in cognitive science*. Cambridge: Cambridge University Press, 1977.

Newell, A., Shaw, J. C. & Simon, H. A. Chess playing programs and the problem of complexity. *IBM Journal of Research and Development*, 1958, *2*, 320–335. (a)

————. Elements of a theory of human problem solving. *Psychological Review*, 1958, *65*, 151–166. (b)

Newell, A. & Simon, H. A. Computer simulation of human thinking. *Science*, 1961, *134*, 2011–2017. (a)

————. *Human problem solving*. Englewood-Cliffs, N.J.: Prentice Hall, 1972.

Raphael, B. *The thinking computer: Mind inside matter*. San Francisco: Freeman, 1976.

Simon, H. A. Information processing theory of human problem solving. In W. K. Estes (Ed.), *Handbook of learning and cognitive processes* (Vol. 5). Hillsdale, N.J.: Erlbaum, 1978.

————. Information processing models of cognition. *Annual Review of Psychology*, 1979, *30*, 363–396.

————. The behavioral and social sciences. *Science*, 1980, *209*, 72–78. (a)

Simon H. A. & Newell, A. Heuristic problem solving: The next advance in operations research. *Operations Research*, 1958, *6*, 1–10.

————. Information processing in computers and man. *American Scientist*, 1964, *52*, 281–300.

————. Human problem solving: The state of the theory in 1970. *American Psychologist*, 1971, *26*, 145-159.

Thomson, R. *The psychology of thinking*. Baltimore: Penguin Books, 1959.

Van den Berg, J. *A different existence*. Pittsburgh: Duquesne University Press, 1972.

Von Neumann, J. & Morgenstern, O. *Theory of games and economic behavior*. Princeton, N.J.: Princeton University Press, 1947.

Voss, J. F. *Approaches to thought*. Columbus: Merrill, 1969.

Weimer, W. Overview of a cognitive psychology: Reflections on the volume. In W. Weimer & D. Palermo (Eds.), *Cognition and the symbolic process*. Hillsdale, N.J.: Erlbaum, 1974.

Wertheimer, M. *Productive thinking*. New York: Harper & Row, 1945.

Wertz, F. J. From everyday to psychological description; Analyzing the moment of a qualitative data analysis. *Journal of Phenomenological Psychology*, 1983, *14*, 197–241.

Wiener, N. *Cybernetics* (2nd ed.). Cambridge, Mass.: The MIT Press, 1961. (Originally published, 1948).

Wilding, J. Bits and spaces: Computer simulation. In A. Burton & J. Radford (Eds.), *Thinking in perspective*. London: Methuen, 1978.

The Man-Made World of Learning:
Remarks on the Potential Value of a
Descriptive Tradition in Pedagogic Research

5

Roger Säljö

If I, as a researcher in the field of educational psychology, were to raise the issue of what we need to know about teaching and learning in order to contribute to the improvement of educational processes, most of my colleagues in the field would consider the question as odd and superfluous. To many it would seem obvious that what we need to acquire knowledge about are the approaches to teaching and learning which can be shown to result in the most efficient learning on the part of the students in question. The task for research clearly is one of inventing new and improved modes of going about teaching and learning and/or establishing what methods are most efficient in a given situation.

A large proportion of the empirical research carried out in this area shares this basic conception of the relationship between research and practice. Researchers in the field of learning, for instance, devote considerable attention to answering questions of whether one particular mode of instruction is more suitable for students with a particular intellectual profile than another, or to ascertaining how to intersperse questions in texts in order to maximize learning efficiency, etc. Yet we all know that quite a considerable proportion of this type of 'main-stream' research — even if stable and reliable results would emerge — can never have significant consequences for schooling. The way the research problems are conceived (and the mechanisms for change which the results point to) are quite often at odds with the way in which educational changes are brought about. At least in Sweden, politicians would never agree to having schools organized so as to maximize the efficiency of learning in the narrow and purely

117

cognitive sense with which most empirical studies operate (and probably it would not help very much even if the outcome variables are multiplied to cover other aspects). There are many obvious reasons for this, and I will not enter this discussion here. For our purposes it is sufficient to conclude that schooling is not a rational and unidimensional process as is tacitly assumed in much of the research endeavors, nor is the potential scope for research evidence to have an impact on education as big as we perhaps like to think. Decisions on educational matters nowadays are so intertwined with general political issues that political arguments and slogans stand a much better chance of leading to modifications in the ways in which teaching and learning is organized irrespective of their support in any kind of research evidence.

Returning to the initial question of what we need to know about teaching and learning, what the research dominating the field can be said to share at a general level is what Marton and Svensson (1979) characterize as a "technical conception of the relation between theory and practice" (p. 483). This conception, it is argued, "implies that research should provide the learner with learning algorithms and the teacher with teaching algorithms, i. e. rules of action based on procedural judgements derived from theory" (ibid).

Without in any way attempting to evaluate the success up to now of research adopting this perspective on the basis of this fragmentary description, it is obvious that in recent years a growing number of people have begun to abandon this line of thinking about the relationship between theory and practice. Many have felt, along with Magoon (1977) that "schooling, teaching, and learning go on without being explicable via traditional approaches" (p. 653). Among the various reasons people have felt making it necessary to broaden the scope of educational research, there is one which will be emphasized here as a point of departure. As Gowin (1972) points out, education and educational phenomena are man-made and as such multifaceted, diffuse, to a large extent hidden in daily routines and practices that have not been very well documented in research, and the changes and modifications brought about are often difficult to predict and follow from arguments remote from the teaching and learning situation as such. In this perspective the very prerequisites for a traditional, hypothetico-deductive model of scientific thinking do not seem to be present. There simply are very limited possibilities of arriving at the kinds of definitions (for instance of what distinguishes various methods of teaching and learning from one another) and deductive relationships upon which this model of thinking relies.

Accepting for the moment this view of educational phenomena as man-made and artifactual, we need to readdress the question of what the contribution of research in this field could be. If it is impossible to generalize in the traditional sense across situations with a reasonable degree of accuracy, the potential use of research as such, evidently seems threatened to many. Such a conclusion — undoubtedly shared by many in the field of education — follows because there is a strong tendency to unreflectively see generalizability as *the* obvious criterion of usefulness. At this stage of the argument, it is important that we should remind ourselves of the fact that the bringing about of change in social and cultural contexts can, and often does, follow a different logic. Hawkins (1971), in discussing the relationship between theory and research in education, touches upon this issue when he argues that "the good teaching I have observed . . . owes little to modern theories of learning and cognition and much to apprenticeship, on-the-job inquiry, discussion, trial — ceaseless trial — within a common-sense psychological framework" (p. 4). If we leave the complex issue of what constitutes good teaching aside for the moment, the significant point about this mode of reasoning is that it implies that the knowledge about educational processes that is potentially action-relevant for those who are directly involved in such activities, is likely to be different from that which is productive when analysing such processes from other perspectives with other knowledge-interests.

Recently this line of reasoning has been carried further by Bassey (1981) who uses the concept of 'pedagogic research' to refer to the kind of educational research which is geared towards the 'classroom level.' To make explicit what distinguishes pedagogic research from other kinds of educational inquiries in terms of the potential relationship to the field, Bassey introduces a distinction between 'open' and 'closed' generalizations, and in connection to this he argues for 'relatability' as an alternative criterion of the usefulness of research.

The value of closed generalizations, according to this line of reasoning, is that they make it possible for a teacher "to relate what has happened in other classrooms to what is happening in his" (Bassey, 1981, p. 84). Such a generalization, based on a detailed account of single events and transactions in educational contexts, has its potential strength in the fact that it "can stimulate his thinking about possible lines of action and it can alert him to possible consequences; it can influence his judgment on the best way of acting" (Bassey, p. 84). In other words, the insight derived from research "can assist him in deciding what to do, but it cannot tell him" (p. 84). Thus, relatability to one's own immediate professional context is an alternative criterion of possible usefulness of knowledge, relying on an alternative conception of mechanisms of change of educational practice. Insights into, and discoveries about, the nature of the communication that develops in educational contexts are there to be reflected upon, but they must not be thought of as being mechanically applicable to other situations. Rather the assumption would be that it takes an intermediate level of judgment of whether what has been discovered relates in any significant way to the context of teaching and learning in which a particular group of people find themselves.

Considering educational processes as artifacts of the social and cultural environment from which they derive, in my view has significant consequences for empirical research. Approaches to teaching, strategies of learning and other aspects of the communication that take place inside as well as outside the classroom, and which are intended to provide students with desired skills and competencies, are transformed into cultural phenomena reflecting the modes of storing knowledge and organizing education that exist in certain societies. The nature of curricula, the mode in which the knowledge accumulated is divided into subjects, the splitting up of the schoolday into lessons of a particular duration, assumptions about the appropriate roles for teachers and students, and all other factors which shape the educational milieu, are conceived as social constructions mirroring traditions and negotiations of the past. Our research conceptualization of human beings would also have to be modified in the sense that the individual, be it a teacher or a student, is no longer to be conceived as "an aggregation of psychological processes following natural laws" (Lundgren, 1979, p. 136, our translation), but rather "as a social being" (loc cit) situated in a certain context and trying to achieve certain ends.

It is precisely within the framework of such a conceptualization of education as a social construction with its own history and firmly institutionalized ways of disseminating knowledge that it becomes necessary to put considerable effort into the descriptive phases of empirical research in order to obtain careful and detailed descriptions of specific instances of the teaching and learning that go on in schools, universities and other educational institutions. The purpose of this increased emphasis on the descriptive elements of research would be to make possible an improvement in the accuracy and analytical clarity with which we are able to discuss educational phenomena. The outcomes of such endeavors would form a basis for making informed decisions through developing *concepts that have a sensitizing capacity* (for a discussion of the sensitizing potential of concepts, see Glaser and Strauss, 1967). At present we are forced to quite a large extent to use a very crude conceptual apparatus when discussing educational phenomena and when, e.g., training future teachers. Concepts like 'project work,' 'lecturing,' 'discovery learning,' etc., are used to refer to wide classes of phenomena that both teachers and researchers know have very little in common in terms of the communication that takes place and the learning that results. As Jackson pointed out some fifteen years ago, it is evident that teachers to a large extent "lack an effective set of descriptive terms for talking about what they do. As a result, they often must fall back on clichés and outworn slogans when called upon to describe their work" (1968, p. 176). To counteract this most unfortunate situation, and to enhance the possibilities of those participating in the educational process to make informed judgements, there clearly is a need for complementing main-stream research with approaches that regard the educational field and the world of teachers and students as yet to be discovered and conceptualized.

Insights into Pedagogic Processes: Some Examples from Descriptive Efforts

To concretize the line of reasoning above, some brief summaries of research following the lines suggested will be presented. A very clear illustration of the advantages of putting considerable effort into familiarizing oneself with the nature of the communication that develops in a particular area is given in the work of Lundgren (1977, 1979). In studying how primary school teachers deal with children who have difficulties in following instruction in elementary mathematics, a revealing observation could be made with respect to how teachers cope with such difficulties in the classroom situation. What was found was that when a child had difficulties in solving a problem of, for example, the kind 83 x 29, the teacher quite often would simplify the task for the pupil by requiring him or her to answer a series of questions of the following kind in a stepwise fashion: 'What is nine times three?,' 'Where do you put the two?,' 'What is nine times eight?,' and so on until the task was solved. In other words, complex tasks frequently were found to be transformed into simpler ones that the pupil could handle. Per se, this mode of proceeding may not be problematic in any sense, and as a matter of fact this is probably a fairly natural way of acting for all of us when we face a situation when someone has problems in learning. However, and this is the critical issue, if, as was shown, specific groups of pupils in a class consistently are given this kind of assistance from the teacher when running into problems of using basic mathematical algorithms, this strategy acquires a different significance and becomes detrimental to any genuine development of competence.

To characterize this phenomenon Lundgren and his colleagues coined the term 'piloting.' The essence of the process of piloting is that the teacher reduces the complexity of the task that the pupil has to handle and transforms it into a task that is already mastered. In the above example, the complex multiplication of numbers of two figures is reduced into a series of multiplications involving only one figure numbers which the pupil has much less difficulties in handling. When the teacher consistently resorts to piloting certain groups of pupils, the possibilities of these pupils ever mastering the more complex task in their curriculum successively diminishes. Quite fast, the gap between the competence of these pupils (i.e. when working on their own and without a teacher to rely on) and the instruction they are being offered may widen beyond the level where they are able to profit from the communication that goes on in their classroom.

The phenomenon of piloting depicts a very significant pedagogic (and educational) phenomenon. Particularly in situations where the teacher has to cope with large differences in previous knowledge, it becomes in many cases the only realistic way of acting. There simply may not be any possibilities for allocating enough time within the classroom situation for dealing with those that have genuine problems in following the instruction. As a concept, then, piloting contains something as intellectually rewarding as a discovery which furthermore can be given a theoretical interpretation through considering the many diverse and conflicting societal goals that an educational system is supposed to meet. It also illustrates quite clearly that learning problems are related to the way in which teaching is organized in the sense that this strategy of communicating is likely to increase when there are large differences in previous knowledge (and this is a major practical problem that Swedish teachers in the primary and secondary schools meet).

For our general line of arguing for a certain approach to the study of pedagogic phenomena, what is significant is the way in which this concept was derived through research, entering the field with a strong familiarity with the domain, i.e. mathematics teaching at elementary level, and without a too strong an adherence to a preconceived conceptual framework of the kind used in most classroom studies. A second important aspect is that through accurate description and through the very coining of the term piloting, it becomes possible to discuss and analyse a certain aspect of teaching and learning at a thematic level.

Another piece of research that can serve as an example of the attempt to gain access to pedagogic phenomena through putting considerable emphasis on the descriptive phase of the empirical work, has been reported by McNeil (1980). In this case the study dealt with the issue of how economic changes and changes in the class-structures of societies were presented to high-school students within the field of history. One of the techniques frequently observed to be used by the teacher for balancing the competing demands experienced in such situations McNeil refers to as 'fragmentation.' The essence of fragmentation as an instructional device, is that the complexities and dynamics of social or economic changes are transformed into a set of isolated facts or statements. In the words of McNeil, fragmentation is the "reduction of any topic to fragments or disjointed pieces of information. Lists" (1980, p. 12). A consequence of this mode of offering instruction is that social processes are trivialized and the dynamic forces underlying change disappear. What remains is 'neutral' information which does not arouse too much discussion or emotion such as lists of political leaders replacing each other, dates, etc. In this sense fragmentation, as McNeil aptly puts it, takes "the issue-ness out of issues" (ibid, p. 13).

That fragmentation is a characteristic way in which schools tend to operate can be given support from other sources (cf. e.g. Young, 1977; Whitty, 1977), and that it is bound to have consequences for the nature of the communication that develops as well as for students' approaches to learning is quite obvious. Whether this is to be considered as 'good' or 'bad' in any sense is of course something that can be discussed at considerable length. The point to be made here, however, is that the concept of fragmentation refers to a rather precise feature of our mode of organizing teaching and learning. If it can be shown to generalize to other contexts with a similar meaning through other investigations, we again have an example of an analytical tool that can be seen as a pedagogic concept revealing an adaptation of communication to a specific way of transmitting knowledge. We can also begin to ask questions about the extent to which this way of telling people about the world creates a communicative environment which is artificial and which systematically is deprived of certain qualities characteristic of full-fledged acts of human communication where people are more deeply involved in the exchange of ideas and more likely to "trade on each other's truths" to borrow an expression from William James.

As a final illustration of research devoting considerable effort to the descriptive elements of the empirical work, a study by Furlong (1977) could be mentioned. In aiming at revealing certain aspects of students' perspective of classroom life, Furlong made some interesting observations on the implicit notions about learning that a particular class of low-achieving pupils investigated, seemed to hold.

When analysing the features of classroom life that stood out as significant to the girls of this class, it could be seen that the activities relating to what was referred to as 'learning' formed such an organizing feature or 'relevance structure.' In the perspective of the girls their judging of whether a teacher was seen as 'good' or 'bad,' depended to a large extent on the notion of whether he or she could 'make them learn'. What is significant from the point of view of how these girls relate to learning, is that they made no apparent distinction between learning something and merely working on the tasks presented to them. Thus, the concept of learning was indiscriminately used

> for it not only referred to situations where the girls actually understood something new (i.e. they 'learned' something in the conventional sense of the word), but also where they simply worked, where they carried out the tasks set by the teachers. Both situations seemed to provide them with feelings of achievement, though learning as new understanding seemed a fairly rare experience. (Furlong, 1977, p. 179)

In a similar vein we have in our own research on learning within an experiential perspective found that there appear to be significant variations in the very way in which people define the task of learning for themselves. This variation in conceptions of learning (which can be described in various ways) can also be related to the way in which learning situations are dealt with and the outcome which is likely to result. Similarly, the conceptions of learning held are in turn related to people's notions of what characterizes knowledge, where corresponding differences can be discerned (Marton and Säljö, 1984).

The point to be made here, then, is that learning from texts can be better understood if we have access to the learner's view of what he/she is doing. Conceptions of learning and knowledge can be regarded as 'premisses for communication' (Rommetueit, 1974) which people rely on as a consequence of a long personal history of what a particular kind of activity is all about. In the study just mentioned, it could for instance be seen how certain students through their tendency to equate knowledge with "information" (or "facts"), had genuine difficulties in coping with parts of a text where knowledge was presented in the form of alternative scientific conceptions of a phenomenon (which in this case was learning). In such cases there was a tendency for some participants to assume that since there was no definite agreement on the nature of this particular phenomenon, what existed and what was presented in the text were mere personal opinions on the part of various people. And since within this conception of learning a strict line of division is assumed to exist between knowledge and personal opinions, there was nothing to be attended to within the overall project of learning from the text.

Concluding Comments

The examples briefly sketched here, point to research efforts which, although working from separate theoretical perspectives, nevertheless share a strong concern for the descriptive part of their studies. This is, I think, the kind of working agreement that has to exist if research based on qualitative methods is to grow. Allowing for theoretical orientations to vary, and focussing on the attempts to achieve explicit relationships that are described in detail between phenomena and the way they are conceptualized, creates a platform for methodological as well as conceptual and theoretical development.

The value of the approach to research outlined here, lies in its potential to develop a language in terms of which pedagogic issues can be articulated. The object of inquiry would be the communication that develops in teaching and learning situations of various kinds (and such situations *do* differ when approached with conceptual tools that allow them to do so); and the frame of reference offered for understanding would pay more attention to the immediate context in which people act (and the culturally mediated conceptual sediments in terms of which it is inter-preted) than do either traditional research approaches in educa-tional psychology or the more recent, macro-oriented sociological analyses. However, this is not to be interpreted as an encourage-ment of indiscriminate empirical analyses of what goes on in educational contexts. Nor is it to be understood as an urge to abandon an 'externalistic' perspective in favor of an 'internalistic' one. Paying an interest in the experiential perspective does not mean a return to a naive position about the role of the educa-tional system within society. What is meant is simply that there is a need for a variation in the foci of research which are being used. Such a variation must be considered as legitimate, since different interest-groups (teachers, administrators, politicians, parents, etc.) relate in different ways to education and thus differ in their knowledge interests.

From a strategic perspective, and for the development of the field of educational research, the success of this kind of endeavor, and its potential impact, depends on whether insights into peda-gogic phenomena can be articulated as an extension of the common-sense interpretation of the world in which teachers and students find themselves. In this respect, an advantage of the phenomenographic approach to research suggested by Marton (1981), lies in its emphasis of describing learning phenomena in terms of their content. Such a turn in the logic according to which cognitive phenomena are conceptualized, opens up considerable possibilities for achieving a language accessible to people without a background in the behavioral sciences. For instance, when a physicist or biologist realises that it took mankind several hundred years to move from one conceptualization of some aspect of the world to another, he or she is in a much better position to understand the learning difficulties of his/her students who may have only a few hours to bridge the same gap. Reflection on such issues leads to change, and in my view those who work in the field of educational psychology could play a vital role in the creation of the intellectual tools necessary for making such reflection possible.

References

Bassey, M. Pedagogic research: On the relative merits of search for generalisations and study of single events. *Oxford Review of Education*, 1981, 7, 73–94.

Furlong, V. Anancy to school: A case study of pupils' knowledge of their teachers. In P. Woods & M. Hammersley (Eds.), *School Experience*. New York: St Martin's Press, 1977.

Glaser, B. G. & Strauss, A. L. *The discovery of grounded theory. Strategies for qualitative research*. New York: Aldine, 1967.

Gowin, D. B. Is education research distinctive? In L. G. Thomas (Ed.), *Philosophical redirection of educational research*. Chicago: University of Chicago Press, 1972.

Jackson, P. W. *Life in classrooms*. New York: Holt, Rinehart & Winston, 1968.

Lundgren, U. P. *Model analysis of pedagogical processes*. Lund. CWK/ Gleerup, 1977.

———. *Att organisera omvärlden. En introduktion till läroplansteori*. Stockholm: Publica, 1979.

Magoon, A. J. Constructivist approaches in educational research. *Review of Educational Research*, 1977, 47, 651–693.

Marton, F. Phenomenography — Describing conceptions of the world around us. *Instructional Science*, 1981, 10, 177–200.

Marton, F. & Saljo, R. Approaches to learning. In F. Marton, D. Hounsell & N. Entwistle (Eds.), *The experience of learning*. Edinburgh: Scottish Academic Press, 1984.

Marton, F. & Svensson, L. Conceptions of research in student learning. *Higher Education*, 1979, *8*, 471–486.

McNeil, L. Knowledge forms and knowledge content. Paper presented at the AERA Annual Meeting, Boston, April 7–11, 1980.

Rommetueit, R. *On message structure*. London: Wiley, 1974.

Säljö, R. *Learning and understanding. A study of differences in constructing meaning from a text*. Göteborg: Acta Universitatis Gothoburgensis, 1982.

Whitty, G. Experiencing school knowledge: The case of social studies. In P. Woods & M. Hammersley (Eds.), *School experience*. New York: St Martin's Press, 1977.

Young, M. School science — Innovation or alienation? In P. Woods & M. Hammersley (Eds.), *School Experience*. New York: St Martin's Press, 1977.

Qualitative Research as
Instructional Intervention

6

Mariane Hedegaard &
Pentti Hakkarainen

Phenomenological Description as a Method
of Psychological Research

For the last 10–15 years, the phenomenological, dialectical and humanistic approach to psychology has criticized the empiricistic tradition of psychological science (e.g., Giorgi, 1970; Duquesne studies, 1972, 1976; Riegel, 1976; Kvale, 1973; Marton, 1978). The main point in their criticism is the use of the natural scientific paradigm as a methodological model for psychology which cannot reflect the entire complexity of the man-world, or lifeworld, relation. The use of the natural scientific paradigm with its claim on operationalism, validity and reliability makes it impossible to attain the goal of psychological research.

Giorgi (1970) formulated the problem of the natural scientific psychology approach in the following way:

> . . . as being empirical, positivistic, reductionistic, objective, analytical, quantitative, deterministic, concerned with prediction and largely operating within the genetic bias and with the assumption of an independent observer. All of these factors have operated in such a way that the paradigm of natural scientific psychology was structured primarily to ask a measurement question and to reveal the quantitative dimensions of reality. It also favored a paradigm that sought specificity and explanations that were within the context of cause-effect relations. This in turn has led to designs that favor isolation of variables with the assumption of a constant relation between specific variables and the conditions of the experiment, but this constancy is understood as being due to external relations between man and the world. (p. 204)

We can agree with the criticism presented by Giorgi and other representatives of phenomenological, dialectical and humanistic approaches directed towards traditional empiricistic psychology. But we would like to question the methodological basis of the new "descriptive approach" to psychology. Our special interest within the phenomenological and humanistic tradition is the work of two research groups: The Duquesne group in USA and the INOM group in Göteborg. Both of these groups have analyzed human learning and tried to develop an alternative for the traditional empiricistic approach. Though human learning has been a main object of research in these groups, the goal of research has been the development of "psychology" in general, which is based on a "new methodology."

We can agree very much with their critique of natural scientific psychology and the traditional experimental approach to psychology. But what we want to question is whether this new "descriptive approach" can get psychology any further than the approach criticized. To answer this question, we have to find out and analyze the criteria against which this new approach wants to evaluate itself, what the content of this type of approach is, and how the methods are specified.

Both Marton and Giorgi, the founders of their respective research groups, have formulated some general criteria for the evaluation of different psychological approaches. These criteria are based on a philosophical conception of science in general, which is manifested in researchers' attitudes towards science. Giorgi uses the term "attitude of science" and Marton "the perspective of science." For example, Giorgi defines what he finds the most fruitful and relevant attitude in the following manner:

> . . . an attitude that requires an opening up rather than closure, one that allows for future possibilities as well as past facticities, and one that does not foreclose the reality or indeterminancy and ambiguity will be a necessary point of departure — because to repeat, the main emphasis is fidelity to the phenomenon as it appears including processes, and *not* to an idea of science that has been developed in a different context. (1970, p. 188)

In turn, Marton distinguishes between two perspectives: a first order and a second order perspective. The first order perspective is a noumenal or matter of fact perspective, and the second order perspective is phenomenal, experiential, the world as perceived perspective. According to Marton, the second order perspective should be evaluated by using the criteria of convenience, simplicity, etc.

What are the methodological implications of the new "attitude of science" or "perspective of science" in psychological research? Phenomenological psychology redefines the essential contents of psychological science using central concepts of phenomenological philosophy. Essential contents of psychological research are, according to phenomenology, the sense and subjective meaning of the world, the "*Lebenswelt.*" This aspect of consciousness makes it possible for the subject to construct the world around him as meaningful. Phenomenology sets a goal of exact science by paying attention to 'facticity,' e.g., take into consideration lived spaced, time, and so on.

The content of the qualitative descriptive approach in Giorgi's version is human intentional relation to the world as an irreducible man-world relation. The object of research is the structure of human consciousness and its variations (Giorgi, 1975, p. 83). Giorgi wants to capture the essence of learning by studying the structure of consciousness and its variations. The essence is revealed by describing different types of general learning based on the subject's description of lived situations. Teaching is not of central concern in this research.

In Marton's approach, the goal and content of psychological research is to construct a map of different conceptions of phenomena in our society, but he does not strive to find out the essence of learning (Marton, 1978, p. 11). The aim of research is to look for categories of conceptions.

> . . . to find and systematic form *or* thought in terms of which people interpret aspects of reality — aspects which are socially significant and which are at least supposed to be shared by the members of a particular society, namely our own. (Marton, 1978, p. 6)

The content of learning should, according to him, be described in terms of what is in the students' minds rather than what is in the textbook. Teaching is then seen as a process where the teacher tries to change the various conceptions which the students have and is not related to the object taught.

Marton states explicitly that there can be no processes without content, and there can be no content without the process in the form of mental activity. Both process and content are seen as aspects of students' conceptions; i.e., as aspects of their thinking rather than of their whole living activity — practical as well as conceptual. Teaching is therefore seen only as a process where the teacher tries to change various conceptions which the students have and is not related to the object taught.

A redefinition of the goal and contents of psychology has led to changes in the concrete research methods. Qualitative descriptions are preferred instead of quantitative measurements, "qualitative" generalizations substitute statistical, propabilistic conclusions. But still the variation of observational data forms the basis of generalizations.

The method in Giorgi's approach is based on the naive descriptions of learning situations of non-academic sophisticated persons. This is the material to which phenomenological analysis is applied in order to reach an in depth understanding of the phenomenon. The meaning of the phenomenon can be found on different structured levels, on a level of situated structure of learning and on a level of general structure of learning (Giorgi, 1975, p. 88). At the situated level, learning is related to the world of the subject and has a specific ideographic content. At the general level learning is related to other phenomena by a theoretical content. The two levels are related because learning cannot be reduced to specific content, and, on the other hand, each content must be understood in terms of the biography or the history of the individual.

Giorgi's method consists of a two stage procedure. At the first stage, the subject answers an open-ended question, e.g., "Please, describe for me a situation in which you have learned." At the second stage, the subject's description of a learning episode is analyzed: 1) Meaning units are located in the description, and their relevatory power for the phenomenon of learning is evaluated by relating the meaning units to each other. 2) The particular relevatory units are transformed from the concrete language of the subjects into the language of psychology. 3) The insight that emerges in the transformation has to be integrated into a coherent description which expresses the essential structure of the learning episode (Giorgi, 1978, p. 13).

By this analysis Giorgi gets a description of "general learning."

One type of general learning can be exemplified from a person's description of learning how to make yogurt:

> Learning is the extension of one's ability to transform situations in the world beyond one's current capabilities through the mediation of a significant other and is accompanied by the awareness that this can be done on demand. (1978, p. 13)

How Giorgi will go further from a sample of "general descriptions" of learning episodes to the essence of learning is still an unsolved problem in his research. Our evaluation is that even if Giorgi's aim is different from that of the INOM-group he ends up with the same *type* of research profile for the phenomenon of learning, which is a conglomerate or perhaps a map of different types of descriptions of general learning episodes. We think that Giorgi perhaps expects some shared structures to turn up from different descriptions of general learning, and as long as he himself is the interpreter of the naive descriptions and also the person who relates these descriptions, there will surely be a chance that "an implicit model of his" could turn up as a model for relating different descriptions.

This is not an outcome which merely deserves criticism, but one which also needs explicitation and explanation. The problem is how to get from the concrete to the general, and which theoretical considerations combine these two poles. We do not find any clear answers in Giorgi's approach, but a procedure for getting from the naive description of a learning episode to the general description of this episode. We still miss explications of the theoretical assumptions for these procedures and a procedure to get from the general descriptions of learning episodes to the essence of learning.

The method developed by the INOM research group is based on open interviews. In their research, the researchers always have some specific phenomena which they want the subjects to develop their conceptions about. Larson (1981, 1982) describes this interviewing procedure and the analysis of the interviews to find different categories of conceptions about a phenomenon. The researchers of the INOM group do not want to find either the ideographic or the typical conceptions, but the variations in conceptions of a phenomenon (Larson, 1982, p. 4).

Larson describes how the variations in categories are found: an alternation between reading and reflection by the researcher of the interview material. It is the dialectics between understanding and reflection which make it possible to go deeper and deeper into the interview material and then find more and more common categories (1981, p. 9).

An example of this method of interviewing and the finding of categories of conceptions of learning can be seen in the work of Säljö (1979a, 1979b) and Marton and Säljö (1979). The research described in these reports falls in two parts: 1) Extensive interviews with 90 students about their method of study and their conceptions of learning, knowledge, education, etc., 2) An experiment with reading a text.

One of the results of this study is clearly illustrative of the INOM group's approach to learning. In the first part of the study, the students respond to the question: "What do you actually mean by learning?"

Five different conceptions of learning turned up in the analysis of the students' answers to this question: 1) Learning as the increase of knowledge, 2) Learning as memorizing, 3) Learning as acquisition of acts, procedures etc., which can be attained or utilized in practice, 4) Learning as abstraction of meaning and 5) Learning as an interpretative process aimed at the understanding of reality (Säljö, 1979a).

These five different categories are then further analyzed so that they can be related to the conceptions of deep approach and surface approach to learning (Marton & Säljö, 1979) which are the two main categories of learning approach specified in the earlier work of the INOM group (Marton, Dahlgren, Svensson & Säljö, 1977).

In the INOM group's research, the problem of moving from concrete descriptions to general conceptions are even more obvious than in Giorgi's research because they do not have an explicit procedure. This problem is touched upon by Säljö (1979a) as a problem for the researcher of projection of his own conceptions into the interpretation of the interview material.

As to the interview material, we can ask first what the criteria are for scoring the material into the five categories of learning conceptions we have mentioned; and next where the criteria are for transforming these five categories into the two main categories of deep and surface strategies — the two strategies which are the theoretical conceptions of the INOM group (Marton, Dahlgren, Svensson & Säljö, 1977).

Theoretically, the INOM group present their method of interpretation as induction, without acknowledging any explicit conceptions of the researcher to guide the induction. Researcher reliability is the criteria for the relevance of the categories, the researcher's perspective on the research is the evaluation basis for the validity of the concepts found. The dilemma now arises as to which conceptions we then get, that of the researchers or that of the subjects — is it really induction without researcher bias? Do we get the real categories of people living in the society? Or does the researcher's perspective, which guides his research, constitute the sole determinant of his results?

We find that this dilemma cannot be solved without taking into consideration the researcher's conception as a theoretical model guiding his search for the subject's conceptions—and then we have a problem of validity; how to relate the conceptions to people's actual life in society.

Summing up, the different problems characterizing the descriptive methods can be seen in a narrow perspective as methodological problems connected to 1) criteria for evaluation of research, 2) content of research and 3) procedure of interpretation.

1. The first problem is to be found in the specification of the criterion chosen for the evaluation of research results. Here the problem is how to relate the descriptive research of an attitude or perspective, to the reality of the actual living of people in relation to nature and society.

2. The second problem is related to the content of research as units of the individual's consciousness, or conceptions. The practical societal aspect is neglected, and furthermore the *object* of learning is not conceptualized as having any meaning for the individuals' *conceptions*, or consciousness, of learning.

3. The third problem is related to the transforming of concrete descriptions or interviews to general learning descriptions or categories of learning. How is one to justify the psychological language used in the interpretation of the concrete into general non-subject bound descriptions?

These methodological problems in the phenomenological descriptive approaches to psychology are related to basic philosophical conceptions of how the relations between appearance and essence of the phenomenon studied are to be revealed.

We will put forward the view that consideration of genesis and intervention can reveal this relationship.

1. *The problem of genesis.* Phenomenological methodology focuses on the variation of conceptions not on the development of conceptions. The phenomenological methodology uses a cross-sectional approach and cannot, therefore, reveal developmental mechanisms. Neglection of genesis leads to some essential questions: Why do people have different conceptions of the same phenomenon: Are some conceptions better explanations of reality than others?

2. *The problem of intervention.* The phenomenological approach concentrates on analyzing isolated individual phenomena; the unit of analysis is the individual's conception or consciousness. The practical, societal aspect of living is neglected, and furthermore the object of learning is not conceptualized as having any meaning for the conceptions or consciousness of the individuals. The methodology, for example, which Marton's group uses, gives as a result a description of different learning strategies. But there is no information about the possibilities of teaching learning strategies.

On the Necessity of Intervention

The phenomenological approaches described above point out some important aspects of psychological research. The content of psychological phenomena is stressed instead of formal logical analysis. In the frame of phenomenological theory, concepts are given a relational character as social constructions and elements of an individual's '*Lebenswelt.*' An attempt is made to understand meaning and intention as psychological phenomena by revealing the individual's biography or personal history.

The phenomenological approach quite correctly stresses the necessity of the revision of psychological research methods so that they adequately correspond to the revised research object in psychology. The solution offered by the phenomenological approach is description of phenomena as they appear. In our opinion, description as a method does not meet the qualitative requirements set by the redefinition of the object of psychological research. This lack of correspondence leads to failures in attaining the goals of phenomenological research.

What are the basic features of research methodology which would be able to reveal the mediated nature of the content of psychological phenomena? A genetic-historical method of analysis is needed.

An essential element of a genetic-historical method is intervention in psychological development. The necessity of intervention was put forward in the classical account by Vygotsky of his analysis of the different stages which the synthesis of two lines of development, 'spontaneous concepts' or 'generalization of things' and 'scientific concepts' or 'generalization of thoughts,' went through. This was carried out by intervention in 'the zone of proximal development' for different children (Vygotsky, 1971, 1974).

A genetic-historical method makes it possible to combine positive aspects of the phenomenological and the experimental approaches in psychology and develop them further. Description alone as method denies the productive aspect of the experimental method. On the other side, the traditional experimental method lacks the positive goal setting of the man-world relation as an integrated whole as the object of research which the phenomenological approach has.

An intervention method aims at the production of psychological formations within 'the child's zone of proximal development.' In the frame of intervention, the genesis of psychological formations is planned, not only described. The historical aspect of the intervention method is connected with the reproduction of the societal genesis of the concepts in a teaching-learning process.

The necessity of an intervention method is clearly demonstrated in the work with deaf-blind children. The use of a descriptive method alone cannot show the essentials of this 'man-world' relation. It is necessary to create psychological phenomena by using intervention in order to describe them as they appear. Experimental work with deaf-blind persons has had important consequences for developing the method of intervention to be used in psychological research in general.

The most fundamental work in the development of instructional intervention is the experimental programme for deaf-blind children developed by Meshcheryakov (1979). His work with deaf-blind children demonstrates very clearly two aspects of intervention: the scope and role of unplanned intervention in the psychological development of the normal child, and the necessity for, and great possibilities of, planned instructional intervention in the case of deaf-blindness.

Deaf-blindness cuts off the most used channels, sight and hearing, and isolates the child from his surroundings. This situation makes it necessary to build up and plan the whole developmental process on the basis of an interventional method. There is no spontaneous development and those influences which in "normal" setting are based on unplanned intervention have to be planned in the case of deaf-blindness. For phenomenological psychology, this situation is very problematic, because there is no research object, no consciousness or subjective perspective in the real sense of the term. As a result of the planned instructional and educational intervention the object of phenomenological analysis gradually appears.

Experimental work with deaf-blind children has some important implications for the analysis of development in general, and specially for instructional intervention. In the "normal" setting it is almost impossible to discern all the aspects of psychological development at the same time. Psychological development as a whole consists of parallel processes which cannot be analyzed simultaneously with the methodological apparatus of traditional psychology. It has been very difficult to discern developmental mechanisms because of the complicated nature of psychological development. The experimental educational programme for deaf-blind sheds some light on these problems. Deaf-blindness reduces significantly parallel developmental influences and the whole developmental process proceeds like a slow-motion picture. At the same time a forced instructional intervention is necessary.

A great deal of intervention is unplanned, occasional instruction. This type of instruction has undeniable developmental effects for the child. For example, Vygotsky stressed the fact that the child learns language and speech on the basis of unplanned instruction. The developmental effect of occasional, unplanned instruction is based, according to Podyakov (1977), on the formation of a horizon of unclear knowledge. Child-mother communication, for example, always includes elements which exceed the child's comprehension. The developmental effect of this part of communication may be explained with the help of the concept of the horizon of unclear knowledge.

The horizon of unclear knowledge is a complicated and contradictory formation. It has a developmental potential and an important role in cognition. But its potential should be converted into developmental effects. Occasional instruction may lead to generalized knowledge which reflects essential relations and dependences correctly. But the research knowledge which is formed on the basis of occasional instruction is unsystematic. In many cases, there are contradictory conceptions at the same time which develop in different directions. Thus, the task of instructional intervention is to form an organized system of knowledge. At the same time, this task means guiding the formation of the horizon of unclear knowledge.

Why is it necessary to talk about intervention and guiding? Why does qualitative description not suffice? The problem is that qualitative description cannot reveal the essence of development though qualitative description may be improved by using longitudinal descriptions, following the process from the very beginning. The necessity of intervention is based on the complexity of man's relation to reality. If the essence of phenomena and objects could be observed without the subject's own activity which practically changes some parts of reality or if the essence were limited to the individual's subjective perspective, no intervention would be needed. But we cannot explain man's relation to reality psychologically, either on the basis of perception or through a subjective perspective; we also have to explain from the perspective of reality. The essence of phenomena, understood as the explanation of development, cannot be revealed without change and intervention. The observation of processes may lead to some elementary conceptions about changes and development, but a deeper understanding and a grasp of the essence of phenomena presupposes the subject's own activity, and intervention in this in relation to the phenomenon. The goal of instructional intervention is to transmit the specific human meaning of our surroundings to form a personal meaning for the child specific to these common human meanings. The first task of intervention is to transform the satisfaction of vital needs into their specific human forms. The second task is to expand the scope of objects and phenomena, giving their human meaning a specific personal sense.

The Main Characteristics of Qualitative Research Based on Intervention Method

For several years, methods for studying aspects of the child's daily life have been put forward (Murphy 1956; Carrew, Chan & Halfar, 1976; Sylva & Painter, 1980); the characteristic of these methods is their use of observation of the child in his daily settings.

The difference between the method of intervention and these methods are in two areas; one being what the object of research is, and the other being how an observer is to behave in the research situation. The traditional methods have the functional and structural aspect of the child's motivational and intellectual development as their object of research. The object of our concern is the content of the activities, and the motives underlying their developmental transformation. The method is one of planned intervention, built upon a theory of the development of the content of the phenomenon under study. In contrast, traditional methods use neutral observation as the technique of research.

A: The levels of intervention

Experimental work by Mesheryakov (1977) has demonstrated the importance of instructional intervention as a prerequisite for psychic development in general. A great deal of instructional intervention has the form of unplanned, occasional instruction in everyday life situations. This instruction aims at the solution of everyday problems, not at generalized knowledge or learning. Developmental effects of this type of instructional intervention are partly mediated through 'the horizon of unclear knowledge.'

Systematized, planned, theoretically grounded instructional intervention results in developmental effects which have a more generalized character. In Mesheryakov's experimental work systematic instructional intervention produced personality traits in a concrete, observable form. Theoretically grounded instructional intervention which aims at generalized developmental effects presupposes molar units of intervention (a synthesis of contents, social interaction, communication, self-reflection).

The theoretical consideration behind this research method is that the object of psychological research should be the life flow of man in relation to society and nature, connected through activity.

The researcher's focus on this life flow should be the qualitative change of man's relation to nature and society, through activity. The methodological considerations of how to research this object area are therefore:

1. The researcher should be part of the subject's life situation for some time. He should be together with the subject in his daily life routines. Anthropology has used this research criterion as its point of departure. Pinxten (1981) argues that psychology should do the same and thereby overcome the difficulties of positivism and phenomenology; their opposition of subjectivism and objectivism.

   To be in the life situations of the subjects makes it possible for the researcher to follow the development of the phenomenon. Development implies the acquisition of the cultural aspects of a given phenomenon through interaction and communication.

2. The researcher has to share the activity of the subjects and thereby he can make interventions to find out what is essential in this activity. So it does not suffice to be in the life situation of the subjects, the researcher must also take part in their activity. Activity is always included in human social relations, and it is determined by the form of their material and mental communication; therefore the researcher must be part of the activity, to find out about its essential inner relations.

   Material and mental communication with the subject both determines the sharing of activity and at the same time is determined by the activity. We can take play as an example to demonstrate this.

   The acting and communicating together is the basic condition for the play to develop, but, at the same time, the participants' knowledge of sharing the play activity determines the communication and the actions shared by the members in play.

   To find out about the inner relations of children's play, the researcher must be a part of it (see Elkonin, 1980). To follow the development of the content of the play and the play motives of children playing, it is necessary to be accepted by the children as part of play even if the activity of the researcher as a very inferior participant, otherwise the researcher cannot take part in the communication; the communication will break down if he intrudes as non-participant.

3. The researcher must have some conceptions about how he is going to intervene, though he ought to be very open to changes and variations. He must have some idea of what to look for and what to ask about. The problem then becomes where the researcher gets the conceptions which guide his research activity.

Our hypothesis is that there have to be two phases in the research process. This hypothesis is grounded on the philosophical analysis of Iljenkow (1972) and on Dawydow's theory of knowledge acquisition (1977). The research process can be paralleled by the process of knowledge acquisition and the development of thinking. Dawydow (1977) points out that there are two qualitatively different modes of knowledge acquisition which result in the development of qualitatively different thinking types, empirical and theoretical thinking.

Empirical thinking develops during daily life activity and is characterized as "practical-perceptible" thinking. The main characteristic of this thinking is that it is closely and inseparately connected with the material acts. The relation of theoretical thinking to reality is much more mediated than that of empirical thinking. Theoretical thinking is guided by scientific conceptions of the object area so that a model of inner relations and their contradictions guides the subject's thinking of the object area. (Podjakow, 1981, p. 30–31).

The development of empirical thinking is necessary as a basis for the acquisition of theoretical thinking. But when the subject acquires the mode of theoretical thinking, his former knowledge will gradually be integrated and transformed by newly developed theoretical concepts.

To parallel the process of knowledge acquisition and the research process implies that we have to conceptualize two phases in the research process. A first phase where the research is closely connected with the life situation of the subjects; the researcher's model of how to invent and ask about it is very vague, and the researcher records more or less intuitively what his impression are of the changes and contradictions in the process in which he participates. From this protocol, some general and vague conceptions about the object of research can be built. In this first phase, the researcher goes to some very vague and fragile general concepts with which to intervene into reality. These will gradually lead to a more connected system of abstractions about the phenomenon under study.

The second phase is to go from these abstractions of the complexity and fullness of real life, to the concrete manifestation of life, where it is possible to verify the abstract model of the phenomena by systematic instructional intervention.

The goal for theoretical research is to conceptualize the concrete so that the concrete determines every step of action in the intervention, and the generalizations subsequently made. The abstract is only the means whereby the researcher reaches the concrete fullness of the phenomenon, it thereby disappears in the general movement; it does not have any meaning in itself separated from the general movement.

B: Communication as a methodological aspect of intervention

Communication can be characterized along the following three dimensions:

1. The researcher will more or less determine the situation. By being there he is an intruder and instead of trying to hide this, it must be explicitated and thematized and thereby used to find what is essential in the phenomenon studied.
2. Communication means exchange. By sharing the activity, the researcher and the subjects communicate through their actions and through their language; what will dominate will depend upon the aim of the research project and the capabilities of the subject.
3. The researcher subject relation in the research situation is not equal though the subject and the researcher are in the same activity. The researcher gives tasks more or less explicit by to the subjects-from single questions to very structured tasks.

To communicate with a child (through action, pictures or language) and at the same time write a protocol is difficult, so it ought to be share by two researchers. But there is also a clear methodological reason for this which is connected with the problem of validity — to be able to conceptualize the actual intervention of the researcher.

When communication is used as a research instrument, it is important that the researcher understands what is going on, and to help here, his view of the subject's communication should be compared with another person's understanding of what the subject is communicating. It is important to get into the subject's perspective and understand how the subject experiences the tasks given. Donaldson (1979) has demonstrated the problems for adults to see the task they give to children from the child's perspective. Donaldson very clearly shows that children in Piaget's task solve other problems than those intended by the researchers, because the meaning of a task is not just understood by the child from the spoken words alone. One way to tackle this problem, as we have said, is to take part in the child's activity, and there should be two researchers in the research situation who are able to discuss the interpretation of the protocols together.

Another important point in securing validity is that the aim of the research project is clear, so that the protocol made in the research situation is always explicitly related to this aim. The protocol is only useful if the aim is explicitated, because what the researcher does, asks, sees and records in the situation is determined by his research goals. How the communication between him and the subject develops is determined by the researcher's motives for doing the research; it determines how much he interacts with the subjects, what mode of communication he primarily uses, what type of task he gives the subjects, etc.

A Research Project*

We will now describe a research project on "evaluating teaching material to preschool children from the children's play with the material" to demonstrate how research can be done according to the criteria mentioned (Hedegaard, 1982). The research project is only developed through the first phase of the research procedure, intuitive interventional communication. The second phase, where planned and systematic intervention should be done, is not reached by this project. This second stage of planned intervention from a theoretical model is carried through in the research of Elkonin on play, and in the research of Meshscheryakov on teaching deaf and blind children.

The phenomenological characteristics of the method used are inspired by Giorgi's research (1976) and can be summarized as follows:

---

* Appendix 1 shows an example of a research protocol and its interpretation on the critical preconceptual level and on the subject oriented level.

1) It is a qualitative method.
2) The researcher is active in the research situation.
3) The researcher describes what is meaningful to him/her.
4) The research situation is an experienced situation both for the researcher and the subject.
5) The researcher focuses on specific themes in the situation.
6) In relation to this theme, the researcher focuses of the subject's motives and intentions through the subject's activities and actions; it is not a behavioral description.
7) The researcher focuses on the themes from the perspective of the subject.
8) The researcher delineates the essential aspects of the phenomena through his interaction with the subjects.
9) The protocols are intended to reflect the conflicts and the problems of the subjects.
10) The protocol which is a result of this procedure is intended to be a basis for further interaction with the subject's, and to allow such interaction to proceed along lines set by the themes of the research.

Interpretation

The results of the communicative intervention in the child's life situation can have the form of a written research protocol, which contains a description of what was going on in the research period. The writing of this protocol implies, as already mentioned, some conceptions about the phenomenon studied. The research protocol should then be interpreted in a way that allows, the results to be seen in a more connected theoretical framework, but the interpretation has to be seen as a further development of the concepts used in the activity phase of researcher and subjects. There is a dependence between research and interpretation; neither can be seen as complete in itself. But although there is a continuity between the writing of the research protocol and the interpretation of this protocol, some essential differences between these two aspects of the research process can be pointed out.

The main differences are:

1. The writing of the research protocol is part of the activity which it describes. The interpretation is separated from this activity.

2. The writing of the protocol implies an interaction between researcher and subjects so that the researcher's writing is based on his experience of this common activity. The interpretation is qualitatively different in this respect, because in this phase there is no contact with the persons written about; the interpreter has a text where he can find relations and connections between aspects of the phenomenon studied, through reflection.
3. The writing ot the protocol is focused on the situation of the subjects and their activity. In the interpretation phase, the focus is on specific themes for developing the theoretical frame and explaining the inner relations between concepts setting aside the specific situation.

In the following, a distinction between a frame of interpretation and levels of interpretation will be pointed out.

Frame of interpretation

The interpretation is a dialectical process between the protocol and the theoretical frame because a theoretical frame is necessary for writing the protocol and starting the interpretation of this protocol. To use a theoretical frame in relation to a specific protocol means both changing the content of the protocol and developing theoretical considerations in this frame.

The writing and the interpretation of a protocol implies preconceptions in the researcher about what he can expect to find through his interpretation. These preconceptions guide the researcher's focus when he reads the research protocol; at the same time it is important that the results of the protocol develop these preconceptions. The content of the research protocol should interfere with, and change the frame of interpretation so that the important aspects of the concrete protocol can be understood in relation to what is important for the phenomenon under study and its development. By this procedure, the preconceptions will gradually develop into reflected conceptions in a theory which reflects the common traits in the development of children in our culture.

Levels of interpretation

a) A CRITICAL PRECONCEPTUAL LEVEL

A first level of interpretation should be a critical commentary on the protocol which indicates the researcher's understanding of what happened in the research period. This interpretation is a sort of running commentary on the protocol (as can be seen from the example) and is important as a check of the validity of the research protocol. The two researchers should here confront their experiences of what happens in the situation. This level of interpretation is also a basis for the next level of interpretation where the theoretical frame is used explicitly.

b) A SUBJECT ORIENTED LEVEL

On this level, the researcher reads through the protocol to focus on questions connected with the theoretical frame. In the example, the foci are 1) the motives and intentions of the child, 2) problems and contradictions in his activities, 3) the child's interaction with the teacher, other children, and adults, 4) the child's capacities and the development of new capacities. This results in a connected & integrated characterization of each subject, with relations between essential traits described for each individual in relation to a specific research aim.

c) A THEMATICALLY ORIENTED LEVEL

This level is based on a collection of the characterizations of the subjects in relation to the specific research aim. By attending to the research foci in these descriptions, the internal relations of the theme of research can be analysed, on the basis of the variations discovered, and some general traits can be found.

APPENDIX

EXAMPLE OF A BOARDGAME SEQUENCE

Game leader: Mariane
Observer: Mirjana
Players: Richard (6), Barbara (6), Sofie (6), Sille (4)

1. Marianne shows a *rake*: "Who wants	
2. this one?"	
3. Silence — the children are look-	No instruction has been
4. ing at their own boards and at	given so they do not know
5. those of the others — they give	what to look for
6. in.	
7. Mariane puts the piece on a	Explanation of the connec-
8. board and explains why she puts	tion between piece and
9. it there.	board, illustrated by example

10. Mariane shows a *paint brush* —
11. "What is this?"
12. Both speaking at once, Sofie
13. and Barbara identify the piece.
14. Richard: "It is connected with
15. paint and I've got it."
16. Barbara hands it to him.

Richard now realizes the task. Explains the connection.

17. Mariane shows a *butterfly*.
18. Barbara: "Here."
19. Mariane asks why, and, both
20. speaking at once, Barbara and
21. Sofie tell the story about the
22. caterpillar that turns into a
23. butterfly
23. Mariane praises them for their
24. knowledge.

Barbara has to be asked for explanation. She understands that piece and placing fit according to different principles, as this developmental connection is the only one in the game

25. Mariane shows a *spoon*.
26. Richard immediately understands
27. that it fits his board and says:
28. "Here."

Now he omits an explanation

29. Mariane shows a *brush*.
30. Without comments Barbara takes
31. it out of Mariane's hand and
32. places it correctly on her own
33. board.
34. Mariane shows a *petrol pump*
35. "What's this?"
36. "A service station" Barbara and
37. Richard reply.
38. Simultaneously, Sille waves her
39. arms and points to the shelf
40. where the toy service station is.

Barbara and Richard both try to be the first one to explain. Sille never gets the chance to express herself; then she uses gestures.

41. Mariane shows a *key*.
42. "It fits the gate" Barbara at
43. once replies and points at it.

Evaluation of the Children Profit from Participating

Understanding the task and independent initiative

The children do not understand the task until the first piece has been shown and its placing explained. Richard immediately understands the idea of the game and at once explains why the next piece fits his board (14). As can be seen from the very beginning, the children conceive of the game as competitive, each of them try to answer first (12, 18, 28, 36, 42).

Problems of the game sequence and attempts at solutions

The competitive element of the game probably motivates Richard to explain the connection between piece and placing on board in the case of the paint brush (14), after all, Barbara is already in possession of the piece. Richard's problem is that he has to act quicker than Barbara. Maybe this is the reason why the next time he sees a piece which fits his board, he contents himself with saying: "Here" (18), not giving himself time to explain. Sille also has the problem of having sufficient time to formulate a response before any of the others has taken the piece or has spoken. Instead she points and waves her arms (38, 39).

Child/child and adult/child interaction

The children's interaction is influenced by competition which is seen when they talk all at once (12, 36) and when they do not take time to explain. The youngest child, Sille, is therefore not given the chance to collect her ideas, although she shows that she would like to do so when she points (38, 39).

The adults try to make the children describe, when they themselves explain and describe (7–9), and when they ask for explanation and description (19, 35). The children would like to answer and explain, but except for Richard's first explanation no independent explanations are given.

Demonstration of experience and the possibility of gaining experience

The children soon understand that they have to find the different connections. Richard, Barbara and Sofie show that they are able to describe such connections (14, 21–22).

Barbara's and Sofie's description of the developmental connection between caterpillar and butterfly shows that their knowledge and understanding of connection go beyond the functional understanding, e.g. the knowledge that a key fits a lock.

It is doubtful whether the children gain new knowledge from this game because 1) the connections in the game do not deal with a common theme nor are they of the same sort. The children are presented with fragments of knowledge, and 2) the competitive element of the game is too dominant, the children cannot concentrate on the content of the game.

References

Aidarowa, L. *Child development and education*. Moscow: Progress publishers, 1982.

Carew, J. V., Chan, I. & Halfar, H. *Observing intelligence in young children*. New York: Prentice Hall, 1976.

Dawydow, W. *Arten der verallgemeinerung im unterricht*. Berlin: Volk und Wissen, 1977.

Donaldson, M. *Children's minds*. Glasgow: Fontana, 1978

Elkonin, D. *Psychologie des spiels*. Berlin: Volk und Wissen, 1980.

Giorgi, A. *Psychology as a human science*. New York: Harper & Row, 1970.

————. Problems encountered in developing a phenomenological approach to research in psychology. In F. Fransella (Ed.), *Personal Construct Psychology*. London: Academic Press, 1978.

Giorgi, A., Fischer, C. T. & Murray, E. L. *Duquesne studies in phenomenological psychology I & II*. Pittsburgh: Duquesne University Press, 1972 & 1976.

Hedegaard, M. *Lege – Lære: En analyse af førskolebørns tilegnelse af færdigheder ved leg med pædagogiske materialer*. København: Forlaget Børn og Unge, 1983.

Iljenkow, E. W. Die Dialektik des Abstrakten und Konkreten im "Kapital" von Marx. In Schmidt (Ed.), *Beiträge zur marxistischen Erkenntnisstheori*. Nordlingen: Suhrkamp Verlag, 1972.

Kvale, S. The technological paradigm of psychology, *Journal of phenomenological Psychology*, 1973, *3*, 143–159.

Larsson, S. Studier i lärares omvärlds uppfattning: Särdrag hos vuxenstuderande. *Reports from the institute of education. University of Göteborg*, 1981, *17*.

————. Studier i lärares omvärlds uppfattning. Ett försök till integration. *Reports from the institute of Education. University of Göteborg*. 1982, *15*.

Luria, A. & Yodovitch, J. *Speech and the development of mental processes in the child*. London, 1959.

Marton, F., Dahlgren, O., Svensson, L. & Säljö, R. *Inlärning och omvärldsuppfattning*. Stockholm: AWE/Gebers, 1977.

————. Describing Conceptions of the World around us. *Reports from the institute of education. University of Göteborg*. 1978, *66*.

Marton, F. & Säljö, R. Learning in the learner's perspective III. *Reports from the institute of education. University of Göteborg.* 1979, *78.*

Meshcheryakov, A. *Awakening to life.* Moscow: Progress Publishers, 1979.

Murphy, L. *Personality in young children.* New York: Basic Books, 1956.

Pinxten, R. Observation in anthropology: Positivism and Subjectivism Combined. *Communication and Cognition,* 1981, *14,* 57–83.

Poddjakow, N. *Die denkentwicklung beim vorschulkind.* Berlin: Volk und Wissen, 1981.

Riegel, K. F. The dialectics of human development. *American Psychologist,* 1976, *31,* 689–699.

Sylva, K. & Painter, M. *Child watching at play groups and nursery school.* Oxford: Giant McIntyre. 1980.

Säljö, R. Learning in the learner's perspective I. *Reports from the institute of education. University of Göteborg.* 1979, *76.* (a)

————. Learning in the learner's perspective II. *Reports from the institute of education. University of Göeborg.* 1979, *77.* (b)

Vigotsky, L.S. *Tænkning og sprog.* København: Reitzel, 1971, 1974.

PART III

Therapy and Research

Psychoanalytic Therapy as Qualitative Research

7

Steinar Kvale

Psychoanalytic therapy is a qualitative research method with a long tradition in psychology. The present analysis is an attempt to learn from this tradition in order to further the current development of qualitative research. First, it is posited that psychoanalysis is *the* qualitative research method which has yielded substantial contributions to psychological knowledge. Second, seven characteristics of psychoanalysis as a research method are outlined. Third, the scientific status of psychoanalytic research is discussed, and finally some implications are drawn for the current development of qualitative research in psychology.

I. THE SIGNIFICANT CONTRIBUTIONS OF PSYCHOANALYTIC RESEARCH

The contributions of psychoanalysis have a central position in standard presentations of psychological knowledge about phenomena such as dreams, neuroses, therapy, sexuality, child development, personality formation, emotions and motivations, unconscious processes, etc. Psychoanalysis is the psychological discipline which has had the strongest impact on contemporary thought, upon culture at large, as well as in other disciplines as anthropology, sociology, the humanities and philosophy. Within psychology, psychoanalysis has been extraordinarily fruitful as a generator of research. The significance of the psychoanalytic contributions to psychological knowledge is a postulate which will not be further documented or argued here. The reference sections of current textbooks, and the Social Sciences Citation Index, may suffice as quantitative surface indicators of the strength of the postulate.

In standard presentations of psychological research methods, the major method by which psychoanalytic knowledge is obtained — psychoanalytic therapy — does not exist. A paradox appears here — central parts of current psychological knowledge are based upon a method which does not exist as a scientific method.

Freud conceived of psychoanalysis as a research method: "It is indeed one of the distinctions of psychoanalysis that research and treatment proceed hand in hand" (1963, p. 120). In an analysis of the status of psychoanalytic theory, in 1959, Rapaport stated: "The major body of positive evidence for the theory lies in the field of accumulated clinical observations" (p. 140). The importance of the intrinsic relation of therapy and research had, however, not been fully grasped within the psychoanalytical tradition: "The techniques of psychoanalysis have been studied, but its methods have scarcely been given systematic thought" (ibid., p. 151). This methodological blind spot of psychoanalysis makes the above paradox even more remarkable — psychoanalytic therapy, which has provided the main research basis for psychoanalytic theory, has scarcely been systematically reflected within the psychoanalytic tradition.

Before discussing the paradox of the non-reflection of the psychoanalytic research method, the specific characteristics of this method will be outlined.

II. PSYCHOANALYSIS AS A RESEARCH METHOD

The present analysis takes the significance of the knowledge acquired and verified in psychoanalytic therapy as given, and asks what the nature of this research method is. This approach contrasts with the more common one, taking the nature of scientific method in psychology as given and rejecting any knowledge not acquired and verified by the traditional scientific methods.

Freud's essays (1963) on therapy and technique constitute the basis for the presentation of psychoanalytic therapy as a research method. It is influenced by Rapaport's (1959) systematizing attempt, and by analyses of psychoanalysis within phenomenological-existential, hermeneutical and dialectical philosophy (Adorno, 1972; Boss, 1963; Habermas, 1971; Ricoeur, 1970; Sartre, 1963). While drawing upon these sources, the present approach is of a more restricted pragmatic-methodological nature — what are the specific characteristics of psychoanalytic therapy which contribute to its strength and weakness as a research method?

A) The Seven Characteristics of Psychoanalytic Research

Seven characteristic aspects of the psychoanalytic research method will be outlined, focusing on general approach more than on specific therapeutic techniques. This description of psycho-analysis is selective, with an overemphasis on the intellectual aspects of the therapy, and a relative neglect of the intensive emotional turmoils and the strenuous working through of conflicts during the therapeutic process. The focus is upon psychoanalytic therapy as a research method and does not involve research on the therapeutic effects and psychoanalysis.

1. The individual case study. Psychoanalytic therapy is an intensive case study of individual patients.

The sheer number of observed events in one psychoanalytic therapy exceeds those of many psychological research projects. In a classical psychoanalysis, the patient comes to therapy for one hour six days a week, over a period of several years. Quantitatively regarded, the enormous amount of observations from a few subjects may correspond to the larger number of subjects in traditional research with fewer observations of each subject.

Qualitatively regarded, the intensive studies of individuals give the therapist a broad context for interpreting the meaning of the patient's behavior. The therapist obtains a unique and penetrating knowledge of the relation of the patient's behavior to his present life situation and to his past history, which may again provide a basis for understanding the more general conditions of human behavior.

The individual case study involves several pitfalls as a research method. There is the danger of overgeneralization from a small number of cases to the population at large; and the focus on individuals as units of study may lead to an individualization of social problems, neglecting their historical and material basis.

2. The open mode of observation. The psychoanalytic mode of observation involves a set of polarities. It takes place in a free and non-directive, as well as a highly standardized, situation; it is open, presuppositionless, and it is guided by theory; it is descriptive and interpretative.

The psychoanalytic situation is open and free. The method of free association asks the patient to follow his associations, to assume a passive attitude towards his own train of thought and dispense with all conscious control over his mental processes. The basic rule requires the patient to report everything that occurs to him without modification or omission.

Whereas the content of the psychoanalytic hour is free and unplanned, the structure is highly standardized, with rules for the patient's reclining on the couch, the position of the therapist's chair, and with prescriptions for the therapist's interpretations and behavior in general. The form of the psychoanalytic situation comes close to a controlled and standardized observational situation.

The psychoanalytic mode of observation is open and explorative, the attitude of the therapist ideally being that of a presuppositionless listener, the therapist should listen with an evenly-hovering attention,,listening to what comes without engaging in selective hypothesis testing. The technique "simply consists in making no effort to concentrate the attention on anything in particular, and in maintaining in regard to all that one hears the same measure of calm, quiet attentiveness — of 'evenly-hovering attention' " (Freud, 1963, p. 118). This entails an openness to the vague, the ambiguous, the contradictory, and the unexpected; the therapist focuses less on whether the patients report factual occurrences or phantasies than upon the psychological meaning of what is said. Freud warned against formulating a case scientifically while treatment is proceeding, since it would interfere with the open therapeutic attitude in which one proceeds "aimlessly, and allows oneself to be overtaken by any surprises, always presenting to them an open mind, free from any expectations" (ibid, p. 120). Freud here recommends the scientific analysis of a case to be postponed until the treatment is concluded.

Psychoanalytic observations are also guided by psychoanalytic theory, everything the patient says is not equally important, some areas of life — such as childhood experiences, sexuality, anxiety — are considered more essential than other areas for the therapy of neurotic behavior.

The psychoanalytic mode of observation is descriptive. Following the principle of an evenly-hovering attention, it entails a non-categorizing approach to what is taking place at the moment, the observations are reported in the form of qualitative descriptions. The descriptive focus is on the meaning of the observed behavior, whereby description and interpretation may be intertwined. The case descriptions are most often expressed in everyday language, sometimes mixed with technical and theoretical terms.

The psychoanalytic observations are, in principle, not intersubjectively reproducible by any observer. They take place in an intensive two-person relation, and they require specific competence, such as extensive knowledge of psychoanalytic theory and a personal training analysis.

The psychoanalytic mode of observation entails several pitfalls for a research method. The lack of systematic observational procedures makes the documentation dependent on the therapist's selective memory and notes; Freud even disclaimed the taking of notes during the therapeutic hour. With the large number of observed events, the structuring of the extensive material becomes highly dependent of the therapist's guiding interest. The private, closed psychoanalytic situation and the lack of systematic recording makes an intersubjective control of the reported observations difficult. The specific qualification of competent observers hampers with an intersubjective control through "neutral" observers.

3. The interpretation of meaning. The interpretation of the meaning of the patient's behaviour is an essential aspect of the psychoanalytic technique. The psychoanalytic interpretation of meaning is open to multiple meanings and layers of meaning of an act. It involves hypothesis generation and hypothesis testing, and raises the issue of validity of interpretation.

Psychoanalysis does not maintain a strict line of demarcation between data and meaning, between description and interpretation. The concept of multiple determination implies that the one and same act may have multiple meanings and motives. The meaning of an act may be ambiguous and contradictory, psychoanalysis entails a methodological tolerance of ambiguity in the interpretation of meaning.

There may be several levels of meaning interpretation. There is a surface level where the meaning of an act or a statement is taken at face value. There is an intermediate critical common sense level of interpretation, where the interpretation of what is said also encompasses the immediate context, including the tone, the expression, and the postures of the speaker. And, there are the deeper levels of interpretation where the meaning of a dream for example is interpreted in the context of the patient's life history and within the theory of psychoanalysis. The levels of interpretation may overlap, and the one and same act may have different meanings at different levels of interpretation.

The focus upon psychoanalysis as a research method leads to an undue emphasis on the interpretation of meaning. A psychoanalysis is a rather non-directive process; the therapist is most of the time listening, sometimes guiding the patient towards certain themes, leaving it up to the patient himself to discover the hidden meanings of his behavior, and with direct psychoanalytic interpretations to the patient being rare during the therapeutic process.

The evenly-hovering attention of the therapist may be conductive for the generation of hypothesis about the meaning of the patient's behavior, and the fruitfulness of psychoanalysis as a method of hypothesis generation is hardly contested. When it comes to the testing of hypothesis, the value of psychoanalysis is more controversial. The standardized, quasi-experimental control of the psychoanalytic situation should, however, not be overlooked. The therapist may carefully time his interpretations and observe the patient's verbal and non-verbal reactions to his interpretations. The same hypothesis about the meaning of the patient's behavior may be tested again and again in different therapeutic hours.

The patient's acknowledgement as well as his rejection of the therapist's interpretations are ambiguous. Freud neither accepted a patient's "yes" or "no" to his interpretations at face value, but considered both as possible expressions of resistance towards to progress of the therapy. Freud recommended more indirect forms of validating interpretations by observation of the patient's subsequent behavior — as changes in the content of the patient's free associations and in his dreams, recall of forgotten memories and alterations of neurotic symptoms (1963, p. 279).

The sensitivity of psychoanalysis at the observational stage, and the creativity at the hypothesis generating stage, may be counteracted by a methodic nonchalance at the hypothesis testing stage. There may occur a tendency in the psychoanalytic literature to quickly overstep the descriptive stage in research in favor of the interpretative stage; the observable symptoms are swiftly passed by an express train to the deeper levels of unconscious meanings and psychoanalytic theory. Here an interpretation-mania may occur, where every possible act is given a multitude of subtle meanings, with overinterpretations on limited pieces of evidence.

Here arises the problem of suggestion, the therapist may validate his interpretations by unwittingly influencing the patient's behavior, the close personal involvement of the patient increasing this suggestibility. And there is the issue of conflicting clinical observations and interpretations from rival schools of psychotherapy.

4. The historical dimension. Psychoanalytic therapy unfolds in a historical temporal dimension, with a unique intertwinedness of the past, the present and the future dimension. The uncovering and the interpretation of the patient's past history is a temporal process over several years with the aim of instigating changes in the patient's future behaviour.

The object of psychoanalysis is a developing subject. The patient's life history, and particularly his childhood, is a central theme of the analysis. Freud's innovation was here to see human phenomena in a meaningful historical perspective. The knowledge of the patient's past history is essential for the interpretation of the meaning of his present neurotic behavior. And the interpretations are a means of instigating the patient to relive the traumatic episodes of his past and thereby surpass their determining effect on his present behavior. In psychoanalysis remembrance of the past is an active force, the therapy aims at overcoming the repression of the past and the current resistance against making the unconscious conscious.

Psychoanalysis is an extremely intensive and sensitive longitudinal method, the same individuals being observed almost daily in a standardized situation over a period of several years. The longitudinal case study of psychoanalysis does not provide merely a quantitative accumulation of knowledge, but focuses on the internal logic of the individual's development, it studies how the original contradictions of childhood have given birth to the present contradictions manifested in the patient's pathological behavior.

The extensive knowledge of the patient's life history gives the therapist a unique context for interpretation of the patient's actual behaviour. His analysis of one single dream may be conducted within the context of several hundred hours of observation of the patient, including many related dreams. The temporal context of the interpretations involves the future, the meaning of the patient's present behavior may first be disclosed by future events. "The full interpretation of such a dream will coincide with the completion of the whole analysis; if a note is made of it at the beginning, it may be possible to understand it at the end, after many months" (Freud, 1963, p. 100).

The historical temporal dimension is essential in the psychoanalytic method; this concerns the historic topic of investigation — the relation of the patient's present behavior to his life history — and the temporal process of the analytic process, where the development as well as the validation of the therapist's interpretations occur over an extended period of time, the aim being the future change of the patient's neurotic behavior. Psychoanalysis is the study of a life history and an attempt to change the course of the life history studied.

The extended temporal context for the psychoanalyst's interpretations and the continual unfolding of this context is limited to the therapist, making a control study of interpretations by others difficult.

5. *The Human Relationship.* Psychoanalytic therapy is a human relationship, it entails a communicative interaction, a reciprocal personal involvement, with levels of disclosure from the patient, and there is a requirement of self-reference for the therapist.

Psychoanalytic therapy involves a complex interaction between patient and therapist. It is a joint venture, an attempt to change a process together with the person involved, the "object of inquiry" participates in the process of investigation. The psychoanalyst listens to what the patient says, and at some points in the therapy communicates his interpretations to the patient, who may react directly verbally to the interpretations, or indirectly through subsequent changes in behavior.

The analytic situation is not a neutral, "objective" relationship, but entails a personal involvement of patient and therapist. The personal contact for an hour almost every day over several years unavoidably leads to a close human relationship; within this comes the specific topic of their communication — the patient's life history and suffering. Freud noticed that if the analyst allows the patient time, devotes serious interests to him, and acts with tact, a deep attachment of the patient to the analyst develops of itself. The long, personal contact may involve feelings of sympathy and antipathy which are essential for the therapeutic process. The patient's feelings towards the therapist, which alternate between love and rage, theoretically interpreted as a "transference" of childhood feelings to the parents to the therapist, are by the psychoanalyst deliberately employed as means in the therapeutic process to overcome the patient's emotional resistance towards a deeper self-knowledge and change.

The personal relation of therapist and patient may involve layers of disclosure, the patient disclosing different layers of his personality according to his involvement in the personal relationship. There may be a continuum of layers of interaction, yielding different depths of knowledge. There are the superficial formal contacts of everyday life, there are the personal encounters in everyday life, and there may be intensive and enduring emotional relationships. Psychoanalytic therapy aims at establishing a unique intense and deep emotional relationship, the nature and the depth varying at different phases of the therapy. At each level, the patient, willingly or unwillingly, discloses different aspects of his personality. The personal involvement and complete trust of the therapeutic relation opens the patient up to layers of self-knowledge that he has not previously been able to encounter.

The influence of the therapist's own feelings towards his patients — termed "counter-transference," are taken into account in a psychoanalytic therapy — not by an attempt of eliminating the personal involvement of the therapist, but by a controlled employment of his subjectivity. The importance of the therapist as person has led to the requirement of a personal training analysis for a psychoanalytic therapist. This involves a principle of self-reference — the same laws of behavior hold for the therapist as for his patient; the therapist should, however, through his personal training analysis and extensive psychoanalytic training have obtained a higher level of self-reflection than the patient starting therapy.

The personal involvement of the therapeutic relationship is contrary to the traditional requirements of scientific neutrality. It may involve the danger of subjective bias in the therapist's interpretations, and a suggestibility of the patient towards accepting the interpretations.

6. *Pathology as topic of investigation.* The topic of investiga-

tion in a psychoanalytic therapy is the irrational behavior of pathological individuals in crisis.

The therapeutic interest is less on the typical or normal behavior than upon apparently meaningless and bizarre behavior such as neurotic symptoms, dreams, slips of the tongue, and the like. Such apparently irrational behavior is considered revelatory of the unconscious processes interfering with rational, normal behavior.

The subjects in psychoanalysis are seldom average, normal, well-adjusted persons, but rather extreme persons suffering from their neurotic behavior. The pathological behavior of these patients may serve as a magnifying glass for the less visible conflicts of average individuals. Pathology is strategic for the study of normal processes. From a psychoanalytical standpoint, the neuroses and psychoses are extreme variations, heightened versions, of normal behavior; they are the characteristic expressions of what has gone wrong in a given culture.

Pathology is a magnifying glass and a driving force for change in psychoanalysis. The patients do not come to psychoanalysis in normal and stable periods of their lives, but at periods of acute crisis, at times when their conflicts become unbearable, when the neurotic symptoms are most pronounced. The neurotic suffering and desperation is a motive for understanding and change; in psychoanalysis, the crises are a locus of knowledge and a driving force for change. The therapist's task is to maintain, and even to increase, the patient's level of suffering during the therapy as a means of combating his resistance to deeper understanding and fundamental changes.

While the focus on the irrational behavior of neurotic patients in crisis may be revelatory of normal behavior, including a questioning of the concept of normality; the pathological subject matter involves several pitfalls for psychoanalysis as a research method. There is the danger of overemphasis of the irrational behavior of man, and the generalizations drawn from neurotic patients may involve a pathologizing of human behavior in general.

7. The instigation of change. The aim of a psychoanalytic therapy is the instigation of changes in the patient's behavior, the mutual interest of therapist and patient is to overcome the patient's suffering under his neurotic symptoms.

The essential dimension of psychoanalysis is the instigation of change and the patient's resistance to change. The pathological factor is not the patient's ignorance of central parts of his past history, but his anxiety and inner resistance to this knowledge. The main task of a psychoanalytic treatment lies in combating, working through, and overcoming the patient's resistances, towards understanding and changing his behavior. "The whole theory of psychoanalysis is. . . in fact built up on the perception of the resistance offered to us by the patient when we attempt to make his unconscious conscious to him" (Freud, 1967, p. 68).

The major forces in overcoming the patient's anxiety and resistance towards deeper understanding and change are his suffering under his neurotic symptoms and his attachment to the therapist. The patient's suffering and his hope of relief gives psychoanalysis a unique access to the normally closed, deeper levels of personality.

The psychoanalytical knowledge is not obtained by external observation, but through attempts to change a pathological process together with the person involved. The patient's resistance to change, which might be a source of error from the viewpoint of pure information gathering, becomes in psychoanalytic therapy a locus of knowledge of the deeper layers of personality. While understanding may lead to change, the implicit theory of knowledge in psychoanalysis is that a fundamental understanding of a phenomenon may first be obtained through attempts to change the phenomenon.

This very strength of psychoanalysis also raises problems for a research method. The guiding interest of change in a patient's behavior may interfere with the requirement of reproducible observations, the validation of different interpretations about the meaning of a symptom is subordinated to the change of the symptoms. The primary aim of a psychoanalytic therapy is not reproducible observations or valid interpretations, but the emancipation of the patient from his neurotic suffering.

B) Alternative Explanations of Psychoanalytic Contributions

The relative importance, and the interdependence of the seven characteristics of psychoanalytic research outlined, will not be further analyzed in the present context. Before turning to the current status of psychoanalytic research, and to the implications for qualitative research in general, some alternative explanations of the scientific productivity of psychoanalysis will be considered.

The major contributions of psychoanalysis may be attributed to Freud's genius, and not to the therapeutic method he developed. The influence of Freud's person on the development of psychoanalysis is not to be overlooked. It can, however, hardly account for other contributions of the psychoanalytic tradition, such as the pioneer works of Jung and Adler, the innovations of the neo-freudians, and the later studies on psychosomatic illness, character structure, authoritarianism, narcissism, etc. Thus, the creativity of psychoanalytic research cannot be due to Freud's genius only. It is, however, possible that psychoanalysis has had an attraction for creative thinkers, or that the psychoanalytic method entails special possibilities for creative researchers to unfold their potential.

The scientific innovations of psychoanalysis may also be attributed to psychoanalytic theory. Psychoanalytical theory is here used in the sense of "clinical theory" (Klein, 1973a), close to the phenomena encountered in therapy, as distinguished from the rather abstract metapsychological theory of psychoanalysis. Thus, the theoretical focus on unconscious processes and hidden meanings, the importance of sexuality and the determination of present personality and conflicts by childhood history, etc., involves an openness to significant areas of human life. Further, psychoanalytical thought has entailed an openness to the revelations of the human situation given by myths, literature and art. On the other hand, psychoanalytic theory also involves rather abstract formalizations and speculations which, together with a tendency to theoretical orthodoxy, may hamper the development of psychological knowledge.

Other therapeutic approaches have also contributed to psychological knowledge, e.g., the non-directive, clientcentered approach of Rogers and the interpersonal approach of Sullivan. This may imply that the therapeutic method in general is conducive to the development of knowledge. In the present context, the focus will be upon the influence of the specific characteristics of the psychoanalytic method, thereby also abstracting from the inherent unity of psychoanalytic theory and therapy.

III. THE SCIENTIFIC STATUS OF PSYCHOANALYTIC
RESEARCH

Psychoanalytical therapy, which has been the main source for
the generation and validation of psychoanalytic knowledge has,
despite the broad impact of psychoanalytical knowledge, had a
rather low status as a research method in the scientific community
as well as in the psychoanalytical tradition.

A) The Seven Characteristics of Psychoanalytic Research —
Vices or Virtues

The seven characteristics of psychoanalytical research outlined
here may contribute to the strength of psychoanalysis as a research method, as well as to its weakness — in particular the
problems of overgeneralization and the lack of intersubjective
control of observations and interpretations. The strength of the
psychoanalytic research method involves the intensive study of
individual cases which may give a comprehensive understanding
of individual development, the open mode of observation makes
possible the discovery of unexpected phenomena, the interpretation of meaning gives access to a depth knowledge of human
existence, the historical dimension gives an extraordinary temporal context for the formulation and the testing of interpretations, the human relationship of the therapeutic situation involves
the trust necessary for a disclosure of the deeper levels of personality, pathology as subject matter provides a magnifying glass for
normal behavior, and neurotic suffering is a driving force for the
instigation of changes and the obtaining of knowledge about
human behavior.

These seven characteristics of the psychoanalytic situation have
mainly been regarded merely as practical aspects of the therapeutic technique, or as sources of error for a scientific research
procedure. An alternative hypothesis is that the very characteristics of psychoanalytic therapy which have led to its rejection as a
scientific method are responsible for the significant contributions
of psychoanalysis. This hypothesis involves a "Gestalt switch" —
the seven characteristics of psychoanalytic therapy, which from a
traditional viewpoint are vices, are in the present perspective the
very virtues of psychoanalytic research.

B) The Positivist Dismissal of Psychoanalysis

A paradox was pointed out in the first section — the psycho-analytic method, which has yielded significant contributions to psychological knowledge, appears non-existing in the presentations of psychological research methods.

From a positivist viewpoint, the distinguishing characteristics of psychoanalysis as a research method systematically violate the basic principles of psychology as a natural science (e.g., Kvale, 1976). The intensive case studies of single subjects break with the traditional criteria of large samples of representative subjects. The open mode of observation violates the requirement of formalized observation procedures and systematic recording of the observations; and the tolerance of vague, ambiguous and contradictory phenomena contrasts with the requirement of science being based upon certain and exact quantifiable facts. The emphasis on interpretation of meaning contrasts with the demands of separating descriptions and interpretations, of distinguishing facts and meaning, as well as with the more drastic relegation of meaning from a natural science psychology. The unfolding temporal context, with changes in interpretation, contrasts with the requirement of science based upon fixed and immutable facts. The human relationship of the psychoanalytic situation with the personal involvement of patient and therapist violates the requirement of detached neutral observers. The focus on the pathological behavior of neurotic individuals contrast with the common study of the normal behavior of average individuals. And the therapist's communication of his observations and interpretations to the patient in the interest of change hampers the requirement of control through repeated observations.

The paradox of the non-reflection of the psychoanalytic research method is now understandable — the outstanding characteristics of the psychoanalytic method systematically, point for point, violate the positivist requirements of natural science research in psychology. It is then logical that the psychoanalytic method, which is disclaimed a scientific status, does not exist in positivist presentations of scientific methods in psychology.

C) The Scientistic Fate of Psychoanalytic Discoveries

With psychoanalytic therapy excommunicated from the scientific establishment and the excommunication tacitly accepted by psychoanalysts, the attempt has been made to verify psychoanalytic knowledge by established scientific methods such as experiments, questionnaires, etc.

The scientistic fate of psychoanalytic discoveries may be illustrated by the study of "the authoritarian personality." Through psychoanalytic studies in the 1930s, a syndrome of an authoritarian personality was uncovered. In the work of Fromm, Horkheimer, Marcuse, and others (1936) at the Frankfurt Institute of Social Research, this authoritarian personality syndrome was traced to family structures and to the social structures giving rise to fascism. The early clinical and marxist analyses of the relation of personality and society were followed by an extensive study by Adorno et al. (1969) in 1950, bridging the gap between clinical and statistical studies. In the 1950s and 60s, the original insights on the relation of personality and ideology were lost in endless series of statistical analyses of test and questionnaire data. One of the authors of the original study (Sanford, 1972) has characterized the subsequent research as a quantitative obsession with the fascism scale — criticizing it and correlating it with other variables. The comprehensive exploratory character of the original study, as well as the psycho-historical nature of the concept of authorianism, got lost in methodic details.

In this context, attention may be called to Sartre's (1965) phenomenological "Portrait of an Anti-Semite" from 1946. Through informal qualitative observations and interviews, he arrived at virtually the same personality syndrome as the psychoanalytic studies and subsequent statistical test and questionnaire studies on authoritarianism (cf. Adorno et al., 1969, p. 971; Hannush, 1974). The correspondence of the two studies may be interpreted as evidence of the validity of qualitative research when conducted by sensitive persons within related theoretical frameworks.

And history may be repeating itself — in psychoanalytic therapies of the 1950s and 60s by Kohut, Kernberg, Mitscherlich, and others, a picture of a new narcissistic personality developed. And, again in relation to the Frankfurt School, this personality syndrome was traced to the family structures brought about by changes in the capitalist society, particularly the breakdown of the traditional authority and legitimity of bourgeois values (cf. Ziehe, 1975; Lasch, 1979). By 1980, the narcissistic syndrome found its way to mainstream psychology, and one may predict a coming construction of a "narcissistic personality scale."

In conclusion, the fate of the authoritarian personality studies, and the likely future of the narcissistic personality studies, suggest that early creative and provocative knowledge, arrived at through clinical studies, decades later find their way into mainstream psychology where they may give rise to extensive research activities yielding little new knowledge.

The results of the attempts to verify psychoanalytic knowledge by traditional methods are in general rather inconclusive and questionable (cf. Rapaport, 1959). Many of the phenomena studied in psychoanalysis only exist in a close personal relationship; in contrast to the deeper levels of personality disclosed in the personal trust of the therapeutic relationship, the replications attempted in the laboratory may only yield knowledge of a surface level of personality. For a human science, significant knowledge of human life would be best obtained by a genuine human relationship rather than through a neutral technical relation.

In face of the general triviality production of attempts to verify psychoanalytically discovered knowledge by experimental statistical methods, it is remarkable that the relative merits of the psychoanalytic method and the traditional scientific methods of psychology have not been more systematically investigated.

D. The Psychoanalytic Identification with the Aggressor

Despite Freud's emphasis on the close relation of therapy and research, psychoanalysis has generally been regarded as a therapeutic method only. While the neglect of the psychoanalytical method is logical from a positivist point of view, the non-reflection of psychoanalytical therapy — the method which has provided the main evidence for psychoanalytical theory — is rather irrational from a psychoanalytic standpoint.

The "lack of clarification as to what constitutes a valid clinical research method leaves undetermined the positive evidential weight of the confirming clinical material" (Rapaport, 1959, p. 141). In particular, as there is no established canon for the interpretation of clinical observations, for distinguishing valid interpretations from speculation, the theoretical edifice of psychoanalysis may come close to a house built upon sand.

After Freud there has been little methodological or conceptual development of psychoanalysis as a research method within the psychoanalytic tradition.

The philosophical analyses of psychoanalysis as a research method were mentioned in the first section, a general discussion of this approach is given by Thomä & Kächele (1973). To this may be added Holzkamp's (1984) argument that a critical marxist psychology has to take the research potential of psychoanalysis seriously. Within the psychoanalytic tradition, the scientific status of psychoanalysis has come into focus after Rapaport's challenge. The issues of verification of psychoanalytic theory and of therapeutic effects is reviewed by Fisher & Greensberg (1977). A review of research on the psychoanalytic process by Wallerstein & Sampson (1971) concludes with emphasizing the necessity of developing the clinical case study, with its compelling power and obvious scientific limitations, into a disciplined research instrument. Despite the recent philosophical and methodological investigations of psychoanalytic therapy as research, the scientific selfunderstanding of psychoanalysts tends to remain rather insecure.

In contrast to the steady output of textbooks on the experimental method in psychology, there hardly even exists a reading on psychoanalytic therapy as a research method. According to the present analysis, the methodological blind spot of psychoanalytic research is not due to its youth nor to the complexity of the method or its subject matter; but has its roots in an irrational self-devaluation of psychoanalytic research.

Psychoanalytic, and clinical research in general, appears today in a troubled position. Not seldom it falls between two stools, dismissed as unscientific or as irrelevant. The therapeutic insights are dismissed by the scientific establishment as unscientific when not arrived at through experimental-statistical methods, or, at the most, accredited a status as preliminary to scientific research. And the findings of clinical research, applying traditional experimental-statistical methods to clinical phenomena, are often dismissed by therapists as superficial and irrelevant for the clarification of the problems they face in their practice.

Habermas (1971) has pointed out a "scientistic self-misunderstanding" of psychoanalysis: while in fact founding a new science of man based on methodic self-reflection, Freud believed psychoanalysis to be a natural science. The continued existence of this scientific misunderstanding today makes it neces-

sary to go beyond the conception of an intellectual misunderstanding and, perhaps as a "wild interpretation", draw in some of
the affective defense mechanisms uncovered by psychoanalysis.

Psychoanalytic research today appears to have a basic lack of
self-confidence and anxiety about scientific status, which inter-
feres with a realistic appraisal of the scientific value of psychoanalytic therapy as research. Current psychoanalytic self-
concepts may contain an internalization of the positivist dismissal
of psychoanalytic research. The research behavior of psychoanalysts may thus be characterized by a tendency towards a formalistic "identification with the aggressor." They may become more
catholic than the Pope himself, borrowing the externalia of the
aggressor — questionnaires, construction of scales, physiological
methods, large samples, complex statistical analysis and computer programs; getting caught in measuring fever. Often lacking
motivation, aptitude and training for the use of these specific
techniques, the results of this academic clinical research may be
meager.

An opposite subjectivistic "reaction formation" may also serve
as a protection against the anxiety about scientific status. Requirements of empirical documentation and logical argumentation are rejected; any inquiry about the validity of interpretations
given are dismissed by referring to the "experienced therapist's
judgement," the publications sometimes coming close to the
unravelling of mystical intuitions. A theoretical orthodoxy may
also occur, where the concepts of psychoanalytical theory are
reified and acquire a life of their own, inaccessible to any logical
or empirical questioning.

From a more sociological viewpoint, psychoanalytic research
today appears caught between a mainstream cooption at the
universities and a "ghettoization" at the psychoanalytic institutes.
The objectivistic and the subjectivistic defense reactions towards
scientific requirements have in common a denial, or a repression,
of the specific character of psychoanalytic research. The conflict
between external scientific requirements and their own therapeutic research may be so anxiety provoking for the scientific self-
respect of analysts that the specific characteristics of therapeutic
research are repressed, the psychoanalytic method becomes an
unverbalized "blind spot." And due to the traumatic nature of
the early confrontations with the scientific establishment, the
repressed phenomena are not open for new learning nor open to

the impact of current developments in the social sciences and in philosophy.

The paradox of the non-reflection of psychoanalytic therapy pointed out in the first section also involves the psychoanalytic tradition, which may be explained by a basic insecurity and anxiety about the scientific status of psychoanalytic research. According to this interpretation, the main problem with psycho-analytic research today is the affective inner resistance within the psychoanalytic tradition against making the specific issues of the therapeutic research method conscious, verbalizing them and working them through towards conceptual clarification.

E) Scientific Assertiveness Training

The current position of psychoanalytic research may be de-scribed as a "methodological learned helplessness," and the appropriate therapeutic intervention a scientific "self-assertion training." A person with low self-esteem may manifest inade-quate behavior by labelling himself and conceptualizing situations in an inaccurate or an irrational manner. Not being able to live up to his irrational ideals, he will respond poorly and evaluate himself as inadequate. The therapeutic task is here to shape more rational self-evaluative statements.

A first step towards a rational evaluation of the research value of psychoanalytic therapy would be, as mentioned in the first section, to consider the substantial contributions of psychoanalyt-ic therapy to psychological knowledge. A further step towards replacing defensive psychoanalytical methodological helplessness by an offensive self-assertive behavior might be to study the self-confidence displayed by Skinner's blatant dismissal of basic tenets of a positivist conception of scientific research in "A case history in scientific method" (1961a). Pointing to the contrast between the ruling conceptions of formalized sciences and his own case of actual research, he takes the latter as the starting point, recommending the reader to adapt the position of a clinical psychologist to his own account of scientific research. It may be noted that while dismissing the mental apparatus of psychoanalyt-ic theory, Skinner (1961b) gives a positive appraisal of psycho-analytic discoveries about human behavior.

It is rather peculiar that psychoanalysts, with their inherent suspicion towards the manifest content of verbal statements, have come to take the idealized presentations of scientific practice at face value. A critical examination of the positivist tenets of science, and an openness towards contemporary philosophy and natural science, would reveal that the positivist philosophy of science has been out of date for some time (Koch, 1959), and that the conception of physics as a model science is based on a series of illusions about the research practice of physics (e.g., Brandt, 1973; Kuhn, 1967).

In contemporary philosophy, psychoanalytic therapy has, as mentioned in the second section, obtained a central position in analyses of the nature of social science research. In phenomenological, hermeneutical and dialectical analyses of psychoanalytical therapy, the specific characteristics of this research have been focal, and their relation to the methods of the humanities are being worked out.

A further step towards a rational self-evaluation of psychoanalytic research would be to investigate whether the seven characteristics of psychoanalytic research — which may contribute both to its relegation from the scientific community, as well as to its creative productivity — may also be found in other research in the social sciences. Such an approach to a realistic evaluation of psychoanalytic research will now be sketched in discussion of the implications of psychoanalysis for qualitative research.

IV. IMPLICATIONS FOR QUALITATIVE RESEARCH

The present analysis has taken the significance of psychoanalytic knowledge as given, and asked about the methodic strength and weakness of the therapeutic method which has been the primary source for psychoanalytic knowledge. This does not involve any glorification of qualitative methods as in themselves progressive, nor does it involve getting caught in the pseudo issue of quantitative vs. qualitative methods in psychology (Kvale, 1983a). Experimental-statistical methods have their definite place in psychological research, but not a monopoly on scientific status.

The alternative is not that psychoanalytic therapy is the one ideal model of research in psychology, nor is it a call for an implementation of therapeutic techniques in ordinary research. Some implications for the development of qualitative research will now be discussed, with respect to scientific status and methodic approach.

A) The Scientific Status of Qualitative Research

It is possible that some of the scientific status problems of psychoanalytic research may also pertain to qualitative research in general. Defensiveness and scientific insecurity may be shown in some qualitative research reports, where the apologia for the method may require more pages than the presentation of the results obtained. Here a positivism in reverse may occur, where the method precedes the problems, and legitimizing the qualitative method itself, rather than leaving the legitimacy of qualitative research to the quality and relevance of the knowledge obtained by these methods.

There are in current qualitative research, tendencies of defense reactions such as an objectivistic identification with the aggressor or subjectivistic reaction formations. For example, the current vogue of qualitative research interviews encompasses rather formalistic content analyses of the interview material, as well as subjectivist anecdotal quotes. The often vague or absent descriptions of the methodic procedures of interview projects, which makes an intersubjective control of the results difficult, may be an indication that the procedures used are believed to be so at odds with scientific requirements that they are kept unverbalized.

The strength and weakness of different qualitative research methods have hardly been systematically faced, nor have the relevance of the traditional criteria of representativity, reliability and validity for qualitative research. Whether the lack of comprehensive analyses of the principal issues of qualitative research is due to its relative novelty, or to a self-devaluation involving inner resistances towards making the basic problems of qualitative research conscious, remains open. The consequence is, however, a lack of a conceptual framework for analyzing the strength and weakness of the current attempts to develop a qualitative methodology.

The eclecticism of current qualitative research is one main problem, the publications on qualitative methodology are often atheoretical and in the form of readings. One exception is the phenomenological tradition, which involves a conception of man and of the scientific study of man (*see* Giorgi, 1970). Whereas phenomenological and existential philosophy has provided a comprehensive context for the reflection of psychoanalytic therapy, it remains open whether it can be developed to provide a correspondingly broad frame of reference for a general development of qualitative research in psychology.

B) The General Relevance of the Seven Characteristics of Psychoanalytic Research

The seven characteristics of psychoanalysis outlined earlier will now be discussed with respect to general relevance, drawing in other examples of research, and suggesting some directions for the development of qualitative research in psychology. The discussion does not concern specific methodic techniques, but general approaches to research (cf. Giorgi, 1970).

1. The individual case study. Intensive case studies of few subjects are neither limited to psychoanalysis, nor to qualitative research. The pioneer work of natural science psychology, Ebbinghaus' experimental and quantitative study of memory, was based on an immense amount of observation on one single subject — Ebbinghaus himself. The current use of large groups of subjects with statistical testing of trivial differences has been criticized by Skinner (1961a) for hampering a flexible research approach and the practical control of individual organisms. Also from a behavioral point of view, Kazdin (1981) confronts the common methodic dismissal of the clinical case study, and discusses how the scientific yield can be improved by different ways of drawing valid interferences from case studies. In a dialectical approach to therapy, the role of sample representativity is replaced by a determination of the relationship between general, specific, and singular aspects in the concrete case (Dreier & Kvale, 1984).

2. The open mode of observation. The open observational approach to human behavior is neither limited to psychoanalysis nor to therapy in general. Piaget, while critical of psychoanalytic concepts and the lack of control in psychoanalytic studies, conceived of his own research as a "clinical method." His method of observation consisted in letting the child talk and in noticing the manner in which his thought unfolded itself. Following up the child's answers and allowing him to take the lead, inducing the child to talk more and more freely, Piaget could get beyond the level of superficial observation and capture what is hidden behind the immediate appearance of things (Piaget, 1923; 1959, in particular the preface by Claparède).

Current evaluation research also includes open observation (e.g., Patton, 1980); "responsive evaluation" and "goal-free evaluation" imply that the investigator should proceed without a fixed design, planned in advance and allow the reality he encounters to determine the process. Without knowledge of a social system's official goals, the researcher would be less prejudiced in discovering the actual goals of a social system.

While the lack of systematic recording of observations is a problem of psychoanalytic research, it is possible that the psychoanalysts' reliance on an evenly-hovering attention has also saved psychoanalytic research from getting lost in endless tape and video recordings and the technicalities of content analysis, and allowing it to remain open to the deeper meanings unfolding during the therapeutic process.

Within the psychoanalytic tradition, Klein (1973a,b) has emphasized the psychoanalytical situation as an extraordinary "laboratory" for controlled naturalistic observation. The research potential of the analytic situation, with its unique therapeutic pact, is hardly exhausted for the study in depth of personality and pathology.

3. The interpretation of meaning. The essential task of psychoanalysis is, according to Klein, the deciphering of the meaning of human encounters. The validation of psychoanalytic interpretations has, however, been considered the Achilles' heel of psychoanalytic research. Different therapists may give different interpretations of the meaning of the same symptoms, and therapists of rival schools may in their clinical practice produce evidence confirming their own theories only.

The problem of rival schools producing evidence confirming their own theories only is not limited to psychoanalysis, but may also occur in the strictly controlled experimental laboratories, cf. e.g., the long and unsettled controversies on the theories of learning. In physics, conflicting paradigms may entail that "Practicing in different worlds, the two groups of scientists see different things when they look from the same point in the same direction" (Kuhn, 1967, p. 149). Before the scientists can hope to communicate, one group or the other must experience a conversion involving a "Gestalt-switch," a "paradigm shift."

The principal issues of the interpretation of the meanings of texts in the humanities have been reflected in hermeneutic philosophy. Canons of interpretation have been developed, e.g. concerning the hermeneutic circle. Conflicting interpretations of the same text do not necesssarily involve an arbitrariness or a subjectivity of interpretation, but rather mean that literary texts, and human existence itself, may reveal a multitude of meaning. In the last decades in Europe, an interaction of psychoanalysis and humanities concerning the interpretation of meaning has taken place. Psychoanalytic therapy has been analysed as a specific form of "depth hermeneutics," and aspects of the psychoanalytic techniques of interpretation have been applied to enrich literary interpretation. The interpretation of texts has even been suggested as a paradigm for understanding human action (Ricoeur, 1971).

The question of the validation of interpretations has been faced from several viewpoints. Habermas (1971) has argued for the development of validation criteria relevant to the psychoanalytic situation, which is neither a literature text nor a standard experiment. Freud's insistence on the validation of interpretations through the future course of therapy goes beyond the traditional criteria of coherence and correspondence and involves the domain of self-reflection, where the self-process as a whole has confirming or falsifying power.

Also starting with Freud's rejection of the patient's "yes" or "no" as sufficient validation criteria, Christiansen (1964) has proposed an increase of the construct validity of interpretations by including the character analysis and the vegetotherapeutic techniques developed by Reich. The problems of multiple interpretations also occur in psychobiographical research. Runyan (1981) lists thirteen different interpretations in the literature about the meaning of van Gogh's act of cutting his ear off. He does not conclude that the interpretations are entirely arbitrary; but suggests procedures for weighing the different types of interpretations. The psychoanalytic concept of levels of interpretation and hermeneutic text interpretation has been drawn in to clarify some of the issues of validity in qualitative research interviews (Kvale, 1983b).

The main problem with the psychoanalytic interpretation of meaning is not the existence of conflicting interpretations, nor the lack of a standard procedure for validating the different interpretations, but the neglect of the specific issues in the validation of psychoanalytic interpretations. The analyses of validity remain scattered and unrelated to each other, there exists no comprehensive analysis and reflection of the specific nature of validity in psychoanalysis at a conceptual level corresponding to the forms of validation developed for psychological tests and experiments.

4. The historical dimension. With the exception of the influence of childhood experiences upon adult behavior, the historical dimension of human existence has received little attention in psychological research. Longitudinal studies and lifespan developmental psychology have focused on the temporal unfolding of life histories, but rarely within a broad meaningful perspective as in psychoanalysis. The recent interest in psychobiographical studies involves a wide interpretative approach to life histories. Psychoanalysis remains a unique context for the formalization and the testing of interpretations about the meaning of human actions, with its extraordinary background knowledge of a life history and its continued temporal unfolding.

5. The human relationship. While the influence of the therapist's person was early acknowledged and taken into account in the psychoanalytic tradition as a "counter-transference," the personal influence of the experimenter on his subject's behavior has only recently come to attention in the research on "experimenter bias," "Rosenthal-effect," etc.

The emphasis on, and the use of, the personal involvement of researcher and subject is not limited to therapy. In the participant observation of sociology and ethnomethodology, the researcher's participation in the social system he is studying is necessary for the obtaining, as well as for the interpretation of, information about the system; and the quality of the human relation will influence the resulting knowledge (e.g. McCall & Simmons, 1969).

6. Pathology as topic of investigation. Pathology has rarely been considered an important topic of general psychological research. The study of the effects of brain damages as an approach to understand the characteristics of normal thought is one exception. In psychology, crises and suffering have seldom been considered sources for a deeper knowledge of human behavior. In dialectics, conflicts and radical changes are the important loci of acquiring knowledge, where new tendencies, superceding the old, are breaking through to realization.

7. The instigation of change. There are several cases, besides psychoanalysis, where the investigation of a phenomenon and the instigation of its change may coincide. Skinner repeatedly emphasizes change of behavior as the means and the goal of his research (1961), and in behavior therapy, the systematic treatment of a case may itself be a research process (e.g., Kazdin, 1981).

Evaluation research (e.g., Patton, 1980) also involves research with a purpose of changing the system evaluated, and in "action research" the purpose of research is to instigate changes in the social system studied in collaboration with the participants of the system to be changed.

A resistance of social systems to insight and change may in some cases of research lead to more important knowledge than the original investigation. Thus in a study of the reliability of grading at university examinations, the statistical results soon became less interesting than the resistance of the university system to this research, which led to an analysis of the power functions of examinations (Kvale, 1972).

Conclusion. The diverse and scattered examples of research practice testify that the seven characteristics of psychoanalytic therapy when regarded separately are not limited to this research situation, but may, to a varying extent, also be found in entirely different research traditions. While neglected in textbooks of psychological research method, the seven characteristics of the psychoanalytic situation are not entirely alien to actual cases of research practice. Not only because of the significant knowledge obtained by the psychoanalytic method, but also due to the more general relevance of some of its specific characteristics, does the general neglect or dismissal of psychoanalytic therapy as research deserve questioning.

It appears worthwhile to investigate more systematically the research potential of the specific characteristics of the psychoanalytic situation for qualitative research in general. Such a venture involves a series of problems, however. The therapeutic method has here been fragmented into seven characteristics, which in actual practice form an indivisable unity. The intrinsic relation of psychoanalytic therapy and theory has been disregarded, and the method has been divorced from its guiding interest and content, the personality change of patients in crisis.

The therapeutic method requires an extraordinary expertise, obtainable only through years of theoretical and practical training, including a self-analysis. Not only the depth interpretation of unconscious meanings, nor the handling of the complex "transference" and "countertransference" of the therapeutic situation, but even making the relevant psychoanalytic observations requires a high level of expertise. While some of the characteristics of psychoanalysis that have been outlined are, as general approaches, common within qualitative research — such as the open mode of observation and the interpretation of meaning (e.g., Filstead, 1970; Giorgi, 1975; Marton, 1981; Mayring, 1983) — the psychoanalytic emphasis upon life history, crises, and an intensive personal relationship with the aim of personality change, has largely been alien to qualitative research. To the extent that these last characteristics contribute to the creativity, significance and deep knowledge of personality in psychoanalysis, the possibility exists that other qualitative research efforts may mainly contribute to relatively surface knowledge of human existence. It may be that the psychoanalytical aim of personality change has counteracted the danger of getting caught in the description of the subtleties of consciousness and a cult of private experience.

With respect to qualitative research, psychoanalysis is less a model to be imitated than a challenge. The question arises whether the relative neglect of the life history and crises, of personal interaction and change is due to the ethical issues involved in approaching these issues for research purposes only, or whether it is due to scientific status insecurity. It is thoughtprovoking that the qualitative research method which has given the most significant contributions to psychological knowledge has not had the acquisition of knowledge as a primary purpose, but aimed at relieving its subjects from their suffering.

References

Adorno, T.W. *Gesammelte Schriften, 8.* Frankfurt: Suhrkamp, 1972.
_____. Frenkel-Brunswik, E., Levinson, D.J. & Sanford, R.N. *The authoritarian personality.* New York: Harper, 1969.
Boss, M. *Psychoanalysis and Daseinanalysis.* New York: Basic Books, 1963.

Brandt, L.W. The physics of the physicist and the physics of the psychologist, *International Journal of Psychology*, 1973, *8*, 61–72.

Christiansen, B. The scientific status of psychoanalytical clinical evidence, *Inquiry*, 1964, *7*, 47–79.

Dreier, O. & Kvale, S. Dialectical and hermeneutical psychology. Reviews of Scandinavian psychology, *Scandinavian Journal of Psychology*, 1984, *25*, 5–29.

Filstead, W.H. (Ed.). *Qualitative methodology*. Chicago: Markham, 1970.

Fisher, S. & Greenberg, R.P. *The scientific credibility of Freud's theories and therapy*. New York: Basic Books, 1977.

Freud, S. *Therapy and technique*. New York: Collier, 1963.

————. New introductory lectures. In: *Standard Edition of the complete psychological works of Sigmund Freud*, *22*, London: Hogarth, 1967.

Fromm, E., Horkheimer, M., Mayer, E. & Marcuse, H. *Autorität und Familie*. Paris: Alcan, 1936.

Giorgi, A. *Psychology as a human science*. New York: Harper & Row, 1970.

————. An application of phenomenological method in psychology. In: A. Giorgi, C. Fischer & E. Murray (Eds), *Duquesne studies in phenomenological psychology*, *II*. Pittsburgh: Duquesne University, 1975, 82–103.

Habermas, J. *Knowledge and human interests*. Boston: Beacon, 1971.

Hannush, M.J. Adorno and Sartre: a convergence of two methodological approaches, *Journal of Phenomenological Psychology*, 1973, *3*, 297–313.

Holzkamp, K. Die Bedeutung der Freudschen Psychoanalyse für die marxistisch fundierte Psychologie, *Forum Kritische Psychologie*, 1984, *13*, 15–40.

Kazdin, A.E. Drawing valid inferences from case studies. *Journal of Counseling and Clinical Psychology*. 1981, *49*, 183–192.

Klein, G.S. Two theories or one? *Bulletin of the Menninger Clinic*, 1973a, *37*, 102–132.

————. Is psychoanalysis relevant? In: B.B. Rubinstein (Ed.), *Psychoanalysis and Contemporary Science, 1*. New York: Macmillan, 1973b, p. 3–21.

Koch, S. Epilogue. In Koch, S. (Ed.), *Psychology: A Study of a Science*, *III*. New York: McGraw-Hill, 1959, 729–802.

Kuhn, T.S. *The structure of scientific revolutions*. Chicago: Chicago University Press, 1967.

Kvale, S. *Prüfung and Herrschaft — Hochschulprüfungen zwischen Ritual und Rationalisierung*. Weinheim: Beltz, 1972 (English summary: Kvale, S. Examinations: From ritual through bureaucracy to technology, *Social Praxis*, 1977, *3*, 187–208).

————. Meanings as data and human technology *Scandinavian Journal of Psychology*, 1976, *17*, 171–189.

————.The quantification of knowledge in education — On resistance towards qualitative evaluation and research. In B. Bain (Ed.), *The Sociogenesis of Language and Human Conduct*. New York: Plenum, 1983a, 422–447.

————. The qualitative research interview — a phenomenological and hermeneutical mode of understanding, *Journal of Phenomenological Psychology*, 1983b, *14*, 171–196.

Lasch, C. *The culture of narcissism*. New York: Warner, 1979.

Marton, F. Phenomenography — describing conceptions of the world around us. *Instructional Science*, 1981, *10*, 177–200.

McCall, G. & Simmons, J.L. (Eds.), *Issues in participant observation*. London: Addison-Wesley, 1969.

Mayring, P. *Qualitative Inhaltsanalyse*. Weinheim: Beltz, 1983.

Patton, M.C. *Qualitative evaluation methods*. London: Sage, 1980.

Piaget, J. La pensée symbolique et la pensée de l'enfant, *Archives de Psychologie*, 1923, *18*, 273–304.

————. *The language and thought of the child*. London: Routledge and Kegan Paul, 1959.

Rapaport, D. The structure of psychoanalytic theory: A systematizing attempt. In: S. Koch (Ed.), *Psychology: A study of a science, III*. New York: McGraw-Hill, 1959, 55–183.

Ricoeur, P. *Freud and philosophy — An essay on interpretation*. New Haven: Yale University Press, 1970.

————. P. The model of the text: Meaningful action considered as a text, *Social Research*, 1971, *38*, 529–562.

Runyan, W.M. Why did van Gogh cut off his ear? The problem of alternative explanations in psychobiography, *Journal of Personality and Social Psychology, 1981, 40*, 1070–1077.

Sanford, N. *Some new perspectives on authoritarianism in personality*. Portland:Western Psychological Association. Presidental Address, 1972.

Sartre, J.-P. *Anti-Semite and Jew*. New York: Schocken, 1965.

————. *The problem of method*. London: Methuen, 1963.

Skinner, B.F. A case history in scientific method (a) & A critique of psychoanalytic concepts and theories (b). In B.F. Skinner, *Cumulative record*. New York: Methuen, 1961, 76–99 & 185–193.

Thomä, H. & Kächele, U. Wissenschaftstheoretische und methodologische Probleme der klinisch-psychoanalytischen Forschung I & II, *Psyche, 1973, 27*, 205–236 & 309–355.

Wallerstein, R.S. & Sampson, H. Issues in research in the psychoanalytic process, *International Journal of Psycho-Analysis*, 1971, *52*, 11–50.

Ziehe, T. *Pubertät und Narzissmus*. Frankfurt: Europäische Verlagsanstalt, 1975.

Existential-Phenomenological Psychotherapy and Phenomenological Research in Psychology

8

Dreyer Kruger

What is Phenomenological Psychotherapy?

Although the ground work of philosophical existentialism was laid by Søren Kierkegaard in the first half of the 19th century, he was not the only existentialist. Others such as Nietzsche and Dostoyevsky may equally lay claim to that title. None the less, his views seem to have influenced clinical psychology more widely than any of the others. On the other hand, Edmund Husserl introduced phenomenological philosophy in 1900. Perhaps it is no accident that Husserl's important work *Logische Untersuchungen* and Freud's *Traumdeutung* both appeared in 1900. For Husserl, consciousness is intentionality and is of central concern for his philosophy. For Freud, consciousness is a peripheral matter and the true reality, the true mainsprings of human action are to be found in the unconscious.

Husserl, especially in the middle period of the *Ideas*, concentrated on consciousness and "bracketed" the world. For a follower of Husserl, psychology will have to be defined as a science of consciousness. On the other hand, the word consciousness hardly occurs in the epoch-making publication of Martin Heidegger's *Sein und Zeit* which integrated existentialism with Husserl's phenomenology; nor does he take it up in his later work. Both Heidegger and another prominent member of the movement, Maurice Merleau-Ponty move away from consciousness to discourse. Furthermore, in Heidegger's work, Husserl's intentionality becomes *care* - the essentiality of Dasein.

As early as 1923, Binswanger had already presented the new perspectives opened up by the work of Husserl for psychiatry. After 1927, he was again the first to discuss the implications of Heidegger's new breakthrough for psychology and psychiatry.

Especially after the second world war in Europe, existential-phenomenology became a powerful movement in both psychology and psychiatry. However, there have been some serious setbacks, for instance, the decline of the Utrecht school. Certainly existential-phenomenology is no longer in the center of the stage in Europe and in psychology, the European has become fascinated with imports from the USA such as behaviorism, psychometric studies, family therapy, community psychology and psychiatry, group therapy, etc. Lacan's *retour à Freud* has exerted a certain influence and fascination.

Existential-phenomenological psychotherapy can, therefore, in no way be said to be a dominant therapy just as existential-phenomenological psychology has not supplanted the major approaches such as psychoanalysis, behaviorism and humanism.

The existential-phenomenological approach to psychotherapy is not simply another way of "doing" psychotherapy. It must question psychotherapy as such — it must ask what it is and what its main concerns and goals are. Our very first concern must be the word "psychotherapy" itself. Is a "therapy" of the "psyche" possible at all? The answer to this at least can be unequivocal. There definitely cannot be anything known as psychotherapy because neither phenomenology nor other major approaches take the concept of "psyche" in its traditional sense seriously. Psychology has not been able to delineate the psyche as a scientifically identifiable entity and certainly has tried to get away from the implied dualism between body and mind as best it can. However, what originally was *soul*, eventually became *mind* in the English language; but more generally the *psyche* in other languages, and now seems to have melted into the brain in "standard" psychologies. That the problem of dualism is not thereby overcome, is a matter which need not be argued here. Condrau (1973, p. 11) points out that in the expression "psychotherapy" a really true interhuman relationship cannot be constituted. Instead of the incarnated presence of the "sick" person, we simply have a scientific abstraction, namely the psyche; while the therapist is subsumed behind his interhuman function, namely, therapy. In other words, psychotherapy literally taken, is a service to a cause (*Dienst an einer Sache*). In medical psychiatric use, psyche simply means not the fellow human being, but a besouled object, or psychic organism, some sort of psychic functional structure. On the other hand, the word "Therapeia" means waiting on, nursing, caring, treatment, which are services which can also be administered to an animal or even a plant. In this way, therapy is supposed to be a therapy of the mind or psyche in which both terms are nothing else but abstract objectified representations for the concrete behavior of human beings.

The essence of psychotherapy is the *word* (Condrau, 1973). For phenomenological-existential psychotherapy, psychotherapy is therefore essentially a language event and psychotherapy happens within the context of language, of speaking, listening and remaining silent. Language only occurs in the context of the co-human and therefore essentially belongs to being human; language co-constitutes being human. Being-together-with-others with the shared things of the world, language and understanding, and the understanding of self and other are the existential foundations of every psychotherapy. In speaking, communication, revelation and the finding of truth come to pass. In language, we find the openness of Dasein, and in language we can actualize our humanness. Without language, it would be impossible for us to understand the meaning of anything that we encounter. It is only through language that human beings are human. By speaking, we are able to let past and future be present; we are able to open up meaning qualities and motivational coherences because the human being is always addressed by what was and by what is and will be. In language, the space for encounter is opened up. Before Freud, the therapeutic words were to be found in the speaking of the physician. After Freud, the word is with the client. The challenge for the client is to find the words for what he is in this world, what he has been and will be. The Freudian transference can, from this perspective, be seen as a challenge to the patient to share his biography with the therapist, to abandon his sole proprietory rights on it for a time and to leave it partially in the hands of the therapist in order to get it back in a better condition. For the neurotic in general, the question is "do you dare to utter the words which you have? Do you dare to say who you really are?"

For Boss (1957; 1975) and Condrau (1973) then, psychotherapy is an inappropriate word. For them what happens between a person called 'therapist' and another person called 'patient' or 'client' in the project called 'psychotherapy' is really the analysis of Dasein. Dasein means "that being who in his own being is concerned with being" (Heidegger, 1972, p. 7). Furthermore, this being also has a pre-scientific understanding of being. It is, as de Boer says (1980), that the human being is a self-understanding being and this should be taken fully into account in all the sciences of man.

This conception of Daseinsanalysis is an extension into psychiatry and psychology of the basic ontological conceptions first explicated by Heidegger. The philosophy of revealing discourse in Heidegger and Merleau-Ponty is important, because in psychotherapy, more than anywhere else, we know that our words can reveal much more than what we are aware of intending. Moreover, the essentiality of care means that what is revealed in psychotherapy, is what matters to one, not simply what one becomes conscious of. The themes of psychotherapy always refer to the main concerns of the client's life.

Is psychotherapy a form of base or persuasive rhetoric (Szasz, 1979) such as we may find in behavior modification? Rhetoric, yes! But hardly persuasive except insofar as the therapist himself takes up an attitude on what the client should be. Admittedly, this is difficult because the therapist can hardly take up a value-free attitude. In existential-phenomenological psychotherapy, the therapist believes that the client should be open to the unfolding of his own possibilities. Insofar as the word is with the client rather than with the therapist, insofar as it is the therapist's task to understand rather than to instruct or to guide, and furthermore, insofar as the therapist does not speak in order to persuade the client but only to help him understand and take up his own self-world-project, the term "base rhetoric" would not seem to apply to the enterprise of psychotherapy. The existential-phenomenological psychotherapist does not start from the proposition that the client's actions are determined; on the contrary, he starts from the proposition that the client is free. It does see psychopathology as a limitation on the client's freedom to actualize his potential and it does make certain assumptions; first of all that man is free, secondly, that being human means being open to the presence of whatever can present itself and thirdly, that the essence of Dasein is care. In other words, the whole therapy rests upon an explicit anthropology in terms of which man is not a thing, mind or spirit, but a dialogue.

Psychotherapy is not a part of the medical profession in its current technological conception. It must, however, always mean some form of healing. It is a *"Heilung durch den Geist"* to use the catchy title of a famous book by Stefan Zweig. However, the word *Geist* should not be taken in any literal sense. Psychotherapy is inevitably a method of healing, where the healing is done within the setting of the freedom of the human being to act as an agent in his own life and to be able to recover his ability to be in charge of his concerns. It would be base rhetoric indeed to argue that the maladies for which people consult psychotherapists are basically brain states requiring treatment in the same sense as somatic states require technological intervention. Psychotherapy only retains its connection with the medical profession insofar as it remains part of the broader enterprise of healing in the sense of making whole.

Ivan Illich (1979) has argued that contemporary medicine has expropriated human health and undermined the human being's ability to take responsibility for his own sicknesses, to doctor himself using folk remedies or simply to wait for nature to take its course. Medard Boss (1975) has pointed out that by accepting physiology and anatomy as the basic sciences for medicine, medicine itself has moved away from its true mission as a healing profession. The ultimate basis for medicine, he argues, is an understanding of man in existential-phenomenological terms. In its concentration on body organs and body parts, medicine has lost sight of the human being as such. Medicine has "forgotten" that when one breaks a leg, one does not have a fracture only, but one's existence is changed in that one cannot walk. A child born without arms is forever precluded from living the very ordinary relationship of being able to body forth his relationship with others by shaking hands.

The existential-phenomenological view of man breaks with the idealistic view of Descartes, according to which man's self is essentially an immaterial entity somehow lodged within the boundaries of the skin. On the other hand, it also breaks with biologistic and materialistic conceptions according to which man is a person in the sense that he is a body having a variety of repertoires of behavior; to use Skinner's famous formulation

(1973) either controlled by schedules of reinforcement (radical behaviorism) or by processes of the central nervous system (neuro-psychological reductionism).

Man is not an encapsulated entity, but exists in the sense that he is always out there in the world. Man is intentional — he never simply thinks, loves or feels joyful. He is always directed towards something. Consciousness is always being conscious of something. Man loves someone or feels joyful about something — be this specific or diffuse.

Being human means always being-with fellow man. Man cannot be seen outside such relatedness. A baby is not first a single being and then enters a relationship with the mother. The baby is gradually constituted as a human being in his relationship with the mother. The 'we' precedes the 'I'. Man is first related to others and only later constitutes himself as an individual with a separate identity.

Man is not a psyche which has a body, neither is he a body of which an epiphenomenon is a psyche. Rather man is lived bodiliness. The bodily sphere of his existence is one way in which he relates to the world.

Man is also his life history and his lived time. Man always lives in the three ecstacies of past, present and future. Time is not a linear continuum but rather a medium in which man lives and which lives in man. Man is always both in front of and behind himself. He is in front of himself in that he lives towards his expectations and anticipations and he is behind himself in that he never fully catches up with these. Man's present is the potentiality and givennesses of the past as he anticipates the unfolding and fulfilment of the future *now*.

Man is the illuminated sphere of being in which the things that are show themselves. He is capable of a standing back and looking at the situation, thus being able to look his existence and his fate in the face.

For phenomenological psychology, the world is not a meaningless system of bare facts or objects such as may be posited on the basis of the natural scientific view. If we refer to things as mere objects, occupying a measurable amount of space, thus composing the world merely in the terms of the Cartesian *extensio* we are impoverishing the rich physiognomy of the world as it is present to us. The world always appears to us as a meaningful structure. It is not mere brute materiality. It always has a face. We live it and are attuned to it in terms of its physiognomy. Emotions are not inner happenings in the psyche accompanied by another set of happenings in the body conceived of as a mechanistic organism. Rather, emotions are the way we live the disruptions of everyday routines. It is the shape the world has when our regular attunement is disrupted.

Whilst it is true to say that disclosure is not achieved by mere appearance, it is also true that we must not look for the essence of the phenomenon behind itself, but rather that we should allow the phenomenon to disclose itself, to speak to us; we should allow the thing its freedom, "let it be"; to understand the phenomenon, we should let it speak to us in all its possible profiles. The thing, the animal, the fellow human being, the world and its horizons always appear to us and show themselves in and as a context of meaning.

Phenomenology and Psychopathology

A reading of Szasz leads us to doubt the relevance of psychopathology for psychotherapy. If psychotherapy is concerned with healing words and with problems in living, then psychopathology, as based on the medical model, is an attempt to conceptualize problems of living as diseases of the "mind."

Anthropological psychiatrists such as Tellenbach, Binswanger, Straus and Rümke have tried to give full existential accounts of the inner meaning of syndromes such as schizophrenia, melancholia, manic depressive psychosis etc.

A somewhat similar procedure is followed by Medard Boss (1975, p. 440-511) who conceptualizes psychopathology in terms of basic anthropological characteristics, derived from Heidegger's ontology, namely, spatiality, temporality, being-with-each-other-in-a-shared-world, bodiliness, attunement or mood, and freedom. In this way, we can classify not only psychopathology, but all human illness.

The classification concerns itself only with conspicuous or pronounced impairment in the actualization of different dispositions of human existence. Obviously, all the essential traits of human Dasein together form a unitary and indivisible structure. It follows that if any of these are disturbed, none of the others are left uninfluenced.

Keen (1978, p. 261-262) has suggested that our ordinary way of describing and understanding neuroses and the other problems that come to the psychotherapist as mere aggravations, or mere quantitative variations of what is to be seen in a normal existence is basically mistaken. What we must look for is the qualitative modifications which take place in Dasein. In reading Binswanger's masterly descriptions of schizophrenic life courses, the qualitative differences from healthy normal existence are striking.

Another procedure is simply to proceed in an empirical phenomenological way using the methods developed at Duquesne University under the leadership of Amedeo Giorgi.

Insightful studies have been made, by W Fischer on anxiety (1982), by Stevick on anger (1971), on fear by Arcaya (1979), on suspicion and delusion by de Koning (1979; 1982), and on guilt by Brooke (1983) etc. A comprehensive study of anxiety and guilt in psychotherapy using philosophical literature, as well as case studies from his own practice, has been made by Gion Condrau (1976). Whether separate phenomenological studies of psychopathological phenomena can be built into a coherent system remains to be seen.

The objection of the phenomenologist agains the psychopathology now available, which is based on organic, behavioral and psychoanalytic models, is that these studies under-emphasize the phenomenon as it is lived and over-emphasize factors such as the genetics of the disorders, the contingencies of reinforcement, etc., without fully understanding what it is that the psychotherapy has to help the client confront. Psychotherapy cannot possibly be an enterprise in which the client is helped by the therapist to dispose of his symptoms in the same way as a doctor, through chemical and other interventions, helps the patient to overcome his physical disorders. If we are successful in our endeavors to build an existential-phenomenology, i.e., a truly human scientific psychology, general psychology, psychopathology and psychotherapy will be much more continuous and integrated with each other than they currently are.

Existential-Phenomenological Psychotherapy — A Brief Summary

In the 20th century, technological thinking has become so pervasive that it almost totally dominates our lives. Heidegger has pointed to the danger that Western man may so betray himself that he may lose the ability to think outside the technological framework at all (Heidegger, 1979, p. 25). Glib talk about mastering and humanizing technology is to reveal how deeply we fail to understand the alienated power of this phenomenon. It may well be that technology is our fate and that we will not be able to master it all. On this, psychotherapists should be quite clear, because, as Van den Berg (1980, p. 49) points out, "in a world of all but omnipotent convergent thinking, phenomenology is cosmotherapy." Psychotherapists must necessarily face the fact that while dominant cultural trends require us to adapt ourselves to a technological world, to be able to think technologically in order to survive at all, the other life of mankind goes on all the same. No person can possibly live entirely convergently and the more he tries, the less he will be at peace with himself. In a world in which a central preoccupation of Western culture is efficiency and leading well adapted, almost anaesthetized lives, psychotherapists are also sorely tempted to look for shortcuts that really work, to develop "psychotechnologies" which are generally applicable and which avoid the slow, often painful, work of psychotherapy. However, psychology is a science of and for man and it must always go "back to the things themselves," prior to the Cartesian split, and the scientific and technological views of life. The practice of psychotherapy may well be an art, as Szasz insists, but psychology should endeavor to be a truly adequate basic science for psychotherapy and other human enterprises. The psychotherapist should have at his disposal adequate descriptions of the phenomena which are central to contemporary existence, should understand how these came into being, why they are characteristic of modern man. He should be able to look critically at the culture in which he lives and to understand how the culture itself alienates man from his body and fellow man. Without such a broad perspective, there is always a possibility that psychotherapy will degenerate into a set of techniques.

A wide variety of views may be considered existential, and people with somewhat different basic assumptions and points of view, have called themselves existentialists. However, the Swiss Daseinsanalytic school (under the leadership of Medard Boss), seems to be a coherent movement with an institute in Zürich (directed by Gion Condrau) as its focus. Americans like Rollo May have contributed much. I. D. Yalom's (1980) highly acclaimed book draws much from Heideggerian concepts in the same way as Medard Boss, but hardly refers to Medard Boss, who enjoyed the close collaboration of Martin Heidegger himself for many years and who wrote a definitive book on the existential foundations of medicine and psychology. Whilst Boss moves from the basic constitutive categories briefly enumerated earlier in this paper, Yalom's existential-psychotherapy takes as its basic themes *death* and *freedom* (also used by Boss), whilst the categories of *isolation* and *meaninglessness* are used by Yalom but not by Boss.

Isolation

Yalom says (ibid., p. 353): "The process of deepest inquiry . . . leads us to recognise that we are finite . . . cannot escape our freedom. *We also learn that the individual is inexorably alone.* (Emphasis mine).

Yalom points to many factors that bring about isolation, e.g. geographical factors, lack of social skill, fear of intimacy, certain personality styles, the break-up of communities, etc. However, in the radical phenomenological view, the individual is always related to others and isolation is always a deprivationary state of this primary relatedness. The "We," as we have seen, precedes the "I." Even the hermit, in isolating himself, is still living a certain relationship with fellowman.

Meaninglessness

The tragic fact that many people find life to be meaningless does not mean that the world is intrinsically meaningless. The idea of the world and the things as being meaningless entities can only have arisen as a result of a long history of Western thought by which all reality was conceived to exist as measurable and calculable in principle. Deriving especially from 19th century physics, the idea is being held that the things of the world are mere objects present in space (as mere extension) and time (as linear continuum), having certain measurable characteristics. In this way, we have become voluntary captives of natural science and its twin brother, technology. Any meaning that things may have, is not intrinsic to them but must have been assigned to them by the subject, which means that our captivity is intimately intertwined with the Cartesian dualistic split.

But this is not the way in which we actually encounter the world. A prison is not a mere collection of stone, steel, walls and doors, watch-towers, open spaces and smaller square ones called cells. The prison speaks to us in its physiognomy; its very facade already has a forbidding character, its guarded steel portals speak to us of its custodial function, its watch-towers of the need for vigilance; it already embodies society's forceful suspension of freedom of movement in respect of those who refuse to live by its norms. A statue is not just a piece of marble hammered into some sort of shape resembling some sort of human being, but the durable embodied presence of the saint, statesman, general or hero in our existence which is always historical.

Things are not meaningful *en soi*, neither are meanings merely conferred on the objects by human beings as embodied subjectivities. Man lives in and as relationship to the world and fellowman, and within this relationship the world, as it is present to us, is always already a meaningful structure.

Meanings, Selfhood and Authenticity

When we were still embedded in tribes and traditional communities the discovery of the structures which specially speak to us as individuals was not necessary, except perhaps for the Shamans, diviners and prophets — later on the philosophers, mystics, poets and reformers. This is because meanings were indisputably given in the cosmology and the tradition. In the 20th century each of us is faced by the challenge of self-discovery. For most of us the problem is solved by adopting current lifestyles, fashions and attitudes. We do as "people do," we believe what other people believe. This is Heidegger's *"das Man."* Mostly, we do not heed the call of conscience, the call from ourselves to take up those challenges of life which are specifically for us; and in this way we fail to arrive at authentic, individual selfhood. Most people never really *dis*cover this failure; they may have twinges about it from time to time, but society offers so much in terms of distractions, occupations, and pastimes, games to play and the production/consumption syndrome that the question is never really faced except when unfavorable developmental and current relational conditions prevent them from being fully absorbed in which case they turn to medical practitioners and other agents of society. Only when the ameliorating assistance rendered by these agents fails to bring relief, do they go to psychotherapists.

The aim then of psychotherapy in the great tradition is to *heal* (that is, to make whole) by helping people to grow towards selfhood. This aim is shared by psychoanalytic, client-centred as well as Daseinsanalytic therapies. It is considerably weaker in therapies like transactional analysis, rational emotive therapies and other strategies to achieve adjustive results. Behavior therapy, if used as a sole approach, opposes the discovery of true selfhood because of its insistence on adaptation and its belief that man is an organism controlled by contingencies of reinforcement which means in the last instance, according to Skinner, the verbal community.

Freedom, Guilt and Anguish

Freedom implies responsibility and guilt. Guilt arises from the very core of being — one always owes something to one's own existence. The call is from ourselves to ourselves. However, the self is not something within us; it is a structure of relations with a cosmic totality which we call the world. One is an authentic self to the extent that this particular set of relationships has been taken into one's own existence as owned. To the extent that one disowns one's unique set of relations, one is guilty in that one has failed to answer the call. If one answers the call there is a growth in authenticity in that one has taken up a set of possibilities as part of one's unique existence. But one does not then become guilt free. One is guilty in that in choosing one alternative, others have been excluded. Man is always in front of himself in that he lives towards the future, and he owes it to himself to take up both future and neglected possibilities. In that we always have to "pay" for possibilities that we have not (yet) taken up, we are also always in debt and thus paradoxically always *behind* ourselves.

Ontological or existential guilt is what one owes oneself and is therefore entirely different from moral or legal guilt. Moralistic guilt or scrupulosity is prominently characteristic of some depressives and obsessives. Selfhood in the above sense is not at all egoistic or egocentric. According to Heidegger the fact that Dasein exists for itself does not mean that it need be solopsistic or egoistic, but it does provide the basis for either egoistic or altruistic behavior or anything in between. It fully accepts the rabbinical saying: "If I am not for myself, who will be for me? If I am for myself alone, who am I?"

Care being the essence of Dasein, authentic selfhood means that man is called upon to care for and tend those relations which specifically speak to him and this means to heed and guide what one encounters to its proper unfolding. By identifying one's existence with these projects, one is doing what one wants to but this will necessarily be a caring for, a tending to, and a letting unfold.

Both guilt and authenticity are central concerns of existential-phenomenological psychotherapy. So is anguish (Angst), which is usually (perhaps less adequately) translated as anxiety. All anxiety ultimately is Dasein confronting non-being. The ultimate source of anxiety is our finitude which means that we have only a limited time to actualize our projects. Thus it is death that constitutes the everpresent background to anxiety, but it is not frequently or necessarily experienced as such. Thus in empirical phenomenological research on the subject, William F. Fischer (1982) found that an anxious situation is constituted by "its power to announce as imminent, a crisis . . . in the individual's family of self-other-world projects and therefore in his unfolding self-understanding." The individual experiences "a burgeoning uncertainty with regard to his feelings of being able, that is, *his lived sense of power* to effectively participate in the activity and to actualize his project is radically undermined" (italics in original). The rest of Fischer's painstaking and penetrating summary should be read but it is clear that anxiety again is a communication from one's own Dasein *to* one's own Dasein. The "object" of anxiety as well as its "subject" is one's own existence, one's family of self-other projects. Thus therapy means helping another to live more authentically, i.e. to find those meaning coherences which specially appeal to him and thus to be able to come to terms with existential guilt and the meaning of life. Living an existence, free of anxiety and guilt, cannot be the aim.

How does the therapy happen? Since Freud, it has been clear that therapy involves self-disclosure to a trusted person, called therapist. Freud called this salient series of encounters "transference" in that the patient relives his basic conflict in reference to the figure of the analyst. Feelings come to light in the relationship because the patient "transfers" feelings held towards parental and other family figures onto the figures of the analyst, and by working through these feelings, the patient can liberate himself from his compulsion to repeat self-defeating patterns of conduct acquired whilst trying to overcome (or cling to) oedipal and pre-oedipal strivings and fixations. "Transference" explains why patients tend to fall in love with their analysts. In the phenomenological view, transference in the strict Freudian conception is an impossibility, a construction used by Freud to overcome Cartesian dualism in which he was trapped much as he was trapped in logical positivism. Feelings are neither material nor immaterial entities of an isolated subject that can be attached first to a mother or father, then detached and "carried over" to another subject, the analyst. Nobody has ever experienced this actually happening. What happens is rather that the patient's reality is so constituted that certain persons are related to as authority figures whether these be bosses, teachers, police officers or analysts. The world of the patient is populated by people towards whom he relates as dependent, but to whom he also feels hostile, insecure, rivalrous and a variety of other possible emotions. The phenomenological therapist does not try to achieve an intense relationship in the sense of transference. He does try to achieve rapport and to make it possible for the client to express himself fully.

The client is never a "patient" in the usual technical-medical sense, who is subject to a process called "therapy" in any other sense than growing towards selfhood; the client is fellowman and the therapist must structure a caring relationship with him. This caring relationship must, however, not be of such a nature that it *takes* care of him, thus relieving him of responsibility, but must rather be a leaping-ahead concern, which enables the client to *take* the responsibility on for himself. This caring relationship is indistinguishable from love of fellowman. The caring relationship hardly differs from Rogers' conditions of unconditional positive regard, acceptance and emphathic understanding. It also includes therapist congruence in the sense that the therapeutic dialogue always also includes a dialogue of the therapist with himself and the client with himself. This dialogue of therapist and client, each with themselves as well as with each other, is perhaps one of the most important aspects of therapy that should be the subject of perceptive research.

After this brief introduction, it should be clear that phenomenological-existential therapy does not necessarily reject the basic insights of Freud, Jung, Rogers and others but that to move towards phenomenological therapy, is to move towards a more comprehensive approach:

a) based on the main approaches of psychoanalysis (mainly Freud and Jung), client-centred psychotherapy and behavior therapy;

b) which recognises the limitations of each of these therapies;
c) starts from a comprehensive view of man;
d) uses a human science approach to do research in psychotherapy and thus
e) strives to overcome the built-in limitations of the current paradigms of psychoanalytic, humanistic and behavior therapies.

I am unable to flesh out this scheme in more detail here except to raise two points briefly, namely:

a) It is important that our psychotherapy be based on a comprehensive view of man. In basic works, such as those of Medard Boss (1975); an exposition of psychological anthropology is derived from Heidegger's ontological categories (existentials) and a study of Heidegger certainly amply rewards the seeker. However, the subject of philosophical anthropology which should be an important source for psychotherapists, starts with Scheler (1928) and other contributors include Plessner (1978); Strasser (1973) and Landmann (1974). The basic stance of being-in-the-world is very wide, but it certainly, if properly understood, overcomes Cartesian dualism.

b) As regards research: few researchers are psychotherapists and hardly any psychotherapists are researchers or even interested in research. It is also regrettable that nearly all research has been done within a logical-positivistic, operationalistic paradigm. In contrast to the highly intuitive insight of the founders of psychotherapy, psychotherapy research tends to involve persistent and excruciating attempts to objectify and quantify experiential and behavioral data in order to isolate variables which supposedly would make up what psychotherapy is.

Psychotherapy and Psychotherapy Research

Much of the current research model is based upon an unquestioning transfer of the contemporary technological medical model to the sphere of psychotherapy. A blatant example of this is the well known research of H. J. Eysenck (1966) who not only failed to ask a single ex-patient for his experience, but unashamedly conceptualized a condition known as neurosis as something that happens to a person or that he "gets," which then has to be "removed" by means of a process called "psychotherapy" after which the "outcome" can be measured by means of some sort of technique analogous to what might conceivably be used in medical practice such as comparing X-ray photographs before and after surgery. Even Rogers (Meador and Rogers, 1973) had to move back to the natural scientific paradigm when doing research. He must have realized a discrepancy here because he said, in reference to a client who refused to take the follow-up tests, that this refusal is "thought provoking," and that "when people accept themselves as persons, they refuse to be regarded as 'objects' no matter how important this is to research. It is a challenging, and in some deep sense a positive thought." Humanistic psychology has not taken up this challenge but psychologists of phenomenological persuasion have.

The reason why we should do psychotherapy research at all should be immediately clear. Whether we are doing Freudian, Jungian or Rogerian client-centered psychotherapy or even behavioral therapy, we are, in a sense, prisoners of the basic insights of the originators. However, none of these paradigms really encompass the whole set of possibilities which constitute human existence.

Therapists, rather than allowing themselves to be influenced by research performed in a distorted operationalist manner, prefer to stay with the paradigm of the founder as modified by later followers and/or by themselves and that fits in with their lifestyles but the result remains that the therapists in each of the main orientations, living their theories, open up differential styles of expressivity for the client in therapy with them. None of these approaches can reveal the total texture of a person's relatedness and possibilities, which is exactly the direction towards which existential-phenomenological psychotherapy should move (Barton, 1974).

One of the most important things that get lost in the standard descriptions and case histories emanating from all schools, is that the vicissitudes of the client are usually given in detail but the client is given no opportunity to explicate his experiences of the therapist and the therapeutic situation. The client expresses himself within the immediacy of the encounter but his reflections on what happened and how he experienced the various themes of psychotherapy are not systematically used to arrive at an understanding of what therapy is. Moreover, it is rather rare for the therapist to explicate his experience apart from what he actually conveyed to the client. While we mostly only have the reports of therapists on how therapy developed, it is important and scientifically more acceptable from a human scientific point of view, if investigations are undertaken by a third party who uses therapists and clients as subjects, or rather as co-researchers. It is, therefore, suggested that an appropriate research method is also to be found in the existential-phenomenological model.

An extensive critique of nomothetic psychometric research has been set out elsewhere (Kruger, 1983). Here my conclusions can partly be summarized by stating that the fatal error of researchers has been that truth can only be disclosed by quantitative operations but in psychotherapy, numbers in themselves have no disclosive power whatsoever. Human life allows itself to be disclosed through explicating qualities, and apart from convergent language, we are always also using qualitative, allusive, metaphorical speech, because life itself is divergent. Psychotherapy cannot be elucidated by the quantitative, correlational approaches of standard psychological research approaches.

The truth requires a patient communion with the phenomenon to let all its dimensions emerge. This is essentially the letting be-ness of the phenomenon (Seinlassen von Seiendem), granting the phenomenon the freedom of letting it speak to the observer as that which it is (Heidegger, 1949, p. 16). Disclosure means that we must be participatively present to the phenomenon in such a way that it can reveal its full contours.

The basic problem that has to be faced in psychotherapy research is how a therapist and client are present to each other. Van den Berg (1980, p. 49) says that "phenomenology is psychotherapy ." Perhaps this can be phrased more precisely that psychotherapy is a phenomenology of *presence*.

The therapist's endeavor is to be present to the client's concerns even when the client is unable to articulate these; the client's endeavor is to move out of his encrustations by having the courage to be present, as ongoing biography, to the therapist. In phenomenological research the communion with the phenomenon is a dialectic of closeness and distance. One must get close enough to the phenomenon to let its dimensions emerge, but one also has to acquire sufficient distance to be able to share one's articulation imaginatively with someone else and compel his agreement. The truth requires a third as witness, otherwise the danger of solopsism rears its head. It is, therefore, imperative that research should not be the task of the therapist who is involved in conducting a specific psychotherapy but that it should be done by a third person who is capable of establishing rapport with both the therapist and the client, involving them as subjects and co-researchers in the research enterprise.

NATURAL SCIENTIFIC -vs- HUMAN SCIENTIFIC RESEARCH APPROACHES

Giorgi (1971a, p. 7) has summarized the natural scientific approach to research. It is empirical, which means that the point of departure for the study of behavior is through *controlled* observation; the variables to be manipulated must be perceived by the senses. Secondly, it is *positivistic* — speculative content must be dismissed or translated into known empirical and mechanical laws. Thirdly it is *reductionistic* in that the phenomenon is made equal to its operational definition.

It is also *quantitative* and *deterministic*. It must be *precise*, and the aim of the procedure is to uncover laws which will enable us to *predict* behavior. Furthermore, it is *analytic* — the phenomenon has to be broken down into its essential elements. Experiments are to be *repeatable* and the observer must be *independent* of the phenomenon under investigation. Giorgi furthermore points out (p. 8) that experimental psychology can be characterized as an approach, a method and a content but of these three, the method is by far the most important. Historically, since the 19th century, the method has preceded the content and assumed a privileged position.

On the other hand, the phenomenological approach to research is characterized by an attitude of openness for whatever is significant for the proper understanding of the phenomenon. The method uses processes of intuition, reflection and description. "The content of phenomenology is comprised of the data of experience, its meaning for the subject and most particularly, the essence of phenomena" (ibid, p. 10).

In a second contribution (Giorgi 1971b, p. 17) it is pointed out that all research need not necessarily be of an experimental nature. Secondly, while natural scientific research concentrates on quantities, the phenomenological approach is directed towards the quality of the experience.

Measurement has its place in psychological research, but that is only after the meaning and quality of the experiaction is known. Furthermore, natural scientific research uses analysis whilst phenomenological research uses explication. We encounter the subject in phenomenological research as intentional and do not try to see his reactions as determined by prior causes or contingencies of reinforcement. We do not consider that, to arrive at intersubjective knowledge, it is necessary for psychological research to use replicable situations. Instead, we can try and point out what essential themes emerge in the study of psychological phenomena. Last, but perhaps most important of all, there is no way in which an observer can be independent of that which he observes. All psychological observation is, as Sullivan pointed out many years ago, participant observation.

Psychological research in the natural scientific, measurement oriented model, sometimes gives results which are rather piquant. Thus Lowe (1964, p. 554) found a higher correlation between a scale purporting to measure anxiety and one purporting to measure guilt than between different anxiety scales! He concludes that "self report measures of anxiety and guilt comprise the same psychological entity whatever that construct should be called." Since guilt and anxiety can be clearly distinguished experientially (Fischer 1982; Brooke 1983), the finding of Lowe hardly takes one any closer to finding out what guilt or anxiety are. The ironic part is that Lowe himself seems to admit that he does not know what he is talking about.

If we now look at the characteristics of phenomenological as opposed to natural scientific research in psychology, we will note a certain number of parallels with the process of psychotherapy itself. In the first place, the process of psychotherapy is not experimentation, but certainly it shows clear parallels with research in the wider sense. Giorgi quotes as an example of non-experimental research in psychology Straus's (1962) paper on memory. This paper starts with a historical introduction to the problem of memory and shows how the engram of trace theory came to be established. He then has a look at the phenomenon of trace and explicates this. When he compares this to certain undisputed facts of memory, he is able to demonstrate convincingly that the phenomenon of memory cannot be properly understood as a trace. *Similarly, every psychotherapy is, in a sense, an unsystematic method of research.* It is exactly by looking at the phenomena presented by the client and by tracing these historically that we come to understand the client.

In the next section, Giorgi opposes quantity -vs- quality. Again, as has been pointed out, the pioneers of psychotherapy did not in the first place look for quantity but for quality. Freud, in his metapsychology, did try to turn his theory into a natural scientific one, and did specify a quantifiable proposition, namely, the libido. However, neither he nor any of his followers have ever made a serious attempt to measure the libido, and as a construct of psychology it really only has hypothetical status.

Essentially the same argument goes for measurement -vs-meaning. The psychotherapeutic approaches of Freud, Jung and Rogers to name but a few, all center around the meaning of symptoms and how these are comprehensible in terms of life history and current goals.

Although psychoanalysis is a form of psychotherapy, it is not analytic in the natural scientific meaning of the term. The same is true for Daseinsanalysis. That we have intentional subjects in phenomenological-psychological research rather than determined reactions is also consonant with all forms of dialogue psychotherapy. It is true that the client comes to the therapist with presenting symptoms which he in no way overtly intends. However, the whole aim of the psychotherapeutic enterprise is to make the client take responsibility for his symptoms, i.e. to see how these symptoms reflect his hidden intentions. The next point, namely, identical repetition -vs- essential theme is also very clearly analogous to psychotherapy. The analyst cannot possibly require a dream to be repeated in order to be able to say that such and such is probably the meaning. However, Jung (e.g., 1974, p. 47-93), especially has used series of dreams in order to elucidate essential themes which for him are the truth.

As regards independent -vs- participant observation, it has been pointed out that psychotherapy is essentially a caring relationship between therapist and client. The understanding that is aimed at in psychotherapy is not achieved by the therapist isolating himself from the client, but rather by an openness to the client's world which he comes to share. Therapy can only really happen once the client and therapist stand out together towards the things of the client's world and thus achieve a shared understanding of these phenomena.

The actual procedures for doing phenomenological research have been set out, e.g., by Giorgi (1971; 1975) W. Fischer (1982) and C. Fischer (1979). As Giorgi points out, the main procedure is to get an effective sense of the whole experience as described, secondly to extract the main themes by first breaking up the material into natural meaning units, thirdly to evaluate each main theme in terms of the total Gestalt, and fourthly, to arrive at a situated, and thereafter an essential structure of the experience. For instance, in regard to the problem of learning, Giorgi states (1975, p. 75) that the research should reflect on the given constituents, still expressed essentially in the concrete language of the subject, and transform the meaning of each unit from the everyday naive language of the subject into the language of psychological science insofar as is revelatory of the phenomenon of learning. The researcher then has to synthesize and integrate insights achieved into a consistent description of the structure of the phenomenon. The procedure raises the problem of interpretation or hermeneutics.

The Problem of Interpretation in Human Scientific Research

What I would like to clarify further is the hermeneutic step. In turning the everyday naive description into psychological language, a hermeneutic step is taken. Perhaps it would be more accurate to say that the problem of interpretation is present in every research step. However, the human being is a self-interpreting being and in our dialogues with ourselves and others, we are always reflecting and interpreting, be it in a pre-articulate manner. In grappling with experiential protocols, the psychologist develops this ability without explicitly thematizing it. Peter Titelman (1975) has discussed Ricoeur's conception of hermeneutics and states that "for a phenomenological psychology that is informed by hermeneutical thinking, reflection and interpretation, in dialogue with description, are paradigmatic modes for comprehending the experience of behavior of the investigator and the investigated" (1975, p. 183). He tries to show that the data of phenomenological psychology have a hermeneutical character because they display four traits that constitute, for Ricoeur, a text in need of interpretation. These four traits are the fixation of meaning, the dissociation of the meaning from the mental intention of the author, the display of non-ostensive references and the universal range of its addresses. For me the second point, namely, the dissociation of the meaning from the mental intention of the author, is specially salient because in psychotherapy, more than anywhere else, we meet the problem that the client's language (including gestures and other forms of body language) disclose more than they are intended to convey. The same would hold for many of our research protocols. It is, therefore, important that phenomenological psychology considers the problem of the logic of interpretation. For this purpose I want to have a look at the conceptions of Jürgen Habermas concerning interpretations in Freud's psychoanalysis and to dialogue this with the phenomenological approach.

For Habermas (1972) hermeneutics is the linguistic analysis of a text. He points out that this analysis suffices in historiography and biography in being considered sufficient to correct mankind's faulty remembrance of its history. However, in the problems faced by psychoanalysis, the text itself is opaque to its author (p. 218-219). Neurosis distorts symbolic structures in the dimensions of linguistic expression (e.g. obsession), the way the person acts (compulsion), and bodily experiential expressions.

For Habermas, neurotic symptoms can be seen as the scars of a corrupt text that confronts the author of the text as incomprehensible. The non-pathological model of such a text is a dream. The author of a dream after awakening, no longer understands his creation.

However, this way of looking at the dream has been opposed both by Jung and the Daseinsanalytic school. Accepting the strict Freudian view means that Freud's causal thinking embodied in his looking 'behind' the phenomenon for the meaning thereof is not overcome. Instead of the "depth" hermeneutics proposed here, we may have recourse to metaphorical understanding. (Compare the example of the prison).

Thus Binswanger (van den Berg, 1979, p. 181) gives the example of a newly married young woman who, in the first night after her marriage dreams that she is flying over a beautiful spring landscape. Why asks Binswanger, should we look for anything behind the dream? The fact that this woman is dreaming of flying over a landscape indicates that that is the way her life is at the moment. No matter what the actual weather is, the landscape in which she is living at that moment is a spring landscape. The verticality of her life is clearly expressed in an ecstatic form. The dream is therefore a metaphor of how her life is at that moment.

It is therefore, not necessary that we should presuppose that what the dream is, is prefigured by a thought or rather, according to Freud's theory, a wish embodied as a thought. Perhaps a dream embodies not what we think or wish, but rather what we "live." We do not necessarily live what we think and, our self-reflections may be mistaken in that we do not live the meanings that we think we live, but rather live a text or script that we do not make explicit, that we hide from ourselves and others. Habermas (p. 220) continues that the technique of dream interpretation goes beyond ordinary hermeneutics insofar as it must grasp not only the meaning of a distorted text, but the meaning of the text distortion itself — it must reconstruct the dream work.

(However, I must comment that the reconstruction of the dream work leading to the latent dream is a step which cannot be justified either in positivistic or in phenomenological-experiential terms. It remains a purely hypothetical procedure.)

The model of hermeneutics therefore, as taken over from the cultural sciences, does not hold for the work of psychoanalytic interpretation. The patient's ability to maintain mutual understanding with his partners is not restricted directly but only indirectly through the repercussions of the symptom. Thus psychoanalytic hermeneutics unlike the cultural sciences aims not at the understanding of symbolic structures in general. Rather the act of understanding to which it leads is self-reflection. Psychoanalysis is therefore essentially a movement of self-reflection.

Obviously one must agree with Habermas that psychoanalysis in particular, and psychotherapy in general, takes place within a self-reflective framework. So does phenomenological research. Not only must the subject reflect on his experience in order to describe it but, if the research asks for clarification, there is a coreflective movement similar to that of psychotherapy.

Habermas points out (p. 247) that through Freud's insistence that psychoanalysis may eventually dissolve into biochemistry, a technological understanding of analysis accords only with a theory that has cut itself off from the categorial framework of self-reflection and replaces the structural model suitable for self-formative processes with an energy distribution model. (This is what Szasz would call base rhetoric.)

Obviously, this is because Freud based his metapsychological thinking on an uncritical transference of the *homo natura* model from the Helmholtz School of Medicine (of which his teacher, E. Brücke, was a member), to psychology. The natural scientific procedure of looking for models is not suitable for phenomenology. Instead of models, psychotherapy and phenomenological research praxis should be prefigured by an explicit anthropology.

In a chapter called "The Scientistic Self-misunderstanding of Psychoanalysis" Habermas points out that Freud's metapsychology does not at all explain his therapeutic work. Freud himself, probably realized this, because he said that his metapsychology was dispensable unlike the psychoanalytic therapeutic method which he regarded as the cornerstone of his work. The reason why Freud moved from the hypnosis and spontaneous catharsis developed by Breuer, is that the patient's remembering, in order to be therapeutically successful, must lead to the conscious appropriation of a suppressed fragment of life history.

Habermas refers to Freud's metapsychology as a scientistic self-misunderstanding. Freud's metapsychological categories and connections were not only discovered under determinant conditions of specifically sheltered communication, but they cannot even be explicated independently of this context. The conditions of this communication are the conditions of the possibility of analytic knowledge for both partners. But surely this raises the difficulty that understanding cannot take place outside the relationship between therapist and client.

The question then is, can we do phenomenological research outside a relationship of trust structured with our research subjects, and the answer to this must obviously be no. The further question of whether we can generalize outside this relationship will be dealt with shortly.

Although Freud regarded psychoanalysis as an empirical science in the ordinary positivistic sense of the term, he regarded the clinical basis of experience as a sufficient substitute for experimental verification. Freudian hermeneutics is metahermeneutics (p. 54) which explicates the conditions of the possibility of psychological knowledge. Metapsychology unfolds the logic of interpretation in the analytic situation of dialogue.

Habermas further states that split-off symbols and defended against motives unfold their force over the heads of subjects, compelling substitute gratification and symbolization. For him, the unconscious thereby acquires a driving instinctual character of something that uncontrollably compels consciousness from outside itself.

According to this conception, the unconscious operates as second nature acting as unconscious *causes* to conscious effects. The unfreedom of neurosis contitutes the subject as determined — allowing for at least a limited causality. Yet, because the unconscious has already been recognized (inter alia, by Habermas himself) as self-deception, this is not acceptable. A phenomenological view would rather conceptualize the power of non-recognized motives as a failure to allow certain features of the client's world to come into his openness; as a refusal to accept the new unfolding world relational possibilities that come to pass within the therapeutic dialogue. Psychotherapy helps the client to liberate himself from being a prisoner of his biography, helps him to let the past be the past.

As regards the way in which symptoms become understandable and the client shows insight, Habermas states (p. 256) that linguistic analysis takes the symptoms and deciphers unconscious motives present in them just as a meaning suppressed by censorship can be reconstructed from corrupt passages and gaps in the text.

He further accepts Freud's theory to the extent that he states that the symptomatic concealment of meaning which is not understood by the subject or others can only become understandable at the level of an intersubjectivity between the subject as ego and the subject as id (p. 257). To this I must comment that all communications take place as a relationship between self and other. Hiding from others means also hiding from oneself - concealing one's true identity from others *and* self. Shorn of its metapsychological self-misunderstanding, psychoanalysis remains basically an interpersonal theory as it nascently was initially when neurosis was thought to result from repressed memories of seductive traumas. Having had to give up this theory, Freud was forced to concentrate on the unconscious and the conscious, the ego and the id as independent entities within the subject, i.e., to set up the interpersonal dialogue within the confines of an undefinable entity called the psyche.

Habermas further points out (p. 261) that the accuracy of interpretative statements cannot depend on controlled observation and subsequent communication among investigators but rather on the accomplishment of self-reflection and subsequent communication between the investigator and his "object." Whether phenomenological empirical research should use this idea has not been finalized yet. Some investigators in fact, do invite the comments of their subjects on the accuracy of the situated structure, or even regard the whole process of explication as a venture which should be jointly undertaken with the subjects.

However, this does raise the problems of whether it would be valid for phenomenological research to dissociate meaning from the intention of the subject without finding out if the subject himself is able to appropriate such a meaning as being inherent in his existence without him having been previously able to articulate it as such. This question is prior to and different from the question of intersubjective validity as formulated for Giorgi (1975), for whom the key criteria for qualitative research is "whether a reader, adopting the same viewpoint as articulated by the researcher, can also see what the researcher saw, whether or not he agrees with it" (p. 96).

Most phenomenological researchers probably *assume* that subjects would appreciate the meanings disclosed by research if given an opportunity to do so. Fischer and Wertz (1975, p. 145) indicate that in some studies researchers go back to the subjects at various stages of analysis but it is not always feasible to do so. If subjects nearly always agree with the meaning structure uncovered by the researcher, it means that this step will nearly always be superfluous. If they do disagree will the researcher then have to check out a new modified description with the subject? Will we perhaps end up by becoming solopsistic in concluding that no general description can ever fully express the experience of a specific individual? Will many of our subjects perhaps be unable to grasp that even though a specific description comprises the structure of his experience, it need not reflect his specific experience as such? I think this question will have to be confronted more systematically than I am able to do at the moment.

Habermas further states (p. 263) that every history is unique. A general interpretation must break this spell — without departing from the level of narrative representation. However, psychoanalysis picks up common themes in order to generate a systematically generalized history, which provides a scheme for many histories with foreseeable alternative courses.

Perhaps one way in which this problem can be tackled is to include the subject more systematically in the later steps of research, i.e. to make the research more explicitedly dialogal. For instance, if body language is prominently a part of disclosure of meaning, researcher and subject should look at a video tape together so that the explication can be based again on the two together standing out towards a common shared reality. This means, the subject is co-opted as co-researcher in a further step. He is asked to stand back and look at himself as a second person together with the researcher. In psychotherapy, the client provides a dream or some other material which is looked at by both therapist and client. Such a text provides a document and thus a way in which the client can look at his production as that of an intimate, intertwined other which he can share as a common reality with the therapist. Similarly, the subject as co-researcher can share research steps with the researcher up to the situated structure level, after which the researcher will be on his own. The subject can confirm or deny that a description embodies his experience but neither he nor the researcher can certify that his experience has been exhaustively revealed. Perhaps we should remember that our interpretation is really a hermeneutic circle and that there is no definite rule that can be laid down as to when full understanding is achieved. It means that the researcher himself will have to feel that he himself cannot take the understanding further. Furthermore, the researcher cannot, like the psychotherapist, probe for "hidden agendas," because he is interested in the *phenomenon* as experienced by individuals rather than in the individual as ongoing biography experiencing a particular phenomenon.

Valuable as Habermas's contribution is, it seems to me that he shows an over-fascination with Freud's dynamic unconscious as a causal construct. I have already shown how it is unnecessary for one to interpret the dream on the basis of uncovering latent thoughts and wishes. I should add here that in the dialectics of human freedom, the negative pole is not "unconscious causal determination" but rather being *habituated* to living a sedimented life pattern, parts of which the person wants to change without being able to see how this is embedded in a larger structure. The importance of metaphor has been highlighted by both Murray (1975) and Romanyshyn (1982). The metaphorical texture of psychological life (Romanyshyn 1982, p. 145; van den Berg 1956,

p. 223–229) can be illustrated by the example of Jean Cocteau, the French playwright who "discovered" his memory in a wall. Certainly, Cocteau's memory is not to be found in the wall looked at as a purely physical structure. But neither is Cocteau's memory to be found in the brain as a purely physical structure. The memory can only be understood metaphorically as a way in which the wall establishes the memory in the present. If we just look at facts in the natural scientific sense, then we will keep on looking for the memory in the brain where we will not find it. At the same time, we will lose the world as a meaningful structure, the world which invites our behavior. It means that the phenomenologist cannot remain fixated to literal vision, neither must he fall into an idealization. Fidelity to psychological experience, says Romanyshyn, must lead us beyond the alternatives of fact and idea, thing and thought, empirical and mental reality towards a metaphorical reality.

Language is our first and last method and framework for understanding; however, we must not allow our understanding to degenerate to the level of language games. In language the thing itself is called into presence (Heidegger) and will have to continue to seek for ways and means of best languaging our meanings in an intersubjectively shareable form. One of the ways of discovering this could very well be by using metaphors more readily.

References

Arcaya, J. A. Phenomenology of fear, *Journ. Phen. Psychol.*, 1979, 10/2, 165–188.

Barton, A. *Three worlds of therapy.* Mayfield Publishing Co., Palo Alto, 1974.

Binswanger, L. *Schizophrenie.* Verlag Günther Neske, Pfüllingen, 1957.

Boss, M. *Psychoanalyse und Daseinsanalytik.* Hans Huber, Bern, 1957.

_____. *Grundriss der Medizin und der Psychologie.* Hans Huber, Bern, 1975.

Brooke, R. *An empirical phenomenological investigation of being anxious.* Masters Dissertation, University of the Witwatersrand, 1983. (Not published).

Condrau, G. Was ist Psychotherapie. In Condrau, G. (Hrsgbr), *Medard Boss zum siebzigsten Geburtstag.* Hans Huber, Bern, 1973.

_____. *Angst und Schuld als Grundprobleme der Psychotherapie.* Suhrkamp Taschenbuch Verlag. 1979.

De Koning, A. J. J. The qualitative method of research in the phe-

nomenology of suspicion, In A. Giorgi, C. Fischer and R. Von
Eckartsberg (Eds.), *Duquesne studies in phenomenological psychol-
ogy, vol. III*, Duquesne University Press, Pittsburgh, 1979.
―――. Suspicion and delusion. In De Koning, A. J. J. and Jenner, F.
A. (Eds.), *Phenomenology and Psychiatry*. Academic Press, London,
1982.
De Boer, T. *Grondslagen van een kritische psychologie*. Uitgeverij
Ambo bv., Baarn, 1980.
Eysenck, H. J. *The effects of psychotherapy*. International Science
Press, New York, 1966.
Fischer, W. F. *An empirical-phenomenological approach to the psychol-
ogy of anxiety*. In A. J. J. De Koning, and F. A. Jenner, (Eds.),
op. cit. Academic Press, London, 1982.
Fischer, C. T. and Wertz, F. J. Empirical-phenomenological analyses of
being criminally victimized. In A. Giorgi, R. Knowles, and D. L.
Smith, (Eds.),*Duquesne studies in phenomenological psychology, vol.
III*. Duquesne University Press, Pittsburgh, 1979.
Giorgi, A. Phenomenology and experimental psychology I. In A. Giorgi,
W. F. Fischer, and R. Von Eckartsberg, (Eds.), *Duquesne studies in
phenomenological psychology vol. I*. Duquesne University Press, Pitts-
burgh, 1971.
―――. Phenomenology and experimental psychology II. Op. cit.,
1971.
―――. An application of phenomenological method in psychology. In
A. Giorgi, C. Fischer, and E. Murray, *Duquesne studies in phenome-
nological psychology, vol. II*. Duquesne University Press, Pittsburgh,
1975.
Habermas, J. *Knowledge and human interests*. Heineman, London,
1972.
Heidegger, M. *Von Wesen der Wahrheit*. Vittorio Klostermann, Frank-
furt am Main, 1949.
―――. *Sein und Zeit*. Max Niemeyer Verlag. Tübingen, 1972.
―――. *Gelassenheit*. Verlag Günther Neske, Pfullingen, 1979.
Illich, I. *Limits to medicine: Medical nemesis*. Penguin Books, Har-
mondsworth, 1979.
Jung, C. G. *Psychology and alchemy*. C. W., Vol. 12, Routledge and
Kegan Paul, London, 1974.
Keen, E. Psychopathology. In R. S. Valle, and M. King, (Eds.),
Existential-phenomenological alternatives for psychology, Oxford Uni-
versity Press, New York, 1978.
Kruger, D. Psychotherapy research and existential-phenomenological
psychology: An exploration. In: Giorgi, A et al., (Eds.), *Duquesne
studies in phenomenological psychology, vol. IV*, Duquesne University Press, Pittsburgh, 1983, p. 8–32.

Landmann, M. *Philosophical anthropology*. Westminster, Philadelphia, 1974.

Lowe, M. The equivalence of guilt and anxiety as psychological constructs, *Journ. of Consult Psychol.*, 1964; 28 (6), p. 553–554.

Murray, E. L. *The phenomenon of the metaphor: Some theoretical considerations*, In Giorgi et al., (Eds.), op. cit., 1975.

Meador, B. D. and Rogers, C. R. Client-centred psychotherapy. In Corsini, R. (Ed.), *Current psychotherapies*, F. E. Peacock Publishers, Ltd., Itasca, Ill., 1973.

Plessner, H. *Hoe de mens bestaan kan*. Sansom Uitgeverij, Alphen aan den Rÿn, 1978.

Romanyshyn, R. D. *Psychological life: From science to metaphor*. University of Texas Press, Austin, 1982.

Scheler, M. *Die Stellung des Menschen im Kosmos*. O. Reichl, Darmstadt, 1928.

Skinner, B. F. *Beyond freedom and dignity*. Penguin Books, Harmondsworth, 1973.

Strasser, S. Fenomenologie en empirische menskunde, Van Loghum Slaterus, Deventer, 1973.

Straus, E. On memory traces, *Tijdschrift voor filosofie*, *24*, 1962.

Szasz, T. *The myth of psychotherapy*. Anchor Press/Doubleday, Garden City, New York, 1979.

Titelman, P. *Some implications of hermeneutics for phenomenological psychology*. In A. Giorgi et al., op. cit., 1979.

Van Den Berg, J. H. *Metabletica*. G. F. Callenbach bv., Nijkerk, 1956.

_____. Phenomenology and psychotherapy, *Journ. Phen. Psychol.*, 1980, *10/2*, 21–49.

_____. *Dieptepsychologie*. G. F. Callenbach bv., Nijkerk, 1979.

Yalom, I. D. *Existential psychotherapy*. Basic Books, Inc., New York, 1980.

Dream Consciousness in Action and Interaction*

Elias J. G. Meijer

In the report of my work presented at the Symposium on Qualitative Research in Psychology in Perugia, I explained that my aim is not merely to do research on the meaning of dreams, but to use dreams in a teaching and a therapeutic context as well. The emphasis lies in the relationship of the dreaming state to the ways of becoming self-conscious. Awareness of one's existence — awake as well as asleep — consists of thoughts, feelings and actions. Usually, dreamconsciousness is best regarded as different, but not incomparable, to waking awareness. Certainly, in the state of sleeping and dreaming there is a lack of adequate conscious response to stimuli and the body is relatively immobile (and comparable to this lack of adequacy is daydreaming — in which a person allows his mind to wander aimlessly along all sorts of imagery, often gratifying wishes not gratified in the alert state), but the content of dreams and daydreams is not unrelated to wakeful experience.

Our waking life demands action. In wakefulness, we mostly directly interact with others or with the surroundings. We are *entranced* by what we are doing — we 'forget' ourselves, and forget, for instance, the mood we are in. We are immersed in society and in our construction of it. We are engrossed in all sorts of activities which exist mainly outside ourselves. In this state, there is hardly time left for *taking notice* of how we are existing in a peculiar place during a certain period. However, our mind and body do in a sense, 'take notice.' They are like a screen on which we can see, hear, etc., reflecting what we think and feel of waking life. Dreamconsciousness recalls this material. The mature integration of active life and recollection of the way we are living is often called health, sanity, or being able to cope. Being conscious of the way we are experiencing wakeful life gives us an instrument for moving towards the goal we set in life.

Another important aspect in studying dreams is the fact that dreams have a communicative function. Although as a rule the character of dreams is private, a person can — if he wants to or is invited to do so — talk about his dreams. Furthermore, it should be stressed that dreams frame embodiments of time and space and represent the activity of the self (for instance, showing mood — which can pass unnoticed in alert wakefulness — and which can have such importance in *psychopathology*).

> In scientific psychology and psychiatry the separation between theory and reality is too strongly marked when the authors define 'a dream' as 'a simple example of a hallucination in normal experience' (Kaplan & Kadock, 1981).

Very many students in psychology and psychiatry state as a big disadvantage of textbooks (e.g., the one by Kaplan & Sadock) that they give hardly any descriptions of patients of flesh and blood. What they miss are descriptions at experiential level. In order to remedy this, dream experience is treated in my work in a manner drawing on Jaspers (1913) as well as Spiegelberg (1975), Boss (1974), Gendlin (1962) and Giorgi (1975). I trained students in small groups:

— to describe clearly what is experienced
— to investigate the connections
— to look at the whole

These steps I combine with Yontef's phenomenological field method (1982) and call it the *phenomenological-interactional method*, which leads to practicing a phenomenologically-based form of interviewing. That is to say 'questioning' in a way that allows the phenomena (i.e., dreaming, consciousness of dream-contents, giving meaning to etc.) to show themselves. The students are invited to interview each other. With the help of sound and videorecording, I supervise their 'openness,' their 'being present' (empty in the beginning), their 'clarity/transparancy' (the questions are congruent and related to the topics brought up by the interviewee).

References

Boss, M. *Fundamentals of psychology and medicine*, 1976 (Originally: *Grundriss der psychologie und medizin*, Hans Huber Berlag: Bern, 1974).

Gendlin, E. *Experiencing and the creation of meaning: A philosophical and psychological approach to the subjective*. Glencoe: Free press of Glencoe, 1962.

Giorgi, A. "An application of phenomenological method in psychology." In A. Giorgi, C. Fischer and E. Murray (Eds.), *Duquesne studies in phenomenological psychology: Volume II*. Pittsburgh: Duquesne University Press, 1975.

Jaspers, K. *Allgemeine psychopathologie*. Berlin: Springer Verlag, 1913.

Kaplan, H. I. & Sadock, B. J. *Comprehensive textbook of psychiatry*. Baltimore: Williams & Wilkins, 1981.

Yontef, G. M. Gestalt therapy: Its inheritance from Gestalt psychology. *Gestalt Theory*, 1982.

---

*Dr. Meijer's Perugia presentation of the use of dream reports in research, therapy and teaching did not lend itself to publication in the present book form. However, it was felt important to indicate the intensely practical application of a qualitative approach to enriching the person's self-awareness. The gap between 'theory' and 'practice' can be minimized in such qualitative work. (Editors)

PART IV

Social Themes

Perception in a
Taboo Situation

9

Frederick J. Wertz

In the late 1940's, a group of experimental psychologists who became known as the "New Look" attempted an integrative movement in perceptual research in order to overcome its previous isolation from other subfields of psychology. Rather than adhering to the previously dominant psychophysical paradigm, researchers began to investigate the effects that perceivers themselves have on perceptual processes. One major line of work undertook to relate perceptual research to psychoanalytic thought and clinical psychology in general. Psychoanalytic theorists had for some time viewed perception in connection with unconscious personality dynamics, that is, as an ego function capable of defending the person against anxiety by *not seeing* anxiety arousing stimuli (e.g., Sullivan, 1953; Schilder, 1924). Although the notions of perceptual defense (avoidance of emotional stimuli) and vigilance (heightened sensitivity to emotional stimuli) had been discussed previously in the New Look literature (Bruner and Postman, 1947; Bruner, 1948; Postman, Bruner and McGinnies, 1948), McGinnies (1949) put the notions of unconscious emotional response to and perceptual defense against taboo stimuli to an experimental test. He found not only that anxiety provoking words produced a higher GSR at prerecognition (below threshold) tachistoscopic exposures but also that they had a higher recognition threshold than neutral words. While these findings implied to many the existence of unconscious autonomic discrimination (subception) and a mechanism that prevented perceptual processes from achieving awareness (defense), it evoked disbelief in others and led to a controversy which to this day has not been univocally resolved.

Following a brief review of the history of this psychology of taboo perception the present work attempts a return to beginnings, that is a qualitative description of perception in an everyday taboo situation. We will then discuss the value of qualitative research of this kind of situation as a fundamental step in the psychology of taboo perception.

A Brief History

McGinnies' (1949) report was followed by a critique from Howes and Solomon (1950), which McGinnies (1950) addressed with a rebuttal. An extensive series of systematic replications of the basic hypothesis and others built on it were then carried out in dialogue with strong, everpresent criticism. One criticism that has been waged from many quarters against the psychoanalytic notion of an unconscious censoring mechanism has been periodically revived in this context (Bruner and Postman, 1949; Luckins, 1950; Howie, 1952; Eriksen and Browne, 1956). It is argued that it is logically impossible for a person to both perceive and not perceive a stimulus, to know and avoid knowing simultaneously. Closely related to this is the theoretical criticism of any attempt to solve this problem by postulating a homunculus, the idea having long been discredited in psychology (Goldstein, 1962; Eriksen, 1958 and 1960).

Alternative explanations of McGinnies' empirical findings have suggested the confounding variables of stimulus frequency and perceptual set and also suggested that it is not so much in the perception but in the response that the selective function occurs. Howes and Solomon (1950) argued that a higher recognition threshold for taboo words is a function of their lesser *frequency* of past exposure and using the Thorndike-Lorge (1944) word frequency tables depicted the function with scatter plots. Others argued that demand characteristics of the experimental situation (rather than emotionality) induce a *set* for seeing neutral words in order to explain their lower threshold (Luckins, 1950; Howie, 1952). Experimental tests supported this explanation (Postman, Bronson, and Gropper, 1953; Lacy, Lewinger, and Adamson, 1953; Freeman, 1954; Kleimer, 1959; Forest, Gordon, and Taylor, 1965; Cable, 1969). Still others argued that the results do not reflect abnormal perceptual processes but rather *response suppression* (Howes and Solomon, 1950). That is, subjects saw the

words but did not report them until the longer exposures provided greater certainty. Notham (1962) and Broota and Khanna
(1974) have supported this experimentally. It has also been
suggested that one need not postulate response suppression inasmuch as the mere past frequency and reinforcement of neutral
and taboo responses would account for their differential probability (Goldiamond, 1958; Goldstein, 1962).

Much of the work supporting the claim of differential perception of emotional stimuli has attempted to confirm the original
hypothesis in a way that discounts the above alternative explanations. The use of the Thorndike-Lorge (1944) tables in this
context was originally questioned by McGinnies (1949) and empirically shown to be inappropriate by Eriksen (1963). Many
studies have controlled word frequency and still found evidence
for defense (Levy, 1958; Chapman and Feather, 1972). Other
experiments have controlled set and still have found positive
results (Blum, 1955; Weiner, 1955; Levy, 1958). Experimenters
have also controlled for response suppression (e.g. by having
subjects respond with taboo words for neutral percepts and vice
versa) and still found significant results (Matthews and Wertheimer, 1958; Zigler and Yospe, 1960; Ruiz and Krauss, 1968).

Despite the persistant criticism and a general disbelief in the
existence of the mechanism of perceptual defense, experimenters
went on to build on McGinnies' original study. Not only defense
but perceptual vigilance has been explored. Experimenters have
predicted whether defense or vigilance would occur on the basis
of personality type and previous performance (McGinnies and
Adornetto, 1952; Eriksen, 1951, 1952, and 1954; Blum, 1954;
Chodorkof, 1954; Spence, 1957). For instance, Carpenter,
Weiner and Carpenter (1956) found that "sensitizers" perceived
emotionally laden stimuli faster than "repressers." Systematic
replications concerning subject variables extended the hypothesis
further. Sex differences were found by Pustell (1957) and Rosenstock (1951), who demonstrated that women repress aggressive
and men sexual stimuli. While Bitterman and Kniffin (1953)
found that high anxiety subjects were no different than normals,
McGinnies and Adornetto (1952) found that schizophrenics and
Stein (1953) found that neurotics were different from normals as
predicted. Kurland (1954) found that "intellectualizers" were no
different from "repressers" but that both groups combined were
more perceptually defensive than normals. Cross-cultural valida-

tions of the general hypothesis of perceptual defense was provided in Italy (Blum, 1957) and India (Kumar, Srvastava, and Divivedi, 1980). Other replications sought to vary the stimuli involved. Eriksen and Lazarus (1952) got positive results with ink blots; Rosenstock (1951) and Wallace and Worthington (1970) showed the effect with varying conditions of illumination; and Smith and Hochberg (1954) demonstrated defense in figure-ground selectivity. Positive results have also been obtained in the auditory (Kumar *et al.*, 1980) and tactile (Levy, 1958) spheres. Daston (1956) went so far as to use the perceptual defense paradigm to test the controversial psychoanalytic interpretation of paranoid schizophrenia (as a reaction formation and projection of homosexual desire) and obtained higher thresholds for homosexual words in cases of paranoid schizophrenia than for other schizophrenics.

Methodological "improvements" such as the use of nonsense syllables and a controlled history of exposure and punishment notwithstanding, the very existence of perceptual defense has remained in question. Erdelyi (1974) provides a fine review of the literature and concludes that research on the problem declined after the convincing methodological critiques by Eriksen and Goldiamond in 1958, when the field accepted the view that the research was plagued with artifacts and rested on artificial foundations. However, Erdelyi goes on to convincingly refute every criticism utilizing both theoretical arguments and emperical references as well as to either dismiss or integrate all the competing theoretical explanations (e.g., learning theory, signal detection theory) of perceptual defense. He accomplishes this from the standpoint of information processing theory, which he believes is the long awaited framework capable of embracing the New Look movement in general and the work on perceptual defense and vigilance in particular. Following the research on selective attention of the 1960's (Dixon, 1971; Maccoby, 1969; Neisser, 1967; Norman, 1969), Erdelyi suggests a scheme of information processing in which selection occurs at various points including fixation (e.g., looking strategies of Spence and Feinberg, 1967), occlusion, pupil size (Hutt and Anderson, 1967a and b), lens accommodation, encoding, construction, rehersal, and output. Thus it is considered a multiprocess and multidirectional phenomenon, the major mechanism being encoding effects in the transfer of information from raw to short term storage:

All that needs to be assumed is that selective control processes in long term memory, following semantic analyses (also in long term memory) take into account a host of factors including wishes, values, expectations, and psychodynamic defense requirements of the organism. Decisions would thus be made in long term memory (note, prior to short term storage, the region of consciousness) as to what to encode and what to reject from short term storage. The material not encoded would thus be permanently lost . . . (Erdelyi, 1974, p. 19).

While one would think that Erdelyi's important article would have rejuvenated research in this area, such does not seem to be the case. In fact, it was in the same year, 1974, that the category of perceptual defense was dropped from *Psychological Abstracts*. Diamant (1975) likens his almost humorous demonstration of perceptual defense to a horse beaten dead that kicked, got up and rode again. York, Mandour, and Jex's (1983) review of the literature yielded only twenty three positive demonstrations of perceptual defense since 1974. York has begun his revival of the area with the first *direct* replication of the original McGinnies study (of course the change in times makes it less than a perfect direct replication), and he found a higher threshold for taboo than neutral words but no significant difference in GSR. York is now involved in a series of systematic replications through which (with finer autonomic indices including heart and breathing rate) he hopes to give evidence of both prerecognition emotionality and perceptual defense in psychopathological populations.

A Methodological Reorientation

In our critical historical study of the New Look (Wertz, 1983b), we too have questioned the methodology and guiding conceptuality of its research. However, rather than viewing its failure in terms of its shortcomings vis-a-vis the virtues of experimental rigor, we have shown that it is precisely the uncritical and premature attempt at realizing such virtues which precluded an appropriate study of perception by demanding kinds of closure which vitiated the phenomenon. We argued that the first step towards comprehending perception of the taboo must be a concrete description of the phenomenon in the lifeworld prior to any attempt to control, manipulate, quantify, etc. While it is Giorgi (1970) who most forcefully argues the position that a methodologically and conceptually open and unbiased contact with everyday life is the rightful, however neglected, starting point for the investigation of psychological phenomena, he is not alone. Neisser, who has been a leading advocate of experimental methodology and information processing perceptual theory (Neisser, 1967) has, influenced by J. J. Gibson, come to call for a basic description of perceptual processes in everyday life rather than an ever increasing technical sophistication of the experiment and an ever more complex inferential postulation of internal information processing mechanisms (which he now dismisses) designed to explain a reality which has yet to be adequately described.

One might wonder at the usefulness of such an approach in the present case since the phenomenon approaches being "unconscious," but Fink (1970) has convincingly argued for the priority of the study of conscious processes in this context. He points out that an everyday familiarity with consciousness has led psychologists to an illusory sense of having already understood its phenomena without having yet conducted a rigorous qualitative examination, which would redefine matters in a way that might very well change considerations of what is called "unconscious." Only after overcoming this naiveté by a thorough-going intentional analysis of consciousness with the descriptive sensitivity and eidetic rigor demonstrated by Husserl (1970), will psychology be in a position to articulate the demarcations, sense, and methodological requirements of what has been called "unconscious" (Fink, 1970).

With these thoughts as a point of departure, the present study attempts a different approach to the matter of "perceptual defense." It is a beginning effort to describe perception in an everyday taboo situation in the hope that our findings will have some bearing on the methodology and theory that have proved so problematic for traditional approaches.

Method

Since the methodological operations, including their development and rationale, are presented in detail elsewhere (Wertz, 1982a, 1984), we will limit ourselves here to a brief summary.

Subjects

Five subjects volunteered to participate in the research, four females and one male. Their ages ranged from 19 to 36 and they represented a range of religions (e.g., catholic, jewish, atheistic), socioeconomic levels (lower, middle, upper), and occupations (e.g., secretary, college professor, student).

Procedure

*Situations.*The primary research situation that will concern us here is a Pittsburgh store called "The Mello News Stand." After being told the name and location of the store, subjects were asked if they would be willing to go there accompanied by the researcher. They were told that what they did and how long they stayed would be completely up to them, and that if they found anything offensive, they could leave immediately. The main section of the store, into which one walks past food, drink, and pinball machines, contains racks of magazines, maps, and newspapers against the right wall and head shop, candy, and cashier counters on the left side. The second section is behind a chest-high partition directly facing the entrance, with a gate marked "Adults Only" on the right side. The right wall in the second section holds "love supplies" and sadomasochistic equipment while the other three walls contain racks of hard core pornographic magazines. Book racks of erotic novels occupy the section's center, and the back wall (left side, facing the store entrance) provides a darkened entrance-way over which hangs a red neon sign "Movies 25¢." Other situations each subject also participated in which are less relevant to the present report were "supermarket shopping" (designated by the researcher) and a "liked" and "disliked" situation which subjects chose themselves.

Data. – After leaving the store, each subject was asked to describe their journey through the store as completely as possible in writing so that everything they lived through there would be expressed in their "Own Description." The researcher described each subject's behavior in the store as an observer, which constituted the "Other's Description." The following day a dialogue was conducted in which the researcher and subject explored the two descriptions more fully to resolve unclarities, provide background etc. in an "Interview." The three sources of data were then integrated in each case in a "Composite Description," which presented a coherent narrative of the subject's course through the situation with the researcher's perspective placed in parentheses.

Analysis. – Each Composite Description was analyzed according to the general procedures of qualitative, psychological analysis articulated by Giorgi (1975), Fischer and Wertz (1979), and Wertz (1983c, 1984). In particular, it was required that the researcher, after receptively gathering the sense of the whole description, reflect upon every statement which expresses the subject's perceptual life so as to identify in each case the constituents of the perceptual process. These were then explicitly related to the overall participation of the subject in the situation. After each Composite Description was analyzed in this fashion, general themes running through the various descriptions were elaborated.

Findings

Before going into the details of taboo perception per se, it will first be necessary to bring into view some of the general aspects of perception disclosed by our analysis (Wertz, 1982b): its intentionality, qualitative diversity, potentialities, extended spatiality, temporality, embodiment, sociality, and embeddedness in a larger existence. Then we will present a sample of one Composite Description and an excerpt from its analysis. Finally, we will discuss several general themes which are relevant to the matter of perception in taboo situations.

The General Psychological Structure of Perception

The most fundamental characteristic of perception, which has been described by Husserl (1913), is its *intentionality*. That is to say that perception is not something internal, closed in on itself, but rather is essentially an opening onto, a way of apprehending the world beyond itself. More specifically, perception witnesses the present surroundings, the field of bodily things. Thus perception may be distinguished from other types of experience such as memory (which intends past events), anticipation (which intends future events), imagination (which intends ficticious matters) and so on.

Perception always apprehends the situation from a certain limited perspective and it may take a *variety of general forms*. It may rest in a state of mere potentiality, as when we are lost in memory, in which case it does not actually disclose the surroundings even though it "can" do so, for we are always already in a situation which is perceivable. In actual perception, it singles out and apprehends something which stands out in the field, the rest

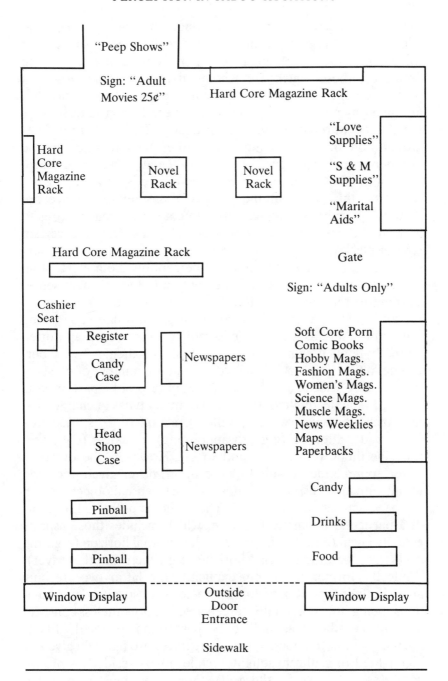

Diagram 1: The Mello News Stand

of which may be called the background. The spatial background admits of four regions of things: those related to the singled-out foreground, those relevant to other immediate interests of the perceiver, those which are wholey irrelevant, and those not perceived which extend beyond the field of actual perception but are given as potentially perceivable. These background spheres are given with relatively little determinacy. The singled-out foreground, on the other hand, may either be integrated into a non-perceptual experience or made a thematic object of perception. In the first case, for instance, the reader is now singling out words on this page but the objects of his/her experience are thoughts properly speaking, unless of course the reader cares to look at the words as themselves objects, manifesting a certain type of black print. Thus we contrast symbolic, imaginal, behavioral, memorial and anticipatory perception from perceptual thematization proper, which is perception in the pregnant sense. Turning to the latter, we find that perception can apprehend a literally infinite variety of objects in any given situation by taking something there as a unitary ensemble of intertwined and often mutually implicit characteristics, that is, as a theme. Every perceptual object (e.g., a bus) affords an infinite number of perspectives; it may be seen as a global whole, in terms of a part or parts (e.g., broken headlights), or by way of many types of characteristics, including sensory (e.g., yellow), action (e.g., still), value (e.g., bad), affective (e.g., disappointing), practical (e.g., useless), aesthetic (e.g., ugly) and so on. However, the object is never apprehended totally by perception, never given once and for all with all its aspects manifest. The perceptual object is given in "perspectives" or "profiles." The object is perceived in terms of a particular noematic structure, which includes those aspects actually given (e.g., the front side), the internal horizon (e.g., the back side), and the external horizon (e.g., the road, the driver). While the former stands out explicitly, the latter two are only given in their typical or virtual character with specific determinations, being only potentially perceivable but nonetheless constitutive of the object as meant by perception (Husserl, 1948). Further, within the noema, certain features are figurally given or highlighted (e.g. the headlights) while others reside less prominently as ground (e.g., the grill). Finally, we must turn to the process of perceiving itself, which admits of its own set of variations. Thematization may be initiated either by proception (e.g., looking for), circumspection (e.g., looking around) or reception (e.g., being struck by). Once an object is thematized, perceptual processes may explicate it in various manners and extents by either avoiding, glancing, grazing over quickly, being captivated or active scrutiny.

It is of great importance that the description of perception includes as an essential matter its *potentiality* (Husserl, 1929) which resides at the heart of its lived meaning. Perception is never limited to actuality but includes its possibilities. Right now I *can* turn around and perceive the area behind me. After doing so and thematizing an African mask on the wall I *can touch* it — indeed I can stick my finger through the eye-hole and feel the back. All the while I *can be struck* by someone calling my name outside the door. These potentialities are not closed in on themselves as if they resided in me but are rather shot through with intentionality and therefore disclose my present bodily surroundings in their own peculiar (and subtle) way, that is, as typical virtualities. For instance, as part of its internal horizon, the feel of the mask's back is not given explicitly as I gaze at the front, either as rough or smooth in particular, but the mask is given as a whole with a "touchable back." It is also meant in terms of its external horizon, that is as being "in my office at the university." Thus one objective correlate of perceptual possibilities is the spatial horizons of the thematized object. We perceive it as extending typically beyond what is actually perceived just as we do its perceptual background, thus inhabiting through perception a *whole spatial situation*. The potentialities of perception are also crucial to understanding perception's *temporality*, for perception includes an ability to reactualize past processes (with regard to both particular syntheses and general habitualities) as well as to forge into new, future domains. In this way perception's past and future are part of its very structure, constituting its everpresent temporal background. In both thematization and explication, temporal syntheses retain what was previously given and anticipate what is to come. Viewing the perceptual process from another related angle, we find that its intentionality, including its actualities and potentialities, is bodily. The perceiver, as a *body-subject* (Merleau-Ponty, 1963), intrinsically requires motility (e.g., walking to the mask and reaching out to it) and is lived as an ensemble of sensory modalities which in syncretic mutual implication constitute the possibilities of touch, sight, hearing, and so on. Since perception is an embodied sort of intentionality, its world relations are (partly) perceptable to other perceivers so that perceptual processes are always lived as *socially situated*. We perceive others perceive us and they thereby become abiding denizens of our world in potentially reciprocal relations with us.

In order to understand the particularity of any given perception - its qualitative form with its spatiality, temporality, embodiment, and relations with others, we found it necessary to view perception as *part of the person's larger existence*, that is, as embedded in an overall life with its behaviors, thoughts, imaginings, rememberings, anticipations, social relations, and so on. We conceptualized the unity of this larger ground of perception as what we called "projective presence." For example, one of our subjects took on the project of shopping in a routine task-oriented presence. In this orchestration of the various potentialities of mental life, behavior was key, for the overall aim was the appropriation of needed foods. Perception moved from the symbolic mode (reading the shopping list) to serving walking behavior (by spotting pathways and obstacles) and appropriating behavior (by thematizing needed foods). Non-needed foods remained in the scanned background and even needed foods were explicated very little, never with active scrutiny, for as soon as the "right thing" (e.g. fish sticks with a crispy crust) was recognized, it was seized and thrown in the basket. This project required very little explicit anticipation and recollection, and the strict pragmatic presence excluded imagination. For contrast consider the perceptuality of this projective presence with that of an employee of the supermarket whose project is to straighten out the shelves or clean the floors and whose presence is lazy, or that of a person going to the supermarket to get ideas for a science fiction novel set there. Inasmuch as the person's world extends beyond a particular thematization to the overall circuit of existence, the person's projective presence extends beyond such phasic unities as pragmatic, routine shopping, which for our supermarket subject had its place in her life as a married, working homemaker.

Composite Description: *Alice in the Mellow News Stand*

Before I went in, I thought it was just going to be a regular type news store with magazines, so that's what I was expecting. Fred said, "If you want to go in, go in. If you don't, don't, or if you want to buy something, do." When he said, "If you find something offensive . . . " I didn't understand what he meant. What could I find offensive in a news store? So I let it go. I had no plans at all. Let it come, let my feelings guide me. I was curious, about the store but also myself since Fred said, "You can do what you want." I was curious also to see what I'd do.

(Alice stopped in front, took a few steps back and seemed to look around, as if to say, "What is this?" She might have caught a glimpse of the soft core porn in the left side of the window, which she then went towards and looked at, as if it would tell her what the store's about.) I always look at the outside of a shop before I go in just to see what type of things they have. I still wasn't clear because a lot of stores have porno magazines. So my quick glance into the window didn't tell me much because I really wanted to go in. I still wasn't completely sure what kind of store it was and I was curious to find out more, but at this point to me it is a relatively typical news stand. The heading over the top is not huge and it's located with a lot of other stores.

Upon entering I knew immediately it was a complete porno shop. I'd been in one and it was the magazines around. The room was broken into separate things with a little door and up on top behind I saw a big thing saying "adult films," "explicit this," "explicit that," and a whole wall of magazines. It was very obvious — the whole atmosphere, which I guess wasn't so different except for the content of the magazines. There wasn't anything abnormal or many people around. My first reaction was just to laugh because of where Fred brought me! It's not a typical place to bring someone and I had no idea, so I was amazed and surprised. I went with it. It was enjoyable. I had no idea what he wanted me to do and didn't even think of it. So I did what I would have done if I were alone and almost forgot that Fred was there. I didn't even know he was watching me.

(Upon entering there was a man at the candy machines on the right and another playing pinball at the left, as well as a black guy mopping the floor in the middle-front. As she passed him, he said, "Don't worry about this," indicating that it was alright to cross the wet floor, so Alice went ahead.) I decided to walk around. I didn't see anyone at pinball or candy machines, for I was looking more for the store itself. I might have vaguely noticed that but it wasn't explicit. I did notice someone mopping and I said I didn't want to walk on his floor but he said don't worry about it so I didn't.

(Alice wandered, care-free, right to the middle of the store, looking all around, at the glass case on the left, and then back to the rest of the store. She seemed drawn to the back of the store and on her way there she glanced down to the second glass case on her left — but not at the cashier, a youngish lady maybe thirty with blonde hair.) At first I saw pipes and paraphernalia and the regular books and magazines. They did not keep my interest because I saw that in the second half of the store was all porno stuff. I felt free. I think if I'd gone on my own I might have been somewhat embarrassed or hesitant, but I was brought to it. Being there for research made me feel I could do anything I wanted to there, freer than I might have otherwise been. So I didn't really have my interest grabbed by the pipes — I just looked quickly because it wasn't what I was interested in. I also wasn't interested in the regular kind of magazines. I wanted to see what the porno looked like.

(Passing by the magazine rack on the right with a quick glance without spending much time there, Alice went right to the back of the store.) I was very curious to see what they had and so I quickly went to the second half of the shop. I was not freaked or disgusted — only curious. I'm always curious about it and there's been a lot of debate on it in Pittsburgh. There are a number of different attractions. One is a psychological one — to see why people are interested, what they get off on through it. At one point I wanted to study it and I applied at a place to work, but I didn't get accepted — too young and innocent looking. A friend of mine once did a study on pornography. It was part of my interest. And at one point in my life a friend — I don't know who — signed me up for a subscription to a very pornographic magazine which I got through all my years at high school. I kept them in my room and my friends would come in and I'd be always shocked and amazed to see how much they'd get into it. That was all part of it. It's interesting how some people are turned off, others turned on, and some want to get into it but think they shouldn't. And then there's the whole idea of whether it alleviates or encourages sexual frustrations. I find it interesting personally also and at times sexually stimulating. The explicitness of it doesn't freak me out or anything — I get off on it. It's a different type of feeling. It is intriguing to see it and feel it and to let yourself go with it, and also to see how you stop yourself from doing it. But I've only had a little experience with it, only enough to make my curiosity stronger.

(Alice seemed pretty relaxed as she took a tour of the back of the store. First she looked over the plastic "love supplies" on the right side of the store. She went over to another section for a

moment, but went back to the love supplies and made her way
along the wall, looking at each thing she passed. Something
caught her eye and she leaned in to look at it closely.) I was
freaked to see a whole wall of artificial stimulators. I've seen
some of them before in porno shops I've been in but I was
surprised to see a whole wall. And I've never seen so many
different types of things. My major reaction was that I couldn't
imagine the uses of them or who would want to or be able to.
You'd have to be a masochist to use some, and how would they
be used? Like a lot of dildo type things, all different sizes and
shapes and one had little rubber spikes on it. Painful, masochistic! There were a couple I couldn't imagine what they were used
for, like a plastic type vagina but it looked like something a
doctor would use to show someone anatomy. Well, the dildos
could be used by either a man or a woman, man with man, or man
with woman. I imagined lots of possibilities but the plastic vagina
didn't make much sense, even to my vivid imagination. Sometimes I'd pass something — like the spiked dildo or vagina,
quickly, and then thinking about it an trying to figure out its use
I'd take a closer look to see its use, and then when I resolved
something I'd move on. I'd never seen so many in my life! A
whole wall full, and so it was very explicit. For some I wondered
if people really use them, but why else would they have them? I
could never get into them, and I'm not just saying that backing
away from it. I personally wouldn't have any interest or get any
joy. Another thing was different flavored lubricants. Ha ha ha!
That was sort of funny. There are all sorts of things people are
putting out for sale, and I just wonder if it enhances, helps, takes
away from the natural thing. My curiosity got pretty much filled
— not completely, it never is. But as far as that part in my life I'd
seen it, thought about it, so I no longer needed to stay.

(Then Alice moved around the back, glancing over the magazines
on the back wall.) I turned my attention to the porno magazines.
On top of each section were listed "Girlie," "Explicit," "Gay,"
etc. And what amused me most was "New Entries." They all
seemed pretty much similar to me since I'm not familiar with
them so I wondered what's the difference between the new ones
and the old ones. The covers of all the magazines were very
explicit and I found I could only quickly glance at each and not
meditate or reflect on any particular one. Most of them seemed to
be women with women (perplexed and slightly disturbed) although some had men. Women with women, in different types of
things and there were men ones but on the covers mostly women,
trios and different variations. I was interested in who was having

sex and the extent of explicitness on different ones — what parts of the body they were showing and what they were engaged in. I thought about the models knowing that often times they do it only for the money. You'd have to be really uninhibited to get into modeling with someone else, maybe exhibitionistic was my little hypothesis. I also thought about what they do on the covers to grab people's interest.

(It seemed she paused for a moment before the movie entrance, seemed inquisitive in this place.) It said movies inside there, which I'm sure they were but it said something about a movie for sale and a price so I was confused. It seemed really expensive. It was really a big sign — that's why I saw it. I didn't think of buying the movie, or the magazines. I wasn't interested in going to the movie.

(Alice went on to the magazines on the other side of the movie entrance, really looking at them rather than just passing by. As she made her way around the full circuit of the store she'd occasionally retrace her steps to get a better look at something. Occasionally she'd look out and see me, then smile.) I was aware of a few other people in there, but only vaguely. I didn't want to impinge on their privacy and I didn't want them to on mine so I didn't really look at the other people except Fred and the cashier. Especially being a young girl and having these men around. I didn't want them to look at me so I didn't stare at them. I noticed, however, that I was only quickly glancing at the magazine covers. I didn't pick any up or look through them or even look at one for a long time. I felt the other people looking at me and wondered what they thought I was doing there looking at those women — if I was gay or perverted, or maybe some other reason. Somehow they'd think I was less good or unnatural. The place seemed mostly for men in general. You usually picture an old perverted man or a young boy in a place like that. It affected how much I looked at the pictures. I felt I didn't really belong there, as if I couldn't spend a lot of time. So I was only quickly observing and stopping myself from really getting into it. I could have gotten into it more. It was both me stopping myself and others looks stopping me — the one other guy back there. Here I am staring at these explicit pictures of other women. It would be more appropriate for me to stare at pictures of men, so that was behind it. Society and myself prohibit my being attracted to women. I felt more free to look at the artificial stimulators, which I wasn't personally interested in. I was more personally interested in the magazines and felt stimulated by them. I felt I shouldn't feel that way and go with it, pick them up. An anxiety might come up. It was alright to glance but not pick them up.

There were porno books in the middle, but they didn't catch my interest because they did not have explicit covers. The more explicit the better. I looked at each of the covers without seeing any of the titles and compared them as to their revealingness and what the people were doing to one another. The more conventional things to me are less explicit. If a woman was just caressing another's breast that wasn't so explicit, but if they're engaged in cunnilingus that's more. I was looking for the more it showed of the body and the more taboo. I guess the ones with the woman making love to a woman, you don't see that a lot. That's what I was interested in and looking at those, I thought they'd think I'm gay. I think I'd be not admitting something to myself if I said I'd never been attracted to a woman, but I've never had sex with one. So those magazines fulfill my curiosity in a way that's more acceptable to society than actually engaging in it. But I don't like the way society reacts to homosexuality at all, keeping people from getting jobs. I worked with people in the gay alliance so I've heard what they're up against and I sympathized so I don't like that view or the fact that I've restricted myself because of it. I was there and felt it, picked it up, was affected, and a victim of it. I also wondered how much the models make, if they enjoy having pictures of themselves taken. Maybe I thought a little about whether I could do it but nothing strong. I never could. No, I'm not saying I never could. It's something I've thought about before and I'll joke about going and being a stripper or something but it's nothing I want to do. It's not a desire in me so it's more thinking about other people and what they get from it.

This store really drew me into it and I completely forgot about the rest of my life. I was engrossed in my thoughts and looking at my reactions. After I glanced around, I'd had my fill and decided to leave. It was fun.

(After coming out of the back she looked over the glass cashier cases and the soft core magazines with news and sports magazines — but these seemed to hold little interest. She then seemed to want something to buy and asked the cashier if she had it. She said she was glad I brought her here. As we waited, she looked down at the newspapers. The cashier came over and said that she didn't have all sizes but laid down a plastic box with what turned out to be pipe screens of four sizes. Alice looked them over and asked about their prices as she looked them over, settling on five of them. Then she went into her wallet for a dollar and some

pennies. The cashier gave three quarters for change and Alice
decided she wanted some rolling papers. She looked over the
display of rolling papers and picked one kind, which the lady got
her. Alice gave 50¢, hunted for and found three more pennies,
and indicated that she wanted to go. I said, "Want to go?" And
she laughingly said "No." I wasn't sure, wondered if she did want
to stay. So I said, "Want to stay?" kiddingly as we left the store.)
As I was leaving, I looked over at the other magazines to see if I
was interested in buying them, but I wasn't. I would have liked to
bought one of the others and I think it was a way to get the desire
out in a more acceptable way to myself. Then I realized I didn't
want one of those. Then I saw the pipes, screens and stuff. I'd
wanted to get back to the pipes to take a closer look at the types
of pipes. I like to see all the different types and styles of pipes
because some people I knew used to make pipes of clay and
wood. There were just normal, typical pipes — nothing unusual
— which is what I was looking for. I got screens and papers,
which I need. It was purely functional — I just needed them. I
saw different types and asked her to get me plain ones — the type
I wanted. I could have stayed longer but I was also ready to go. It
was fun. I enjoyed it. It was an adventure.

An Excerpt from the Analysis of Alice in the News Stand

Alice's project of helping with the research by going into the
Mello News Stand is the overall framework within which perception takes place. The inside of the Mello News Stand is the goal of
her project despite its indeterminateness and accordingly prior to
her actually being there Alice's perception's function is to show
the way there. Since her goal is not present in the immediate
surroundings, perception thematizes them strictly as indications
of the way inside. We could call this behavior orienting perception "Ambulatory Perception." Alice sees the general style of the
store she's intending to enter. All that needs appear is its normality, i.e. that it is marked by a regular sign and is there next to
other stores. Perception renders the store in its routine enterabil-
ity. Were her project to guess at the inside of the store from the
outside, she no doubt would have perceived the outside differently. She would have seen the signs indicating "Adult Movies,"
"Love Supplies," etc., but given her project *to go inside*, only
those features relevant for entering are perceived. Similarly, she
doesn't see the pinball and candy machine or the people using
them in the hallway prior to the interior of the store but does see
a man mopping the floor because he is in her way. He tells her to
walk over the wet floor and Alice hears this motility-relevant

aspect of the situation and thematizes nothing else of the man. In this situation where the project's goal lies outside the immediate surroundings, behavior has the privilege, dominates Alice's orientation, and perception functions in the service of the movement through the immediate situation towards the goal of the project. Only once inside the store, where Alice's projected goal immediately surrounds her, does perception go beyond motility-relevance and begin to see the surroundings positively for their own sake, thus directly fulfilling the project's aim. In the openendedness of Alice's indeterminate project and curiosity, her gaze sweeps over the whole store globally and is surprised to find herself in "a complete porno shop." Another subject went into the store strictly to get a newspaper without any curiosity whatsoever and did not see any pornography nor was his expectation of a "normal news shop" disrupted. But Alice's expectations are loosely held in the orchestration of her openended project and curious presence which thereby allow for a surprising perception. Hence it would seem that the significance of expectations and their weight in determining perceptual process is not an invariant function but one which varies according to project and presence — particularly with their indeterminateness or openness.

We find in this situation that perception, in revealing a situation well beyond Alice's expectations, can play an essential role in the evocation or emergence of a project. But when we look at this process closely, we find it impossible to place full responsibility upon perception, which always points us back again to Alice's project and presence. The project of exploring pornography is evoked by the pornography in the store looking "more interesting" than the drug paraphernalia or regular magazines. But this quality of interesting attraction, which genuinely emanates from the percept, occurs not in isolation, but only on the basis of Alice's implicit history and desire. This percept holds within it the intertwining of Alice's intentional history and a situation quite beyond it. Particularly, pornography has come to be lived by Alice as a potential answer to questions she has and a potential fulfillment of still outstanding desires. Only in light of this sedimented meaning does it stand out figurally in the store and captivate her perceptual interest. Alice's openended curiosity thus allows the unexpected to emerge but the unexpected is still not the totally unfamiliar, and it evokes a hitherto latent project which in turn brings it to ever greater articulation in the situation. The pornography is beckoning, familiar, yet also indeterminate and intriguing. And we must also remember that it is the good status of the research project which allows Alice to perceive more

fully what under other circumstances she might be too embarassed to investigate, which would then appear more physiognomically forbidden.

Now Alice's project is more determinate, i.e. to explore the
pornography, and her presence has intensified to the point of
intrigue. Her project prescribes a very specific place or function
to perception. She intends to go with her spontaneous attraction
to pornography by looking at it, feeling it, thinking it over, and
reflecting upon her responses. Thus perception is *one* mode of
contact among others. It is however, the primary way in which
hitherto unfamiliar realities present themselves. Perception is
then built upon and surpassed by "higher functions" such as
imagination, thought, and reflection. In other words, the goal of
Alice's project is not simply to *see* these things but to understand
them and herself as to their place and significance in the world.
Thus perception will give a basis for this understanding; it will
provide clues, but it will only be a point of departure. However,
perception attempts to see it all and see it in detail, for Alice is
intrigued by what lies before her and her overall understanding is
dependent upon perception. Alice begins by scanning a "whole
wall of artificial stimulators" which is something suprising and
new to her. She then runs over individual items looking at their
differences in size, shape, etc. In this array, she is particularly
interested in those she's never seen before in terms of their use
and bodily experience, for to understand them is to know what
they're used for and how they feel. While perception does not
present their use and bodily experience directly, these are horizons which are elaborated in imagination and thought. For instance, "the long slendor insertability and painfully protruding
spikes of a dildo-like thing" leads to various images of different
people using it in different ways and thoughts about masochism.
Similarly, a "plastic vagina-looking thing" is imagined first as a
doctor's model but this is dismissed and Alice looks more closely
for use-implicative features, then imagining "men trying to use
it." Perception is thus a gateway to imagination and thought
regarding the total situation in which these items have a place.
Following from Alice's project and presence as an intrigued
appropriation of the unfamiliar, perception gravitates towards
and dwells with the more strange looking things whose use and
bodily experience are not yet understood. Her interest is in the
novelly explicit, thus in the explicating. Perception thus functions
as the gateway to greater intellectual understanding. How different Alice's seeing would be if she was in a routine task-oriented

presence going to pick out something specific and quickly leave, or if her presence was that of disgust and being repelled. Instead perception is the initial embodiment of Alice's open intrigue as she looks around, sees the general style or group-type of things before her, and differentiates the various individual things passing over the relatively familiar and interrogating in detail the unfamiliar.

Most interesting in this situation are the changes which perception undergoes as Alice's project of exploring pornography becomes more personally interested and her presence becomes "turned on" or aroused by women on the magazine covers. This transformation or modification of her project and presence emerges out of latency or potentiality when evoked by perception as her open scanning of the magazines reveals "mostly women in very explicit poses." Once, however, she does become personally interested and aroused, the counter-project of being positively judged and the counter-presence of self-consciousness complicate Alice's hitherto straight forward perception. Perception expresses and reflects both conflicting projects and Alice's moreover ambivalent presence by becoming partially restricted — hesitant or inhibited. Rather than becoming captivated by and actively scrutinizing the details of these pictures of women, Alice glances quickly over the covers, never daring to open up any of the magazines and look inside (which incidently, she couldn't have done even if she wanted to since they are covered by plastic. Indeed, that she didn't even see the plastic shows how far from looking inside she was). In other words, perception sees but does not see, in a double movement of turning towards and turning away. This doubleness reflects respectively the project of exploring her sexual attraction to women and the project of being judged as good and normal. It also reflects her ambivalent presence which on one hand is increasingly aroused and intrigued by the women and on the other hand turns back upon herself and regards her activity as gay or perveted. Perception is thus not lived straight forwardly but is eclipsed; it avoids dwelling with and completely articulating the aspects of the field which it is projected towards. Perceptual involvement is lived as taboo and therefore disengages itself or better put, is restricted to a limited engagement which allows only a superficial, quickly glancing surface contact. This is possible because perception itself can become an object of experience, be judged, and the meaning it reveals when this occurs is that the person is involved in a forbidden relationship with what perception thematizes. Through perception, Alice is entering into a more or less intimate sexual relationship with other women and to this extent it can be negatively judged, lived as taboo, and restricted.

On an "objective" scale — however this could be devised — the masochistic artificial stimulators might be considered equally if not more taboo than the pictures of women, and so one might predict more perceptual avoidance of the former. But this is to ignore the immanent meaning of Alice's project which was other-oriented and more intellectual/spectating as she perceived the artificial stimulators. Thus perception was a spectating of things which she is not personally drawn towards sexually. This was not lived by her as taboo and she was free to lean in and look closely. It is only when her project and presence have a more personal and intimate orientation that perception is lived as taboo and restricted. If her interest in the women's pictures was purely an intellectual curiosity about others, Alice might have looked more closely. Also, if Alice did not care about how a personal homosexual involvement would be judged she might have looked more closely. Thus the crucial features of implicit personal intimacy and investment in the object and the negative valuation of this investment must be considered to understand the perceptual avoidance of the taboo.

It should also be noted that perceptual avoidance is not total. There is no problem of how Alice avoids something she doesn't see. Indeed she sees what she avoids, but at first only by a quick glance revealing a general style of thing whose particular graphic details are turned away from and never explicated. Perception can see enough to avoid seeing any more. We find another variation of seeing and avoiding seeing in Alice's relation to the other people in the store. These she doesn't even thematize but sees in the background, vaguely out of the corner of her eye as it were. These she sees even less fully than the pictures of women for they remain on the periphery, constituted in their typicality by a sense of forbiddenness. These are two different ways perception may avoid seeing something after a limited, nascent viewing (e.g., fleeting theme or background). These correspond to different kinds of forbiddenness, as defined by the person's value bestowing projects.

The quick glance and the fleeting theme do not alone necessarily constitute a taboo perception. Alice also glances quickly over the regular magazines and ordinary pipes as she walks out. Restricted seeing in this case is different in that it is simply the passing over of the irrelevant. While in the case of perceptual avoidance there is a definite intention to see the thing in greater depth as well as the intention to avoid that relation with it, in the present case the fleeting themes are not taboo but irrelevant to Alice's project and therein lies the basis of the limited perception. In one case the percept is of a forbidden thing and in the other of an irrelevant thing though superficially the quick glancing and fleeting theme may appear similar in both cases.

We find a wholly different kind of perception when Alice takes on the project of buying needed screens and papers with a strictly task oriented presence. This project is more determinate and less open, which is reflected in perception's strict looking for a certain size screen and certain type of papers. Perception is pragmatic and as soon as the predetermined things are seen, rather than being perceived further, they are behaviorally appropriated. Here we could call perception appropriative. It operates by looking for and identifying for appropriation without articulating its object any further.

General Considerations Regarding Taboo Perception

Prethematic perception. Perceptual objects, taboo included, do not come out of nowhere but are from the beginning situated in space and enter the perceptual field through the background. The background is a rather complicated phenomenon which may be given in several different ways, many of which are difficult to describe on account of their inarticulateness. Indeed, the perceptual background seems to admit of gradations which blend innocuously into the totally unperceived. For instance, as our subject Brian enters the News Stand, the food machines, the smoking paraphernalia and the pornography remain in the background. They are not given in detail or even as objects per se but rather as general spatial areas like "the entrance way" and "the far end of the store." They are potential themes and the person may engage in definite relations with them without ever even thematizing them, let alone explicating them. For instance, our subject Sara responded to the cold of the freezer section in the grocery store by putting her hands in her pockets without ever making a theme proper of this background phenomenon. Brian avoided "people" in the supermarket as soon as they were given according to their general style in the periphery of his field without ever focusing on them perceptually. Thus vague areas of the background are beckoning, neutral or forbidden physiognomically and are approached, passed over, or avoided without being clearly perceived in individual distinctiveness and detail.

Inexplicit perceptual thematization. Thematized perceptual objects, taboo included, are not given all at once in full explicitness. Even when an object is thematized, it may be largely indeterminate as perceived. It may be given globally as a whole, as to its type, or a part or feature may be highlighted with much of the object remaining in the more inarticulate noematic ground or internal horizon, thus being only potentially explicable. For instance, our subject Karen thematized both the pinball machine and the pornography section of the store and turned away from both so quickly that the fleeting perception only gave "a regular pinball machine – the usual" and "a gate to the section that said 'Adults Only' indicating the presence of pornography."

Unactualized potentialities of perception. Why are these perceptual realms which lack clear, distinct, actual givenness not perceived more extensively? Of course, it is intrinsically impossible to thematize every object in a situation or to explicate every feature of even one thematized object, but what determines which are not thematized and/or not made to show themselves explicitly? Perceptual powers are not exercised on either one of two accounts: *irrelevancy* or *forbiddenness.* According to the teleological structure of his perception, in which Brian is busy looking for magazines, the food machines and smoking paraphernalia are irrelevant and thus remain in the prethematic background. Karen thematized the pinball machine but since she "never liked to play," its explication was completely irrelevant. On the other hand, sometimes relevant things and features of things are not seen clearly — beyond that, they are actively avoided. These matters have great relevance, not the least of which is their forbiddenness. In the news stand, our subject Sara's perceptual telos is "things which provide information about the social life of the store's clientelle, particularly as it relates to women." She doesn't thematize and explicate the walls and ceilings of the store due to their irrelevance, but what could better fulfill her intention than the pornography? Indeed, she admits a perceptual interest in the pornography and her perception even includes an intention to explicate it, but there is also a counter-intention to avoid this area on account of its forbiddenness. In other words, the teleological stucture of perception includes a restriction of possibilities which can override other goals and thereby render otherwise relevant potential themes and features as to be avoided. This complex teleological structure of forbidden perception is reflected in a double movement, a seeing and not seeing (clearly), a fulfilling and avoiding intention that occur at the same time, thus an arrested or eclipsed actualization of the perceptual process.

Forbidden perceptual explication. The perception of thematized objects may be limited by its globality or partiality. For instance, Sara's perception operates in the manner of a distanced glancing over and then avoiding "more pornographic-type magazines than ever before." Perception is too far away and fast moving to explicate this global typicality more fully. Indeed, this type of perception repeats past synthesis of meaning rather than forging new determinations of the object in the present. In the front section of the store with the soft core magazines, Sara recognizes "a few familiar titles" but the bodies on the front covers remain "a blur" in the noematic ground while the hidden inside remains so as a socially informed horizon of the objects: "A type of printed material pertaining to sex and not to be looked at." In its recognition of familiarity, perception retreads the past synthesis which originally presented the object as taboo, forbidden, and a *type* of thing to be avoided. A similar process occurs when thematization highlights a "suggestive" *part* of a taboo object. For instance, Sara sees the gate and sign "Adults Only," which is familiar enough to indicate "an even worse, more awful type of pornography," which she does not even gaze at in order to explicate at all. It remains, as it always has been, an internal horizon with no positive, distinct details but pervaded with a physiognomic awefulness, forbiddenness. Yet, there is an intention to see; Sara struggles to overcome this habitual teleological structure of perception. However, as she looks beyond the gate and apprehends what lies behind it, she remains restricted to globality given through a distanced glancing at familiar aspects like "racks of book cases for printed material — maybe books or magazines" (notice the indeterminacy of meaning expressed by "maybe" which indicates more possibility than actuality). So much is allowable; it is going up close to explicate beyond typical matters that have only been "heard about" which is forbidden. Hence, she never focuses upon the 25¢ movies even though they are announced by a gigantic red and white blinking neon sign, the leather goods and "marital aids" that occupy a whole wall, or any of the materials on the racks. Sara avoids the "pornography section" prior to any explication.

Forbidden thematization. In Sara's case, there is at least the thematization of the pornography section, even if it is quickly avoided on account of forbiddenness. It is also possible that matters residing preobjectively in the background are avoided prior to clear thematization on the basis of peripheral perception or prethematic scanning. Sara would have proceded in this fashion had she not "struggled to face the pornography." Prior to approaching the soft core pornography on the "regular rack" she sensed it was there out of the corner of her eye and as she approached it, her head twisted away, back towards the nonpornographic magazines. Then she stopped just before arriving in front of it and moved back to the middle of the store (a safe distance away) before turning to actually thematize these magazines. One of the subjects in a pilot study felt a "seedy aura" in the back of the store and left without ever "taking the chance" to look at it. This is what occurs when Alice avoids people in the supermarket. Afraid they will "think she is strange" talking to herself into a tape recorder there, she looks away and moves away as soon as she catches a "glimmer" of another person approaching. Thus without ever thematizing them rendering any details explicit, peripheral auras, glimmers, and types of background things may be avoided. This, like the short circuiting of explication (and any perceptual process), can be habitualized and come to be more automatic (undeliberate).

Public and private contexts of forbidden perception. Existentially, perception is not neutral with regard to its objects; perceiving is a manifestation of the person's involvement in the situation, a biographically meaningful appropriation and integration of objects into a circuit of existence. We must remember that perception is therefore a social act to a significant extent perceivable by others, and it may be precisely this horizon of perception that is avoided. In other words, one may restrict one's perceiving so as not to be caught in the act of involvement, which means being understood by others as having a stake in the object with all it implies. In this case perception could actualize its possibilities in private, for activity would only be forbidden in public, places where perception is potentially visible to others. Here it is not seeing per se but rather being seen seeing that is taboo. Sometimes dark sunglasses are enough to forgo the arrest of perceptual actualization in this context. On the other hand, however, one may refrain from actualizing perceptual possibilities in a situation even in privacy because the implications of being involved with an object, no matter how personally interesting from other angles, are not integratable into the overall biographical flow of the perceiver. Perception, we remember, defines his peculiar spatio-temporality (e.g., a dubious past), and therefore one may be loathe to perceive some things even in private on account of its meaning for the perceiver himself.

Taboo projects. To understand the mutual implication of taboo perception and the perceiver's social spatio-temporality at large we must go beyond perception to the person's overall projective structure that is the ground of perception's peculiar perspectivity. Our analysis has found that in many situations the person is living not one but an ensemble, a family of projects (Wertz, 1982). These may be relatively separate, parallel, or hierarchically integrated (mutually supportive). Further they may be harmonious or at odds, even incompossible with each other. It is the latter case which occurs in taboo situations. For instance, Brian finds himself spontaneously aroused by and attracted to the soft core pornography, which may be viewed as a subproject of appropriation emerging in the course of his routine look over the magazines, yet another subproject implicit until now in his involvement is that of maintaining a socially appropriate and acceptable (as defined by him) stance there. The latter social-self subproject precludes and overrides the former sexual subproject, eclipsing and frustrating it soon after its emergence. In such cases as these, there is not unity but some manner and extent of fragmentation in mental life. Sara's project is to explore the store's social horizons, particularly women's place there, and the pornography assumes its relevance accordingly; however, she finds herself unable to overcome her "automatic" tendency to act like a "good, normal woman" which to her means avoiding such things. Alice is able to live her project of exploring the pornography as long as this exploration addresses its pertinence to others. For instance, she closely inspects the marital supplies and leather equipment that others would use, imagines and thinks over the consumers' involvements with these things, and contemplates what it is like for the magazine models. This is all harmonious with the social legitimation conferred by her helping with research. But when Alice becomes aroused by the women in the pictures thus herself engaging in a homosexual subproject, she renunciates this goal for that of being seen as "sexually normal." Indeed the subproject of not standing out conspicuously and vulnerable to condemnation is implicit in much of our psychic life and may be considered trans-situational. In Brian's case, it had to do with not allowing himself to be sexually aroused by the magazines in public (so he picked up a *Scientific American*). In Sara's case, it had to do with avoiding pornography, which her "parents have always said is sinful." In Alice's case it has to do with not appearing homosexual. These subprojects of social selfhood are visible in the present situation insofar as the person spontaneously begins to project their transgression, but the morality here expressed is deeply sedimented as a habituality that pervades many situations implicitly without the least bit of deliberation and even, as we see in Sara's failure, despite considerable voluntary efforts to surpass it.

Perceptuality in taboo projection. We found in the Mello News Stand cases in which two subprojects have two manifestly different and conflictual intentional relations to the same object. In these cases perception exhibits a compromise which expresses both projects by both seeing and turning away from the object in question. Perception is fleeting and turns aways before explicit thematization occurs. For instance, when Alice comes to the pictures of homosexual acts, her perception changes to fleeting glancing, these magazines presenting the dual physiognomic characters of attractiveness and forbiddenness, reflecting the equivocality of her overall orientation. As long as both subprojects are pursued, perception continues to display this dual structure of apprehension and inhibition/avoidance. If social/self acceptability were given up then the object would be extensively adumbrated by perception, but in our cases, the equivocality is terminated by abandoning the forbidden object-relation. Perception expresses this by decisively turning away from the taboo thing and thus participating in the fulfillment of the subproject of an affirmable, "normal" self. This achievement requires a selective perceptual avoidance, an abandonment of actual perceptual processes. This shows us that the perceived object is not the only matter of significance in perception but equally at stake is the self or "who" of the perceiver — his future, relations with others and so on. Brian describes these horizons of his turning away by saying that seeing pornography "has no future" for him, that he would reproach himself and expect others to do so as well were he to take up an involvement with pornography. Perceptual thematization is not accidental or isolated but implies the relation of the whole person to the world.

Ambivalence and embarassed self-consciousness. Ambivalence is a presence which takes up the project in a bipolar movement. In an ambivalent presence, the person is on one hand oriented towards the goal of the project but on the other falls away from its end through outright avoidance, inhibition, and/or self-conscious petrification. Alice had the greatest difficulty carrying out the task of reporting her experience into a tape recorder as she walked through the supermarket. Every time she began to look around and start her report she became overcome with embarassment and anticipations of being judged as "crazy" by the shoppers, which led her to stop speaking and turn the tape recorder off so as not to "look funny, stupid, different or out of place." The self-conscious pole of ambivalence is anti-functional; to the extent that it holds sway over the person's presence as a whole, it undermines the project. Alice's project became frozen in negative judgments in the face of which her spontaneous activity flinched and was objectified. What is an issue here, as we have seen above, is the "who" implicit in the situation of the project, particularly in terms of its forbiddenness. Sara's curiosity about the Mello News Stand comes to a halt inasmuch as her tense flight from the pornography is deeply rooted in her past and constitutes a habitual presence to the type of object whose involvement in her life implies that she is "sinful, a prostitute or a nymphomaniac." The dominance of the avoidance pole of her ambivalence is involuntary and persists despite efforts on her part to muster the "courage" to explore the pornography. Alice's straightforward engagement with the pornography becomes similarly ambivalent and overtaken by embarassed self-consciousness in which she considers other people as thinking she is "sexually abnormal, a queer" and so on. To this extent, the "who" or "self" of this project is first disengaged by objectification and then abandoned as the subject's "own."

Anxious, ambivalent perception. Much of our data leads to the general conclusion that anxious embarassment can be a modification of presence that is antithetical to perceptual thematization of taboo objects. As part of this overall inhibited, social/self oriented stance, actualizing the possibility of thematization and explication may be undermined and at least partially given up. The taboo object is either never thematized in the first place or turned away from and becomes at least parathematic and at most permanently relegated to the unperceived background. As long as the ambivalence remains, perception is restricted to a limited engagement of background sensing of or quick, superficial, glancing surface-contact with the taboo object. An example of this is Alice's fleeting encounter with the magazines which is itself lived as an expression of her sexuality for which she is responsible and socially accountable. As soon as the ambivalence is resolved in the direction of a repudiation of the straightforward involvement, no further thematic perception occurs at all. If there is any extensive properly thematic perception in the moment of self-conscious embarassment, it is either of other people (e.g., "they-'re watching me") or of the perceiver him/herself (e.g., "I feel tense, out of place, and awkward"). More likely, however, there is neither thematic perception nor any manner of dwelling in anxiousness self-consciousness but rather an attempt to take another stance and route in the situation which involves a non-forbidden perceptual process.

Four variations of anxious perceptual avoidance. At a more specific level, we can distinguish four typical occurances of perception as it is anxiously lived. In the first case, perceptual thematization is freely executed and it is not of itself embarassing but is guilty as an accomplice; that is, however innocent itself, it is part of a larger activity whose visibility to an other is embarassing and therefore it is curtailed along with the total activity.

> For instance, when Brian is locked out of his hotel room he is looking for moving parts on the lock as he pulls and pushes at it, shaking the door. As he hears the elevator open, he becomes anxious and concerned about appearing to be a thief breaking into a room, at which moment his problem solving object–relations, including the lock-perception, are curtailed.

In the second case it is perceptual thematization itself that is embarassing and vulnerable to negative judgments of an other.

> For Brian, extensively gazing upon the soft core magazines in the New Stand is an activity which is itself shameful despite (or perhaps because of) his arousal, so he gives it up and looks for a *Scientific American* to absorb himself in.

In the above cases, perceptual powers would be exercised more fully in a private or secret context since it is the potentiality of being seen that constitutes the anxiety. The object itself does not appear forbidden but rather it is the perceiver's visible involvement with it that is forbidden. In the third case, the object appears forbidden directly to the perceiver himself. Often in this case explication of the thematized object never occurs or if it does, the first sign of the taboo realm is enough to repell further interrogation.

> While the soft core pornography was amusing to Brian (though not to be publicly indulged in), as soon as he sees the sign "Adults Only" as indicating a type of thing which is so repulsive and evil that it has no place in his world, he turns away. Any further involvement would imply *to him* a "desperate" and "irresponsible" self. This presence to "that sort of thing" has habitually been Brain's stance, which involves an eclipse of perception upon which a certain integrity of his existence depends, for the kind of life in which such an object has a thematic place is wholey repulsive, alien, and "not for him."

The fourth case, which we have discussed previously, occurs when the person becomes anxious in the face of a background pretheme prior to even focusing on it.

> Brian is generally uncomfortable regarding other people in the supermarket. As soon as they appear in the periphery of his perceptual field, he looks the other way, for instance at the cheeses. He avoids looking directly at others, "especially their eyes" and stays clear of them quite effectively without ever perceptualy thematizing them.

Others and self as themes for anxious perception. When the taboo object itself is abandoned by perception though the person has not yet surpassed their anxious presence, others and the self sometimes become perceptual themes. Although others are often avoided perceptually at times, the anxious perceiver may thematize and even explicate them. In doing so there is a specific attunement to the other's regard of the perceiver, particularly his negative regard. People are seen in terms of their possibility of seeing and/or judging the perceiver. For instance, Alice sees a lady in the supermarket "give me a strange questioning glance." Even if the other is not concerned about the perceiver they are perceived in terms of this *capacity*, which is part of the internal horizon of the other. This manner of perceiving the other actually or potentially "having regard for me" is consistent with the overall self-concern of this presence, which is perhaps more often lived imaginally or in thought as Sara does when she thinks they might view her as a prostitute or nymphomaniac. If the self proper is thematized perceptually, it is often the body's own tension, inhibition, stiffness, awkwardness, spellbindedness, alienation or out-of-placeness that becomes prominent as it does in Sara's case, which is also consistent with the eclipse of spontaneous straightforward activity characteristic of this presence.

Social perception in general. The issue of perception's visibility for others takes on an interesting flavor when the object of perception is the other person, for it expresses an investment *in* an other person *to* an other person. Thematization and explication are nascent moments of a *relationship*. Brian tries to catch a bartender's eyes with his own to let him know he wants a drink and avoids the antagonistic-looking hotel porter because he wants nothing to do with him. Thematization and explication invite a reciprocal relationship while turning away curtails it. Part of Brian's inconspicuousness in the supermarket is achieved by never gazing at others and especially their eyes. Perception is a social intention which contacts and distances as it thematizes and turns away. The woman at the bar who doesn't want to be "hit on" avoids the others with her eyes, thereby closing herself to the reciprocal relation of which perception would be a first embodiment. The expression "hey, whatcha lookin' at, boy?!" testifies to the perceived person's threatening rejection of this nascent relationship when to the perceived, the perceiver "has no line on" him. Hence, whether or not — according to one's projects — a person is willing to become so engaged determines to a great extent the manner of social perception. Whether one looks longingly, never dares to look, or steals fleeting glances at an other follows from the manner in which one projects his appropriation of and appearance for the other.

So-called social "rules" of perception are no more than actual habitualities constituted in concrete relations with others. The vicissitudes of perceptual life which hinge upon its visibility and vary according to one's projected social relations can become habitualized and even instituted as societal or cultural norms. In this way others' values may infect perception though they are never the only determining agent or even the privileged one since a person may take on the project of being oblivious to, dominating, being with, or for others. In the News Stand, Alice avoids thematizing those she senses in the background because "it's impolite to invade people's privacy; I don't want them to do it to me." This social "rule" would have no bearing on her perception except that it is part of her project to be, or at least be seen as a polite person, perhaps by virtue of the potential and/or anticipated consequences of being (seen as) impolite. In the intermission of a concert, Brian "glances in moderation" at a "nicely arranged woman." This perception reflects the sexually restrained presence which goes along with much of social life and certainly such a dignified event as a symphony concert. Similar "rules" are expressed in statements like "it's impolite to stare," "don't examine your food before eating it," "never look in a woman's purse," and in such good manners as being attentive to one's guests and maintaining eye contact with a conversatión partner. Our perceptual habits are fraught with social prohibitions which we unreflectingly abide by. Indeed, the people we freely stare at, touch, listen to, taste and smell carefully and extensively are extremely few in relation to pure possibilities. Perception has its own etiquette which once habitually instituted requires no actual others to be present for perception to function according to what are ultimately their demands.

> Since various human possibilities are forbidden from and remain "mere possibilities" in actual perception, that area which is the threshold of the real, such things as pornographic magazines and movies reveal forbidden themes to the vicarious and imaginal (or at most quasi-real) intentions of people who are still interested in thematization and explication. The social isolation and lack of integration of such themes with "the rest of life" is obvious. It is interesting to note how popular filmmakers "respect" their captive audiences so as not to "offend" them by their treatment of taboo subject matters. To that extent films mimic ordinary, conventional perceptual experiences of taboo objects such as those we have been discussing. In *Tatoo* when Bruce Dern's character has a sexual encounter with the stripper in a glass booth, we are shown only a *part* of the encounter, that is her upper body and the reflection of his face in the glass. In *The Hunger*, the sensual bloodsucking is shown in fast paced cutting that amounts to only the most fleeting and quickly eclipsed *glances*. In *Return of the Jedi*, when Jabba the Hut does what no one actually sees to

Princess Leah, the camera moves from their faces — on his a lascivious, drooling, tongue-twitching look and hers one of excited revulsion — to the tenderminded robot, C3PO, who *turns away* and proclaims in mock humanness, "I can't bear to watch." When the camera returns to the couple, Leah is lying tamely with Jabba in a revealing (but not too revealing) harem outfit, neck collared on a chain, held by the monster, whose phallic tail twitches alongside her legs. The closest many get to genuine thematization and explication of such horrors *in context* is by the vicarious experience afforded by reading such texts as those of writers like Genet (1964) who was "hot for crime" and Vassi (1981) whose "catalogueing of the entire range of erotic experience" led him also to feel that he "would always be a criminal in the eyes of a world that despised both its animal and angel natures" (p. 222). The writings of those who transgress provide conventional man with the explicit expression of his own most forbidden possibilities of existence.

Taboo perception and cultural objectivities. We see that perception implies culture from yet another angle when we recognize that the perceived world, as it transcends any individual's projective presence, is largely culturally constituted. Man meets the other not only in his gaze and demands but in the very objects that surrounds these relations. As Merleau-Ponty says, man creates his own milieu, which implies that the world perception is given to apprehend, and in which it exercises its possibilities and finds its limits, is already a cultural world. We live in a perceptual world in which fashions themselves play at revealing and concealing the human body. It is a world in which certain doors are already closed and others open, the places already made. The Mello News Stand, as a perceivable place, could be analyzed in its own right, namely as a cultural-historical artifact preloaded with perceptual meaning. The fact that sexual objects are profoundly proliferated in imaginal, symbolic and artificial forms, their separation from the rest of the store, the partition that partly obstructs vision, the gate that requires effort to open, the sign barring children from the enterance, the economics of the store all say something about our culture that is worthy of reflection. Our culture constitutes many of our perceivable places and places limits as well as provides opportunities; it forbids and invites perception which apprehends such significance immediately. This leads us to our discussion of the laboratory.

Discussion

Ecological Validity of Experimentation

Without empirically based qualitative description, consider-ations of the ecological validity of experimentation is psychology are left to unsystematic and informal observation. One value of analyses of the present kind is that of providing an appropriate kind of scientific rigor for answering the question of the extent to which experimental research applies to ordinary situations, which are presumably the ultimate object of psychology. Our findings in this regard call our attention to serious *ecological invalidity*. For instance, to the extent that objects are taboo for the subject only by virtue of an implicit yet intrinsic external horizon of worthless self and forbidding others, the experimental infliction of a history of punishment by electric shock would not even approximate the constitution of "taboo" meaning. Our general conclusion, largely consistent with Neisser (1976), is that the researched phenome-non has been transformed under the demands of experimental manageability (i.e., for isolation, manipulation and quantifica-tion) to such an extent that the experimental phenomenon fails to correlate in essential ways with taboo perception in everyday life.

Stimulus objects. Our qualitative distinction between percep-tual thematization proper and what we have called submerged perception, or perception integrated in non-perceptual experi-ence becomes relevant for the consideration of the ecological validity of words and pictures as stimulus objects in perceptual experimentation. While words and pictures can be the objects of purely perceptual experience and are often that for their technical creators (e.g., printers), ordinarily and as a rule in experimenta-tion the actual object of experience is a thought or image, which correlates with linguistic or imaginal psychological activity though it is grounded in perception. In other words, experimentation has been studying taboo reading and picture viewing, which are qualitatively different from taboo perception in its pregnant and most authentic sense. It is beside the point whether recognition thresholds for reading the word "chair" correlate with those for seeing a chair because even if they do, the essential psychological structures of the two experiences are not the same. Words and pictures are used because they are easily controlled — isolated, manipulated, and quantified — but this gain is outbalanced by the cost in the form of perception studied. An interesting case is that of nonsense syllables. While one might think they are purely perceptual since they don't symbolize anything, it is more likely that they are perceived as symbols simply deficient in meaningful reference. The wedding of experimental manageability and genuine perception would lead more in the direction of squiggles and zig-zags, though even these are probably seen as indeterminate symbolic representations.

Perceptual processes. The process of perceiving tachistoscopically generated material of any sort is highly peculiar qualitatively. It is initiated by an unusual sort of "looking for" which protends an indeterminate object given beforehand as to its type (e.g., a "word") which is followed by a "being struck by" the specific actually perceived. The perceived has a very limited spatiality beyond itself which its meaning intrinsically draws from (external horizon) and does not admit of any richness of hidden aspects of its own (internal horizon). Its temporality is limited to an instantaneous flash largely unrelated to what has come before and what is about to be perceived next. To the greatest extent possible perception is reduced to actual perception, stripped of its potentialities. The limited spatiality and temporality of the perceived do not allow very much explication and none of the more extensive types. The perceived addresses only one sense modality and often cannot be apprehended by others (e.g., one cannot touch a word projected on a screen). The limitation of the embodied subjectivity of perceptual processes extends further into an almost complete restraint of motility. The perceiver is reduced to a receiver of isolated material lacking in dimension. Rigorous qualitative analysis of perception in experimental situations would be necessary for a truly sophisticated contrast with ordinary perception, but our brief considerations make it clear that essential constituents of everyday perceptual process either take on highly peculiar forms or are totally missing from laboratory perception thus drastically reducing its ecological validity.

Recognition threshold. What the experimenter retains as data of this process, the dependent variable, is but a rather small and highly abstract part of its occurance, recognition threshold. While it could be argued that this is not a properly psychological index of perception at all, we will limit ourselves to its ecological validity as an index of selectivity, for which it was originally intended by the New Look (though it has become an end in itself for many). First it must be recognized that the singling out of something present in the perceptual field is not the same as the amount of time it takes to recognize what a thing is, despite the appearance of the latter to the quantitatively minded as an index of sensitivity. In fact, the experimental subject, with his eyes already fixed in the proper place and the material already determined by the experimenter, is not engaged in selectivity at the moment he is attempting to catch the fleeting image. Experimentation which purports to study selectivity in this way presupposes it rather than examines it. Viewing the matter more empirically, recognition time and selectivity do not correspond to each other. We found many instances in which objects which could be recognized quickly and easily were not thematized and those which took considerable time to identify were thematized. A case in point is Alice who in the news stand selected objects which took many seconds to recognize and consistently passed over instantaneously identifiable things. Even if threshold usually correlates with selectivity (which is dubious), the point is that they are qualitatively different matters of such variable relations as to indicate a most questionable validity of threshold as an index for selectivity despite its quantitative manageability.

Empirical Findings

In the context of experimental methodology, the existence of distinctive processes on the part of taboo perception, apart from such other variables as past experience and set, has been difficult to maintain. Despite the discontinuity of experimentation and everyday life, it is possible for us to address the same conceptual problem from a different empirical standpoint. While we are not, of course, in a position to say whether taboo perception operates at a higher threshold than normal perception, our research does support the thesis that the former is different from the latter. Our analysis has been able to bring to light the *qualitative* differences between taboo and normal perception. We too have found a significant relationship between anxiety and perception. Our findings also shed some light on relationship of perception to past experience and set, which have confounded many experimental studies. Finally, our findings suggest a possible clarification of the discrepancies among experimental results.

"Subception" and "defense." Although a great deal more work with appropriate methodological refinements is needed for a comprehensive treatment of "subception," we found empirical

evidence of perceptual apprehensions which hold much significance for the perceiver without involving any thematization proper. Sara felt the cold in the supermarket and put her hands in her
pockets without ever making that cold or the warmth of her
pockets perceptual themes and Alice, in her disliked situation,
apprehended her car's gas pedal in her effective driving routine
without its objectification. What is distinctive in the case of taboo
perception, for instance when Sara twists away from the soft core
pornography before ever looking directly at it, is that these
background "prethemes" have the significance of forbiddenness,
inimicality, and anxiety provocation which often overshadow
whatever attractiveness they also possess. They are apprehended
as such by an attuned bodily subjectivity and thematization is
avoided. What has been called "defense" is from our vantage
point renunciating the objectification of forbidden prethemes or
virtual/potential themes. In contrast, for normal perceptual processes, relevant prethemes (whether entering the background
intentionally or serendipitously) are given, however vaguely with
a univocal physiognomy of invitingness which calls out a direct,
straight-forward involvement with them that constitutes the project for which they are relevant. To the extent necessary for
project actualization, they are then actually thematized so as to
emerge as clear, distinctive perceptual objects. Following the
process of taboo perception beyond thematization when it occurs,
we find a second level of limitations pertaining typically to the
manner and extent of explication. In this case "subception" and
"defense" again pertain to a failure to actualize perceptual possibilities which vaguely imply matters forbidden from articulation.
When a taboo object or an object possessing taboo features is
thematized, the intention of extensive explication, however relevant, is renunciated much in the way we have described thematization itself above. That is, when the object is thematized, its
significance as a whole, whether it is focused on globally or in
terms of a part, includes something forbidden which is not yet
actually in clear view but remains largely implicit or virtual and
the possibility of making it distinct by the relevant explicating
synthesis remains unactualized on account of being lived as "off
limits." Most importantly, we have found that to understand this
peculiar process we must recognize the external horizons of the
object as meant, namely the "bad self," the "condemning others,"
and "other related forbidden things" which play intrinsic roles in

the constitution of the perceptual sense (noema) "taboo." It is only in terms of the specific projective presence with its concrete labor in the total system self-others-things that perceptual possibilities are held back from actuality, because it is in this situation that the taboo phenomena do not fit, are not integrated.

Anxiety and perception. We have also found empirical evidence of a relation between anxiety and perception. To the extent that subjects became anxious, perceptual processes may suffer. While it has been suggested that anxiety causes perception to be "defensive," which in turn reduces anxiety, we conceived the matter somewhat differently. We are careful not to view anxiety as a state of the organism (enclosed within it) and perception as a neutral reception of stimuli. Rather than viewing anxiety and perception in this external, accidental relation of reciprocal causality, we view them as mutually interdependent and interpenetrating aspects of one projective presence. In the present context, anxiety only arose on the basis of perceptual processes, but perceptual processes which apprehended the object as "inimical," which implies anxiety. Since our view of the perceptual noema includes its affective characters and since we recognize mood itself as an intentional relation to a certain object or situation, anxiety and perception do not appear to be separate variables but play a single melody as it were, one embedded in the overall projective presence. Only inasmuch as Sara is living the project of exploring pornography as well as being a virtuous woman as defined by her parents is the pornography given as relevant–but–forbidden (implying) condemning others and a loathed self she is on the threshold of becoming). Anxiety's narrowing and disintegrating sense of being stripped of possibilities (e.g., "I should not, must not, cannot") and perception's disengagement from the taboo constitute two closely intertwined aspects of the same conflict ridden projective history. The equivocal projection is manifested through both emotional ambivalence and a perceptual struggle of turning towards and away at once in concert with behavior, thought, and a host of other aspects of psychic life which also attest to the same failure at integration. We rediscover the same relationship between anxiety and perception at the second level of perceptual process, explication. Alice does actually thematize magazines picturing homosexual activity, for she is genuinely attracted by virtue of her sexual exploratory project, however she is also attempting to maintain a normal, acceptable self for others. While it is consistent with her projected sexuality for others to glance in passing, it is not fitting with this structure to pick up and explicate the magazines. The disintegrating uncanniness of anxiety and the failure of perceptual explication are again but two sides of the same coin. Being affected by forbiddenness and the loss of perceptual agency are essential moments of the maintainance of a self-world structural dominated by others, in Alice's case that of a secretly nascent homosexual relation which appears normal.

> Probable limitations of this conception can be elaborated on the basis of Fischer's (1971) excellent work on anxiety, in which he distinguishes neurotic and healthy *types* of anxiety. Strong indications are that our subjects manifested a significantly (though by no means completely) *neurotic* presence. That in the face of which neurotic anxiety operates is a lived sense of others as disapproving judges and that about which one is anxious is a disgusting, worthless self one is about to become, all of which must be avoided. In a neurotic presence, the person does not experience himself as owning and directing the course of his life but rather his feelings, actions and sense of worth are tied up with others' values and opinions. On the contrary in a healthy presence, the uncertainty of anxiety is lived with a sense of agency in the face of reassuring others, which would allow for a more open and fullsome exploration of the situation at hand including a perceptuality which freely actualizes its possibilities.

Perceptual set and past. Our analysis disclosed a most intimate connection between perception and extraperceptual aspects of mental life like behavior, thought and emotionality (as indicated above). We found that thematic and explicit remembering and anticipating which precedes perceptual processes as well as prethematic and implicit retentive and protentive aspects of perceptual process itself can be most decisive for the life of perception. For instance, the fact that Alice has no past experience with some erotic materials and consequently very indeterminate expectations regarding them must be considered in understanding the long time consumed in recognition and explication, a fact supported by experimentation. However, when we consider perception beyond recognition time, matters complexify. Generally, (that is, for all kinds of perception,) we do not find an invariant relationship of causality between these variables and perceptual selectivity (thematization and explication). Rather, past experience and set assume their specific relationship with/in perception according to the person's overall projective presence, the whole of which they are parts. For instance, when Brian and Alice walk into the news stand, both expect an "ordinary news stand," however Brian sees "a good magazine rack" whereas Alice sees "a complete pornography shop." Approaching the issue holistically instead of atomistically and causally, we see it is not set in and of itself that is crucial for perception but the way the expectation is lived and held according to the overall projective presence. Brian enters with a habitual, narrowly appropriative intention which renders everything but magazines irrelevant whereas Alice's project is more indeterminate and her presence more openly curious. Brian holds his expectations tightly and Alice holds hers loosely. The significance and weight of a given set for perception is not generally a linear, invariant function but varies according to the sort of openness entailed in the projective presence. Similar considerations apply to past experience. Whether a person thematizes familiar things as Sara does in the news stand, or novel things as Alice does depends upon the overall intentional orchestration of experience in which perception takes up a determinate relation to — that is, either relives or surpasses — its past. In other words, perception is not necessarily a slave of either anticipations or past perception, though these always have a bearing, but as an original function can transcend both; whether it does so or not is intelligible only in the larger context, the person's projective presence.

Set and past of taboo perception. However, when we take up the specific case of taboo perception and broaden our considerations of past perception beyond its mere frequency to its significance, the issue becomes fascinating and difficult. Although the matter deserves closer scrutiny, it makes sense to say that when taboo subprojects are renounced, perceptual processes do seem to remain tied to past syntheses of meaning and anticipations based on them. Sara sees the gate and what others have said about such places in the past is anticipated as the section's inner horizon, perception then simply fulfilling this categorical sense by explicating only "a lot of printed matter that you're not supposed to look at." To the extent that perceptual possibilities are *not originally actualized* in relation to the taboo, retained and anticipated meanings constitute the crucial however subtle and implicit noematic structure without ever being surpassed. This implies that in taboo type perception, set and past experience, far from being confounding "independent" variables in relation to perception, assume such a status as to be intrinsically constitutive of the very phenomenon! It could be that it is this subtle experiential process, occuring in a zone of immanent meaning sometimes beyond the reach of external experimental manipulations, that has made these matters so resistant to systematically replicable experimentation. For one instance, consider an experimenter who attempts to eliminate any set for neutral words by telling the subject that "some of these will be dirty words" and who then finds no evidence of perceptual defense. It could be that his manipulation not only removes the set for neutral words but also the very taboo character of the critical words inasmuch as the subject takes up the legitimate project of being a good subject by seeing quickly what the experimenter clearly encourages him to. Thinking he was manipulating something external to taboo perception, the experimenter does not realize he is participating in the very constitution of the subject's perceptual experience inasmuch as the latter implies the temporal unfolding of a total self-others-object structure of which the experimenter and the laboratory are a part. It may be impossible according to the *eidos* of the phenomenon to unconfound these variables and it is quite possible that the apparent instability of the phenomenon as reflected in divergent experimental results is a consequence of blind, unanalyzed manipulations whose subtle significance for the phenomenon are quite variable. To rigorously clarify the confusing and apparently contradictory results of experimentation in this area, it would be necessary to perform qualitative analyses of the subjects' experience of these experimental situations in depth and detail with special attention to how the subject live the self-other-object experimental structure in relation to their larger temporality.

Implications for Perceptual Theory: General Comments

Perception has remained something of an alien to psychological conceptualizations. After its problem-fraught treatment according to the empiricistic orientation of psychophysics, who at least viewed perception as a psychological process in its own right, perception has lost this status and has been viewed as behavior and more recently as cognition. The latter tendencies pertain to the problem at hand through those who claim that what is mistakenly considered perceptual defense is reducible to a be-havioral or neurological response and through those who explain the phenomenon on the basis of an information processing model. Let us briefly consider how our treatment of perception differs from these theoretical developments as well as how it relates to the general notion of the unconscious.

Perception and behavior. Qualitative analysis carried to the *eidetic* level allows us to distinguish perception from behavior and identify the original and unique structure of the former. Although we also recognize a two-way dependency and in some respects a syncretic relationship between the two, perception is an *apprehension* of the surroundings whereas behavior is a *transformation* of them. Perception distinctly does not at all change its objects whereas the very object of behavior is change. It is precisely in this difference that this close relationship unfolds, for without motility changing one's perspective on an object, apprehension is paralyzed and without apprehending the situation, motility looses its bearing. In view of these eidetic insights, the structure of taboo perception has been located in its peculiar way of apprehending meanings in the surroundings rather than re-duced to verbal response or any behavior which could be brought under the control of the "contingencies of reinforcement" which would themselves have to be perceived to have any meaning at all for the person. Not only is perception different from "response" at the molar level of behavior but it is also of an essentially different nature from neurological activity in the broadest sense (including afferent impulses) and therefore requires *psychological* concepts which reflect its intentional structure as a distinctive and irreducible apprehension of the situation.

Perception and information processing. The basic problem of cybernetic models of perception as well as any view that encapsu-lates perceptual processes inside of the subject (whether con-ceived mentalistically or physiologically), is that they do not reflect the *intentionality* basic to perception. When perceptual theorizing sticks close to its eidos, it thinks in terms of world relations, for it is in the world, not in the perceiver that perception apprehends its meaningful objects. The fact that perception in-volves awareness, which is always awareness *of something for itself*, makes it different from anything like a computer or any manner of mere internal manipulations or energy transforma-tions. The relationship of the whole embodied person to his situation and that between a cybernetic mechanism to physical energy are radically opposed to each other. Erledyi (1974) admits that the problem of consciousness is "tricky" for such models and that it is "always awkward to link a phenomenal concept to a functional model" (p. 13). The model's intrinsic inability to reflect the phenomenal is a consequence of its blind functioning devoid of intentionality.

It follows that perception's place would be problematic in the model. Entering into this model, this "world" within the world, theorists have located consciousness in short term storage and, assuming with common sense that perception is conscious, have located perception there. Erledyi notes the arbitrary nature of this convention and takes advantage of the fact that the model "does not formally demarcate a specific locus of perception since the concept is judged to be simultaneously too arbitrary and too vague" (p. 13) by conceiving perception more broadly as spanning the whole series of events from information intake to consolidation in long term memory, which makes it "a vast region of processing space" (p. 14). Such lability in the handling of consciousness and perception betray the fact that theorists have already committed themselves to a model which is not precisely tailored to these phenomena. This commitment entails viewing the world as meaningless stimuli rather than significant situations and then having to account for meaning and consciousness by the internal operations of the processing apparatus. The key to perceptual organization is long term memory, presumed to intervene in the processing of information at virtually every step, including the receptor systems, afferent storage, iconic storage, encoding, rehersal and consolidation, and output generation. A full analysis would have to show that each of these "processing stages" is problematic vis-a-vis perception. For instance, perceptual experience in its phenomenal givenness is a *non-encoded*, direct apprehension of *things* of an essentially different structure than semiotic experience or any quasi-symbolic cybernetic reality. More generally, Merleau-Ponty (1962) provides a radical critique of any theory which attempts to explain perception by recourse to memory inasmuch as it implies an infinite historical regress and ultimately always presupposes what it attempts to explain — the original perception.

Erledyi claims that in order for subception and perceptual defense to be explained, one only needs to *assume* that long term memory performs selective control processes on the basis of a semantic analysis of information that takes into account such factors as wishes, values, expectations, and psychodynamic defense requirements of the organism. But this is no small assumption! This idea, which is in fact quite fantastic, gains integrative potential only inasmuch as it invites the *ad hoc* postulation of infinitely mixed and colorful cognitive control mechanisms in the new black box of long term memory. But how a world of significance as rich and diverse as the one we live in ever gets constituted on the basis of blind manipulations of meaningless information is the question with no answer. We agree that such matters as wish, expectancy and so on have a bearing on perception, but perception is an *original* function which operates with them, not on meaningless information but in a meaningful world. The world is immediately disclosed by each of these modes of experience, which *in concert* constitute our involvement in the world. Since these processes are all conscious and available to reflection, they need not be postulated hypothetically. This is not to say that these processes or their relations are so obvious, simple, or clear that they do not pose problems for reflection. It took the genius of Husserl to begin to discover the profound eidetic insight that not all consciousness is actual, let alone thematic, explicit and reflective. That consciousness includes its potential and relates to the world directly though not necessarily clearly and distinctly, is a revelation that has completely eluded information processing theorists whose model reflects only a sequence of actualities. To comprehend "subception" and perceptual defense" there is no need to posit an unconscious semantic analysis inside the organism which yields perfectly clear comprehension lacking only in its arrival in short term storage.

Perception and "the unconscious." As Fink has noted, the fundamental error which has riddled considerations of what is called "unconscious" is a misconception of consciousness. In this context, the misconception (in the thought of Freud and many after him) takes the form of conceiving consciousness as the awareness of clear, distinct, representations. We have found, on the contrary, as Merleau-Ponty (1963) has suggested, that there are many ways for consciousness to be conscious, ranging from the mutely prethetically lived to the articulately known. Many are not actually thematizing or explicating, let alone reflective, but are only so *potentially*. Yet this does not mean they are nothing.

These possibilities have their own illuminating powers and corre- latively meaningful wordly matters with internal and external horizons through which they are situated in the overall self- others-things structure and related to in specific ways. So much could be said of Freud's "preconscious," but what about the "systematic unconscious"? Here we find realms of sense which are not only given according to vaguely lived virtualities rather than actual representations but which possess a physiognomy of forbiddenness and are avoided prior to thematic explication. Thus despite its being lived, this domain remains primitive and unintegrated into the actual course of psychic life on account of its obliquely, preobjectively apprehended incompatibility of meaning. Merleau-Ponty (1963) has said that to comprehend the unconscious we must simply admit that the life of consciousness is itself not fully integrated. This is demonstrated in our case inas- much as taboo projects in the structure of bodily self-others- objects are eclipsed or transformed by counter-intentions which preclude the fittingness of the forbidden intentions thereby con- stituting a fragmented, equivocal existence only part of which is owned. Taboo realms are relegated to the fringe of existence, the actual circuits of which circumvent them just as the agnosognostic patient does his damaged limb. It is interesting in this regard to remember Freud's profound insight that what man cannot master he is condemned to repeat. For perception, mastery of a certain relevancy means apprehending it in a manner objective and explicit enough to fulfill the person's project, which means forg- ing original determinations in the present that open onto a hitherto merely possible future. Taboo perception is not merely slower perception but perception with no future; this futureless- ness has been dictated by others, under whose sorcery the perceiver is "undone," Our above reflections on the manner in which the past and others constitutes the present and close down the future of taboo perceptual processes reveal a breakdown in the temporal and self-as-agent possibilities of perception that is structurally analagous to what Freud demonstrates at the level of personality per se. Later psychoanalysts (e.g., Guntrip, 1971) have conceptualized this overall personality structure in a more consistently psychological (i.e., less biologistic) manner. The turning towards and turning away of perceptual processes are but one moment of a split-ego life which is both "libidinal" and "anti-libidinal" (Fairbairn) in relation to surrounding objects, which are correlatively attractive ("good") and inimical ("bad").

Some Clinical Connections

The habituation of this peculiar psychological structure, in which perception occupies a distinctive place on account of the person's apprehension of *the real*, takes on a dramatic and pervasive character in psychopathology. For instance, the socially phobic person is painfully isolated and desirous of others' warmth/friendship while relentlessly attuned to their potential for criticizing, humiliating and rejecting him as well as his own potential awkwardness, incompetence and foolishness in social settings. The project of preventing these possibilities (which are everpresent horizons) from realization requires continuous sharp but fleeting thematization of others as well as an excruciating self-consciousness that guide a skillful avoidance of anything other than safe (e.g., superficial) relating, which precludes perception of much of the situation. This structure is sedimented into a largely automatic routine with tremendous perceptual restrictions that continue to haunt the person even beyond the actual presence of other people. Perhaps the most problematic existential condition in this regard is what Laing (1962) calls "ontological insecurity" with its anxieties regarding engulfment, implosion and petrification. One may protect one's fragile self from the trecherously overpowering others by developing a schizoid way of existing, i.e., by relegating perception and behavior to a "false self system" that mechanically conforms to the others' social order and reserving the spontaneity of one's "real self" for the realm of thought and fantasy (with their omnipotent power and inaccessibility to others). The perceptual world in this context becomes "occupied territory" and any attractiveness or meaningfulness for the person himself becomes an extremely remote possibility.

> One patient focused on his own ludicrousness when a co-worker mentioned a giant car dealership (which he knew my patient drove past every day for six years) because he never noticed it. He ended the conversation quickly so the co-worker wouldn't discover how "out of it" he is. Though he fantasizes going places and having desirable relations with people, his habitual avoidance of others' gazes and his "don't bother me" bodily expression, which emerges in precise proportion to the desirability of the relationship, preclude any development of relations (including the vaguely anticipated perception of the other person as not interested and feeling "bothered" by rebuff). One of his major problems in being with others is that since he perceives little outside of direct work-

relevancies, he feels he has nothing to talk about. His central concern is to avoid the criticism of his bosses and to this end he absorbs himself in his computer work from nine in the morning until ten at night. Once he bought a magazine to acquire some experience that would be useful in conversation, but reading only heightened his sense of himself as uninformed and ignorant so he closed the magazine permanently. An attempt to explore a bar was short-circulated when he saw himself in a mirror on the wall, for he looked uncomfortable and out of place to himself and immediately left to spare himself the agony. His alienation from the wider sphere of perceptual reality, which is the common social sphere, is one facet of his feeling "apart" and "from another planet."

Since the constitution of taboo perceptual zones includes external horizons implicating the self and others (thereby being situated in a total person-world configuration), a therapist, as a part of this whole, may play an essential role in its transformation. The therapist can glimpse "the pearl at the bottom of the sea," that is the most authentic intentions of the patient's self which have been eclipsed and have failed to reach out to actualize their world relations. His acceptance rather than destruction of this hitherto nascent and potential self-world unfolding is necessary for it to be actualized and integrated in an existence which thereby becomes more whole, less alienated and fragmented. Anxiety may be lived in a healthy rather than neurotic way (Fischer, 1971) thanks to this crucial change in the meaning of the Other in the patient's world. This new context allows the person's agency to be gradually resumed and the previously forbidden perceptual reality entered into. Not least important in this emancipation from the sorcery of the annihilating Other is the patient's perception of the therapist, which is itself likely to be taboo. "Unconscious transference resistance" actually involves the very peculiar perceptual structuration we have been discussing, and it will be the therapist's place not only to "analyze" it but forcefully *be* an understanding, encouraging, trustworthy presence in the patient's world. This means supporting his secret and newly emerging intentions by affirmatively *sharing in the attractiveness* of the region they begin to articulate.

The Limits and Future of the Research

Obvious limitations of the present research along the lines of generalizability pertain to the small number of subjects and the peculiarities of the taboo situation they participated in. Much more could be learned from enlisting more individuals and researching their involvement in the diverse variety of other situations in which taboo perception operates. Of course, due to the formidable demands of qualitative research, in which extensive data must be collected with each subject and every statement analyzed, such work can move forward only gradually through limited steps as the present one. In this difficult a realm such "systematic replications" of the present study could not help but substantially extend and correct our preliminary exploration.

Further research is also needed to take up the phenomenon of the transcending or overcoming of taboo in perception, that is, the process in which the person overthrows taboo meanings and integrates forbidden realms perceptually. Though the struggles of our subjects did not move in this direction to a very great extent, this variation on the theme of lived taboo perception is of great importance. To address this problem centrally, research would have to be designed so as to bring within its grasp an appropriate empirical data base for handling the matter.

In order to make more sense of the still baffling findings of experimental research, it would be possible to replicate the crucial experiments with a wider and more descriptive data base so that the subjects' involvement could be qualitatively as well as quantitatively analyzed. This could contribute not only to the debate about apparently contradictory results that have already arisen but might also suggest more critical experimental designs to the extent that these can make an important contribution.

A related area requiring qualitative research which we have not even begun to address here is the matter referred to as "perceptual vigilance," the heightened perceptual attunement to taboo objects. What exactly is involved here (e.g., the extent to which these objects can be rightly regarded as "taboo" for such subjects) and how this phenomenon relates to the one under consideration here would have considerable bearing on this area as a whole.

Finally, our research has consistently focused on perception but it provides a method and conceptual approach which with appropriate modifications could be extended to the areas of taboo behavior, memory, imagination, thought, and so on. These could be taken up one at a time (of course, viewing the one under consideration in the context of the others) as we have done, or in concert. It would seem that the very character of the taboo would be unique in each mode of experience yet still attest to commonalities with the others. For instance, the fact that behavior is more visible than perception and imagination is less so doubtless holds significance for their respective taboo processes.

References

Bidderman, M. E. and Kniffin, C. W. Manifest anxiety and "perceptual defense." *Journal of Abnormal and Social Psychology*, 1958, *48*, 248–252.

Blum, G. S. An experimental reunion of psychoanalytic theory with perceptual defense and vigilance. *Journal of Abnormal and Social Psychology*, 1954, *49*, 94–98.

————. An investigation of perceptual defense in Italy. *Psychological Review*, 1957, *3*, 169–175.

————. Perceptual defense revisited. *Journal of Abnormal and Social Psychology*, 1955, *51*, 24–29.

Broota, K. D. and Khanna, B. K. Perceptual defense or response suppression: an experimental investigation. *Indian Journal of Psychology*, 1974, *49*, 158–166.

Bruner, J. S. Perception under stress. *Psychological Review*, 1948, *6*, 314–323.

Bruner, J. S. and Postman, L. Emotional selectivity in perception and reaction. *Journal of Personality*, 1947, *16*, 69–77.

————. Perception, cognition and behavior. *Journal of Personality*, 1949, *18*, 14–31.

Cable, D. C. Perceptual defense or set: A reexamination. *Psychonomic Science*, 1969, *16*, 331–332.

Carpenter, B., Weiner, M., and Carpenter, J. T. Predictability of perceptual defense behavior. *Journal of Abnormal and Social Psychology*, 1956, *52*, 380–383.

Chapman, C. R. and Feather, B. W. Modification of perception by classical conditioning procedures. *Journal of Experimental Psychology*, 1972, *93*, 338–342.

Chodorkoff, B. Self perception, perceptual defense, and adjustment. *Journal of Abnormal and Social Psychology*, 1954, *49*, 508–512.

Daston, P. G. Perception of homosexual words in paranoid schizophrenia. *Perceptual Motor Skills*, 1956, *6*, 44–45.

Diamant, L. Perceptual defense – down but not out. *American Psychologist*, 1975, *948*.

Dixon, N. F. *Subliminal perception: the nature of a controversy*. London: McGraw Hill, 1971.

Erdelyi, M. A new look at the new look: perceptual defense and vigilance. *Psychological Review*, 1974, *81* 1–25.

Eriksen, C. W. Perceptual defense as a function of unacceptable needs. *Journal of Abnormal and Social Psychology*, 1951, *46*, 557–564.

————. Defense against ego-threat in memory and perception. *Journal of Abnormal and Social Psychology*, 1952, *47*, 430–435.

————. Psychological defenses and ego strength in the recall of completed and incompleted tasks. *Journal of Abnormal and Social Psychology*, 1954, *49*, 45–50.

————. Unconscious processes. In M. R. Jones (Ed.), *Nebraska Symposium on Motivation: 1958*. Lincoln: University of Nebraska Press, 1958.

————. Discrimination and learning without awareness: A methodological survey and evaluation. *Psychological Review*, 1960, *67*, 279–300.

————. Perception and personality. In J. M. Wepman and R. W. Heine (Eds.), *Concepts of personality*. Chicago: Aldine, 1963.

Eriksen, C. W. and Browne, C. T. An experimental and theoretical analysis of perceptual defense. *Journal of Abnormal and Social Psychology*, 1956, *52* 224–230.

Eriksen, C. W. and Lazarus, R. S. Perceptual defense and projective tests. *Journal of Abnormal and Social Psychology*, 1952, *47*, 302–308.

Fink, E. On the problem of the unconscious. In Husserl, E., *The crisis of European sciences and transcendental phenomenology*. Evanston: Northwestern, 1970.

Fischer, C. T. and Wertz, F. J. An empirical phenomenological study of being criminally victimized. In Giorgi, A., Knowles, R. and Smith, D. (Eds.), *Duquesne studies in phenomenological psychology: volume 3*. Pittsburgh: Humanities, 1979.

Fischer, W. F. The faces of anxiety. In A. Giorgi, W. F. Fischer, and R. Von Echartsberg (Eds.), *Duquesne studies in phenomenological psychology: volume 1*. Pittsburgh: Duquesne, 1971.

Forest, D., Gordon, N. and Taylor, A. Generalization of perceptual defense. *Journal of Personality and Social Psychology*, 1965, *2*, 137–141.

Freeman, J. T. Set or perceptual defense? *Journal of Experimental Psychology*, 1954, *48*, 283–288.

Genet, J. T. *The Thief's Journal*. New York: Grove, 1964.

Giorgi, A. An application of phenomenological method in psychology. In Giorgi, A., Fischer, W., and Murray, E. (Eds.), *Duquesne studies in phenomenological psychology: volume 2*. Pittsburgh: Duquesne, 1975.

————. *Psychology as a human science*. New York: Harper and Row, 1970.

Goldiamond, I. Indicators of perception: I. Subliminal perception, subception, unconscious perception: An analysis in terms of psychophysical indicator methodology. *Psychological Bulletin* 1958, *55*, 373–411.

———. Perception. In A. J. Bachrach (Ed.), *Experimental foundations of clinical psychology*. New York: Basic Books, 1962.

Goldstein, M. J. A test of response probability theory of perceptual defense. *Journal of Experimental Psychology*, 1962, *63*, 23–28.

Guntrip, H. *Psychoanalytic theory, therapy and the self*. New York: Basic Books, 1971.

Howes, D. H. and Solomon, R. L. A note on McGinnies' "Emotionality and perceptual defense." *Psychological Review*, 1950, *57*, 229–234.

Howie, D. Perceptual defense. *Psychological Review*, 1952, *59*, 308–315.

Husserl, E. *Cartesian meditations*. The Hague: Martinus Nijoff, 1929.

———. *Crisis of European sciences and transcendental phenomenology*. Evanston: Northwestern, 1970.

———. *Ideas: general introduction to pure phenomenology*. New York: Collier, 1913.

———. *Experience and judgment*. Evanston: Northwestern, 1948.

Hutt, L. D. and Anderson, J. P. Perceptual defense and vigilance: Prediction from the Byrne Scale of Repression-Sensitization. *Psychonomic Science*, 1967, *9*, 473–474. (a)

———. The relationship between pupil size and recognition threshold. *Psychonomic Science*, 1967, *9*, 477–478. (b)

Kleimer, R. Perceptual defense or set? *Journal of Social Psychology* 1959, *49*, 95–103.

Kumar, A., Srvastava, S. N., and Divedi, C. B. Visual and auditory perceptual defense of early and late adolescence. *Perceptual Motor Skills*, 1980, *50* 882.

Kurkland, S. H. The lack of generality of defense mechanisms as indicated in auditory perception. *Journal of Abnormal and Social Psychology*, 1954, *49*, 173–177.

Lacy, O. W., Lewinger, N., and Adamson, J. F. Foreknowledge as a factor effecting perceptual defense and alertness. *Journal of Experimental Psychology*, 1953, *45*, 160–174.

Laing, R. D. *The divided self*. Baltimore: Penguin Books, 1962.

Levy, L. H. Perceptual defense in tactile perception. *Journal of Personality*, 1958, *26*, 467–478.

Luckins, A. S. An approach to social perception. *Journal of Personality*, 1950, *19*, 64–84.

Maccoby, E. E. *The development of stimulus selection*. In J. P. Hill (Ed.), Minnesota Symposium on Child Psychology, volume 3. Minneapolis: U. Minnesota, 1969.

Matthews, A. and Wertheimer, M. A "pure" measure of perceptual defense uncontaminated by response suppression. *Journal of Abnormal and Social Psychology*, 1958, *57*, 373–376.

McGinnies, E. Emotionality and perceptual defense. *Psychological Review*, 1949, *56*, 244–251.

————. Discussion of Howes' and Solomon's note on "Emotionality and perceptual defense." *Psychological Review*, 1950, *57*, 235–240.

McGinnies, E. and Adornetto, J. Perceptual defense in normal and schizophrenic observers. *Journal of Abnormal and Social Psychology*, 1952, *47*, 833–837.

Merleau-Ponty, M. *Phenomenology of perception.* Evanston: Northwestern, 1962.

————. *Structure of behavior.* Boston: Beacon, 1963.

Murdock, B. B. Perceptual defense and threshold measurement. *Journal of Personality*, 1954, *22*, 565–571.

Neisser, U. *Cognitive psychology.* New York: Appleton-Century-Crofts, 1967.

————. *Cognition and reality.* San Francisco: Freeman, 1976.

Norman, D. A. *Memory and attention.* New York: Wiley, 1969.

Notham, F. H. The influence of response conditions on recognition thresholds for taboo words. *Journal of Abnormal and Social Psychology*, 1962, *65*, 154–161.

Postman, L., Bronson, W. C., and Gropper, G. L. Is there a mechanism of perceptual defense? *Journal of Abnormal and Social Psychology*, 1953, *48*, 215–224.

Postman, L., Bruner, J. S., and McGinnies, E. Personal values as selective factors in perception. *Journal of Abnormal and Social Psychology*, 1948, *43*, 142–154.

Pustell, T. E. The experimental induction of perceptual vigilance and defense. *Journal of Personality*, 1957, *25*, 425–438.

Rosenstock, I. M. Perceptual aspects of repression. *Journal of Abnormal and Social Psychology*, 1951, *46*, 304–315.

Ruiz, R. A. and Krauss, H. H. Perceptual defense versus response suppression. *Journal of Psychology*, 1968, *69*, 33–37.

Schilder, P. *Medical Psychology.* Englewood Cliffs: Prentice Hall, 1924.

Smith, D. E. P. and Hochberg, J. The effect of punishment on figure-ground perception. *Journal of Psychology*, 1954, *38*, 83–87.

Smith, G. Visual perception: An event over time. *Psychological Review*, 1957, *64*, 306–313.

Smock, C. D. Influence of stress on perception of incongruity. *Journal of Abnormal and Social Psychology*, 1955, *50*, 354–356.

Spence, D. P. A new look at vigilance and defense. *Journal of Abnormal and Social Psychology*, 1957, *54*, 103–108.

Spence, D. P. and Feinberg, C. Forms of defensive looking: A naturalistic experiment. *Journal of Nervous and Mental Disease*, 1967, *145*, 261–272.

Stein, K. B. Perceptual defense and perceptual sensitization under neutral and invoked conditions. *Journal of Personality*, 1953, *21*, 467–478.

Sullivan, H. S. *Interpersonal theory of psychiatry*. New York: Norton, 1953.

Thorndike, E. L. and Lorge, I. *The teacher's wordbook of 3,000 words*. New York: Columbia, 1944.

Vassi. *The Erotic Comedies*. Sag Harbor, New York: Permanent, 1981.

Voor, J. H. Subliminal perception and subception. *Journal of Psychology*, 1956, *41*, 437–458.

Wallace, G. and Worthington, A. G. The dark adaptation index of perceptual defense: A procedural improvement. *Australian Journal of Psychology*, 1970, *22*, 41–46.

Weiner, M. Word frequency or motivation in perceptual defense? *Journal of Abnormal and Social Psychology*, 1955, *51*, 214–218.

Wertz, F. J. *Dialog with the New Look: A descriptive approach to everyday perceptual process*. Unpublished Doctoral Dissertation, Duquesne University, 1982a.

_____. Findings and value of a descriptive approach to everyday perceptual process. *Journal of Phenomenological Psychology*, *13*(2), 1982b.

_____. From everyday to psychological description: Analyzing the moments of a qualitative data analysis. *Journal of Phenomenological Psychology*, *14*(2), 1983a.

_____. Procedures in phenomenological research and the question of validity. In C. Aanstoos (Ed.), *Exploring the lived world: Studies in the social sciences*. Carrollton, GA.: West Georgia College Press, 1984b.

_____. Some constituents of descriptive psychological reflection. *Human Studies*, 8, 1983c.

_____. Revolution in psychology: Case study of the New Look school of perception. In A. Giorgi, A. Barton, and C. Maes (Eds.), *Duquesne Studies in phenomenological psychology, volume 4*. Pittsburgh: Duquesne University Press, 1983b.

York, M., Mandour, T. and Jex, S. Perceptual defense–a replication. Paper presented at the Annual Meetings of the Eastern Psychological Association, Philadelphia, 1983.

Zigler, E. and Yospe, L. Perceptual defense and the problem of response suppression. *Journal of Personality*, 1960, *28*, 220–239.

Approaching Social Attitudes

10

Peter D. Ashworth

1. Methodology as Compounded of Approach and Technique

The intellectual atmosphere of contemporary social and psychological sciences, with its continued emphasis on quantification, prediction, and the delineation of causal influences on behaviour, forces an understandable defensiveness onto the discussion of qualitative methods. Proponents of qualitative research are called on to explain where the reliability and validity can be found in what they do. Even if the work is reliable and valid, how can these features be demonstrated? In what sense are the methods rigorous, when judged in terms of the standards of rigor of methods based on quantification? How does qualitative work escape 'subjectivity'?

Of course, we continually face such questions. One response is to turn attention to our qualitative praxis, and to attempt to sharpen up the display of evidence — trying to show that the claimed results of research are derived in a rule-governed and publicly-accessible way from some kind of 'brute data'. In other words, there is a tendency to rest on a defence of the adequacy of technique.

Another line of defence, which may be linked to the first, is to concede the lack of rigor intrinsic to qualitative techniques, but to claim that they have a valuable early role in the scientific process. An important, recent, representative volume on qualitative methods, Smith and Manning (1982), makes a defence on exactly these grounds. For them, there is no difference between qualitative and quantitative research in terms of the 'paradigm' guiding the approach of the researcher. Rather, 'soft' techniques can be useful in feeling one's way to 'intimate knowledge' of the things being investigated, but ideally this descriptive basis will give way to 'hard,' quantification. Thus:

This volume . . . seeks to reduce the specious distinction between qualitative and quantitative methods. We desire that researchers will be led by this book and other volumes of the Handbook to introduce quantification into their descriptive studies and thus to cross-check their rich firsthand observations. Researchers should also strive for continuity in their research programmes by continuing to elaborate their studies by using the more focussed methodologies of experimentation and survey research. Conversely, we hope that others will be led by this book to base their abstract quantitative analyses on firsthand observations of the empirical social world. Perhaps the low percentage of explained variances that characterise much quantitative and evaluative research is a consequence of inappropriate impositions of research designs and accounting schemes on the empirical social world. These often do not adequately capture the reality being studied. Instead of simply doing artificial scientistic social research, it is important to develop quantitative studies based on intimate knowledge of the empirical social world. (Smith and Manning, 1982, p. xvii)

So, qualitative studies have the role of increasing sensitivity to reality so that the researcher can form more adequate hypotheses concerning causal variables which will then be rigorously tested using the tighter techniques of quantification. It seems, then, that debate on 'qualitative methods' tends to narrow down to questions of technical praxis. But this kind of defence, justifiable in some ways, misses the point if it is not supported by a defence of another, more fundamental sort. Qualitative *method* is a term which is much broader than qualitative *technique* in its scope. And it is on methodology in its broadest meaning, not merely on technique, that the argument for a qualitative alternative rests.

A terminological distinction, then. Where 'method' of research is spoken about, often all that the speaker has in mind is technique. It is dangerous, from the point of view of defending and developing qualitative methods to follow this confused usage. The virtue of qualitative methods does not lie in adequacy of technique considered on its own, but in the total *approach* (Giorgi, 1970) which qualitative methods adopt towards the human subject-matter of the social and psychological sciences.

Methodology involves questions of technique, certainly, but these are only addressed in a correct manner if taken in the context of the approach which is adopted to the object of the science. Methodology is compounded of approach and technique.

If we stick to the technical level, then we know that qualitative techniques are rightly regarded as second best. They fail in terms of control. The data produced does not relate sufficiently directly to the hypothesized relationship between variables to allow a clearcut test to be made. And so on. But, as I say, sticking purely to the technical level misses the point. It is at the level of approach that the argument for qualitative methods must be made. Technique must not be abstracted from the total context of methodology.

As Giorgi points out, there is resistance from colleagues in the human sciences when issues as fundamental as this are raised. In general, positive approaches, and thus the supremacy of quantitative techniques, are taken for granted as unproblematical. A great deal of effort goes into the establishment of this belief in the process of socializing new members of the scientific community. Yet this is where the debate has to be staged.

Now, the question of approach having been raised as central, it is necessary to discuss more fully the meaning of approach, and set it in its correct place in the structure of understanding of methodology.

2. Approach as Hermeneutic Fore-Understanding

A very general characterization of methodology is needed if a proper understanding of the role of approach is to be achieved. It must be a perspective which suits all kinds of approach. Whether an approach or overall method is *right* or not in some particular context is for the moment not our concern. The aim just now is to come to a view concerning the role of approach.

Since all science, whatever else, is aimed at making sense of some aspect of the world (not a definition which demarcates science, I agree, but it is general enough to cover any effort which has pretensions to scientific method, which is, for our purposes, more important than its power to exclude any particular sense-making activity), the general theory of interpretation, *hermeneutics*, seems an appropriate source for concepts which will elucidate the role of approach in methodology.

"Interpretation, in the sense relevant to hermeneutics, is an attempt to make clear, to make sense of an object of study," so scientific efforts fall within its sphere. "This object must, therefore, be a text or text–analogue, which is in some way confused, incomplete, cloudy, seemingly contradictory — in one way or another, unclear. The interpretation aims to bring to light an underlying coherence or sense" (Taylor, 1973, p. 47).

Any attempt to make sense of an aspect of the world, then, begins with a confrontation with something which, though already somewhat formalized (the primary sense of hermeneutics being the interpretation of written text), is in need of clarification. The kind of 'formalization' required of objects of study before an interpretive effort can be applied to them can be judged by the following list of possible objects: dreams, categories of responses, written or spoken accounts of experience, any documentary source or material that can be transformed into a written form, and so on. As Ricoeur (1971, p. 537) indicates, "Meaningful action is an object for science only under the condition of a kind of objectification which is equivalent to the fixation of discourse by writing."

A methodology, then, is an attempt to render a confused 'text' clear, and this enterprise is a hermeneutical one.

Now, the process of interpretation depends on a pre-existing stance: a fore-understanding of the 'text.' And, indeed, this fore-understanding will determine what is taken as the 'text' to be interpreted. "In interpreting, we do not, so to speak, throw a 'signification' over some naked thing which is present-at-hand, we do not stick a value on it; but when something within-the-world is encountered as such, the thing in question already has an involvement which is disclosed in our understanding of the world, and this involvement is one which gets laid out by the interpretation" (Heidegger, 1962, pp. 190f). To make it plain, the 'text' found within-the-world of a social psychologist interested in attitudes and whose fore-understanding of attitudes is a behaviorist one will be such as to allow an interpretation in terms of behavioral regularities to emerge: the involvement gets laid out in the interpretation. A very different interpretation will be produced by work which is guided by a cognitive fore-understanding.

We can now say some very general things about approach, taken as the fore-understanding with which an interpreter engages with the 'text' that is the object of the science.

The fore-understanding specifies the kind of technique which is appropriate to lending clarity to the 'text.' If human behavior, for instance, is presupposed to be the lawful outcome of the interac-

tion of a number of discrete variables without 'personal' participation, then certain techniques are suggested. If there is thought
to be personal involvement in the free staging of human action,
then other means of shedding light on the 'text' are required.

Immediately, it can be seen how intimate the connection can be
between approach, technique and content of a human science.
The fore-understanding, manner of interpretation, and 'text' are
mutually-referential. Techniques get their meaning as ways of
revealing the nature of phenomena in the context of the world
which is opened up by a particular fore-understanding.

Interpretation, it must be recognized, is dialectical (Palmer,
1969). The 'text' is questioned in the terms suggested by the
researcher's approach, and the answers shed light on the standpoint of the original fore-understanding. In contrast to any realist
qualms, it must be emphasized that there can be no 'objective'
'text,' and no unique reading or interpretation of it. Other fore-
understandings, other approaches to the text will give rise to
other interpretations.

Two points deserve mention here. Firstly, the 'hermeneutic
circle' of textual clarification leading to a new understanding of
the fore-understanding, and so on, is quite general. Ricoeur
considers the cycle of hypothesis – test – reformulation of hypothesis (moving from Reichenbach's realm of discovery through
the realm of justification and back) to be an equivalent process.
Secondly, it has to be accepted that there is always a problem of
grounding the interpretation. There is no escape from an ultimate
appeal to a shared understanding of the clarified text based on
acceptance of the fore-understanding of the approach to clarification. Acceptance of the interpretation rests on acceptance of the
fore-understanding which generated it.

In sum, then, we have shown that approach, or hermeneutic
fore-understanding has a directing influence on any interpretive
or clarificatory enterprise. Yet we saw in the previous section that
discussion of methodology, and therefore debate about the value
of qualitative methods, gets stuck at the level of technique.

By shifting discussion of qualitative methods to the realm of
approach, we can hope to uncover some most fundamental features of methodology in the human sciences. What are the fore-
understandings of the various qualitative and quantitative methodologies? When these are uncovered it may be possible to make a
judgment as to their relative appropriateness for the subject

matter they are intended to clarify. For, despite the truth of the statement that there is no 'objective' 'text,' there is a certain recalcitrance of reality, such that there is a possibility of inappropriateness in approach.

The example of the analysis of the nature of social attitudes seems to be a good one for demonstrating the divergences which occur in fore-understandings, and the ways in which failure in clarifying phenomena may be seen to be due to inappropriateness of approach. At this level, qualitative methods provide ways of allowing clarification to appear which supercede the results obtained by quantitative methods.

3. Fore-Understanding and Methodological Error in Attitude Research

Defence of qualitative method should not be primarily at the level of technique, it seems. Rather, the inappropriateness of the *approach* adopted by those methods which start with the aim of quantification may be revealed, and contrasted with the fore-understanding of qualitative research.

In this section of the paper, the two central types of approach to the study of social attitudes will be considered. Their explicit fore-understandings are best seen by assessing their definitions of attitude. But implicit fore-understandings can also be sought in the kinds of questions which they address to the 'text' of social attitudes. Such questions reveal the 'unsaid' fore-understandings — which, though not always explicitly avowed are nevertheless there, for were these fore-understandings absent, the questions to the forefront in the literature would surely be rather different.

To set the scene, some general background to the two theoretical views which are to be scrutinized.

"An attitude is a mental and neural state of readiness, organised through experience, exerting a directive or dynamic influence upon the individual's response to all objects and situations with which it is related" is Allport's (1935, p. 810) influential definition, which he optimistically regarded as synoptic of the different definitions which he surveyed in that paper, which could be the basis of scientific consensus. McGuire (1969) has however examined a wide range of orientations to the study of social attitude, and rejects the idea of a consensus. Indeed, he differentiates between five distinct perspectives, among which we must consider here two broad types. These are, on the one hand, behaviorist notions which regard the concept of attitude as labelling the *probability* of a certain response within a given stimulus situation, and, on the other hand, the view of cognitive social psychologists that attitude refers to a mental *disposition* which is taken to account for the observed behavior — a "real and substantial ingredient in human nature," as Allport put it.

A definition of the behaviorist sort is exemplified by DeFleur and Westie (1963): "The attitude — is an inferred property of the responses, namely their consistency. Stated in another way, attitude is equated with the probability of recurrence of behavior forms of a given type or direction" (p. 21).

A thoroughgoingly dispositional viewpoint is that of Newcomb, Turner and Converse (1966) who argue that attitudes may be regarded as both cognitive and motivational entities:

> From a cognitive point of view . . . an attitude represents an organisation of valenced cognition. From a motivational point of view, an attitude represents a state of readiness for motive arousal. An individual's attitude toward something is his predisposition to be motivated in relation to it (p. 40).

Clearly these authors would see behavior as indicating an underlying attitude, rather than viewing attitude as a term which merely draws attention to behavioral regularities. Attitude is a mental disposition. The holder of the attitude is ready to display certain tendencies of thought, feeling and action.

In the probabilistic and dispositional approaches to the psychology of social attitude we have clear instances of the tendencies, typical of 'natural science' psychology, discussed by Merleau-Ponty (1965) as empiricism and intellectualism. Let us now consider the two approaches in turn.

a) *Fore-Understanding, Direction of Research and Flawed*
   Method in Cognitive, Dispositional, Attitude Theory

Brannon (1976) points out that most social psychologists have been unwilling to accept definitions of attitude as a response probability. They presuppose that attitudes are mental phenomena which involve more than can be drawn from the study of objective behavioral regularities. In Secord and Backman's (1964) text, for instance, we discover that "The term attitude refers to certain regularities of an individual's feelings, thought

and dispositions to act towards some aspect of his environment"
(p. 27), a definition which is certainly dispositional, but which
also raises starkly a question about the nature of attitude. The
problem of dispositional attitude theory, to anticipate, is that it
attempts to cover every meaning of the perceptual world through
the furnishing of the person with a number of internal variables.
The world would be meaningless stimulation without attitudes,
and his actions would have no coherence.

A consequence of the dispositional view of attitude is that the
psychologist who adopts it is thereby enabled to retain a commitment to the natural scientific approach while attempting to comment relevantly upon the world of his subject's actual experience.
But, if experience is an outcome of purely attitudinal ordering,
and attitudes are purely internal variables, this places an enormous burden on the system of inner variables. The features of my
world and the determinants of my behavior must be pregiven in
my system of attitudes.

A prime example of the ever-present difficulty that dispositional attitude theory faces is the problem of attitude — behavior
inconsistency. As Newcombe, Turner and Converse point out:

> It is not hard to find examples of people who behave systematically
> in ways that seem contrary to their attitudes . . . Since we have
> suggested that attitudes are important keys in understanding the
> long-range organisation of behaviour, and such lack of correspon-
> dence is a matter of concern to us . . . The notion of attitude as
> stored dispositions is useful only in the degree that behaviour can be
> seen as dependent in some way on such dispositions. If individuals
> are capable of behaving in ways which seem to correspond poorly
> with their attitudes, of what use is the notion of attitude at all?
> (p. 47).

So, if the explicit fore-understanding of cognitive, dispositional
attitude theory is that regularities of behavior are due to an inner
furniture of variables, then, in the attempt to cope with the lack
of attitude — behavior correspondence, we may see covert presuppositions which are implications of this fore-understanding.

b) The Problem of Behavior and Attitude as Revelatory of Cognitive Fore-Understanding

Allport's influential early definition of attitude, it will be recalled, treated it as a disposition involving a readiness to respond

in a certain manner to the attitude object. This surely means that attitudes will manifest themselves in behavior. Given this implication, it is somewhat embarrassing to the dispositional view that research aimed at disclosing a link between attitude and action often arrives at the conclusion that the relationship is at best weak. (The specific studies will not be detailed here. Reviews are numerous, e.g., Brannon, 1976; Calder and Ross, 1973; Schuman and Johnson, 1976; Wicker, 1969). The bold assertion of Krech, Crutchfield and Ballachey (1962, p. 146) that, "The actions of the individual are to a large extent governed by his attitudes," although a natural consequence of the dispositional view, seems in the face of the evidence to be incorrect.

The generally equivocal relationship between attitude and behavior shown in the many studies he reviewed led Wicker to argue that researchers in the social sciences should not lightly claim that a piece of attitude research had, in itself, any serious implications for behavior. Brannon observed that, "By the late 1960s the old commonsense assumption that attitudes influence actions was rapidly disappearing from the technical and professional literature" (p. 147).

However, this situation is an uncomfortable one for dispositional attitude theory, and many authors, including Wicker and Brannon, have been dissatisfied merely to leave attitude and behavior as distinct domains. Efforts have been made to that there *is* an impact on behavior from attitudes, but that the conceptualization and measurement of attitudes and behavior are in some ways inadequate to reveal this — various conceptual and methodological adjustments may remedy the discreditable situation (Ehrlich, 1969).

Significantly, the various adjustments suggested do not arise from a radical reflection on attitude and behavior in their appearing as phenomena, but from a perusal of the terms of the attitude-behavior correlation, directed by a desire to make it stronger through an alteration of the modes of operationalization of the variables. This is, of course, a normal strategy in attempting to save a theoretical model which appears to be threatened by the evidence. It is recalled that the evidence is based, not on direct tests of the model (in this case, the causal model of an influence of the independent variable, attitude, upon the dependent variable, behavior, but rather on tests of relationship between operationalized variables. So the problem may lie with the mode of operationalization rather than with the model itself.

On the *attitude side of the correlation*, it is well known that the reliability of questionnaire and rating scale measures may be problematical (Ehrlich, 1969). Construct validity may also be open to doubt. Thus Tittle and Hill (1967) found that different measures produced rather different assessments of the attitude held by an individual.

A large number of measures of additional features of the attitude, beside a simple assessment of like / dislike, has been suggested in order to increase the prediction of behavior. Fazio and Zanna (1978) advocate the inclusion of measures of certainty and 'latitude of rejection' (the extent to which near, but different, attitudes are rejected) in the predictive equation. Crane and Martin (1978) suggest that intensity and centrality measures will improve the correlation.

The debate about the tridimensionality of attitudes enters at this point as well, since various authors (e.g., Ehrlich, 1969; Bagozzi and Burnkrant, 1979) have argued, either that attempts be made to include separate measures of different components in the regression equation predicting action, or that concentration on one of them (the action tendency aspect of attitude) could be expected to improve prediction of behavior.

Ehrlick's suggestion that the conative aspect of attitude be the focus of interest in operationalization can be associated with other views on how to improve the measure of attitude in the service of prediction. Fishbein, while insisting that attitude is a matter of affect, goes on to state that attitude, in concert with certain other determinants (which will be treated below), gives rise to 'behavioral intentions', and it is these that best predict action.

Fishbein argues that behavioral intentions are virtually the only way that specific behaviors can be predicted with any success. Assessment of attitude — if it is to relate to specific intentions to respond, rather than very general tendencies of behavior — should be aimed at scoring the evaluation of that specific action. Ajzen and Fishbein (1977) place strong emphasis on this approach to the assessment of attitude:

> A person's attitude has a consistently strong relation with his or her behaviour when it is directed at the same target and when it involves the same action. Generally low and inconsistent relations are observed when the attitudinal and behavioural entities fail to correspond in one or both of these elements' (p. 912f).

Let us pause briefly here to assess this move of cognitive attitude theorists, for it is typical of a strong contemporary tendency. There appears to be a retreat from the general and synthetic view of attitude, towards a microscopic, analytical approach. In the service of prediction from a measure of attitude to an observed behavior, the dispositional concept has been retained after a fashion, but the focus is limited to his preparedness for a certain line of action.

In arguing that behavioral intentions are the only way to predict specific behaviors, and that assessment of attitude must be aimed precisely at the particular behavior being predicted, Fishbein effectively demands that *the subject supply the values of variables which will map out the total situation as it appears to him.* So the very pointed assessment of behavioral intentions moves away from attitude research, in a sense, into the realm of predicting one's own behavior. And, unfortunately, although Fishbein's approach does often give rise to high correlations (as in his own most recent reports, e.g., Ajzen and Fishbein, 1980), this is by no means always the case (e.g., Linn, 1965; Wicker and Pomazal, 1971; Crane and Martin, 1978). We will return to the Fishbein model below.

The attitudinal side of the attitude — behavior relationship is a matter of intense debate, then. It is more unexpected to discover that the *behavioral side of the correlation* is also problematical — after all, attitudes are understood to be 'covert,' whereas behavior is supposed to be clearly observable. Yet Ehrlich (1969, p. 29) writes:

> While the operations for attitude scale construction are relatively well standardised, the operations for observing and recording behaviour, particularly in natural settings, are generally unstandardised and problem specific.

Accordingly, Tittle and Hill found that the relationship between attitude and action could be increased by the careful selection of cases of attitude-relevant behavior, and by combining these to give an index of behavior. This confirms a view of Fishbein about the predictive capacity of general measures of attitude being limited to general trends of behavior, rather than specific behaviors.

Thus far, then, attempts to rescue the attitude-action correlation have focused on the problem of operationalization of the two classes of variable. The question also arises as to the existence of 'other variables' which affect the subject's mapping of attitude into action-variables which are often attitudes themselves, or are of exactly comparable formal status, being dispositions.

Many authors have considered the social situation of expressing an attitude in comparison to the social situation of action, to discover whether there might be specific characteristics of the two situations which will reduce the degree to which questionnaire response will concord with attitude-relevant behavior. Ehrlich, for instance, argued that assessment of a subject's attitude to a certain object should be supplemented by assessment of his attitude to the situation in which that attitude would be expressed. In affinity with this suggestion, Fazio and Zanna (1978), Regan and Fazio (1977) and Zanna, Olson and Fazio (1980) have shown, in a series of experiments, that the correlation between attitude and behavior was increased when the subject had direct and consistent prior experience of the situation of behavioral expression of the attitude.

The idea of treating reference groups as a supplementary source of variation is mooted by Schuman and Johnson (1976), who cite evidence supporting the efficacy of such variables. Similarly, Warner and DeFleur (1969) argue that action is subjected to various social constraints, so that the individual's attitudes to social norms of behavior need to be taken into account.

Brannon suggests that the relevance of attitudes to the guidance of behavior in a given situation is subject to personal criteria of 'congruity.' He writes, "The degree of normally-perceived fit between an attitude and a behaviour under standard conditions, the relation which knowledgeable members of the culture would expect without knowing any special circumstances of the case" is congruence (p. 173).

Although there are puzzling aspects to this statement, it seems that, as well as investigating the specific attitude, a researcher should explicitly assess the cultural norms of expression of that attitude — and should assume that the subjects 'know' these norms.

The same perspective is seen in Brannon's argument that attitude and action have different consequences for the individual. Broadly — although this is not an iron rule — action is more personally costly than the holding of attitudes. Hence an attitude may have to be very strong if it is to lead to action. Campbell

(1963) couches this idea in 'natural science' language through the notion of 'behavioural threshold.' But the point is that 'another variable,' beside attitude itself, is being suggested in order to increase the attitude-behavior relationship.

Now, almost all the refinements to the enterprise of the prediction of behavior from attitudinal variables which have been mentioned above have been incorporated in the *expectancy / value model of Fishbein*. It emphasizes, as has been indicated already, the use of specific behavioral intentions with a view to prediction, instead of very broad and general attitudes. It treats attitude as simply a score on a scale of like / dislike or agree / disagree, regarding cognitive components as so strongly correlated to this affective dimension as to be unworthy of separate assessment, and treating conation as deriving from affect. However, this derivation is modulated by awareness of norms surrounding the projected action. Thus intention to perform the action will only be expressed if the positive aspects of his attitudes to the action and its social meaning outweigh the negative ones.

Expressed algebraically, the relationship between behavioral intention and action is given by:

$$B \approx BI = \sum_{i=1}^{n} \left\{ B_i \cdot a_i \right\} w_0 + \sum_{j=1}^{m} \left\{ (NB_j) \cdot (Mc_j) \right\} w_1$$

where:

B is actual behavior

BI is behavioral intention

n is the number of beliefs about the proposed action

B_i is the strength of such a belief

a_i is its evaluative component

m is the number of normative beliefs concerning the proposed action

NB_j is the strength of such a norm

Mc_j is the motivation to comply

and w_0 and w_1 are weightings which are associated with a person's tendency to act in accordance with norms or his own attitudes (Fishbein, 1973).

As has been said, there is evidence in support of this model, in the sense that correlations are then indeed improved (e.g., the reviews of Schuman and Johnson, 1976; Eagly and Himmelfarb, 1978).

However, there has been dissent. Schwartz and Tessler (1972), testing the Fishbein model in an early form, found that behavioral antecedents (i.e., 'other variables') still affected the relationship between attitude and behavior — they were not all accounted for in the various elements of the formula for behavioral intention. The relationship between the variables has also been the subject of disagreement with the Fishbein model in research published by Smetana and Adler (1980). They modelled the relationship between all 'theoretically relevant components' using path analysis, and found that the putative independence of the normative and attitudinal terms of the Fishbein equation was not borne out (though they did find, in contrast to Crane and Martin, 1978, that behavioral intention predicted behavior).

Thus we find that the Fishbein model does not cover all the relevant variables, and that the relationship between the ones it does include may not be stable. This last point is brought out clearly in the work of Bentler and Speckart (1979) who tested the Fishbein model in comparison to two other regression models, in which the variables were combined in different ways. In one of the alternative models, behavioral intention mediated attitude and normative beliefs (as in Fishbein), but attitude was also supposed to have its own independent effect on behavior. And in the other alternative, a measure of prior behavior was also brought in as a factor directly influencing current action. Goodness-of-fit- statistical comparison of the models favoured the second alternative rather than Fishbein's.

> For this sample it is apparent that attitudes and past behavior, or some other factors linearly related to these antecedents, are contributing strongly to the occurence of behavior without the regulation of intentions (p. 461).

With Fishbein, our survey of the attempts within orthodox dispositional attitude theory to deal with the vexed attitude-behavior problem is complete. Through careful analysis of the terms of the causal chain, and refinement of the means by which they are operationalized, it is hoped by these authors that the predictability of behavior may be increased. It is presupposed that behavior is the product of dispositional variables, because cognitive psychology places on the person the burden of investing the world of physical stimuli with meaning — it is intellectualist.

The consequence of this attempt to furnish the person with a sufficiently rich set of dispositional characteristics to be able to act in the world, was to, firstly, focus in on the specific instance of a certain action (so as to limit the realm to be predicted), and secondly to specify the variables and their formal interrelationships. Fishbein develops what amounts to a very complex picture of the inner realm of the individual caught on the verge of action. One could justly argue that, for Fishbein, the accuracy of prediction is limited only by the extent to which his equation — or the operationalization of the terms within it — fail to include all aspects of the subject's imaginative evocation of the situation wherein his attitude-relevant action is to be performed, or fail to account for the refractoriness of the world to the subject's prediction.

There is no need to detail this criticism further here. Plainly dispositional attitude theory is intellectualist. It imposes a dualism on the world by attempting to provide an 'inner man,' an inner copy of the real outer world of meaningless stimuli.

Although it seems that Fishbein's model might have to give way to some other regression equation in the light of recent results, the problem here is a general one, and is not to be shrugged off by the replacement of one dispositional model by another. *No* such model, no combination of variables, will be final, because action in the world is not of a form that such models can mirror.

This argument, then, is that such models are, in principle, insecurely founded. An indication of this is the fact that 'cognition' in cognitive attitude theory (e.g. the pivotal notion of behavioral intention in the work of Fishbein) is not a matter of conscious openness to the world, but it is merely the event of the interaction of discrete, externally-related variables, whose meanings do not mesh together as having an inner sense. My attitude to something, and the norms which I understand to surround it, are not linked in any way so as to have shared significance as parts of a totality, which is necessarily focused on that thing by virtue of its being part of my world. Of course, when treated as discrete variables, at one moment one regression equation will picture their interrelations, at another moment, and when the interest of the culture or the person shifts, another model will cover the 'facts' more adequately.

The primary methodological flaw in dispositional attitude theory is one of inadequate fore-understanding: an inappropriate approach. The apparent virtues of quantitative techniques flow from the requirements of approach.

c) Fore-Understanding and Flawed Method in Behaviorist, Probabilistic Attitude Theory

The behaviorist, probabilistic treatment of attitude is in line with the positivist standpoint, which demarcates science from other forms of knowledge by its reliance on observables, and the demonstration of relationships between them. (In fact, the dispositional approach also moves in this direction, but such a position is more overt, and more clearly confessed by the behaviorists.)

For psychology, positivism entails a third-person, exterior stance and a refusal to countenance any interiority. The unobservability of Allport's dispositional 'mental and neural state of readiness' leads the behaviorist to reject that definition of attitude. De Fleur and Westie believe that attitude as a scientific concept must invoke no mental entity. Attitude for them is merely a term which registers the observer's acknowledgement that there are certain regularities of response. Thus the behaviorist accords attitude the status of an intervening variable (MacCorquodale and Meehl, 1948) — a link between stimulus and response which is not to be taken as referring to any 'hidden' process.

In response to DeFleur and Westie, Weissberg (1964) argued that a probabilistic view which treats attitude as an intervening variable effectively reduces attitude research to the barren state where its main theoretical term has no meaning. Alexander (1966) took this complaint further, pointing out that DeFleur and Westie's definition "anchors attitude to the specific, external stimulus situations to which the individual responds." Whereas cognitive attitude theory views attitude as an "inner state variable that exists dispositionally," Alexander wrote, DeFleur and Westie "are denying its independence of the stimulus situation in which responses are observed" (p. 280). The concept of attitude is superfluous: one might simply deal directly with response probabilities. DeFleur and Westie seem to confirm this interpretation when they write (in a statement reminiscent of the cognitive theorist Fishbein discussed above): "Attitudes appear to be most usefully conceptualised as *specific*, in the sense that they may be viewed as probabilities of specific forms of response to specific social objects" (p. 30).

As Kvale and Grenness (1967) have been particularly clear in pointing out, there is a truth in behaviorist fore-understanding in that it rejects the erroneous approach of cognitive psychology in its logical conclusion in intellectualism. The 'myth of the inner man' — the idea that human behavior is to be accounted for in terms of a set of mental variables which map the world 'internally' — is correctly dismissed.

But environmental determinism is not an acceptable alternative. The essential structure of consciousness, intentionality, links self and world in a manner which the idea of determinism does not express. The general criticism is directly applicable to the probabilistic view of attitude. DeFleur and Westie, in correctly attempting to resist dualism, and therefore in trying to avoid a concept of attitude which invokes a distinct, subjective, inner world, have mistakenly adopted the orientation which Merleau-Ponty terms "empiricism." This is rooted in the external, physical, 'objective' world, and having no concept of consciousness. The approach of 'natural science' psychology is selected: the image of a causal chain of discrete variables, interacting extrinsically (*partes extra partes*) only. The 'empiricist' prejudice leads to error in that the perception and activity of the person does not have any inherent connectedness, but is in a certain sense arbitrary. Stimuli and responses are discrete variables without inner relationships of meaning.

If so, there is a problem for empiricists in the presence of an attitude. In general, language habits are assumed to underlie the conditioning of attitudes. And techniques similar to those of cognitive theorists may thus be employed in investigating attitudes.

In attitude theory we seem to have the situation where, on the one hand, probabilistic definitions treat attitude as an accidental event, in that it is devoid of inherent meaning; on the other hand, dispositional views require that *all* meaning be vested in the attitude-holder. As Merleau-Ponty (1965) put it, both empiricism and intellectualism miss the "originality of the perceptual world" (p. 219).

> Where empiricism was deficient was in any internal connection
> between the object and the act which it triggers off. What intellec-
> tualism lacks is contingency in the occasions of thought. In the first
> case consciousness is too poor, in the second too rich for any
> phenomenon to appeal compellingly to it. (1962, p. 28)

Both cognitive and behaviorist approaches to attitude are
grounded in fore-understandings which, despite differences, have
a major similarity: The person is taken to be the inert locus of
action of a number of causal variables, which have only external
interaction with each other (one does not affect the inner nature
of the other). Given this approach, techniques are used which
seem to be informative about these 'variables,' their mode of
interaction, and causal influence. The meaning of the situation to
the person is not to be a theme of research when this fore-
understanding is adopted. The mistake is one of substituting the
causal order for the moral order. And for obvious reasons, this
error having been made, quantitative techniques are preferred to
'soft' qualitative ones.

*The important point in all this is that the flaw of methodology
shown in both dispositional and probabilistic attitude theory is first
and foremost in the fore-understanding, the approach of the theorists. Qualitative methodology is best defended on this basis prior to
a defence in terms of technique.*

4. Fore-Understanding of Attitude as Intentional Relatedness

How can psychologists study lived experience and meaningful
action, then, if an analysis in terms of systems of variables is
inappropriate? Clearly the starting point must be some description of features essential to all experience. Phenomenologists
from Husserl (1977) through Merleau-Ponty (1962) to Ey (1978)
have provided descriptions of this sort, and it is right to rehearse
some main points of them here.

The fundamental discovery, of course, is intentionality. All
consciousness is consciousness *of* something; an object-focus is
always present (or 'intended').

> Subjectivity is not a simple and absolute attribute of conscious-
> ness. Certainly it involves a subject, but it is always — as has been
> increasingly repeated since Brentano — consciousness of some-
> thing, that is, invincibly bound to the laws of the objectivity by
> virtue of which it is being constituted.

> This bilateral subjective — objective reality, this essential ambi-
> guity forms the ontological structure of conscious phenomena:
> they are neither completely objective nor completely subjective.
> (Ey, 1978, p. 5)

Thus objects of awareness — even of perceptual awareness —
are not, cannot be, sense-data copies of objects in the 'outer
world.' One does not see meaningless sense data to which a
meaning is later attached. My percepts are 'relatednesses' intrinsically. They have a meaning which is bipolar. On the one hand
the object, on the other hand the self. So that the percept is
inextricably caught up in a net of meanings. It is a part of my
life-world.

The fact of intentionality as the key structure of consciousness
is precisely what prevents one from considering awareness as a
question of the interaction of a multitude of variables with no
intrinsic relationship to each other.

> Internal experience gives no mere mutual externality; it knows no
> separation of parts consisting of self-sufficient elements. It knows
> only *internally* interwoven states, interwoven in the unity of one
> all-inclusive nexus. (Husserl, 1977, p. 5)

In sum, "The field of consciousness is circumscribed and
oriented by its *sense*" (Ey, p. 99), and this sense is constituted by
the meaning of something for the self. This is the structure of
intentionality.

This sketch is by itself insufficient except as a bare introduction
to the phenomenology of consciousness. In particular, the meaning of 'self' in the description of intentionality is controversial
indeed (e.g., Gurwitsch, 1941; Sartre, 1957; Schutz, 1942, and
Spiegelberg, 1981). This question bears heavily on the theory of
social attitudes, and will be considered again shortly. For the
moment, it may be asserted as an aspect of the fore-
understanding with which we approach attitude, that the self pole
of intentionality is not to be taken as reflective self awareness, or
as self knowledge, but merely unreflective presence to the attitude object.

To maintain the phenomenological stance towards the objects
of experience as *purely* objects of experience in order to describe
their essential characteristics, is something which requires effort
and circumspection, especially in an area like social psychology in
which the matters of reflection are the subject of so many theo-

ries, and cultural and personal presuppositions. To discover what *attitudes* essentially are, in their appearing, for instance, demands that we set aside the presuppositions which probabilistic and dispositional orientations adopted, and return 'to the things themselves.'

MacLeod (1947) reminds us of other prejudices which must be set aside. Among these it is particularly relevant to mention organism-centeredness, the genetic bias, and the sociological bias. As far as attitude is concerned, the genetic bias must be suspended, since it involved the assumption that attitude would be adequately treated by attempting an explanation of the occurrence of attitude in earlier states of the organism. Rather, we must concentrate on the description of attitude as it actually presents itself. Suspension of the sociological bias sets aside the desire to treat attitude as a predicate of the social structures defined by sociological research.

With the suspension of the prejudice of organism-centeredness, a feature which MacLeod regards as central to the phenomenology of attitude appears. Organism-centeredness is a tendency of thought which, in a way, mirrors the sociological bias, in that it focuses on attitude as a predicate of the individual. Our concern, however, is to describe attitudes, pure and simple. References to society and the person must be bracketed unless they appear in the phenomenon itself. Such bracketing of organism-centeredness reveals, according to MacLeod, that attitude appears, not as a state of the *self*, but as a state of the *field*.

"Attitude appears as a state of the field." What does this mean? Are we entitled to take it as the starting point of a phenomenology of attitude? The feature that is being pointed to is one which all attitude theorists implicitly accept, without specially remarking on its significance, that attitudes do not refer directly to the attitude-holder, but to their *object*. All attitudes are of something — the stimulus for behaviorists, cognition of the attitude object for dispositional theorists.

In our discussion of dispositional fore-understandings of attitude, it was clear that it was possible to view attitudes as incorporating cognitive, affective and conative meanings. But a predominant tendency is to regard the affective as definitive of attitude. This is not to say that cognition is absent: certainly not. There is an object focus of all attitudes. Affect and cognition, then. What about the vexed (for dispositional theory) question of conation, the question of whether an action-tendency is a necessary part of attitude?

Audi (1972) is helpful here, indicating *reasons* which an attitude situation might present for acting (or refraining from action). The important point here is that the affect and cognition do not constitute causal variables which motivate action, but are a state of the field of awareness and therefore might provide the person with reasons for desiring change in that field.

So Audi points out that, where an attitude object is positively evaluated, the desire may be that it should prosper, advance, increase — or merely remain in the present state. Where it is negatively evaluated, the desire may be that it should be modified, avoided, destroyed, hindered, etc. In the possible situation of a neutral evaluation, the concomitant desire may be that the attitude should be neither favored nor disfavored, or that it should be considered further, or that it should be left to follow its own course, or whatever.

We now have some sort of fore-grasp (Heidegger, 1962, p. 191) on the phenomenon of attitude as affective, cognitive and conative. We also see it as a structuring of the field of experience rather than an attribute of the self as such. It is to be understood as intentional.

Yet individuals may reflect upon their perceptual world and find in it evidence concerning their own personal nature. The attitude is there in the percept, certainly, directing interest and assigning meaning to the parts of the field (cf. Ashworth, 1980). But in thus structuring the field, attitude "arranges round the subject a world which speaks to him of himself, and gives his own thoughts their place in the world" (Merleau-Ponty, 1962, p. 132).

A preliminary reflection on the phenomenology of attitude has shown that it is an *intentional* phenomenon, having an *object focus*, and constituting a *structuring* of the *field* of awareness by predominantly *affective* meanings, and conative implications may be present. Such structuring may be *prereflective*, but a person may develop a thematic awareness of their attitudes and treat them as *self predicates*.

With such a fore-understanding we may now approach the empirical attack on attitudes. The course of further methodological decisions, the question of technique, is plain. Quantitative techniques are not likely to be adequate to the uncovering of attitudes when they are taken to be intentional. Here we are not confronted with variables, but with meanings of a certain kind.

5. A Sketch of Descriptive Empirical Research Based on a Fore-Understanding of Attitudes as Intentional

As a *consequence* of the new approach, descriptive techniques of research are employed. They are, in fact, the preferred kind of technique — not a 'soft' approximation to a quantitative ideal — because they allow the expression of first-person meanings.

a) A Qualitative Technique

The focus of this paper is, of course, on the aspect of methodology which has been labelled 'fore-understanding' or 'approach.' *The question of technique is not treatable with any degree of seriousness within this context.* However, it is right to give a sketch of the way the empirical research on attitudes has proceeded, though the claims made will not be properly justified. (Detailed examples are given in Ashworth, 1985.)

The aim of the empirical technique in this research is to obtain descriptions which will be *revelatory* of aspects of attitudinal structuring of the field of awareness. We are not here engaged in hypothesis testing but with discovering meanings.

The qualitative technique is based on the descriptive procedures pioneered by the Duquesne group. There are two stages. In the first, individuals voluntarily wrote a short account in response to the invitation: "I am asking people about their experience of holding attitudes. It would be very helpful if you would describe as carefully as possible a *situation in which you were very aware of holding a certain attitude.*" This protocol is then appraised in the manner recommended, deriving 'meaning units' which generate situated structures displaying key features of attitude (a procedure which has as its main virtue the demand that the material be reflected upon seriously and creatively in as many aspects as possible). This having been done, the second stage of the research involves a lengthy taped interview with the person who produced the original account. Often there turned out to have been misunderstandings about the original description. Always the interview brought out new implications — and often also produced more telling instances of attitude situations. The interviews are analyzed in the same painstaking way as the original protocols.

Such techniques are regarded by experimentalists as least rigorous because of the lack of specification and control of variables. But in the light of a fore-understanding of attitudes as intentional, these kind of techniques should be understood as most rigorous. They do not immediately falsify the field as a system of interacting variables but rather interpret it as a field of meanings.

Reading of the data provided by the qualitative technique is aimed at shedding light on the nature of attitude. The original accounts are read from this viewpoint, and the interviews are guided by the interviewer in the direction of clarification of the attitudinal structuring of particular events.

b) Some Aspects of the Nature of Social Attitudes

Again, only a sketch. The empirical technique provides data which elaborate on, change subtly, and in other ways alter the way in which the fore-understanding of attitudes as intentional now appears. Three key aspects are noted here: (i) The tridimensional view of attitudinal meanings, (ii) The relationship between the self and attitude, and (iii) The relationship between the self and others as thrown into reflective awareness by divergences of attitude.

(i) Cognition, Affect and Conation.

Attitude is a state of the field, not a state of the self, and 'within' the field it has an object focus. It is hard to specify the object. Since affect is the prime feature of attitudinal consciousness, the object of the attitude may be said to be whatever 'cognition' (a dangerous word, since the object is in the field, not in the mind) carries the affective meaning that constitutes the attitudinal structuring of the field. The whole situation may thereby be implicated. To borrow a term from perception, the center of intentional directedness might best be called the 'figure,' or the *figural concern* of the attitudinal awareness.

A clarification of the 'affective component' is also necessary. The specification by Fishbein of the individual's position on a scale of like / dislike or agree / disagree as the means of operationalizing 'attitude' as a dispositional variable is reminiscent of

Spinoza in its parsimony. It does not concord with the evidence of our subjects' descriptions, where affect was found in many distinct modes.

Unless one wishes to adopt some sort of elementalism, and claim that each emotion 'consists of' pleasure or pain together with certain cognitions — a point of view which is both out of keeping with the felt meanings, and also leads (as did Spinoza's view) to the conclusion that there are as many affects as there are affecting situations — it is clear that the whole gamut of emotions may appear in descriptions of attitude.

Conation also deserves consideration here. Several of the descriptions were centrally concerned with 'what is to be done' on the basis of the atttitudinal situation. If we are prepared to allow the possibility of a null category, in which the attitudinally structured field means precisely that no action is implied — either through a 'dynamic equilibrium,' a dilemma, a conflict of meanings, or through an implication which is to 'let be' — then it can be said that attitudinal consciousness *does* involve, as an essential component, conation.

(ii) Self and Social Attitude.

Consideration of the attitude descriptions suggests a typology of three 'levels' of self-awareness in attitude situations. In the first type, the attitudinal structuring of consciousness of situation is pre-reflective, and there is no thematic self-awareness involved. The second level comprises instances in which there is a reflective awareness of the attitudinal nature of the situation. At the third level the figural concern is with the self-as-attitude-holder.

At the *pre-reflective* level, then, the experience is "lived rather than known" (Merleau-Ponty, 1965, p. 173), in the sense that the figural concern of awareness is 'out there' in the world, rather than engaged in reflection on experience. Neither is the self a matter of thematic concern. The person is aware of something in such a way that the awareness can be said to have the structure of attitude. But there is no concern with the self as the holder of the attitude, there is not even a turning of attention to the experience as such, as there would be in reflection on 'my experience of such and such an object.'

Here we concur exactly with Sartre's (1957, 1958) analysis of the self. There has to be an absolute distinction between the 'self' as mere presence — that 'presence to itself' which is definitive of all conscious life — and awareness of self. At the first level of attitudinal awareness of the field, self is not thematized.

Now, strictly, the first level of attitude structuring does not enter into the descriptions which provide our data. They are necessarily based on occasions of reflective awareness of attitudes. Nevertheless, several accounts included the moment of change from pre-reflective to reflective awareness. This constitutes the evidence for a distinction of levels.

Reflective awareness of attitudinal experience involves the ever-present possibility of turning from the world that one is experiencing to the consideration of the experience itself.

Figural concern with self as attitude-holder is the third type of attitudinal awareness. In reflection the self has already appeared. But we are now interested in the move to a focus on the self. The move to awareness of the self as holding the attitude, and the contribution to the self concept that this may make.

The self concept which reflection on attitudes helps to form, then, is especially a matter of distinguishing the self from others. A matter of social individuation. Without exception, descriptions of attitude situations have shown some reference to the attitude as 'mine' in contrast to the attitudes of others.

(iii) My Attitude and the Others'

Attitude as a predicate of self, as a posture, disposition, personal orientation, appears in the third level of self consciousness, then. However, there is a second series of concepts which are treated as synonymous with attitude, and which refer to my self in relation to other selves: perspective, viewpoint, standpoint. That attitudes are given personal meaning for the self by comparison with others' attitudes (or my own at another time) is clear from the accounts, as we have just seen.

Many authors, including the 'symbolic interactionist' social psychologists (Ashworth, 1979), seem to think that the interpersonal aspect of attitudes is adequately expressed by analogy with perceptual 'perspective.' I and the others have different 'points of view,' but they can be treated as merely different slants on the same thing. Schutz (1973) also takes this line: each individual 'perceives' or defines the situation from his own point of view — his 'biographically-determined situation.'

Now, there is good reason for social scientists to adopt this notion of attitudes. Interaction between people depends on some sharing of definitions of the situation, and discrepancies have to be 'negotiated' if communication is to continue. So it is easy to presuppose that social attitudes are negotiable, and that 'reciprocity of perspectives' extends to attitudes. (This position is also adopted by Ashworth, 1980.)

However, is this analogy a true one for attitudes? Is it not the case that the admission that other people have different attitudes is very different from the admission that they are seeing the same physical object from a different spatial perspective?

In spatial perception, my view of an object essentially implies the existence of other perspectives. Each perspective has equal status in terms of 'acceptability' or 'merit.' This surely is not the case with attitudes.

Such writers as Schutz and the symbolic interactionists underestimate the place of conflict in social attitudes. But there is a further reason for a rejection of the perspective analogy. At the third level of attitude awareness, people come to a knowledge of themselves as 'attitude holders,' grasping this as a 'fact' about themselves. And this is a matter of contrast or conflict with others. One is distinguished from others partly through one's different attitudes.

There is, however, a truth in the analysis of Schutz and the rest. Certainly interaction will break down if some accommodation is not reached on particular attitudes. The problem is the bland assumption of the success of negotiated definition of the situation when attitudes may be so intrinsic to the selfhood of participants. This lack of a correct estimation of the seriousness of attitudes may lead to a neglect of the intricacies of the processes by which accommodation is achieved. There may be complete lack of negotiability of the attitude. However, instances of accommodative plays include toleration (cf. Hamrick, 1980); circumspection in the 'expression' of one's own attitudes, and role distancing or detachment.

References

Ajzen, I. and Fishbein, M. Attitude - behaviour relations: a theoretical analysis and review of empirical research. *Psychological Bulletin*, 1977, *84*, 888–918.

———. *Understanding attitudes and predicting social behaviour*, Englewood Cliffs, N. J.: Prentice - Hall, 1980.

Alexander, C. N. Attitude as a scientific concept. *Social Forces*, 1966, *45*, 278–281.

Allport, G. W. Attitudes. In C. Murchison (Ed.), *Handbook of Social Psychology*. Worcester, Mass.: Clark University Press, 1935.

Ashworth, P. D. *Social interaction and consciousness*, Chichester: John Wiley, 1979.

———. Attitude, action and the concept of structure. *Journal of Phenomenological Psychology*, 1980, *11*, 39–66.

———. Phenomenologically-based empirical studies of social attitude. *Journal of Phenomenological Psychology*, 1985, *16* (1).

Audi, R. On the conception and measurement of attitudes in contemporary Anglo – American psychology. *Journal for the Theory of Social Behaviour*, 1972, *2*, 179–203.

Bagozzi, R. P. and Burnkrant, R. E. Attitude organisation and the attitude - behaviour relationship. *Journal of Personality and Social Psychology*, 1979, *37*, 913–929.

Bem, D. J. Attitudes as self - descriptions: another look at the attitude - behaviour link. In Greenwald *et al.*, 1968.

Bentler, P. M. and Speckart, G. Models of attitude - behaviour relations. *Psychological Review*, 1979, *86*, 452–464.

Brannon, R. Attitudes and the prediction of behaviour. In B. Seidenberg and A. Snadowsky, *Social Psychology*. London: Collier - Macmillan, 1976.

Calder, B. J. and Ross, M. *Attitudes and behaviour*, New Jersey: General Learning Press, 1973.

Campbell, D. T. Social attitudes and other acquired dispositions. In S. Koch (Ed.), *Psychology: A Study of a Science* (vol. 6). New York: McGraw-Hill, 1963.

Crane, M. and Martin, S. S. Attitudes: the keystone or millstone of social psychology. Intensity, centrality and behavioural intention as modifications of the attitude - behaviour relationship. *Sociological Focus*, 1978, *11*, 185–198.

DeFleur, M. and Westie, F. Attitude as a scientific concept. *Social Forces*, 1963, *42*, 17–31.

Eagly, A. H. and Himmelfarb, S. Attitudes and opinions. *Annual Review of Psychology*, 1978, *29*, 517–554.

Ehrlich, H. J. Attitudes, behaviour and the intervening variables. *American Sociologist*, 1969, *4*, 29–34.

Ey, H. *Consciousness, a phenomenological study of being conscious and becoming conscious*. Bloomington: Indiana University Press, 1978.

Fazio, R. H. and Zanna, M. Attitudinal qualities relating to the strength of the attitude - behaviour relationship. *Journal of Experimental Social Psychology*, 1978, *14*, 398–408.

Fishbein. M. The prediction of behaviours from attitudinal variables. In

C. D. Mortensen and K. K. Sereno (Eds.), *Advances in Communication Research*. New York: Harper and Row, 1973.

Giorgi, A. P. *Psychology as a human science*. New York: Harper and Row, 1970.

Greenwald, A. G., Brock, T. C. and Ostrom, T. M. (Eds.). *Psychological foundations of attitudes*. New York: Academic Press, 1968.

Gurwitsch, A. A non-egological conception of consciousness. *Philosophy and Phenomenological Research*, 1941, *1*, 325–338.

Hamrick, W. S. Towards a phenomenology of toleration. *Journal of the British Society for Phenomenology*, 1980, *11*, 116–130.

Heidegger, M. *Being and time*, Oxford: Basil Blackwell, 1962.

Husserl, E. *Phenomenological psychology*. The Hague: Martinus Nijhoff, 1977.

Kroch, D., Crutchfield, R. and Ballachey, E. *Individual in society*, New York: McGraw - Hill, 1962.

Kvale, S. and Grenness, C. E. Skinner and Sartre: Towards a radical phenomenology of behaviour. *Review of Existential Psychology and Psychiatry*, 1967, *7*, 128–150.

Linn, L. S. Verbal attitudes and overt behaviour: A study of racial discrimination. *Social Forces*, 1965, *43*, 353–364.

MacCorquodale, K. and Meehl, P. On a distinction between hypothetical constructs and intervening variables. *Psychological Review*, 1948, *55*, 95–107.

MacLeod, R. B. The phenomenological approach to social psychology. *Psychological Review*, 1947, *54*, 193–210.

McGuire, W. J. The nature of attitudes and attitude change. In G. Lindsey and E. Aronson (Eds.) *Handbook of Social Psychology* (vol. 3). Reading, Mass.: Addison - Wesley, 1969.

Merleau-Ponty, M. *Phenomenology of perception* London: Routledge and Kegan Paul, 1962.

———. *The structure of behaviour*. London: Methuen, 1965.

Newcomb, T. M., Turner, R. H. and Converse, P. E. *Social psychology*. London: Routledge and Kegan Paul, 1966.

Palmer, R. E. *Hermeneutics*. Evanston: Northwestern University Press, 1969.

Regan, D. T. and Fazio, R. H. On the consistency between attitudes and behaviour: look to the method of attitude formation. *Journal of Experimental Social Psychology*, 1977, *13*, 28–45.

Ricoeur, P. The model of the text: meaningful action considered as a text. *Social Research*, 1971, *38*, 527–562.

Sartre, J. -P. *The transcendence of the ego*, New York: The Noonday Press, 1957.

———. *Being and nothingness*, London: Methuen, 1958.

Schuman, H. and Johnson, M. P. Attitudes and behaviour. *Annual Review of Psychology*, 1976, *2*, 161–207.

Schutz, A. Scheler's theory of intersubjectivity and the general thesis of the alter ego. *Philosophy and Phenomenological Research*, 1942, *2*, 323–347.

_____. *Collected papers 1: The problem of social reality*, The Hague: Martinus Nijhoff, 1973.

Schwartz, S. H. and Tessler, R. C. A test of a model for reducing measured attitude - behaviour discrepancies. *Journal of Personality and Social Psychology*, 1972, *24*, 225–236.

Secord, P. and Backman, C. *Social psychology*. New York: McGraw - Hill, 1964.

Smetana, J. G. and Adler, N. E. Fishbein's value x expectancy model: an examination of some assumptions. *Personality and Social Psychology Bulletin*, 1980, *6*, 89–96.

Smith, R. B. and Manning, P. K. *A handbook of social science methods, volume 2: Qualitative methods*. Cambridge, Mass.: Ballinger, 1982.

Spiegelberg, H. Gurwitsch's case against Husserl's pure ego. *Journal of the British Society for Phenomenology*, 1981, *12*, 104–114.

Taylor, C. Interpretation and the sciences of man. In D. Carr and E. Casey (Eds.), *Explorations in Phenomenology*. The Hague: Nijhoff, 1973.

Tittle, C. R. and Hill, R. J. Attitude measurement and the prediction of behaviour: an evaluation of conditions and measurement techniques. *Sociometry*, 1967, *30*, 199–213.

Warner, L. G. and DeFleur, M. L. Attitude as an interactional concept: social constraint and social distance as intervening variables between attitudes and action. *American Sociological Review*, 1969, *34*, 153–169.

Weissberg, N. C. Commentary on DeFleur and Westie's 'Attitude as a scientific concept'. *Social Forces*, 1964, *42*, 422–425.

Wicker, A. W. Attitudes vs. actions: The relationship of verbal and overt responses to attitude objects. *Journal of Social Issues*, 1969, *25*, 41–78.

Wicker, A. W. and Pomazal, R. J. The relationship between attitudes and behaviour as a function of specificity of attitude object and presence of a significant person during assessment conditions. *Representative Research in Social Psychology*, 1971, *2*, 26–31.

Zanna, M. P., Olson, J. M. and Fazio, R. H. Attitude - behaviour consistency: An individual difference perspective. *Journal of Personality and Social Psychology*, 1980, *38*, 432–440.

The Experience of Breaking the Rules

11

Florence J. van Zuuren

Introduction

The research described in this article may be divided into three phases. It is rather difficult to provide one introduction to the entire research. The fact is, there has been a clear development in the way of questioning and in the methods used, which development will be discussed in this article.

The original motive for this research stems from our clinical experience with phobic patients, especially those who suffer from agora — and social phobia. Whatever specific causes their fears may have, these are considered to be irrational, and in experiencing and displaying them phobic persons stand out as non-conforming. This in itself renders situations even more problematic for them and is part of the vicious circle they find themselves in.

In fact, all kinds of mentally disturbed behavior can be regarded as behavior that is deviant from and in breach of the norm (Becker, 1963; Goffman, 1963; Scheff, 1966; Lemert, 1967). What this implies is that the clinician should not only look at the symptomatic features of individuals, but also at the rules they deviate from. By rules we do not mean etiquette rules like Emily Post's, or other explicitly stated rules such as legal ones, but the psychologically more fundamental, implicit rules. Scheff (1966) calls them 'residual rules': the rules that go without saying, for which society does not provide a specific category and the violation of which is unthinkable.

In agora- and social phobia, problems manifest themselves mainly in public places, and there is evidence that agoraphobics experience particular problems with anonymity (Van Zuuren, 1976 and 1982). Part of what they feel can perhaps be experienced in a milder form by non-phobic individuals when they try to sensitize themselves to the rules in these situations or when they deliberately induce a feeling of abnormality by breaking one of these residual rules themselves.

The use of non-phobic individuals as subjects has several advantages such as the study of the very beginning of abnormality. Besides, they can be trained in verbalizing their feelings and comportment as accurately as possible — a skill which most agoraphobics for instance do not have, apart from the fact that all phobic persons are too much preoccupied with their strong fears to notice more subtle situational varieties. And, finally, non-phobic individuals may be able to create means to make rule-breaking experiences more bearable, means that phobic persons have never thought of and which could be very helpful to them.

But even if practical applications should not materialize immediately, a research as mentioned above may still be of general theoretical interest. The fact is that it may provide an insight into the meaning and impact of norms in the lives of individuals, how they deal with them, how they adapt them to their wishes, bargain, compromise, and live on the very margins of them.

This way of considering normative determinants of behavior is characteristic of the symbolic interactionistic tradition (Mead, 1934; Blumer, 1962 and 1969). It tallies with a more qualitative research attitude as advocated by some sociologists and social psychologists working within this scope (e.g., Cicourel, 1964; Glaser & Strauss, 1967; Smelser, 1976). In other branches of psychology there is also a revival of qualitative methods (Giorgi et al., 1971, 1975 and 1979).

We will now describe the various phases of our research. For the sake of readability we confine ourselves to a few illustrations regarding the results.

PHASE ONE: A FIRST EMPIRICAL APPROACH

The aim during this first phase is to gain some understanding of what it feels like, and exactly what it means not to conform to the normal order of things in public, particularly in anonymous situations.

It seemed to us that a way of doing the just mentioned theme justice would be by calling in the help of a person willing to experiment on him- or herself in order to obtain the above-mentioned experiences. Our subject was a male student of psychology, who experimented on himself over a period of several months.

First of all, he wrote down in how far he had felt (slightly) uncomfortable in public situations he had been in during the day. He did so in order to become more conscious of these feelings. Soon after that, he entered certain situations more frequently, so as to gain more (unpleasant) experiences. He then analyzed these experiences, which gave him some insight into the prevailing implicit norms. This insight, in turn, was helpful in inventing ways to violate these norms. Thus, he experimented with walking along a pavement, and then suddenly turning round; with looking at other people too long, or approaching them too closely; or with wearing the wrong kind of clothes. At first, these 'observations' took on a fairly unplanned character. Gradually, they were thought up beforehand. The subject tried to enter these situations without forethought, though, and as open-mindedly as possible.

After each observation the subject made a detailed report of his experiences which was then discussed with the investigator and a second supervisor (a sociologist). The subject also commented on these discussions. During this process some ideas developed about the substance and methodology, which, in fact, intermingled with one another. These ideas will be discussed briefly now.

The most important and fundamental norm which the subject encountered, was the so-called 'accountability rule': it is desirable that, when in public, it may be seen whom you are (or what your function is), and what you are about to do. Even if you are not doing anything special, you have to indicate it in some way or other. This corresponds to one of the main themes of ethnomethodology, which states that people keep to a 'practical sociological reasoning' in everyday life, that is to say: they account for their actions in a reflexive manner. They make the organization of their lives 'accountable' by constantly showing that their actions, or the things said, felt or thought are purposeful, rational and legitimate (Garfinkel, 1967, p. 10; for a discussion on motives, accountability and attribution theory, see also Ashworth, 1979, pp. 131–157).

Besides, it appeared time and again that at the very last moment the subject almost automatically resorted to the use of tricks in order to avoid or soften the feeling of non-conformity, in spite of his open-minded attitude. Such an arsenal of artifices could very well be of general importance to people to maintain themselves in various social situations. The fitness and range of this arsenal could also play a part in the genesis of agora- and social phobia. Therefore, further research will be directed towards these artifices. These will hereinafter be called 'coping modes,' a term that is sometimes used for reactions to life events or stress in general, emphasizing the adaptive character of these reactions (Lazarus, 1966; Haan, 1977; Vaillant, 1977). In order to gain more insight into these we search for different varieties and try to label them.

On the whole, in this phase it became apparent that a subject breaking the rules will provide very informative and original material. The subject himself described his piece of work as a useful experience, whereby he had got to know himself better, and had expanded his behavioral repertoire.

PHASE TWO: THE DEVELOPMENT OF CATEGORIES

For this part of the investigation we deal with the same issue as in Phase One, although the emphasis is now on categorizing modes of coping, used by individuals when they break implicit rules.

Data Collection

Altogether fifteen rule-breaking assignments have been formulated. These do not make extremely high demands upon the subjects, in order not to discourage them. They are variations on the themes of Phase One, most of them taking place in totally anonymous situations, while some involve a face-to-face interaction in otherwise anonymous situations.

More precisely: four assignments have to do with standing still in a street for no specific reason (also: in a crowded place; in front of a shop; for a fixed period of time). Then there is pacing up and down the street, and the same in a tram. Another assignment is to take a seat next to another person in a tram where there are enough empty seats left. Several assignments take place in a supermarket: making just one insignificant purchase; just standing still somewhere inside; doing the same but then waiting for somebody (a stooge) and this also for a fixed amount of time. Two assignments have to be carried out in a shop where in one case the subject has to buy an unusual quantity of cheese (175 grams) and in the other he/she has to buy twice the same (normal) amount of cheese within some ten minutes. The last assignment is supposed to be the most difficult: raising your voice in a tram when talking to an acquaintance (a stooge) about private matters.

This time several subjects participated in the investigation in order to elicit more varieties of coping behavior. One subject, a male psychology graduate, carried out all the assignments (Loose, 1982). Nine others (undergraduates in psychology: males and females under 25 years old), each had to carry out about half of the assignments.

The assignments are handed out to the subjects on separate sheets. The instruction is to try to accomplish the task; if someone finds this too hard, however, he/she is allowed to quit at any moment (which does not release the subject from the obligation of writing a report). In this way we hoped to avoid ending up with completely phobic subjects.

Each subject works alone and writes a report as soon as possible after carrying out the assignment. In this report, the course of events has to be described and also one's own behavior and feelings as experienced while carrying out the task. No further guidelines are given in this phase. On handing in the report there is a discussion with the investigator who tries to clarify opaque aspects of the written material (if any) by asking rather straightforward questions (e.g., "Are you a regular customer in this shop?"). Sometimes the answers are 'revealing,' in the sense that they alter the meaning of a passage significantly. No intensive interview about the subjective meaning of diverse aspects of the situation is taken in order not to sensitize the subject too much, for this would interfere with the performance on the next assignment. When feelings are absent in the report, however, this is pointed out to the subject.

The written reports, together with some clarifying notes from the investigator, form the raw material in this phase of the study.

Data analysis

First of all, the investigator reads all the reports on a particular assignment to see if there is any implicit material about a certain violated norm. This results in a conclusion for each assignment.

In developing categories of coping modes one has to work extensively and systematically. Much of the method, at that time, was borrowed from Glaser and Strauss (1967). They advocate an inductive way of developing theories, in which continual comparative analysis is an essential element (*see also* Swanson, 1971, p. 145). For the sake of convenience we shall describe our method step by step, although in fact there is no clear separation line.

The first step is to read each report again to answer this question: "How does the person behave from the moment he receives the assignment until some time after its accomplishment?" Here the word "behave' includes feelings and thoughts as well. During the reading *fragments relevant to this question are selected*, the selection criterion being that the fragment has some kind of *signal-value* now that the investigator has relegated his common-sense knowledge to the second place. This attitude of distancing oneself from the too well-known world, though without denying one's knowledge, is essential for succeeding in this job of selection (*see also* Giorgi, 1976).

The result of this step is a list of fragments on the left half of a blank sheet for each written report. To get an idea one complete report will be presented: subject III, assignment 9 (buy twice the same quantity of cheese in a shop, with about 5 or 10 minutes in between). The relevant fragments are in italics; feelings are indicated by a dotted line.

> "*Thinking out matters in advance turned out* to have negative effects in the previous assignment. For this reason *I decided just to carry out* the assignment today and *to see what would happen. The only thing I decided beforehand* was to *carry out the assignment in a local shop where I have been once or twice.*
> The assignment took place in the Kerkstraat from 2.26 p.m. till 2.45 p.m. When I entered the shop the (woman) owner stood behind the counter taking money from a customer and talking to the little son of this woman. When the chat about Easter eggs was over, the mother left and the child followed reluctantly, perhaps still hoping for a sweet. I ordered four ounces of ripe cheese, answered the woman's question ('medium'), paid and left, passing some new customers. This part of the assignment took about five minutes.
> I walked further down the street, sat down on the pavement and made a few notes. I felt uneasy about returning to the shop and *was inclined to leave it at this.*
> After about five minutes I walked back *in the direction of* the shop,

feeling more and more embarrassed. *I noticed that the following sentence circled through my mind:* "Four ounces of cheese *once again*, please". *I told myself: skip that 'once again'. I asked myself what I should do if the woman asked me something* like "Weren't you here just now?" *Could I confine myself to simply answering "Yes"? I suddenly realized how striking I look* with my pink coat and pink trousers. After about eight minutes *I found myself* in the shop again. The woman had to come from behind and when she saw me she smiled and asked "Forgotten something?" *I could not restrain myself from nodding and answering her question with "Yes, four ounces of cheese once again, please".*

While she was cutting the cheese and we both kept silence (there were no other customers) I began to feel foolish and *I got the idea that she thought I had already finished the other amount of cheese on the street. As a matter of fact I did eat a slice.* But so what? Why should I have to explain this? Nevertheless, *my inner feelings told me that I had to* because this silence made me more and more tense. *I broke the silence by talking about the weather: not talking was too hard for me, and I did not want to explain about the cheese with some kind of a pretext. And after all: the weather wàs nice.* Then I paid and left."

In the discussion afterwards it turned out that this subject had been especially afraid of being accused of voracity. Maybe this is a personal problem of hers. Further, she had ensured that between her two visits other customers had entered the shop.

The next step is a real interpretive one and amounts to what we call preliminary categories. The investigator tries to label each fragment in more psychological terms which indicate the functional meaning of the behavior described. These labels are written on the right-hand side of the sheet. Here we have the beginning of categories. These categories are connected with the fragments on the left by lines. It soon turns out that several fragments connect with the same category. They form, so to speak, the beginning of an operational (or should one say: ostensive) definition of the category. There are also some fragments that seem to connect with more than one category. This may lead to relabeling the already developed categories by reconsidering the *context* of the fragment or the added clarifying notes. Here we learn from Giorgi (1971, p. 53) that " . . . in order to understand the functional significance of any behavioral act one must understand its relationship to the whole."

Still, we are left with fragments for which it is impossible to choose. Sometimes due to lack of contextual information. Besides it is not unlikely that some behavioral segments are multi-functional in character. For the person such a behavioral segment serves several ends at the same time.

Having thus examined the reports the next step is to compare the thus formed categories. Some are co-ordinative, others seem to be subcategories of the same main-category. Some are to be united, eventually under a new label. It is important to look for similarities as well as for differences. Again, some inventiveness is needed to find a proper label that covers the subsuming fragments. This is also a matter of interpretation and further abstraction. It continues till only those (main-)categories remain which in our opinion differ in functional respects. Nevertheless, they still have to be considered sensitizing concepts, not as definite ones (Blumer, 1954, p. 7). The categories thus developed include all the selected fragments. The fact remains, however, that a few fragments can be categorized in more than one way.

The final step in Phase Two is the ordering of the categories. Important here is the relation main-/subcategory and also, to some degree, the time dimension. The most condensed result here is a tentative scheme of coping modes. It reflects various ways in which people may try to fit in their own rule-breaking behavior into a more or less normal public situation. This scheme is not exhaustive. New categories may be required for other subjects and different assignments. In the following we will describe the categories.

Categories of Coping Modes

In table 1 the tentative categories are summarized. There is some chronological order in this scheme, but there are modes that can be used in another order as well. The behavior to be categorized starts when the assignment is given. The subject may either *refuse* the assignment (perhaps this will make him or her feel less at ease towards the investigator) or *accept* — with or without some kind of reserve.

Acceptation is followed by a phase of *orientation*. For some subjects this simply means that they go at it blindly without having any thoughts beforehand. Others leave undecided for themselves when and how they will carry out the assignment in order to let this happen more or less spontaneously. Most subjects prepare themselves cognitively. Sometimes this means they have negative preoccupations ("I shall make a fool of myself"). In other cases thoughts are more neutral ("How shall I set about it?"), eventually combined with actively searching for information and making choices beforehand (e.g. the subject in the protocol given before chooses a well-defined shop). Also, there can be positive expectancies ("It seems exciting to me").

The task itself can be carried out *in conformity* with the intention of the assignment, but there can be also much *avoidance*. In the most extreme case the subject eventually shrinks back, but it is also possible to carry it out only partially or to interrupt of simplify it otherwise (e.g. standing still in the street for only half a minute; buying cheese twice in a crowded shop). Sometimes the implication is that the performance can hardly be called rule-breaking anymore. In that case the subject has broken a rule concerning the intention of the assignment itself and will have to find a solution for that. This may be done with essentially the same modes as were used in carrying out the rule-breaking task itself. What we see here is an empirical demonstration of the situation under investigation being an interaction between subject and investigator (see also under "Some further comments on the method").

When the assignment is indeed carried out in a rule-breaking way the subject faces the problem of straightening himself out with his environment, one way or the other. The first thing one can try is to *accentuate normal* behavioral aspects, either by intensifying these aspects in one's own behavior ("I tried to look as normal as possible"), or by extending them (e.g., having a chat in a shop; grasping the opportunity to be polite to other customers). The intensifying can even take the form of compensatory behavior (e.g., taking a seat next to someone while at the same time creating as much distance as possible).

Depending on the circumstances, this accentuation of normal behavioral aspects will enable the subject with enough skills to carry out his rule-breaking task without problems. As it were, so much goodwill is created with the 'normal' that the bystanders will accept the rule-breaking. In other cases, this strategy does not succeed and a more embarrassing situation results.

In such rather awkward situations the subjects have recourse to two main coping modès, which both include subcategories. On the one hand, they can try to *legitimate* their behavior, on the other hand (or: at the same time) they can try to *escape* possible unpleasant *social consequences* of their behavior. These two modes refer to two important aspects rule-breaking persons have to cope with, one being that some kind of fusion has to be made between two conflicting realities, the other being that possible (unpleasant) social consequences have to be dealt with. Both modes will be discussed now.

Legitimizing one's behavior turns out to be the single mode most used in this series of tasks. It consists of 'cognitively' dissolving the discrepancy between the act of rule-breaking and the prevailing norms by shedding a new light on the course of events. This can be done, first, on a meta-level, on the one hand by using an <u>accounting excuse for oneself</u> (thinking "I am doing this for the sake of the investigation," "other students behave in the same way"; or, when the task is not fulfilled: "I have some moral objections to. the assignment"), on the other hand by meta-communicating that one is aware of riding roughshod over the rules, that is using an <u>accounting excuse for others</u> (e.g., smile apologetically; ridicule it; and, towards the investigator when the rule-breaking did not succeed, say one felt sick).

Legitimizing can also take place *within* the situation (in contrast tó the meta-level, where the legitimizing concerns the situation-as-a-whole). It turns out that here the subjects mostly adapt their own reality to the normative reality of others: they <u>pretend</u> to behave in a way that is understandable and functional in the situation (e.g., standing still *as if* waiting for somebody; *as if* being interested in the shop-windows). There is also the possibility that the subjects distort reality in the direction of their own rule-breaking behavior (thinking that people suspect you of voracity, or mistake you for a prostitute in the street); this is called '<u>misattribution</u>' here.

Altogether this coping mode of legitimizing seems to have its roots in the 'cognitive need' for order: the world within and the world without have to be consonant; behavior has to be accountable, for oneself as well as for others.

As far as one uses the other main coping mode, *escaping* possible unpleasant *consequences*, one has given up trying to accomplish a cognitive order. Then one follows the ostrich policy and saves what can be saved. Our subjects made use of three main variants. First, one can manipulate one's attention. This can mean to try not to think about unpleasant situational aspects, and also seeking distraction, either in a fantasy-world or in the actual surroundings (e.g., counting pavement-stones while standing still). Secondly, one can try to withdraw socially. This can be done by 'marginalizing' one's presence, that is resorting to the borderlines between one situation and the other, to the effect that one 'is' only partially in the actual situation. One can try also to send out as few signals as possible ('not attracting attention'), which is often combined with secluding oneself from feedback (e.g., avoiding eye-contact; sneaking out of the situation). The third way of escaping unpleasant consequences can mean a rather serious attack on the psychic constellation of the person: withdrawing the self. The person does not ascribe his behavior to himself anymore, but only plays a part. Sometimes this mode takes the form of depersonalization.

There is, of course, the tendency with coping modes to see whether they are effective or not. For this reason the subjects often try to get some (extra) *feedback* about their behavior ("do they actually believe me?"). Here a complication arises when a subject of all possible modes uses the social withdrawal mode. In still trying to check the effectiveness, the subject undermines this very mode at the same time. Sometimes this gives rise to particular after effects (e.g., the subject looks back once more when she is far out of sight).

If all the preceding modes have failed while there is definitely some serious rule-breaking behavior, the subject runs the risk of getting very anxious and of becoming depersonalized. This hardly happened to our subjects. As an exception a subject does not resort to any coping mode at all while still intentionally breaking a rule. Such behavior is labeled *keeping straight on*. In order to succeed in this you have to be very self-confident.

Some General Findings

Just as in Phase One there is a dialectic between method and results: some results have serious consequences for the method to be used,,some methodological peculiarities are in fact substantial results.

First, it is striking to note how much effort was needed to keep the subjects motivated. The personal attention of the investigator in the discussions following the written reports was indispensable as a source of stimulation. In spite of the many encouragements it was repeatedly proved that the subjects put off their tasks till the very last moment: it seems as if there is no suitable moment for a rule-breaking task, until the deadline approaches.

Another, unexpected, result is that while reading the subjects' reports and talking these over with them, the investigator very soon felt closely acquainted with these persons. It was as if the essence of their way of life came out. This can be taken as an indication of the individual specificity of the reactions, although this effect is not immediately evident from the scheme of table 1.

On the whole, the reactions during the assignments were highly diverse. Notwithstanding their mild character, some subjects found them very threatening. One subject gave up (later she explained she was going through a difficult period in her life). Another subject provided a minimal performance and even broke off some tasks at a very early stage; he himself related this to his latent homosexuality, especially in the street-situations. Some others did not have any problems at all, or even liked their experiences. Afterwards most subjects were positive about their participation. In accordance with the findings of Phase One there is the feeling of extending one's behavioral repertoire and the idea of having experienced something fundamental to the effect of getting to know oneself better. In the routine of everyday-life this does not happen very easily.

PHASE THREE: ELABORATING CATEGORIES AND INTEGRATION

In this phase it is possible to work in a more structured way than we did before, still keeping the same aims in mind. The categories developed so far will be further differentiated, extended and, eventually, modified.

Data Collection

Again some norm violations are thought out, seven in total, two of which are, in fact, 'positive' norm violations (numbers 4 and 6), which renders them especially interesting in a comparison with the negative ones. At the start of this series a so-called 'zero-assignment' is added. It does not consist of a norm viola-tion, but has to be carried out in order to make the subject familiar with the procedure, including the writing of a report. Nevertheless, it will be interesting to see in which ways the assignment-character changes otherwise normal behavior. .

The exact (translated) formulations of the assignments are as follows:

0. Buy one or more stamps in a post-office.
1. Go to a place where furniture is sold and make use of a piece of furniture for some time, without having the intention to buy.
2. Go to a pub/coffeehouse, stay there a while and leave the place without having ordered anything at all.
3. Go to a pub/coffeehouse/cantine where some tables are occupied while others are still free; take a seat at a table occupied by people you do not know and have a drink.
4. Queue up somewhere in a row and wait till people are standing in front of you as well as behind you; then allow the person behind you to go first, someone who seems physically able to wait.
5. Enter a strange, large building for no specific reason and go to the top floor; then leave the building.
6. Make sure you have a seat in a tram which fills up; then offer your seat to a healthy looking person of your own age.
7. Gate-crash a reception alone.

Seven undergraduates in psychology participated in the study. This time they are all women (coincidentally) and under 28 years old, except one married woman of over thirty who also runs a household. Each subject has to carry out all the assignments. The married woman, however, gave up after assignment three. For the sake of standardization, more instructions on the report-writing are given than in Phase Two. Some concern the form (typewritten, not too short, not too long, anonymous). Besides, the subjects are asked to mention several topics in their reports, but *only if* they consider them relevant. These topics are:

- how did you look upon the assignment beforehand?
- under which conditions did you start?
- how exactly did you behave during the assignment?
- did you have any particular feelings?
- did anything else happen?
- what were the reactions of other people, if any?

Table 1: Tentative scheme of coping modes

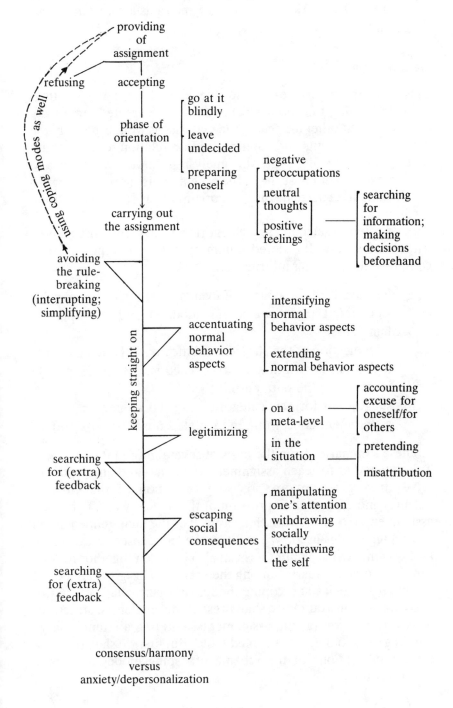

- how did you finish the assignment?
- general remarks or thoughts which flashed through your mind.

Data Analysis

This time the categories already developed form the starting-point in reading the reports. This anchorage creates some freedom to look at other aspects of the material as well, especially the chronology of events and coping modes in relation to the feelings of the subject. All in all, the analysis is more thorough and systematic than in Phase Two, the accent being more on integrating various aspects than on categorizing each single behavioral segment.

In addition to selecting and categorizing fragments, the investigator makes a well-ordered summary for each report, which contains the following information:

- a synopsis of the course of events together with a conclusion about the *main* coping mode(s) and its supposed handiness;
- an indication of the subjective difficulty of the assignment;
- a factual description of the reactions of other people involved (if the data permit this);
- suggestions for new categories and subcategories;
- a statement concerning the violated norm (if possible).

These summaries form the basis of several more integral steps. Taken together for each assignment and compared among themselves they give a more precise formulation of the violated norm(s) and an overall impression of the difficulty of a particular assignment and of the variations as well as the main tendencies in the coping modes used. We call this the 'condensed structure' of an assignment. The summaries can also be taken together for one subject and be compared among themselves. This gives an idea of the main strategies and coping modes of a particular person.

By way of illustration we shall present the condensed structures of two rather contrasting assignments: entering a strange, large building, and joining an occupied table. But first we shall describe some modifications of the scheme of coping modes and some general results.

General Results

Altogether, the scheme developed during Phase Two proved to be a suitable foothold for categorizing. This applied mostly to the assignments which did not lead to a face-to-face contact, such as assignments 5 and 7. It turned out that some of the problems regarding the location of the fragments could be resolved by discriminating between the form and the function of the behavior, as Lazarus and Launier (1978) propose.

Besides, additions and new categories were arrived at. We shall give two examples here. One subject enlisted the 'home-front' so that she would stick to her intentions: she discussed her plan for an assignment with a friend, and visited her immediately afterwards to tell her about it; she also set an alarm-clock for a certain number of minutes, before setting out for an assignment, and took it with her to force herself to stay in the assignment situation during a fixed period of time. The functional significance of these behaviors might be summarized as *enhancing one's motivation.* Another subject composed herself by repeating sentences to herself such as Ellis (1962) recommends to his patients, e.g., "And if I make a fool of myself, so what, I shall never see these people again." This leads to a further differentiation of the category 'escaping social consequences' into *'escaping* them' and *'stressing* their *relativity.'*

Both the positive norm violations (assignments 4 and 6) showed a remarkable shift. Here, the subjects themselves did not particularly feel the need to legitimize, but their 'victims' did so all the more. They were all surprised, without exception, asked questions about the reason for the gesture and invented reasons. Cicourel's statement (1972, p. 257) certainly applies here: "Through the use of basic or interpretive rules the participants supply meanings, and impute underlying patterns. . . ."

In general, it is worth noticing that each assignment hits on special themes which are strongly subjected to norms in our culture. The consequences of assignment 2 (to order nothing) were the most dramatic. Two subjects were soon expelled from a coffeehouse. The others were allowed to stay, but this was because they resorted to an excuse (usually: 'I am waiting for someone'). The norm which was violated during this assignment (the obligation to consume) was probably statable very explicitly for all the participants: it is rather a legal rule than a residual one.

Its violation appeared to instil the fear of social degradation: one does not want to appear to be a tramp.

The respect for someone else's property lays behind assignment 1 (the improper use of a piece of furniture); and breaking this rule made some subjects feel like a kind of thief. Sexuality and aggression reared their ugly heads over assignment 3 (to join an occupied table). This shows how well the impulses related to these, are regulated when one keeps to the norms. Sexuality may also play a part in assignment 6 (to offer your seat to someone in a tram). Assignment 4 (allowing someone to go first in a queue) indicates the importance of time in a culture where everyone appears to be in a hurry; however, the subjects did not receive the gratitude they had expected here. One subject felt like a burglar when she was doing the fifth assignment (to enter a large building). Assignment 7 (the reception) was performed by very few subjects, and was unimaginable to some.

Finally, assignment 0 (buying stamps), which is not a norm violation at all, showed its own effects in that it worsened the performance of some subjects: one person experienced a lot of anticipatory anxiety, another stuttered, and a third came home with the wrong stamps! Focusing on a routine task seems to lead to behavioral impairments.

Illustration 1: Entering a large building for no specific reason

This fifth assignment has been chosen to serve as an illustration because it demonstrates some of the categories developed in Phase Two rather well, while at the same time the reports can be briefly summarized. This is so because this assignment distinguishes itself from the others in that there is no face-to-face interaction.

Six (female) subjects carried out this assignment; they will be referred to as A, B, D, E, F and G. Subject C gave up before assignment 4. Subject F performed the task twice (F1 and F2). The length of the reports varies from rather short (subject E: 13 lines) to medium-long (subject B: 45 lines). Most of the subjects experienced no serious problems during the task, some even found it exciting. Only subject G was rather tense.

Some facts summarized. What strikes first is the framework in which the subjects place the assignment: three of the six subjects had rather extensive experiences with this kind of rule-breaking: on holidays subjects B and D sometimes enter buildings in order to enjoy the beautiful view from the top floor. Subject E entered strange buildings as a kind of game when she was a child.

The choice of buildings is rather diverse. Subject D chooses a hotel (one she is curious about); subjects B, E and G choose an office and subject F both times enters a public service office (without knowing this though). In all these buildings there is a porter present. Only subject A chooses a big shop. This is not in accordance with the intention of the assignment (shops hardly exclude any category of persons) and besides there is no porter either.

On entering, all subjects immediately use the lift to transport themselves up and down. This seems to be the normal thing to do. Only subject A who goes to a shop takes the staircase. Subject F starts walking in her first trial and takes the lift from the fourth floor to the top one (the ninth), subject G ends her assignment by walking all the way downstairs.

There seem to be good reasons for these exceptions. Probably subject F starts with walking because she is the only subject who has not orientated herself beforehand (*see below*): all of a sudden she discovers the steps and she grasps this opportunity to keep moving. The pedestrian conclusion of subject G's assignment is probably related to the fact that on the top floor she has become rather tense, which makes waiting for a lift rather trying. Her departure has more or less the character of a flight (see also below).

Coping modes. The categories developed in Phase Two are quite appropriate for this assignment (see also table 1). *Legitimizing* turns out to be the most important mode here. In the present assignment this does not mean legitimizing one aspect of one's behavior: one's whole presence in the situation has to be legitimized. Four of the six subjects mention to have thought of an *accounting excuse for others* before entering the situation:

> "I came here to bring somebody upstairs something he has forgotten" (subject G);
> "I came here to see a friend, called Peter Jones" (subject B);
> "I would like to look around a bit" (subject D)
> unspecified: subject F.

Subject A does not use an accounting excuse for others, probably because she does not violate a norm anyway.

Some other behaviors serve a legitimizing end as well, in that they preclude being discovered in an illegitimate state. For instance, three subjects explicitly mention how important it is to seek the necessary information in advance:

"Happily I immediately see the lift, so I shall not have to look for it" (subject B);

"From the outside I looked inside to see where the lifts were, so that I could walk straight to them" (subject G);

"I followed him with my eyes and in this way I was able to localize the lifts" (subject E).

By having the necessary information at one's disposal in advance, one prevents making an insecure impression. Or, stated otherwise, by creating a goal-directed impression one precludes further questions.

In the same vein some subjects make use of *intensifying normal behavioral aspects* on entering the building. This too precludes further questions:

"I go straight to the lift" (subject B);

"I walked to the lift confidently" (subject G).

Of all subjects person F experiences most pregnantly what it means to be unable to legitimize one's presence: she is all alone on a top floor which is being repaired: all of a sudden she feels like a burglar and she makes a hurried exit.

Maybe some other behavior patterns than those already mentioned do have a legitimizing function as well. Here, as well as in the previous examples, we see the importance of distinguishing between form and function of a behavioral segment. In the following instances there can be a question of *pretending* something intelligible and functional in the situation:

- two subjects look rather extensively out of the window on the top floor (subjects B and G);

- two subjects lean their bicycle against the wall of the building, perhaps pretending something like "I belong here" (subjects E and G).

But there are behavior segments which serve other ends as well. Twice some vacillating is mentioned between searching for *feedback* and *withdrawing socially*:

"I keep an eye on that side of the hall without looking at the faces of the people most probably sitting there" (subject B);

"I caught the eye of the porter and immediately looked around me" (subject D).

Subject F describes how she tries *not to send* out any *signals* on the top floor:

"Very softly I walked through the swing-doors".

Once out of the situation it is easier to look for feedback openly:

"I felt eyes staring at me, but when I turned round I saw this was not the case" (subject G).

As for the *orientation*-phase we already mentioned that for this assignment it turns out to be crucial to seek the necessary information beforehand. Subjects B, E and G succeed in this, whereby subject E makes use of observing another person to get the information she needs. Subject F omits to get information in advance: she does not even know what kind of a building it is she enters which seems to be the reason she immediately takes the first staircase she sees.

The most embarrassing part of the assignment is to stay on the top floor without having anything to do there, while the journey itself can no longer be an excuse. This part of the task then is the most avoided, shortened and escaped one:

"I stayed in the lift and went down immediately" (subject E — she is alone in the lift);

"I ran downstairs to catch the lift one floor lower" (subject F);

". . . but I decided to walk downstairs immediately" (subject G).

Three other observations are worth mentioning. Subject A does not need any legitimizing as far as the shop-assistants are concerned; but it turns out that she uses an *accounting excuse for herself*:

"Thinking of the assignment takes away the meaninglessness I would have felt otherwise."

Subject B, who avoids the porter on entering the building, greets him rather exuberantly when leaving (he is talking to other people at that moment): in sight of the haven this subject is more daring. She shows the same tendency in assignment 2. Subject D has chosen a building (a hotel) she is curious about and wants to visit; this is also characteristic of her. We call it a 'hedonistic' choice.

Reactions of other people involved. Notwithstanding the subjects' preoccupations about it, this assignment hardly provokes any reactions in others. Only the porter of subject G just glances at her. The other porters do not even have their attention free to look around. It seems that the guarding function of a porter is first of all a preventive one. One passer-by in the stairway may have looked puzzled, also to subject G. With other subjects some 'normal' interactions take place in the lift, but nothing special happens.

Specifying norms. Here too, the subjects do not mention much spontaneously. According to subject A the assignment is not rule-breaking (she chose a shop!). Subject B states that not knowing each other in a big building is a normal state of affairs. This means that once one has passed the porter, there is nothing to worry about. Subjects D, F and G expect to be stopped and questioned ("Why are you here?", "What are you looking for?"). These same three subjects and also subject B think up an accounting excuse beforehand. In a more extreme case this assignment pushes somebody into the role of a burglar, as subject F experiences.

Illustration 2: Joining an occupied table.

Contrary to the previous illustration this third assignment does involve face-to-face interactions; it fits less well into the scheme of categories. Six (female) subjects performed this assignment, whereby subject E made two attempts in the same café (E1 and E2), and subject G tried two different coffeehouses (G1 and G2). Subject A did not dare or want to carry out the task, but she did write a report on her motives.

The reports are rather longer than in the previous illustration, running from 24 lines (subject C) to 77 lines (subject G). The subjects mainly judge this assignment in comparison to assignment 2 (not to order anything), and find it relatively easy. However, subject C feels some resentment, and subject G only just has the nerve to do it. Subject A feels that the assignment is against her principles. She is only willing to join a woman, but at the same time finds it very unpleasant to confront particularly a woman with rule-breaking behavior. The assignment touches on a personal problem of hers, namely her attitude as a lesbian towards men and women in public.

These last three subjects are also the ones to suffer from after effects. Subject A feels guilty towards the investigator, subject C finds the whole situation very embarrassing (she is the only one who has been forced to leave), and subject G is left with some suspicion of the cashier.

Coping modes. Accentuating normal behavior aspects is the most important coping mode used during this assignment: *extending* of normal aspects occurs, and also *compensation* to some extent. This may be demonstrated clearly by the way in which the subjects sit down. Three subjects ask for consent before sitting down:

B : "I do ask, though, whether the chair is unoccupied";

F : ". . . but first I did ask whether the chairs were free";
G1: "I asked whether the chair was occupied; when no answer came I repeated my question";
G2: "I asked the girl whether the chair next to her was free."

Subject E makes contact by eyeing the person concerned from another table first, ensuring in this way that she is welcome. Subject G2 first sits down turned away, and joins the table only later.

The normal order is also accentuated by the carrying of attributes. Four subjects already have their consumptions with them when they arrive at the table, the fifth (F) has a newspaper with her, and subject A also plans to do this, but she does not perform the assignment in the end.

It may be concluded that all the subjects try to ease or compensate for their intrusion of territory on arrival. They indicate to their 'victims' that despite the rule-breaking they respect his or her space and that they do not want to claim his or her attention. A systematic exception is subject C.

The same tendencies are carried on while sitting jointly. Two subjects report that they light a cigarette, and one subject reads a newspaper. Subject D avoids visual contact while smoking, and takes care to keep the smoke away from her victim. Conversation develops with two subjects; in subject E's case after her victim has clearly shown an interest, and in subject F's case via her newspaper. Subject B is deliberately staring at her victim. This is meant to be provocative (a gesture towards the investigator?). Subject C does not use any of these means.

Not so very many other coping modes are used. *Withdrawing the self* shows in subject C ("I turned the knob, and then I behaved as if I were nuts"). Perhaps some aggression towards the investigator is shown in the way this is formulated. Subject E uses *legitimizing* to end the contact: she reveals the true reason for her advances, and gets up. It is noticeable that subjects D and G make very good observations. Subject G, at the same time, is very irresolute: she keeps on cycling back and forth to find a coffeehouse suited for the task, and this costs her a great deal of energy. Subject A *legitimizes* herself to the *investigator*: she uses circumstances beyond her control as an excuse. She also resorts to empty promises: "Perhaps I shall do it some other time." Subject D says that she gets to know herself better. Perhaps this is also a gesture to the investigator.

Reactions of other people involved. – There are some specific features in the interaction with the victims. We shall now simultaneously examine the choice of victim, the victim's reaction, and the way in which the contact is terminated. Here follows a schedule:

A: a woman (in imagination);

B: a man on his own; he does not allow for contact to be made, and leaves without saying goodbye;

C: two people in conversation; the man asks if Mrs. C could go and sit somewhere else, and calls the waitress; C has to leave;

D: a man on his own, who has a large newspaper lying in front of him; he inches away, paper and all, looking at her out of the corner of his eyes, and eventually leaves without saying goodbye;

E1: several people at a table for regulars (no real rule-breaking);

E2: a man on his own; a conversation develops; E gets up after legitimizing herself;

F: a man on his own on a long bench; a conversation develops via her newspaper; the man says goodbye and leaves;

G1: two silent people; the daughter gets up, and the mother then inches away; eventually G gets up herself;

G2: two people in conversation; the girl consents, when asked, but looks around quickly at an empty table; after that she does not have a very active contact with her boy-friend anymore, they both avoid visual contact with G, and leave before their cups are empty.

It is noticeable that nearly all the subjects choose a victim in accordance with their own sexual inclinations, but this could have happened accidentally. Further, it is striking that the twosomes do not like the contravention at all, whereas this does not necessarily apply to those who are alone. It is difficult to ascertain whether the intrusion causes the victim to leave early. It certainly does in one case, and possibly in three.

Specifying norms.–Finally, we shall examine the formulations of the contravention as these are found in the reports. Here follows another schedule:

A: – "you do not only make a fool of yourself, but you also infringe on someone else's rights; you encroach upon personal space; you force yourself on someone; it is a form of aggression; this is even more unpleasant for women, who fairly often have to endure such behavior from men";

- "I know what I am doing, but I do not know how it leaves others";

B: - "this contravention by a woman towards a man could mean that she is interested in him";

- "to join two people as a third person is more of a contravention than to join one person as a second one";

- "to sit down opposite someone is worse than at a diagonal angle";

C: - "this rule-breaking would be very serious against a couple who are deeply engaged in conversation";

D: - "strangers can regard it as a threat when approached too closely";

E: - "it is less serious to infringe upon the interpersonal space of someone on his or her own than it is of several people engaged in an intimate conversation; it concerns private space in the latter case, and that makes you an intruder";

- "to go and sit opposite somebody on his own often means looking for contact";

F: - -

G: - "it is really disturbing to join people who are involved in a conversation."

Firstly, the accountability rule from Phase One manifests itself again: you should not leave someone else in puzzlement or with false impressions (subject A). Further, the formulations above demonstrate that norms serve a.o. to regulate sex (subjects A and B) and aggression (subjects A and D). Safety from either of these is jeopardized when breaking the rules.

It is also interesting to note that individuals on their own ('singles') are considered to be more 'open' than duo's, who may be in conversation. As many as four subjects mention this spontaneously, and it is also in accordance with the actual reactions of the victims. In either case different names are given to the contravention: in the case of a single person it is called an 'infringement' (which can also have a sexual connotation), while in the case of a duo the subjects speak of a 'disturbance' as well. This means that with singles the violated norm concerns their personal territory, with duo's their involvements as well.

SOME FURTHER COMMENTS ON THE METHOD

Much remains to be said about substantial aspects of the results, particularly in relation to other categorizations of coping behavior (e.g. Lazarus & Launier, 1978) and also to their usefulness for phobic persons. In relation to this it is encouraging to see that many of the descriptions given by our subjects strongly resemble those which phobic patients give of their situational problems.

However, we shall let these matters rest for the moment, and briefly look at some methodological questions. First, we want to stress that the relationship between subject and investigator requires special attention in a research of this kind. The subjects not only have to deal with the interactionary situation in which they break a rule in front of strange people, but they have also more or less committed themselves to the investigator to break a certain rule. The same peculiarities may come to light in the relationship between subject and investigator as those that manifest themselves during the breaking of the rule in front of bystanders. The investigator has to pay special attention to these (*see also* Cicourel, 1964, p. 73–105). Instead of considering them as a barrier, one can regard these peculiarities as revealing for the problem in question. What may first seem a disadvantage can turn out to be an extra source of information. In the same vein Hagan, in this book, considers obstacles in an interview situation as useful information.

Another methodological question is the obligation one feels to account in detail for one's method. Particularly when it concerns the moment at which new verbal labels for categories are invented, these accounts are not only difficult to give, but also interfere with one's train of thought. The way seems to show itself here. In the same vein Michelangelo allegedly referred to the art of sculpture: "it is only a matter of freeing the shape that is already there from the surplus marble."

If one is, nevertheless, going to account for one's method in detail, it means that one is, in fact, going to analyze one's own way of thinking, which then in itself will become a subject to research. It is perhaps not accidental that a fairly large number of investigators within the qualitative tradition direct their research to such topics as thinking and learning. Another thing, however, is that the more one tries to account for one's method, the more time and energy will be taken up by discussions on the methodological side of the research. And this is precisely what the traditional quantitative psychology is always blamed for! An important ideal of practicing qualitative psychology is to let the subject of the research come into its own, as far as this is possible.

One may ask why the investigator should always try to justify the method used. Obviously, one might think that it would provide an indication of the reliability, or to put it even more strongly, of the degree of truth of the results.

The next question would be whether the degree of truth can only be measured from the method used. One might also argue that the degree of truth is something which will manifest itself. The better a statement holds in practice, the more valuable it is, and the more truth there (obviously) is in it. We are approaching the extreme pragmatic point of view taken by William James. In his opinion, the truth of a statement does not lie in the fact that the statement should be an exact copy of reality. What matters is how far the statement is verified by subsequent occurrences (James, 1907, p. 201). This point of view seems compatible with a qualitative way of practicing psychology. It even forms an extension to both the school of thought behind radical behaviorism (Skinner) and phenomenology (Sartre), as expounded by Kvale and Grenness (1975, p. 40–49), whereby knowledge is ultimately seen as a form of action.

SUMMARY

The purpose of this research was to gain a better insight into what people experience when they find themselves in a public situation in which they do not conform to the social order. An attempt has been made to evolve a method whereby these experiences may be put forth as pregnantly as possible. A suitable way of tackling this, proved to be to instruct subjects to break residual rules, and to analyze their written reports, if necessary complemented by verbal information, in a qualitative manner.

One of the most salient results is that the subjects manage to avoid or ease their unpleasant experiences every time by trying to assimilate their rule-breaking behavior into the situation in some way or other. Attempts have been made to divide these coping modes into provisional categories, so that we had something to go by when we considered the next data. These data prove to elucidate interesting aspects of normalized social life, as well as specific ways, in which individuals deal with precarious situations.

References

Ashworth, P. D. *Social interaction and consciousness*. Chichester: Wiley, 1979.

Becker, H. S. *Outsiders, studies in the sociology of deviance*. Glencoe: Illinois, 1963.

Blumer, H. What is wrong with social theory? *American Sociological Review*, 1954, *19*, 3-10.

――――. Society as symbolic interaction. In A. M. Rose (Ed.), *Human behavior and social processes*. Boston: 1962, 179-192.

――――. *Symbolic interactionism: Perspective and method*. New Jersey: Englewood Cliffs, 1969.

Cicourel, A. V. *Method and measurement in sociology*. New York: The Free Press of Glencoe, 1964.

――――. Basic and normative rules in the negotiation of status and role. In D. Sudnow (Ed.), *Studies in social interaction*. New York: The Free Press, 1972, 229-259.

Ellis, A. *Reason and emotion in psychotherapy*. New York: Lyle Stuart, 1962.

Garfinkel, H. *Studies in ethnomethodology*. Englewood Cliffs: Prentice Hall, 1967.

Giorgi, A. The experience of the subject as a source of data in a psychological experiment. In A. Giorgi, W. F. Fischer & R. von Eckartsberg (Eds.), *Duquesne studies in phenomenological psychology, Vol. I*. Pittsburgh: Duquesne University Press, 1971.

――――. Phenomenology and the foundations of psychology. In J. K. Cole & W. J. Arnold (Eds.), *Nebraska symposium on motivation: conceptual foundations of psychology, Vol. 23*. Lincoln, Nebraska: University of Nebraska Press, 1976.

Giorgi, A., Fischer, C. T. & Murray, E. L., Eds. *Duquesne studies in phenomenological psychology, Vol. II*. Pittsburgh: Duquesne University Press, 1975.

Giorgi, A., Knowles, R. & D. L. Smith, Eds. *Duquesne studies in phenomenological psychology, Vol. III*. Pittsburgh: Duquesne University Press, 1979.

Glaser, B. G. & Strauss, A. L. *The discovery of grounded theory: strategies for qualitative research*. Chicago: Aldine Publishing Company, 1967.

Goffman, E. *Behavior in public places; notes on the social organization of gatherings*. New York: The Free Press of Glencoe, 1963.

Haan, N. *Coping and defending: Processes of self-environment organization*. New York: Academic Press, 1977.

James, W. *Pragmatism, a new name for some old ways of thinking*. New York: Longmans, Green and Co., 1907.

Kvale, S. & Grenness, C. E. Skinner and Sartre: Towards a radical phenomenology of behavior? In A. Giorgi et al. (Eds.), *Duquesne Studies in phenomenological psychology, vol II*. Pittsburgh: Duquesne University Press, 1975.

Lazarus, R. S. *Psychological stress and the coping process*. New York: Mc Graw-Hill, 1966.

Lazarus, R. S. & Launier, R. Stress-related transactions between person and environment. In L. A. Pervin & M. Lewis (Eds.), *Perspectives in interactional psychology*. New York: Plenum Press, 1978, 287–329.

Lemert, E. M. *Human deviance, social problems and social control*. New Jersey: Englewood Cliffs, 1967.

Loose, R. *Subjectieve consequenties van regelovertredingen*. (Subjective consequences of rule-breaking behavior). Graduate essay, Amsterdam, University of Amsterdam, Department of Psychology, 1982.

Mead, G. H. *Mind, self and society — from the standpoint of a social behaviorist*. Chicago: Chicago University Press, 1934.

Scheff, T. J. *Being mentally ill*. Chicago: Aldine Publishing Company, 1966.

Smelser, N. J. *Comparative methods in the social sciences*. New Jersey, Englewood Cliffs: Prentice Hall, 1976.

Swanson, G. E. Frameworks for comparative research: structural anthropology and the theory of action. In I. Vallier (Ed.), *Comparative methods in sociology: Essays on trends and applications*. Berkeley/Los Angeles: University of California Press, 1971.

Vaillant, G. E. *Adaptation of life*. Boston: Brown and Company, 1977

Zuuren, F. J. van Slachtoffers van de openbare orde — een culturele benadering van de agorafobie. (Victims of public order: A cultural approach to agoraphobia). *Bulletin Persoonlijkheidsleer*, 1976,4, 103–137. Amsterdam, University of Amsterdam Press.

──────. Fobie, situatie en identiteit — een studie over de situatievermijding en identiteitsproblematiek van twee soorten fobici. (*Phobia, situation and identity; situation avoidance and identity problems in two kinds of phobics*). Dissertation. Lisse: Swets & Zeitlinger, 1982.

Interviewing the Downtrodden

12

Teresa Hagan

This paper is an account of the problems found when attempting to employ interviewing as the main means of data collection in a research context. The problems are laid out to show how and in what ways a traditional approach to interviewing could not provide the desired data. Comment arises from a particular project but can be regarded as highlighting the real problems any honest researcher must deal with when interviews are the important source of data. There is a brief overview of the research interest, followed by a consideration of some generally recognized principles of good interviewing drawn from the natural science paradigm in relation to what actually happens in practice. Concrete examples from interview material are used to demonstrate how such principles, derived from construing interviewing as an objective eliciting device, are not tenable and introduce gross distortions in the interview itself — the very thing they are meant to be overcoming in the pursuit of unbiased data. It is further shown that when an alternative, phenomenologically-based approach to interviewing is adopted, the concerns of the researcher are quite different and the defects previously outlined can be regarded as strengths of interviewing as a means of attaining relevant data.

Research Context

The research concerns the problem of underusage of child health care facilities, particularly of infant welfare clinics which depend for their effectiveness on the voluntary take-up of services by mothers themselves. Much concern has been expressed, for example, by the Dept of Health (Acton, 1978; CPAG/DHSS, 1978) about the poor attendance of certain mothers. Those groups of people who make least use of the health care services in general can be regarded as those most in need of help (Hart, 1978). The medico-sociological literature abounds with instances of the poorer health status of the lower social groupings in comparison to the rest of society (Townsend and Davidson, 1982). Many writers draw attention to the widening of the gulf in health status between the social classes, with the poor becoming progressively poorer (Holman, 1978). They typically reside in the more deprived inner city areas, notorious for poorer uptake, and poorer provision of services (Spencer, 1978).

The Problem of Underusage

Concern about what is seen to be a growing sociomedical problem is evident not least because of the alarming consequences attributed to gross underusage. It has been implicated, for example, in what have been called 'cot deaths' (Emery, 1979) — the research in sum presenting a picture of gross inadequacy on the part of some parents who seem to be completely outside the medical care system (McWeeny, 1977). Research into the reasons for low uptake has been controversial to say the least. Classically problems of late /non attendance at clinic have been attributed to the mothers themselves couched in terms of supposed irresponsibility towards their children's welfare (DHSS, 1977; Pringle, 1977). Where the fault is felt to lie is clear by the type of research undertaken which mainly sets out to determine what it is about this group of people which makes them behave in such a self harming manner. There have been attempts to measure 'mothercraft' and accepted standards of health by monitoring the length of time which elapses between a mothers' recognition of symptoms in her child and concern as shown by summoning medical aid (McWeeny and Emery, 1975). Others have tried to measure physiologically the mother's sensitivity to her infants behaviors, which is thought to regulate care giving responses (Weisenfeld and Klorhan, 1978). Barriers in client/ professional communication have been highlighted, the degree of social distance between them being considered as indicated by the working class patients' inability to recall or understand medical instructions or their difficulty in the application of logical thinking (Baric, 1967; Herbert 1976).

Such contentions appear well supported by the consistently positive association found between formal educational achievement and use of preventative health services (Ashford, 1970). Numerous studies see the problem as one of negative attitudes towards health care on the part of the underusers (e.g. Court, 1977), whereby they are seen as irresponsible, unable or unwilling to take responsibility for themselves. It is contended that they typically regard events as being outside their control, fatalistically living in the present with no systematic planning for the future. Their standards of family care being judged to be particularly low (Collver, 1967; Pringle, 1977).

Their lifestyle is judged to be feckless, whilst their motivation is not of the right sort when they do approach helping agencies, as they only go to get a bed booked for confinement or to receive monetary benefits (McKinlay and McKinlay, 1972).

Research Reviewed and an Alternative View

Thus it seems that health care planners and research workers have been genuinely perplexed by this group of people who, apparently willfully, do not do what is generally considered to be best for them. They are seen as defaulters who will not conform; this is clearly reflected in the 'at risk' type of identificatory research done, and leads to inevitable discrimination and negative appraisal. Even the notion of positive discrimination in favor of such groups, whereby special task forces of health carers will be specifically responsible for reaching them, cannot be taken at face value. Despite its well meant conception, it still rests on the assumption that these people must be made to follow convention for their own good. They are not usually treated as rational human beings who make decisions for themselves on the basis of information available to them. The implicit assumption behind such research is that the consumer's point of view can add little to an understanding of the problem (thus the preoccupation with trying to identify characteristics predictive of usage). Even where attitudinal studies have been carried out, they have not asked the consumer for her views of services, rather the consumer's reported lifestyle has been scrutinized. The biggest gap in research to date must be that even where clients themselves have been interviewed with a serious intention of discovering their views, the nonuser has effectively been ommitted due to the sampling procedures adopted, the tendency being to include those most easy to locate, for example, in a clinic or hospital setting where a captive sample can be found. Further, a number of studies explicitly question the usefulness of interviewing underusers at all, as expressed intentions (Collver, 1967) or beliefs often bore no relation to subsequent behavior; respondents had expressed favorable attitudes towards the service offered, and/or acknowledged the importance of it, but not made any use of it themselves.

Where lower social class members have been interviewed, they do not do "well" at all, in that what they say is subject to the researchers own judgment which sets out to look for causative factors (whether they be perceptual, motivational or whatever in nature) which can be contrasted with more desirable middle class attributes. Even though subjective (qualitative) research on the whole has been disregarded in favor of what are considered to be more objective modes of enquiry, the subjective is nevertheless inferred. The researcher typically interprets the objective facts (partial though they may be) according to whatever notion of motivation he adheres to. More recent research (Graham, 1979) and comment (Burkeman, 1980; Chalmers, 1980; CHC, 1980) has questioned the validity of what has been termed 'blame the victim' research. They have indicated that failure to use services may be due to the inappropriateness of the provision itself in meeting the needs of clients and have taken seriously the clients' point of view (Oakley, 1980; Graham, 1978) — though here again the underuser has not been sought out for interview. Nevertheless, a considerable amount of dissatisfaction was found even amongst users, whose problems were not well understood by the providers of services, apparently.

My study was undertaken to investigate the reasons offered by mothers themselves for their selective uptake, concentrating on those who would be regarded as underusers, the aim being to find out what their contacts with the services were like *in their own terms*. To this end, it was decided to employ interviews, which it was hoped would allow for an exploration of the underuser's point of view.

Some Considerations about Interviewing

There are all sorts of considerations which need to be taken into account when utilizing interviewing in research; decisions and choices have to be made as to how to proceed and what importance to attach to what kinds of data. The natural science paradigm draws attention to certain aspects of interviewing which can be contrasted with the matters which would concern a phenomenologically-based approach.

From the natural science paradigm many considerations have been brought to bear on the validity of interviewing as a means of accessing unbiased and reliable data. Such matters as the varying ability of people to recall events accurately; the effects of time delays between an event and its retelling; problems to do with influencing the interviewees responses (with leading questions, for example, and many other matters have been explicitly dealt with by most writers. It is clear that interviewing is acknowledged to be a highly subjective exercise but it is construed as one which can be controlled for such distorting factors. The idea behind the rigors of interviewing seems to be that as in alaboratory experiment, if one holds all other factors constant then differences in response will be a product of different attitudes within respondents.

When liberated from the constraints of natural science, interviewing can be construed in quite different terms. It would not be likened to a laboratory experiment, rather it would be seen as a social encounter of a particular kind. In this paper the intention is to focus on the importance of the interview situation itself as a social encounter and the implications of this for the conception of interviewing as an objective eliciting device, and for the interpretation of the resulting data. This has been neglected in most methodology texts, and most often totally ignored as an important consideration. Usually excluded from the analysis is any consideration of the ways in which the researcher carrying out the interview participates in constructing the data. If the interview schedule is regarded as a stimulus given to elicit a response, then this requires that an event has a standard effect on all who are subject to it, which can never be the case with human beings because what is of crucial importance is the meaning the event has for the person-which defies standardization. What a respondent says in an interview is usually taken to be indicative of some underlying predisposition within the person and not as a result of the shared meanings and expectations operating in the interview itself. The interviewer is thought to be taking part in an impersonal and technical relationship over each aspect of which she can exercise control with predictable/specifiable consequences. At the outset she must assume she knows how people tend to react to certain stimuli and just bear in mind these biases and allow for them in order to get at the truth. At least such ingredients as empathy, intuition and imagination are indicated by such a stance if not acknowledged to be operating in the interview itself. What follows is an attempt to look at the ways in which meanings, expectations and shared rules of conduct are negotiated between persons participating in an interview in contrast to the positivistic picture of isolated individuals merely responding to each other in a controlled social context.

Interviewing in Practice

When trying to converse with the respondents taking part in my research, and obtain useful, important information of real relevance to them, it proved impossible to follow the rules of rigor which can be found in most methodological texts. Those which deal with health-related research interests were mainly consulted (e.g., Treece and Treece, 1977; Selwyn, 1978). Overall, the advice given on how to carry out valid and reliable interviews assumes too much control over what goes on on the part of the interviewer. It ignores the social context in which interviews take place and the part played by the interviewer in the construction of data. This paper then, attempts to look at some generally recognized principles of good interviewing in relation to what actually happens in a research situation, showing not only that they are not tenable, but that they introduce gross distortions in the interview itself, the very thing they are meant to be overcoming in the pursuit of unbiased data.

The advice given can be regarded as relating to four main problematical areas of interviewing:

A) When it is considered appropriate to use interviews.
B) The question of relevance and irrelevance, and what can be regarded as true and unbiased data.
C) The interpersonal relationship in the interview situation itself, which amounts to the problem of keeping optimum conditions constant.
D) The analysis/processing of data to produce relevant unbiased results.

A) The Appropriate Use of Interviewing

The richer data which one can get from interviewing a person, as opposed to their filling in a questionnaire, is thought to be necessary where one wants to 'put flesh on the statistical bones'; in other words they are to be used as an adjunct to 'more objective, quantitative' methods. Often they are only recommended for pilot work (e.g. in the construction of an attitude inventory), or to amplify and check up on questionnaires. Semi-structured interviews are recommended for use when one wishes the respondents to express themselves at some length, bearing in mind that they must be carefully worded and have enough shape to prevent aimless rambling. In general the researcher is warned off using unstructured interviews, as these require considerable skill—due to the built in hazards of redundant information, questioner bias and questionable relevance of content.

All of this seems to relegate the interview data to a position of secondary importance at the outset, and it is usually justified by a need to make a research report a little more interesting. Not everyone would agree that they are of such limited usefulness. Where one wants to discover a person's view of a situation the interview itself can provide the areas of relevance, to be subject to statistical treatment if this is considered necessary. If one has already decided on the areas of relevance and only requires instantiations of them then there seems little point in interviewing. In this respect, there seems to be little difference between interviews and questionnaires, neither being particularly suited to tapping the views of respondents themselves. When interviewing is considered from the natural science viewpoint as an objective eliciting device, it becomes stripped of all usefulness as a means of accessing important and genuine information from respondents. It is then judged according to the criteria by which other scientific techniques are assessed in the natural sciences. As a result the data must be regarded as less then satisfactory, of only secondary importance, soft (i.e. subjective) and consequently unreliable.

The reorientation involved in adopting a phenomenological perspective restores interviews to a position of central importance in research, not a mere adjunct to other methods; they are considered *a main means of access to the respondent's life world*. The aim is to obtain rich and detailed descriptions of the respondent's own concerns opinions and actions in her own words, rather than eliciting bits of behavioral responses to precategorized stimuli. One is more interested in how matters appear to the respondent than in how to fit answers into prefigured categories

— the first step being uncensored concrete descriptions which come prior to any efforts to control, manipulate or quantify what is said. Such descriptions are not treated like physical variables; the focus is not on control but on understanding the meanings intended.

The respondent is given the freedom to choose her own areas of importance and to put emphases where she feels they should be, so that anything which she feels is worthy of mention is registered as data. It is important then that she be allowed to structure her descriptions in her own way and not be tied to a rigid schedule or form. Subjective bias does not arise in the way it does as a positivist understanding of interviewing, as the subjectivity of the researcher is the very means of access to the meanings and themes which make up the qualitative description. All of the description is seriously considered precisely as the respondent described it, before the particular concerns of the research focus are applied and allowed to organize the material. The subjectivity /or concerns of the researcher are made explicit in this regard rather than assumed to be controlled factors. The dialogue between the researcher and respondent possible in an interview allows for the exploration of the respondents concerns. From a phenomenological perspective, it is contended that a human science of psychology, can be practiced with rigor and discipline and yet do justice to the phenomena, without seeking its transformation into quantitative data (Giorgi, 1970). The situated naive descriptions of the respondents lifeworld which can be obtained from interviewing are then considered as of primary importance to an understanding of the world of the subject.

B) The Question of Relevance in the Pursuit of Unbiased Data

The question of relevance, although usually considered only in relation to digressions from the main focus of research on the part of respondents, can make itself felt right at the start of the inteview on first approaching a potential respondent. In some cases, I have found myself unable to make the desired enterprize either intelligible and/or interestingly worthwhile and was refused cooperation. Others were anxious to please, offering to help in any way they could but were not sure they had the credentials to participate usefully. This is an important consideration, as some of those approached obviously had no idea how to act in such a situation and were well aware of this. Approaching respondents and inviting their participation in a project presupposes an appreciation of the researchers aims and, in some ways, a general appreciation of social concerns — which may be true of the middle class well educated respondent who is familiar with such things but is patently not true of the lower class respondent who has no idea of the part she is being asked to play and therefore cannot comply.

The interview situation then requires the respondent to see herself as an object worthy of study, who holds opinions and views on (in this case) motherhood, which she is only too willing to divulge. It was evident that some respondents had never been asked for their participation in this sort of activity before and found the whole idea very strange indeed. This was not always the case: for some the experience of motherhood and views on health care facilities were seen as issues to be discussed in this manner, but for others they could not see what I wanted at all. This does not mean they would have nothing to say for example about being a mother, but just that they had never considered treating it in this way, as a topic to be discussed. From the replies given on approaching potential respondents it is possible to see the lack of correspondence between my concerns and theirs. In particular one of the aims of the study, to help improve provision for the consumer was not one that they shared. They were quite content to have nothing to do with it, or just did not see it as a changeable thing, it was seen as a given, to be ignored or endured. In declining my invitation to take part, the following was not uncommon;

> 'I don't think I can help you there, love; It's got nowt to do with me . . . . I don't go . . '

i. *Idealized Interviewing*

In the advice pertaining to approaching potential respondents, one is encouraged to expect to find an interested, motivated and receptive person who has a general understanding of what the interviewer has in mind. They are expected to understand the general importance of academic work of this sort and to be friendly and cooperative. We are given to believe that most people cnnot resist such an opportunity to talk about themselves.

Some of those in my sample who agreed to be interviewed were distinctly uncooperative throughout, either by poking fun at the whole exercise as not something to be taken seriously, or chose to take on a disinterested enactment of the part whilst making sure nothing of any real consequence was said. The former situation usually resulted in chaos where the interviewer was questioned in return, justifying herself at every stage, as the respondent did nothing to hide her total scorn for the whole encounter, while the latter took the form of a rigid question and answer (monosyllabic) routine throughout. Both can be seen to be flagrantly flouting the rules of the encounter for their own reasons. In some cases then the smooth running encounter one is led to expect did not happen at all.

Carrying out interviews then is not a mechanical procedure to be applied across a sample of respondents, rather it should be possible to allow the reality itself encountered to determine the process. Where the best intentions of the researcher were not perceived and there was a lack of correspondence between the research concerns and theirs, the researcher is called upon to be convincing, able to reassure clients that their interests will be respected. The ways in which such interviews proceed reveals something of the client's concerns. The researcher was treated as an intruder and subject to the distancing used to keep authorities of all kinds at bay. Rather than writing them off as 'difficult' clients, it was necessary for the researcher to treat their concerns seriously and question the perspective of the researcher for its relevance to their situation. The need to be adaptable, then, is not a fault but a necessity to access matters of real importance to the clients. Rather than approaching respondents with what are thought to be technical and manipulative interviewing skills, there is a need for an open, genuine and sympathetic approach which treats the interview as a personal encounter.

ii. *Unbiased, Objective Questioning*

The researcher is advised to first of all stimulate the respondent with questions which are relevant and meaningful to her situation, which does not seem too difficult until one closely examines the ways in which questions are responded to. To illustrate, it is useful to look at the assumptions built into question asked, which quite unwittingly can contain alien and often amusing notions for the respondent. One question in my schedule concerned the part played by the respondent's husband/partner in antenatal preparation, as antenatal classes now seek to encourage fathers-to-be to get involved. For some, the very idea of a man taking part in antenatal preparation was highly amusing, if not alarming. It was not considered to be an appropriate activity for a man at all. At the very least this made clear to the respondent that she was talking to someone with very different ideas to her own. This could be regarded as merely illustrative of public resistance to new trends in provision, but such considerations apply to much less obviously contentious areas of discussion.

When asked what advice they were given by their doctor on confirmation of their pregnancy, I was made to realize that this was not an accurate way of talking about their experiences with doctors, as one respondent put it;

> Advice?, . . What do you mean, advice, he don't give yer advice . . . they don't talk with yer, he just telt me to go up to clinic and take these pills (iron tablets).

It became clear that 'advice' was far too equal a word to use to describe their dealings with doctors; they were given authoritative directions to follow. To merely answer my question would have been to totally misrepresent their experiences.

Even the apparently harmless common sense notion of planning to have a child was not seen as such by all respondents. A number of them construed planning to have a child as referring to their desire to have one or their willingness to care for a child. It was obviously seen to be a moralistic issue, to do with whether they approached the advent of motherhood in the correct way. Such answer as;

> Oh yes love, I wanted her, she was a wanted baby

and —

> Well I definately haven't had any regrets about having her.

show the mothers to be answering to the implied charge of irresponsible feckless breeding, which was not meant by the questioner. It became clear that the whole notion of planning to have a child was a middle class one, to do with organizing one's family around a career, which was hardly relevant for some respondents.

The problem illustrated here, is one of looking at the researcher's own analytic concepts which were completely divorced from the terms in which respondents themselves understood and described their experiences. The answer to such dilemmas is not simply a question of finding a less value laden word to substitute, as even though there may be one, it will have it's own nuances of meaning which differ markedly from person to person.

The important issue is not one of unbiased objective questioning, but of ensuring precision in meaning. Whereby:

> *Such discrepancies should not be overlooked or hidden by the interviewing method, but seen as an important feature of human discourse.* An interviewing method which claims fidelity to the phenomena would acknowledge that there are a multitude of meanings in any 'text' and allow for the exploration of meanings intended, to examine how a respondent has understood a question and show a willingness to acknowledge new material brought to light. Efforts at clarification should not be haphazard but built into the method and lead to self correction and thus precision in meaning. To avoid premature analytic/explanatory constructs in the questions and analysis, key terms would be developed and employed after contact with the data and not before. Where the interpretation of meaning is regarded as the important task, it seems necessary that the researchers' own involvement with the phenomena be searched and articulated through self searching and openness to others.

iii. *Facilitating a Relaxed Conversation*

Most outlines of the interviewing method suggest that the researcher start off the interview with non-threatening impersonal questions, for example the filling in of background details in order to put the respondent at her ease and allow her time to relax into the interview proper-when more pertinent, potentially emotive topics can be broached.

What at first sight seems trivial to the researcher can in fact be highly symbolic for the respondent. One example of this was the first part of my schedule which required the respondent to go through a tally of amenities she had available to her, which was meant to be a purely fact gathering excercise. From the full transcriptions of the taped interviews, it can be noted that none of the respondents who lacked any of the amenities simply ticked them off as present or absent. Some were anxious to stress that they could manage very well without, for example, as washing machine; while others stressed the hardships and difficulties involved in managing without one. Both were at pains to show a concern for hygene and cleanliness, 'as any good mother should'. It was also apparent that it could be quite distressing to confront a person with what could be seen as a discreditable agenda of inadequacies they must admit to, it being obvious that I, or the agency I worked for, considered such amenities to be at least desireable if not necessary to good mothering, (or I would not have asked about them).

From the analysis of the full transcript of the interview, a prime consideration of the respondents is revealed — to be seen and to portray themselves as good mothers. To merely categorize presence/absence, to amass quantitative data, would ignore this major concern. Their concern was with dignity rather than accuracy of reporting, showing the overiding importance of treating the respondent as a human being and not something to be measured in any abstract way. The interview is more accurately to be seen as an interpersonal encounter, and not a technical matter with procedural rules which can be adhered to and administered in a clinical way. In this regard it would seem to be more important to listen to what comes, without selectively testing hypotheses, so as to take a non-categorizing approach to what is taking place at the moment.

iv. *Invalid Self Reporting*

In the advice regarding what to expect in interviews, one can find a mixture of tolerant amusement and patronizing contempt for the respondent, with suggestions as to how to correct for tendencies in human nature which may distort one's data. For example we are warned that the unscrupulous respondent may use the interview as a platform on which to air their prejudices, it being implied that only the most naive researcher would take what was said seriously.

This can hardly be regarded as an objective excercise in any sense as the researcher must judge when this is happening to the extent that it is a false account, and disgard it. Here again there are some guidelines, the researcher is advised to discredit certain tendencies which, incidentally, one would expect the least privileged to display. Where a person overstates the case (it is thought) to extract more benefits, or where the person makes excuses (false ones) to make up for apparent inadequacies.

The bitterly angry accounts given by some of the respondents in my sample of the treatment they suffered at the hands of the services would most certainly have to be regarded as prejudiced. Instances in which they were deliberately ignored, publicly ridiculed or accused of child neglect do not avail themselves to reasonable, unbiased recounting. The events were experienced, and recounted, as stark threats to their self respect; in the interview it is vital to self esteem that the respondent 'redress the balance.' It is important that the professional be seen to be at fault and themselves to be innocent of any blame. This is clearly in evidence in the following account:

> A particularly impoverished respondent was advised by her health visitor to help herself to some second hand clothing which was available at the clinic. She reluctantly complied and sorted out some suitable items, a task which entailed considerable cost to her self-respect as she was seen to be scrounging by the other mothers there. The humiliation was made worse by a member of the clinic staff demanding payment for the items, which she had been led to believe were free.
> 'Well I didn't know you had to pay for 'em, and she were right snotty about it, . . . so I had to put them all back 'cos I didn't have the money to pay.'
> When informed that the health visitor had offered the clothes freely the staff member backed down and allowed her to go, demonstrating to the respondent that she had acted wrongly, probably 'fiddling' the money for herself. In good faith the respondent had agreed to demean herself by accepting second hand clothing, only to find when she got to the clinic that she was to suffer uncalled for public degradation.

When relating an incident or event, distortion is inevitable as the person is anxious to portray herself as a respectable citizen who should not have been treated otherwise. In this respect, it is not unusual to find mistakes on the part of professionals gloriously described as proof of their ineptitude. Disqualifying a professional who has wronged a client from any claim to credibility often entails relating numerous examples of their incompetence.

Thus the doctor who reprimanded one client for wasting his time, is subsequently held responsible not only for the possible loss of the child but for many other events deleterious to her well being; 'It said on bottom of bottle (home pregnancy test), to go see your own doctor, so I went, and he says . . . It's gastric stomach you've got. I'd been badly . . . and thought I was losing the baby,. . . but that doctor still insisted it were wind I'd got . . . . up to me really showing and then they changed their minds. If I'd have took any notice of him I'd of done something heavy and lost it!'

and later;

'that doctor of mine, he shouldn't have the job he's got, he don't even examine the bairns properly. . .he didn't see that she (the baby) has got a bad chest . . . and he gives wrong medicine out, . . . it would have killed a child to give what he said. . . .'

It can be seen that not only do the aggrieved find it necessary to bolster their self respect by giving a one-sided account of how they were wronged, but in general a person will tend to make their lives seem more socially praiseworthy that they were, better planned or more intentional. Such considerations are not taken into account in the rigorous prescriptions for interviewing as laid down by positivist writers. They are not to be seen as important expressions of the person's life situation, but corrected for as blatant distortions of the truth.

Overstatement, understatement, lying and contradictions are common in interview data, and would usually be written off as unreliable reporting. However where the researchers task is one of understanding the respondents perspective, such glib judgments would not be permissible. If the respondent believes what she claims, then there are real consequences in that she may well act on the basis of such beliefs, whereby it would be important to accept them as her truth. They could be more carefully investigated by trying to find the meaning of the distortion for her by empathic interpretation, backchecking and making sense of the interview as a whole. In this way the analysis would be particularly sensitive to the respondent's own interpretation of her situation, and tolerant of ambiguity, contradiction and the unexpected, which may quite accurately reflect how she feels.

In any case, in qualitative research, this is where our interest lies — in getting as close to the persons understanding of her life world as possible rather than amassing facts as they appear to the researcher with her assumed access to objective reality.

v. *Minimizing Redundant Data*

The interviewer is advised to control the content of the conversation by not allowing respondents to wander off the point, to keep bringing them back to the areas of relevance. This is usually referred to as the problem of minimizing redundant data of no use to the researcher, and focuses on the tension between what the respondent wishes to talk about and the interviewer's concerns as a researcher. In some ways the interviewing technique can be regarded as specifically trying to control those who do not stick to the rules of interviewing, those who do not treat it as a fact gathering excercise. They define the situation in their own terms and have no idea of what the researcher has in mind, which makes them unsuitable as respondents. As the conversation is primarily structured by the questions asked, the appearance of diversions could be regarded as indicative of the success of the encounter in terms of how relaxed and informal a very artificial situation has become, the respondent having been allowed to define her own areas of relevance. In this sense some areas of importance may emerge almost in spite of the interview. In some ways, diversions can be regarded as rich descriptions of the respondents concerns, in that they always reveal something of the world of the describer and cannot be dismissed so easily as irrelevant. One example from my research concerns the account given by one respondent about the recent loss of her car.

> The car had been a bargain, the only one she had ever had, which held out the possibility of getting around more easily. Unfortunately her husband had not been able to get hold of the ownership documents-leading them to believe that it must have been stolen. Rather than risk conviction, they got rid of the car quickly, only to discover that the new owner had no problem in obtaining the relevant documents.

This was one in a long line of disappointments in life she had suffered. Her plans often came to nothing, every attempt to better her lot being flouted by forces outside her control. She feels hard done by, undeserving of the bad luck which comes her way. She expresses similar sentiments towards the services, in terms of the possibility of hope being held out (eg. in terms of extra money to buy necessities), soon dashed by administrative punitive red tape (rendering her not entitled to claim). She does not have a specific attitude reserved solely for the services, they are only one more trial of many in her powerless existence.

Constraints in the Interview

The researcher is not meant to influence the respondent in any way which would bias her response. However respondents are well aware of the encounter as an interview and realize there must be rules governing what is to take place, even if they are not always clear about what these will be. It is commonplace to find respondents actively negotiating guidelines in the interview itself. They overtly offer statements for validation by the researcher both in terms of relevance for the interview, as in:

I don't know if this is what you're after but . . . . . .

or —

Should I tell you about (an incident), will that do?

and also in terms of the social acceptability of what has been said as in:

Is this the sort of thing that most people say?

Respondents do not treat the researcher as the objective reporter which some would pretend, and so they do not give clearcut answers which are untainted by the interviewer and amenable to categorial analysis.

C) The Interpersonal Relationship in the Interview

Advice mostly takes the following form: The interviewer is advised to create a friendly and pleasant atmosphere to gain the respondents confidence by smiling and showing enthusiasm, in response to which the respondent will usually react positively. Most people are thought to be happy, curious and quite pleased to be interviewed. If the interviewer is totally responsive and receptive to whatever the respondent may say, by maintaining an appearance of spontaneity and naturalness, it will lead to an interview highly charged with information. This is meant to create a climate in which an ordinary person's ability to talk is freed from ordinary constraints. The researcher must remain friendly and warm towards her subjects, but not so friendly that the subject responds personally, rather than stating her opinions on the topic. The researcher wants the person to express herself as a subject and not as a personal friend.

Interview data is replete with examples of the respondent reacting to the researcher on a personal level, rather that acting as a subject proper, which seems to require her to strictly tie her answers to questions posed in an objective impersonal way. This is clearly shown in the more obvious example offered here when the respondent was talking about her immediate feelings on becoming a mother:

> You'll think me terrible for saying this but, I never did like N, (baby's name) when I'd first got her, she were always crying and cranky. I think she were windy most of the time and I just didn't like her at all. I know it sounds stupid but it took me a long time to love her.

The respondent is clearly well aware of the socially unacceptable nature of what she is about to say, and comments on how she thinks such an admission will be construed in personal terms by the researcher at the time.

Whilst it is unlikely that the respondent will respond as to a personal friend, the hope that she will be freed from the ordinary constraints which govern normal interaction between people is also unfounded. In some ways the interviewer will always be seen as a judge, as in any social encounter. In every case it is clear that the respondents felt they were being held to account for themselves. Even if one manages to get away from the more institutionalized idea of a judge, as a professional possessing social power over the respondent, one can never escape from the inevitable judgments people make about each other as a matter of course. In the interview then as in any social encounter, the respondent will try to ensure that she is seen to be a worthwhile person in possession of socially desirable values, no matter how clinical the interviewer tries to be.

In the following example, the respondent wishes to display herself as being a knowledgable person to the researcher. When asked whether she felt well on discharge from hospital, she mentions her painful scar resulting from caesarean section:

> . . . it's about a foot long . . . but it's right good surgery, not like a frankenstein scar, you know,

> . . . it's got the stitches that dissolve themselves. I don't suppose
> you will know this but apparently there's five layers from the
> womb to the outside skin in a woman . . . .

The apparently spurious addition of such 'facts' has little to do
with the question being asked, but serves a more important
function for the respondent, that of ensuring she is seen to be well
informed about such matters.

i. *Value Free Questioning*

The researcher is advised to make every effort to ensure his
statements are value free, and to have an impartial and unbiased
approach towards the respondent which is thought to come
through concious effort. Some writers acknowledge the impossibility of making value free statements and recognize that it is not
simply a matter of not loading questions in a particular way. The
aim however remains to cut out bias by correcting for potentially
value laden distortions. It is suggested that, if the cultural norms
will tend to pull a response in one direction the wording should be
loaded in the other direction to maintain a balance. In this way
the researcher can make it easy for the mother to admit to
unacceptable things. In one text, the example of bedwetting in
childhood is given, suggesting that if the question assumes the
child to still be wetting the bed, a mother will find this easier to
admit to, whilst for those who are not, a mother will proudly
refute the assertion. The main concern of the researcher being to
facilitate a true response.

Such 'physical loading' imagery seems to oversimplify what is
going on in an interview, and also assumes too much control over
what people will tend to do. Here the mother's concern to be seen
as a success is seen as likely to distort the optimum balance, so
that if one corrects for this tendency at the outset then a true
response will be elicited. This would only be true of the most
gullible respondent and in any case constitutes a definate bias in
its own right.

Leading questions as such cannot really be avoided in interviewing, as even the act of raising certain issues to be discussed
must be acknowledged to be encouraging the respondent to talk
about some things rather than others. Whilst it may be true, that
grossly innaccurate assumptions built into questions are vehe-
mently denied by those who are innocent, this is not always the
case and if the assumption is particularly offensive to the respon-

dent, this can have disastrous consequences for the remainder of the encounter.

In phenomenologically-informed interviewing, value free questioning does not arise as such, it is more important to try to elucidate the respondent's viewpoint as understood by the researcher; as a point of method, the researcher is required to be aware of their own presence and of interpersonal processes, making for more accurate interpretations. It would be more useful to rigorously investigate assumptions built in and influences on answers given than to imagine such matters to be controllable and predictable.

ii. *Preserving the Anonymity of the Interviewer*

We are told that the interviewer must not be involved in a relationship with the respondent, as perceived non involvement will encourage her to impart a confidence. It would seem to depend rather on in what way the interviewer is seen to be involved and the consequences are never as predictable as this suggests. The ideal is for the interviewer to remain anonymous so as not to bias what might be said in any particular direction. This seems impossible to achieve as at best the mysterious anonymous researcher can only hope to receive non-commital, evasive replies which anyone would give to a total stranger. The very fact that she is carrying out a project in this area at all provides enough trappings for the respondent to decide who she is talking to, even if she only assumes the person to be interested or knowledgeable about such things. More importantly the respondent will ask, and needs to know, enough about the researcher to decide what to say and how to act in the encounter, as can be seen in the following example where the respondent was asked to assess how useful she had found her health visitor to be.:

Respondent: – Do you know Mrs X very well then?'
Interviewer : – 'No, not really, I don't have much to do with them, they just put me in touch with people . . . .'
Respondent: – 'Oh, she's right fussy, have you noticed? . . .I just don't like fussy people. . . and she always comes round when I'm in the middle of doing something.'

It is not just a simple matter of perceived non involvement that is important. The respondent needs to know of possible allegiances before deciding what to say, as otherwise she could be guilty of social indiscretion and find herself denigrating a close colleague.

When confronted with questions from the respondent, we are advised to use non-directive techniques, which essentially means to be evasive in response to a direct question. Again it is not a simple matter of avoiding saying anything in case the response is affected: whether the interviewer chooses to answer directly or not will 'distort' the conversation. To be seen as unhelpful or uninterested is as much of a distortion to the respondent's perception of the interviewer as anything specific which might be said. The idea of a balanced, non-involved encounter with another person is based on a false conception of what human interaction is like.

iii. *Non-Judgemental Responsiveness*

The interviewer is warned to avoid biasing responses by the giving of approval or disapproval during the encounter. Rather, one is often encouraged to give non-judgmental responses like 'I see' to whatever the respondent may say. It can be most inappropriate to respond in this way to whatever is said. For example, in response to a very sad, distressing story, such a non committal response does not avoid bias in any way, as it can totally devalue what has been said and would most probably be received as disapproval. Often, when relating a well told story, the respondent anticipates an appropriate response. She would expect surprise or amusement to be shown, for example, to indicate that the punch line had been appreciated. To react otherwise would amount to a gross distortion of the encounter, only serving to make both parties acutely embarrassed.

There is a need for the interaction itself to be analyzed thoughtfully and any judgments arrived at made explicit. From a phenomenological perspective, it is maintained that significant knowledge of human life is obtainable by a genuine human relationship not a technical one.

iv. *Standardizing Input*

In order to standardize stimulation across the sample, one is advised to stick to the interview schedule, which will ensure flow and variety of pace. It is felt to be important that the wording and order of questioning is adhered to in order to minimize any bias which may creep in. The respondent who is talking freely, however, will not adhere to the order of the schedule. She will cover topics before they are introduced and continually reintroduce those of importance to herself. On occasions she will express an opinion which would make it most embarrassing and destructive to the encounter for the next question appearing in the schedule to be broached.

In relation to the wording of questions, it was also found necessary to rephrase some questions to ensure the respondent had understood. What are regarded as factual questions are seen as anything but factual to the respondent because, for example, some of the questions did not naturally arise for her, they required her to reflect on her experience and reprocess it into other terms in order to provide a response. When asked to enumerate problems encountered during the first few months of motherhood, for example, it was clear that their experience was not seen in these terms:

> Respondent: – 'Well I mean things did happen, yeh, but I mean I didn't have no problems with her (baby), she were alright most of the time . . . '
>
> Interviewer : – 'I really meant anything that had worried you in particular, when you were first coming home . . . '
>
> Respondent: – 'You mean with her not feeding proper, and stuff like that? . . .We got all that sorted out in the end . . . so nothing really, no . . . no problems. . . '

She prefers not to regard such minor difficulties as *problems* she faced. Such a treatment would make what occurred seem worse than it was; the connotations are all wrong, implying failure or lack of ability. In any case mothering was not seen in terms of problem solving, it was not something to be thought about in this way, you just get on with it.

Question Construction

The type of questioning to be used has received much discussion, but it is generally acknowledged to be best to use non-restrictive, open ended questions in order to elicit the most valid response as this gives the respondent room for manoeuvre, and little guidance as to how to respond. In some cases, rather than allowing the respondent more flexibility, open ended questions merely befuddled and silenced them. Such questions give no indication as to what the researcher is looking for, and require the respondent to have confidence in her views and to be able to define areas of relevance. A number of respondents did not feel comfortable when faced with open ended questions. For example when asked what they thought of the clinic, they asked for more clarification, as in 'What do you mean, in what ways?', or avoided specifying by saying they had never really thought about it. When specifically asked about certain aspects of the clinic, they had no difficulty in providing an answer.

In other instances where respondents showed reluctance to express a point of view, this was due to the constraints operating in the interview itself. They expressed their need for time to think about what to say, and were not happy to blurt out whatever came to mind. They wanted time to consider what their opinion might be, now they were being asked for one, and also what such an opinion might say about them.

Following a set text and rigid question construction would be of little value where the concern is to let the world of the respondent reveal itself in an unbiased way. Ensuring the person has understood questions as intended calls for flexibility to elaborate; the researcher should feel at liberty to rephrase questions, discover distortions and on occasions to formulate the underlying message and send it back to the respondent for verification.

D) Analyzing Interview Data

When one comes to attempting an analysis of the data, most of the guidelines give priority to the minimizing of processing time. To this end the interviewer need not wait until all data has been amassed, some analysis can take place during the interview itself. One strategy suggested is the judicious use of a pencil during the encounter, whereby the researcher marks down the pooint in the interview where it is felt something of importance is being said.

The experienced interviewer is considered capable of judging on the spot what is to be regarded as important, as the full transcription is considered to be totally unwieldy and full of redundant data. Such immediate discriminations can only be based on the preoccupations of the researcher and imply that one already knows at the outset what sort of things one is looking for.

The criteria suggested for marking points are such things as where the respondent talks with great feeling, where a particularly clear or vivid example is given or where something particularly unusual or striking is said. Such an approach would result in the exclusion of the less articulate respondents contributions. What is not said in an interview can sometimes be as revealing as what is stated. The less articulate respondents' interviews defy analysis by any of the more traditional methods which scrutinize the data with the above considerations in mind.

One of the respondents in the present study, never completed a sentence to the end, most often she gave up on whatever it was she had started to say. She would begin an answer in a lively fashion which gradually tailed off to mumbling as she struggled to find the right words. Overall she was evidently disgruntled by her contacts with the services but could never have made a passionate convincing case for herself. She expressed doubts as to whether she was ever taken seriously by the health professionals and had grown used to being turned away. In sum the interview could be taken as an example of the persons ability to speak for herself in general and expressive of her hopelessness neither of which would be amenable to the categorial analysis of manifest content, but could be seen as important to a consideration of her underusage of the services.

i. *Categorial Analysis*

Most often interview data is subject to categorial analysis, whereby the content is grouped according to the researcher's own system, with topic headings derived from pilot work. This interpretative process is not as straightforward and uncontentious as it appears. It requires the researcher to make judgements at each stage, which are rarely made explicit.

It is conceivable that the respondent may have been describing events to illustrate quite different points, of importance to her, from those which the researcher reads into the data; some interpretations can amount to a gross distortion of the data. One example from my own research illustrates the problem of trying to group responses under general categories. Some of the mothers in the sample felt they had been left to care for their child alone with no help forthcoming from the child's father. They had to carry all of the responsibility for the welfare of their child alone and felt that this was the reason for their unhappiness and depression. This seemed from the researcher's point of view a reasonable and important identification of a problem faced by mothers. There were, however, other respondents in the sample who also experienced a minimal lack of involvement on the fathers' part, but would not identify this as contributing to their depressed state. They expressed amazement and gratitude towards their husbands for the minimal contribution they were prepared to make:

> Oh he's (the father) really good with him (the baby), he loves him, he doesn't have much to do with him . . . but you can tell . . . one time he helped clear up the mess the bairn made without saying a word to me about it . . . and now he's started to say some things to him . . .

In this particular case it is clear that she does not expect much help from her husband at all and to identify this as one of her problems would not be a faithful analysis of the data.

Lack of clearcut criteria for interpretation generally, and the distortion of grouping as similar, experiences with distinct meanings for the respondent, are only two of the many problems which face the researcher who attempts to analyze interview data by traditional methods.

A more appropriate analysis of interview data has been offered by (Giorgi, 1975) which seeks to develop interpretative procedures which can be used with rigor to do justice to the richness of qualitative data rather than seek its transformation into quantitative results. The reorientation involved draws attention to quite different areas of concern than those which assume a natural sciences paradigm. The respondents' contributions are not regarded as responses to stimuli but as descriptions of aspects of their worlds, the task of the researcher being to let the world of the describer reveal itself through description. It is necessary to adopt interpretative procedures, as lived meanings are not always known explicitly but must be discovered and articulated. Criteria of validity and rigor change in relation to the concerns of a qualitative approach. (Other contributions to this volume detail such changes. Only a few indications of the contrast with positivist approaches are made here.)

Interpretation is fulfilled by a rigorously specified means of engaging the naive descriptions and discerning their psychological sense, a process which entails bracketing, intuiting and describing. As a first step, all of the data obtained is seriously considered and presented precisely as the subject described it before any other concerns are allowed to organize the material. Any preliminary analysis would be considered premature in this respect. The researcher is then required to deliberately put aside all preconceptions and try to see what meanings the respondent is conveying. Each part of the data is investigated as to its meaning in the respondents terms and only later for its relevance to the research interest, any judgments are made explicit. Thus the possibility of genuine discovery is maintained by the systematic search for meaning. The procedure is descriptive and interpretative as the researcher is not interested in some "objective accuracy" of the respondents views, rather an attitude of maximum openness and a bracketing of all prejudice are the desired features. Importance is not assigned on the basis of frequency of occurance across the sample or clarity of expression. An attempt is made to articulate the essential meanings, not always self evident.

Any structuring of the data depends on an articulated guiding interest which could be gone through by another person. It is acknowledged that there is much of interest in the data which is not immediately relevant to the research focus.

Validity is not based on how close one has got to experimental control but on fidelity to the data which can be achieved in a number of ways. During the interview answers can be rephrased and fed back to the respondent for verification, the aim being to achieve an accurate understanding of her perspective. When oriented to the research interest, others can carry out the analysis and compare interpretations to bring to light any bias.

Some Concluding Comments

It is not so surprising to find that expressed intention on the part of the respondent bears little relation to subsequent or (as in my research) past behavior; the interview itself is recognized as an interpersonal encounter so there is a strong likelihood of socially acceptable things being said. One clear example from my research would be the respondents apparently contradictory stance towards clinic attendance. When asked why they thought some people never went, they were quick to locate the fault in the under user:

> Well, I think they just can't be bothered, they're too idle and would rather be playing bingo. . . . they can't care much about their bairns can they?

Later in the interview when asked about their own attendance, they were forced to admit:

> Me, oh I never went myself.

Clearly the respondent does not regard herself as a lazy, uncaring mother, the criticism given of non users is rather a reflection of the respondents concern to be seen to hold 'correct' views/socially desireable values, which she probably expects the researcher to hold. The interviewee is concerned with staging a socially praise-worthy persona, whereby it is perfectly understandable for one to both acknowledge the importance of an issue, and yet choose to ignore it in behavior.

When the interview is acknowledged to be an interpersonal encounter it is clear that as with any such encounter, the normal constraints governing interaction will be operating. It is important to realize that the researcher will be getting 'edited highlights' from respondents, which display what the person wants displayed, and also a reluctance to talk about events which cannot be depicted as socially praiseworthy. It serves no good purpose to ignore or pretend such things are not going on when a person is interviewed in a research situation. Interviewing does not become an objective data eliciting excercise merely because it is convenient/necessary for the researcher to construe it as such.

Such an analysis of the interviewing technique could have been offered by a hardline behaviorist, who wishes to strip interviewing of any credibility as an acceptable style of research, to show that it can never be a truly scientific, objective method. The conclusion given is for psychologists to stop wasting their time trying to study such impossibly subjective areas as self reporting. However in acknowledging the problems of interviewing as an objective eliciting device it was intended only to point out how it is being treated in psychology as something which it is not and could never be, regardless of how many safeguards or balances were built in. It becomes clear that the criteria and methods of the natural sciences cannot be applied unproblematically to the concerns of the social sciences which require their own appropriate modes of investigation.

References

Acton L. *Reaching the consumer in the antenatal and child health services.* In CPAG/DHSS. London: DHSS, 1978.

Ashford, J. R. & Pearson, N. G. Who uses the health services and why? *Journal of the Royal Statistical Society,* London, 1962.

Baric, L. *Exploration of social characteristics in research.* Manchester: The University Press, 1967.

Burkeman, S. *Carrots are for donkeys.* London: Community Health Council News, 1980.

Chalmers, I. Perinatal health services: An immodest proposal. *British Medical Journal,* London, 1980.

Collver, A. *et al.* Factors influencing the use of maternal health services. *Social Science and Medicine, Volume I,* London, 1967.

Community Health Council. *Report of the working group on maternity services.* London: Community Health Council, 1980.

Court, D. Has the court report been misunderstood? *British Medical Journal, Volume II,* London, 1977.

CPAG/DHSS. *Reaching the consumer in the antenatal and child health services.* London: DHSS, 1978.

DHSS. *Reducing the risk.* London: HMSO, 1977.

Emery, J. L. Identification of some infants at immediate risk of dying unexpectedly. *The Lancet,* London, 1979, 343–346.

Giorgi, A. P. *Psychology as a human science: A phenomenologically-based approach.* New York: Harper & Row, 1970.

————. "An application of phenomenological method in psychology." In A. Giorgi, C. Fischer and E. Murray (Eds.), *Duquesne studies in phenomenological psychology: Volume II.* Pittsburgh: Duquesne University Press, 1975.

Graham, H. *The first months of motherhood.* London: Health Education Council, 1979.

————. *Problems in antenatal care.* York: University of York, Department of Sociology, 1978.

Hart, N. *Health and inequality.* Colchester: University of Essex, Department of Sociology, 1978.

Herbert, G. W. "Social problems: Identification and action." In K. Weddell, *et al* (Eds.), *Early identification of educationally at risk children, educational review.* Birmingham: University of Birmingham Occasional, 1976, Chapter 14.

Holman, R. *Poverty: Explanations of social deprivation.* London: Martin Robertson, 1978.

McKinlay, J. & McKinlay, S. N. *et al.* Some characteristics of utilizers and under-utilizers of health and social welfare services. *Journal of Health and Social Behaviour,* 1972, 369 ff.

McWeeny, P. M. & Emery, J. L. Unexpected post neonatal deaths due to recognisable disease. *Archives of Disease in Childhood*, 1975, 191–196.

McWeeny, P. M. The use of child health services related to cot deaths. *Journal of Institute of Health Education*, 1977, 13–18.

Oakley, A. *Women confined: Towards a sociology of childbirth*. London: Martin Robertson, 1980.

————. *From here to maternity: Becoming a mother*. London: Martin Robertson, 1979.

Pringle, M. K. *The needs of children*. London: Hutchinson, 1977.

Selwyn, B. J. An epidemiological approach to the study of users and non-users of child health services. *American Journal of Public Health*, 1978, 231–5.

Spencer, N. J. *Nottingham child health clinic survey*. Nottingham: University of Nottingham, Leverhulme Health Education Project, 1978.

Townsend, P. & Davidson, N. (Eds.) *The black report: Inequalities in health*. London: DHSS, 1982.

Treece, E. W. & Treece, J. W. *Elements of research in nursing*. London: Mosby V. S., 1977.

Weisenfeld, A. R. & Klorhan, R. The mother's psychophysiological reactions to contrasting affective expressions by her own and an unfamiliar infant. *Developmental Psychology*, 1978, *14*, 294–304.

About the Authors

André de Koning: His contact with J. H. van den Berg at Leiden University, led him to Duquesne University as a visiting scholar and lecturer. After working some years for the Area Health Authority in Lincoln and Sheffield (U.K.), he obtained a Thyssen Fellowship to work with H. Tellenbach in Heidelberg. Together with F. A. Jenner he edited and contributed to *Phenomenology and Psychiatry*. He was appointed as consultant psychologist by the Maria Hospital in Tilburg, The Netherlands in 1979 and has since then completed his training as an analyst with the Belgian Society for Analytical Psychology (C. G. Jung). His interests lie in the analysis of attitudes and assumptions and their modification to release individual development.

Address: Maria Ziekenhuis, Department of Psychiatry,
Dr. Deelenlaan 5, 5042 AD Tilburg, The Netherlands.

Amedeo P. Giorgi: Received his Ph.D. from Fordham University. He is currently professor of psychology at Duquesne University and a founder and editor of the *Journal of Phenomenological Psychology*. He is author of *Psychology as a Human Science*, and one of the editors of the *Duquesne Studies in Phenomenological Psychology* book series.

Address: Psychology Department, Duquesne University,
Pittsburgh, PA 15282, U.S.A.

Lennart Svensson: Received his training as a researcher at the University of Goteborg in Sweden, where he was appointed assistant professor in the Department of Education from 1973 to 1979. Since 1979 he has held a position as researcher at the Swedish Council for Research in the Humanities and Social Sciences. His work has mainly concerned two fields: research methodology, and skills of understanding and learning among groups of adults. The first work has concerned the development of an approach to research and the second work has concerned descriptions of mature students (especially university students) approaches to understanding and learning within some different subject matter areas.

Address: Department of Education, University of Goteborg,
Box 1010, S-431 26 Molndal, Sweden

Yrjö Engeström: Research assistant at the Academy of Finland/ University of Helsinki, Department of Education. Research interests: the formation of a theoretical and dialectical relation to reality through instructional interventions; the theory of activity. Co-editor of the book *"Learning and Teaching on a Scientific Basis"*. *"Methodological and Epistemological Aspects of the Activity Theory of Learning and Teaching"* (Aarhus, Denmark, 1984) Author of the book *"Learning Activity and Instructional Work"* (Helsinki 1983; *in Finnish*).

Address: Marjantic 22 a, 006 10 Helsinki 61, Finland

Christopher M. Aanstoos: Received his B.A. from Michigan State University and M.A. and Ph.D. from Duquesne University. He is currently an assistant professor of psychology on the graduate faculty at West Georgia College. His research interests and publications are in the areas of cognition (especially thinking, perception and imagination), and the historical, theoretical and methodological foundations of psychology. Currently he is completing a book contrasting the phenomenological and cognitivist approaches to thought.

Address: Psychology Dept. West Georgia College, Carrollton, Georgia, 30118, U.S.A.

Roger Säljö: Professor of communication in the Department of Communication Studies at the University of Linköping, Sweden. His research interests are within the fields of learning and thinking with particular reference to the communication that goes on in pedagogic contexts, and its consequences for the development of human intellectual repertoires.

Address: Dept. of Communication Studies, Linköping University S 581 83 Linköping. Sweden

Mariane Hedegaard: Associate professor, Institute of Psychology, University of Aarhus. She has published works on concept learning and on the methodological basis of research in teaching and learning, as well as on the way in which children become related to the world.

Address: Institute of Psychology, University of Aarhus, Asylvej 4, DK-8240 Risskov. Denmark

Pentti Hakkarainen: M. Ed. 1970, Lic. Ed. 1972, senior researcher at the Institute for Educational Research University of Jyväskylä, since 1970. Research interests: Activity theory, learning motivation, moral education.

Address: University of Jyväskylä. Institute for Educational Research, Seminaarinkatu 15, SF-40100 Jyväskylä 10, Finland

Steinar Kvale: His dissertation at the University of Oslo had the title *"Prüfung und Herrschaft"* (1972 (Examinations and power)). He is now professor of educational psychology at the University of Aarhus. He has published articles in the areas of memory and grading, dialectics, phenomenology and behaviorism, and recently on qualitative methodology.

Address: Institute of Psychology, University of Aarhus, Asylvej 4, DK-8240 Risskov. Denmark.

Dreyer Kruger: Holds a doctorate in psychology from the University of South Africa. He has worked as a social worker, vocational psychologist, personnel consultant and clinical psychologist. In 1966 he became professor at the University of Fort Hare and in 1974 transferred to Rhodes University where he is currently professor and head of the Psychology Department and also practices part-time as a psychotherapist. He has published extensively and is the author of, *inter alia, An Introduction to Phenomenological Psychology*, published by Juta's, Cape Town and Duquesne University Press, Pittsburgh. He is editor of *"The Changing Reality of Modern Man: Essays in Honour of J. H. van den Berg."*

Address: Psychology Dept. Rhodes University, Grahamstown 6140,
South Africa

Elias J. G. Meijer: Clinical psychologist and psychotherapist. Since 1974 he has been working as a co-ordinator of psychopathology at the Department of Clinical Psychology at the State University in Utrecht, The Netherlands.
His special interests are: Daseinsanalysis; The meaning of dreams in therapy and in normal life; Self-consciousness; Gestalt Psychotherapy and Pesso System Psychotherapy.

Address: Instituut voor Klinische Psychologie, Trans 4, 3512 Utrecht,
The Netherlands.

Frederick J. Wertz: Received his degree in phenomenological psychology from Duquesne University. He teaches psychology at Fordham University and practices psychotherapy in New York City. Having researched perception, birth, criminal victimization, children's experience of parental divorce, abnormality, and consumer psychology, his overarching interests include the research methodology and philosophical foundations of psychology.

Address: Division of Social Sciences, Fordham University,
Lincoln Center, New York, NY 10023

Peter D. Ashworth: Principal lecturer in psychology at Sheffield City Polytechnic, U.K. He is author of *"Social Interaction and Consciousness"* (Wiley, 1979) in which an attempt is made to integrate research on the social psychology of "mental processes" within an existentialist/symbolic interactionist framework. His current research is entitled: "Existentialist psychology and the negative way".

Address: Dept. of Applied Social Studies. Sheffield City Polytechnic,
36 Collegiate Crescent, Sheffield S10 2BP. England.

Florence J. van Zuuren: received her Ph.D. at the University of Amsterdam which was published under the title "Phobia, situation and identity" (1982). She works at the Personality Department of the University of Amsterdam as a researcher and psychotherapist.

Address: Psychologisch Instituut, Weesperplein 8, 1018 XA
Amsterdam. The Netherlands.

Teresa Hagan:

Address: Dept. of Applied Social Studies, Sheffield City Polytechnic,
36 Collegiate Crescent, S10 2BP. England.